ANGLISTISCHE FORSCHUNGEN
Band 416

Begründet von
Johannes Hoops

RUSSELL WEST-PAVLOV

Imaginary Antipodes

Essays on Contemporary Australian Literature and Culture

Universitätsverlag
WINTER
Heidelberg

Bibliografische Information der Deutschen Nationalbibliothek
Die Deutsche Nationalbibliothek verzeichnet diese Publikation in der Deutschen Nationalbibliografie; detaillierte bibliografische Daten sind im Internet über *http://dnb.d-nb.de* abrufbar.

Gedruckt mit Unterstützung der Deutschen Forschungsgemeinschaft

COVER PHOTO:
Melbourne, Yarra North Bank, 2007
© Tatjana Pavlov-West

ISBN 978-3-8253-5925-6

Imprimé en Allemagne · Printed in Germany
Druck: Memminger MedienCentrum, 87700 Memmingen

Gedruckt auf umweltfreundlichem, chlorfrei gebleichtem und alterungsbeständigem Papier

Den Verlag erreichen Sie im Internet unter:
www.winter-verlag-hd.de

Acknowledgements

I wish to record my debt here to the colleagues who were instrumental in these essays being written and published in their original places of appearance: Richard Aczel (Cologne), Heinz Antor (Cologne), Jens Elze (Berlin), Leigh Dale (Wollongong), Madelena Gonzalez (Avignon), Steffi Hobuß (Lüneburg), Stefan Kohl (Würzburg), Frank Lay (Cologne), Andrew McCann (Hanover NH), Justus Makokha (Berlin), Monika Müller (Stuttgart), Heidi Plucknett (Sydney), Gerhardt Stilz (Tübingen) and Jennifer Wawrzinek (Berlin). I also wish to acknowledge the contribution of all those anonymous readers whose comments and feedback allowed me to improve the essays in their original and subsequent versions.

Thanks are due to the editors of the various journals or essay collections where most of the chapters in this book appeared. I am grateful for their kind permission to reprint those pieces here. An early version of Chapter 1 appeared in *Zeitschrift für Anglistik und Amerikanistik* 50: 2 (2002). A version of Chapter 2 was published in *Sleuthing Ethnicity*, edited by Monika Müller and Dorothea Fischer-Hornung (Associated University Press, 2003). Part of Chapter 4 was printed in *Konversionen: Fremderfahrungen in ethnologischer und interkultureller Perspektive*, edited by Iris Därmann, Steffi Hobuß and Ulrich Lölke (Rodopi, 2004). A version of Chapter 5 appeared in *Frontier Skirmishes: Literary and Cultural Debates in Australia since 1992*, edited by myself and Jennifer Wawrzinek (Winter, 2010). Parts of Chapter 6 were published in *Border-Crossings: Space and Culture in Contemporary Literature*, edited by Justus Makokha, Jennifer Wawrzinek and myself (Winter, 2011). An early version of Chapter 7 was printed in *Anglia* 119:1 (2001). Chapter 8 is a modified version of an article originally published in *Hungarian Studies* 13:2 (1998–99). Chapter 9 was printed in another form in *Flight from Certainty: The Dilemma of Identity and Exile*, edited by Anne Luyat and Francine Tolron (Rodopi, 2002). Chapter 10 is a modified version of an article in *Who's Australia? – Whose Australia? Culture, Society and Politics in Contemporary Australia*, edited by myself (WVT, 2005). An earlier version of Chapter 11 appeared in *New Reckonings: Australian Literature Past, Present and Future: Essays in Honour of Elizabeth Webby* (special issue of *Australian Literary Studies* 23:2 [2007]), edited by Leigh Dale and Brigid Rooney. Chapter 12 was printed in a different version in *Subverting Masculinities: Hegemonic and Alternative Versions of Masculinity in Contemporary Culture*, edited by myself and Frank Lay (Rodopi, 2000). Chapter 13 was co-penned by myself and Jens Elze and appeared originally as a longer article in *Anglistik: Mitteilungen des deutschen Anglistenverbands* 22: 1 (2011).

Thanks are due to Heinz Antor for once again making a space in this series for Australian literary scholarship, to Katharina Reinartz for her expert formatting of the manuscript, and to Rowan Payton for his precise and detailed proofreading.

I wish to thank Tatjana Pavlov-West for permission to use her photographic work for the cover image. All other photos in the book are my own and were taken during a sabbatical at the University of Melbourne in 2006-2007. Photo credits are as follows:

This book is dedicated with love, as always, to my wife Tatjana, and to our three 'offshore Australian' children Joshua, Iva and Niklas.

Contents

Introduction

David Malouf's first novel *Johnno* (1975) is a tribute to Brisbane in the 1950s and 1960s, and a record of the ambivalence often felt in that period towards their place of birth by Australians with intellectual and cultural aspirations.[1] Malouf dramatizes this ambivalence by splitting his Antipodean subject into a Manichean duo: Dante, who remains in Australia, and Johnno, who leaves the country powered by dreams and ambitions. The tragedy of the narrative is the failure of communication which dogs the relationship between the two characters. Only after Johnno has died does the narrator-protagonist come to realize what has really connected them. Read as a parable of the dichotomies structuring the twin poles of Australian cultural life for much of the nineteenth and twentieth centuries, expatriation and a search for an autochthonous culture, *Johnno* alludes not only to the cultural peregrinations of its author but of generations of Australian artists and intellectuals.[2]

Though Australian expatriation continues to be a significant phenomenon,[3] the dichotomy of the cultural metropolis in Europe or America, and the 'Arabian desert of the human mind' denigrated by A. D. Hope[4] has surely dissolved. In the age of electronic communication much cultural or archival material from abroad is a mere mouse- or touchpad-click away. And at the turn of the twenty-first century, Australia has become a cultural and intellectual actor able to hold its own in many respects with Europe, the UK or North America. However, even today residual traces of the ambivalence portrayed by Malouf in *Johnno* can be detected in the cultural domain. The relationship between Australian cultural studies done in Australia and the same work done abroad remains at times an ambivalent one. A large number of Australian academics and intellectuals work abroad, and a number of them are working in the area of Australian studies. An even larger number of non-Australians work on Australian topics from overseas. An unacknowledged politics of authenticity, in which place of birth, nationality (sometimes acquired late), place of institutional affiliation, and place of publication all play a significant role, operates in complex configurations to regulate relations of symbolic power and the acquisition of cultural capital.[5] At times a reverse 'cultural cringe' may be suspected of continuing the work, as a reaction formation, of its mid-twentieth-century antecedent. To be sure, the avail-

1 David Malouf, *Johnno* (Ringwood VIC: Penguin, 1976).

2 See Stephen Alomes, *When London Calls: The Expatriation of Australian Creative Artists to Britain* (Cambridge: Cambridge University Press, 1999); Simon During, 'Out of England: Literary Subjectivity in the Australian Colonies, 1788–1867', in Judith Ryan & Chris Wallace-Crabbe (eds), *Imagining Australia: Literature and Culture in the New World* (Cambridge, Mass.: Harvard University Press, 2004), 3–21, and *Exit Capitalism: Literary Culture, Theory, and Post-Secular Modernity* (New York: Routledge, 2010), 57–94.

3 See *Parliament of Australia: Department of the Senate.* Legal and Constitutional References Committee. 'They still call Australia home: Inquiry into Australian Expatriates'. March 2005. http://www.aph.gov.au/senate/Committee/legcon_ctte/completed_inquiries/200407/expats03/report/report.pdf. Accessed 29 April 2010.

4 A. D. Hope, 'Australia', in John Tranter & Philip Mead (eds), *The Penguin Book of Modern Australian Poetry* (Camberwell VIC: Penguin, 1991), 16.

5 See on this topic, Pierre Bourdieu, *Homo academicus* (Paris: Minuit, 1984).

ability of archival material and the proximity of a community of scholars may dictate the quality and innovation of the work being done in the respective domestic and offshore sites of Australian studies. Indeed, there may be occasions where some work in Australian Studies can be better done from abroad than in Australia. This is in part the contention of the final chapter of this book. Certainly the demand that offshore Australian literary studies be treated as an equal partner is one of the tangential points made in Graham Huggan's recent *Australian Literature: Postcolonialism, Racism, Transnationalism* (2007).[6]

It is within this complex and variegated field of intellectual lines of force and lines of flight that the present collection of essays has emerged. This collection summarizes the work I have done on Australian literature across a period of fifteen years from the platform of a number of German university positions. The essays in this volume were written between 1997 and 2011 during my time in Cologne, Magdeburg, Lüneburg and Berlin. They are explicitly the work of an expatriate scholar viewing contemporary Australian literature from a European perspective. This will be abundantly evident, in many cases, from the continental orientation of the theoretical underpinning of their readings. The unashamedly outside perspective they present envisages a largely 'imaginary Antipodes' whose character is probably at times more or less hallucinatory. That character, I suggest, far from merely gesturing at a referent whose original is elsewhere, 'positive unoriginality' in Meaghan Morris's classic formulation,[7] might well bear being taken seriously in inverted form so as to enable a view of Australian culture as an assemblage of imaginations more or less rooted in a place whose reality informs their semiotic work: an Antipodes as imaginary from the home perspective as from abroad.

This book moves across four broad areas of enquiry: first, indigenous literary production; second, white settler identities; third, immigrant identities; and finally, the global construction of Australian literature. Part one points to an underlying sense of place which I have discovered as much in the Mark Brandenburg in recent years as in the Australian bush. The expatriate view on indigenous sense of country in a sense differs in no wise from that of all non-indigenous Australians, whose access to indigenous place can only ever be secondary and derivative, though it can certainly be acquired, as indigenous rituals of 'introduction to country' indicate.[8] Part four gestures towards the transnational view of Australian literature which of course forms the constitutive and enabling condition of possibility of the collection itself. The two parts in between, dealing with settlement and immigration, describe vectors which are also mutually constitutive of each other, and deeply intengled in the condition of expatriation, and in turn hold the bracketing states of being, indigeneity and transnationalism, together and apart via a productive set of tensions. My underlying claim in constructing this collection in such a manner is that though these four 'conditions' of Australianness describe distinct modes of belonging to country, they tend none the less to overlap and inflect each other. What they produce

6 Graham Huggan, *Australian Literature: Postcolonialism, Racism, Transnationalism* (Oxford: Oxford University Press, 2007).

7 Meaghan Morris, 'Metamorphoses at Sydney Tower', *New Formations* 11 (Summer 1990), 11.

8 Stephen Muecke, *Ancient and Modern: Time, Culture and Indigenous Philosophy* (UNSW Press, 2004), 69.

together is a 'folded' conception of Australian identity whose various facets and surfaces make up an undulating fabric of located identities which are connected in many ways, some very loose, some exceedingly intimately, with country. The expatriate (or transnational) mode within which the pieces collected in the present volume have been composed is never identical with but also never separate from those others with which it communicates in fluid forms of connectivity.

Four ways of imagining Australia

Part One responds to the ethical imperative of prior indigenous ownership of the continent by opening the volume with three diverse approaches to indigenous literature. The first chapter is self-referential in the sense that it broaches the question of white readership of indigenous writing. It implicitly examines its own conditions of possibility by scrutinizing the manner in which a white addressee is specifically constructed and positioned by the use of apostrophe in indigenous poetry. The second chapter continues in its concern with the issue of reading indigenous literature as a white reader. The chapter interprets Sally Morgan's classic *My Place* (1987) as a detective narrative which involves the white-majority reading public in a quest for its own history of discrimination as much as it records the protagonist's search for an elided family history. Chapter 3 switches perspective somewhat, zooming out to frame the broader context of indigenous writing, exemplified here in Kim Scott's *Benang* (1999), from the point of view of the ongoing biopolitics which has managed and governed indigenous lives since 1800. The final note, however, draws attention once again to that primordial element of indigenous culture which underpins all social existence, whether indigenous or non-indigenous, in Australia: namely, the land.

The first part of the book thus takes up the notion of the priority of indigenous being on the southern continent. At a very superficial level, this is a temporal priority, reflected in the indigenous claim for 10,000 years of history preceding European occupation. However, the argument of temporal priority carries with it a number of risks, for it inevitably buys into the European logic of modernity and pre-modernity, translating into civilization and primitiveness, which underwrote the colonial conquest and dispossession of indigenous people all around the globe. Moreover, if we accept the plausible thesis proposed by Tony Swain in *A Place for Strangers* (1993), a logic of temporal success was quite foreign to pre-contact indigenous societies. Rather, he claims, indigenous cosmologies awarded complete primacy to space. This primacy operated in the interests of an ethos which encouraged a sense of social selfhood as embedded in a place endowed with a sacred quality and conveying custodial responsibility for the environment. Notions of temporal progression came gradually via the first contacts with Makasarese and Melanesian visitors from the North, and then, brutally and apocalyptically, with European invasion in the southwest.[9] The ethos of country suggests, then, that there is a presence of the land which is immune to modern temporalities in a sense which

9 Tony Swain, *A Place for Strangers: Towards a History of Australian Aboriginal Being* (Cambridge: Cambridge University Press, 1993).

can only approximately gestured to by such colonial formulations as the 'timeless land.' Such turns of phrase merely negate what is taken to be a stable given of temporality.[10] Rather, the land itself would have to be understood as an agent with its own non-linear temporality, enduring and underpinning all the societies which subsist in it, making them, perhaps unwittingly, residues of place.[11] Indigenous culture, especially in its linguistic manifestations, even when operating in the imposed colonial language of English, would thus be obeying the imperatives of a non-temporal logic of country, which gives birth to life, and places custodial responsibilities upon all the inhabitants of the land. The land itself would generate an ethos and an ethics which interpellates those who inhabit it, much as Lévinas' 'Other' pre-exists the subject and imposes an archaic responsibility upon the subject which brings it into being. When placed within the linguistic-literary framework which is the primary interest of this volume, the land would speak not so much a content or a message, but would lay down the very possibilities of language itself, *le dire* in Lévinas' terms,[12] something more primordial than Buber's intersubjective dialogism,[13] an 'interpellation' which makes speech possible as it calls the speaking subject into being. The three chapters in Part One thus record my own shift of perspective away from a notion of temporal priority, reflected especially in the double temporality of detective fiction as elucidated in my reading of Morgan's *My Place*, and the temporality of biopolitics in Kim Scott's *Benang* (1999), towards an atemporal ethos of place which latently informs Chapter 1, and becomes explicit at the end of Chapter 3.

Having posited the axiological and ethical priority of indigenous culture as manifest in contemporary indigenous fiction, the book shifts its concerns in Part Two towards settler culture. Starting from the assumption that indigenous culture interpellates settler societies, the three chapters in this section interrogate the ways in which white settler culture have responded to this interpellation. Chapter 4 examines the phenomenon of the 'white Aboriginal,' a putative figure of cultural synthesis as proclaimed in Germaine Greer's maverick manifesto *Whitefella Jump Up* (2003).[14] However, in texts such as Patrick White's *A Fringe of Leaves* (1976) and David Malouf's *Remembering Babylon* (1993), Liam Davison's *The White Woman* (1994), and Stephen Gray's *The Artist is a Thief* (2001), the 'white Aborigine' figure progressively modulates into a sign of appropriation rather than of reconciliation. Chapter 5 examines a rather less masked form of cultural domination and inscription: that of the fence as a marker of territorial possession, management and (from the settler point of view) 'improvement.' In a number of contemporary texts, ranging from Rodney Hall's *The Second Bridegroom* (1991), via Doris Pilkington-Garimara's *Follow the Rabbit-Proof Fence* (1996) and Philip Noyce's subsequent 2001

10 Eleanor Dark, *The Timeless Land* (1941; Sydney: Angus & Robertson, 2002).

11 See my *Spaces Fiction/Fictions of Space: Postcolonial Place and Literary DeiXis* (Basingstoke: Palgrave Macmillan, 2010), in particular 1–15, 37–57, 184–211.

12 Emmanuel Lévinas, *Ethique et infini* (Paris: Livre de poche/Biblio essais, 1988), 82–83; *Autrement qu'être ou au-delà de l'essence* (Paris: Livre de poche/Biblio essais, 1990), 64–67.

13 Lévinas in conversation with François Poirier, *Emmanuel Lévinas – Qui êtes-vous?* (Lyon: La Manufacture, 1987), 123–24.

14 Germaine Greer, *Whitefella Jump Up: The Shortest Way to Nationhood*, *Quarterly Essay* 11 (2003).

film adaptation, through to Kate Grenville's *The Secret River* (2005) and poetry by Anthony Lawrence, the fence is analyzed as a material semiotic form inscribing both the text of the land and the spaces of texts. The final chapter in this section addresses what was, symbolically, at least, undoubtedly the most significant event in the recent history of indigenous Australia: the 1992 High Court 'Mabo' decision, which confirmed the ongoing validity of native title. Tragically, Mabo appears to have had relatively little impact on Australian culture (just as it has had only a minor impact on the real practices of restoration of indigenous land ownership). One of the few literary texts to have directly registered the invisible seismic reverberations of Mabo was Andrew McGahan's *The White Earth* (2004), which this chapter analyzes in terms of the text's dominating metaphor, that of disease.

Part Three turns to what for a long time was the underlying malaise motivating white attempts to appropriate indigeneity: namely, an enduring sense of exile and disorientation in the new continent. There is a widespread consensus now that this sense of deracination often performed an alibi function, eliding the more acute uprooting and destruction of autochthonous indigenous culture on the Australian continent. This alibi is evinced, to give one example, in Paul Carter's enumeration of 'the relative failure of Whites in Australia to incorporate Aboriginal concepts into their language' with the result that 'English here continues to float, as it were, off the ground' and 'its poetic power to evoke the living space remains patchy.'[15] The real material depredations effected by the European settlers did indeed cut off the white settlers from those inhabitants who might have mediated a closer relationship to the land. But the resulting sense of alienation also masked its own historical origins in genocide. If we reject, with theorists such as Sartre, Foucault and Deleuze, the notion of repression, exile and genocide emerge as two sides of the same coin, paired mechanisms complementing each other neatly up until the present day. None the less, the configuration of exile has shifted significantly in the last quarter century with late waves of immigration from South-East Asia, parallel to major, if uneven and often ambiguous recalibrations of the relationships between indigenous and non-indigenous Australians.

The first chapter (Chapter 7) in Part Three examines the concept of exile in David Malouf's work, focussing on *12 Edmondstone Street* (1986), suggesting that it is a term without a binary other. There is no originary home by which to measure exile. Rather, it is an underlying condition of literary existentiality. Similarly, I show in Chapter 8 how David Martin's autobiographical fictions *Fox on My Door* (1987) and *My Strange Friend* (1991) hollow out possible origins of their stories, building a political ethics upon the absence of a moment or site of originary belonging. What emerge instead are networks of contingent, politicized and ethical relationships. Malouf and Martin write against the background of late-nineteenth-century immigration experiences (Malouf's grandfather), mid-twentieth-century expatriation (Malouf's own trajectory) and post-war immigration (Martin's immediate context). The third chapter in this section (Chapter 9) addresses a number of works by the Australian-Canadian author Janette Turner Hospital, from *Charades* (1983) and

15 Paul Carter, *The Road to Botany Bay: An Essay in Spatial History* (London: Faber, 1987), 136–37.

Borderline (1990) to *The Last Magician* (1992) and *Oyster* (1996). Hospital's writing denies, in very postmodern fashion, the possibility of some sort of originary belonging as a foundation for artistic identity, yet her markedly hermeneutic preoccupations never cease to interrogate the bases for interpretation and meaning-making. The fourth chapter (Chapter 10) addresses more recent immigration experiences, namely the late-twentieth-century wave of immigration – not from Europe, but from East and South-East Asia – that has fundamentally inflected the character of contemporary Australian society. The work of Brian Castro (*Birds of Passage*, 1983), Yasmin Gooneratne (*A Change of Skies*, 1991) and Hsu-Ming Teo (*Love and Vertigo*, 2000) reveals other trajectories in which the figure of crossing supplements that of the absent origin to destabilize excessively closed notions of national identity.

Reflections upon the migrant experience in Australian literature often focus upon the experience of arrival, integration and settlement, or alternatively, upon the experience of departure and expatriation. Sometimes they bracket these two vectors of migration together by documenting both departure and return.[16] Most critical narratives of the immigrant experience remain curiously myopic, however, focussing on the content and the form of such narratives, their story and discourse (which can in some cases be strongly inflected by their protagonists' stories of uprooting), but generally ignoring the larger migratory flows of literary production itself. National literature, even when it deals with transnational experiences and incorporates those turbulences into its forms, is framed by a conception of literary canonicity whose borders are those of the nation.

In reaction to this customary sense of closure, the fourth part consists of three pieces which seek to broaden the scope of Australian studies, pointing it in the direction of a transnational literary discipline. The first in this trio (Chapter 11) is an anomaly in this collection, reading a film rather than a literary text. It interprets the classic *Crocodile Dundee* (1986) as an example of the manner in which a version of Australianness was propagated around the world. The contours of the global market rather than domestic versions of Australian identity were from the outset the defining criteria for the selection of the traits from which a henceforth hegemonic portrayal of Australianness were constructed. The penultimate chapter (Chapter 12) addresses the question of translation, thus raising the implicit issues of polylingualism at the heart of a national literary discipline which has long ignored the patent multiculturalism of many of its writers and of the society whose culture it maps. The chapter analyzes the disruptive functions of a stubbornly residual polylingualism manifest in texts such as Angelika Fremd's *Heartland* (1989) and Morgan Yasbincek's *liv* (2000). It paves the way for a more theoretically analytical and panoramic final chapter (Chapter 13), co-written with Jens Elze. This concluding piece combines these perspectives of the two previous chapters. It takes the question of polylingualism even further, suggesting that translations of Australian literature themselves constitute the 'outside' of the national literary canon in the sense that a Möbius strip has an 'outside' which is integrally unified with its 'in-

16 See for instance John Hughes, *The Idea of Home: Autobiographical Essays* (Artarmon NSW: Giramondo, 2004).

side.' The final chapter argues for a conception of Australian literature which encompasses the 'offshore' derivatives of the 'original,' 'native' texts as an integral part of a transnational literary corpus in which many texts have parallel lives in several languages, and may be accessed by readers around the world in one or more of those co-existing versions.

Rhizomatic or aborescent?

This book thus traces a broad arc across three basic concerns: from an initial engagement with indigenous issues, or their engagement with us (as non-indigenous readers), it moves, via the question of immigration and exile, to the emerging horizon of a transnational or postnational contextualization of Australian literature in a global context. These three successive stages of reflection are not conceived, however, as a chronological sequence. They should be understood far more as palimpsestic or simultaneously interwoven layers of spatialized meaning. It is impossible to separate them from each other. This reciprocal enmeshing of layers of meaning can be illustrated variously. First, the indigenous layer of meaning is overlaid, irrevocably, by the white settler layer of signification: unlike much briefer episodes of hegemony and genocide at a continental scale, such as the ten-year Nazi domination of Europe, settler nations have been in place for several centuries and cannot possibly be dislodged. Any re-assertion of native title, or, more radically, re-establishment of indigenous sovereignty, must be negotiated within the framework of existing settler sovereignty, even if it is to radically question that latter sovereignty.[17] Similarly, the immigrant experience cannot be held apart from that of the expropriation of indigenous territory, even though later immigrants may have arrived long after the colonial first-contact conflicts, continent-wide settler expansion and the assimilationist biopolitics of the last century. Any immigrant arriving on Australian soil gains a place made possible by the marginalization of the erstwhile indigenous owners. The agency of an unchosen, perhaps even unsuspected set of prior circumstances framing the present, as Judith Butler has shown,[18] inevitably condemns the freshly-disembarked migrant to an unwitting entanglement in the problematic of conquest, genocide and the ongoing struggle over land rights: 'We make our conquests too. | The ruins at our feet are hard to see,' writes Les Murray.[19] Finally, all of these narrative layers must be articulated within a global matrix. The global boom in indigenous art, to take only one example, shows to what extent the indigenous layer of meaning has taken on a global significance of astonishing proportions. In sum, constant flows of immigration and re-migration, with corresponding ebbs and flows of labour power, expertise, talent, accumulated quotidian experience and evolving narratives, mean that all these layers of meaning are ineluctably intertwined with the global palimpsest. These layers of meaning can be teased apart

17 See Bain Attwood, 'Historical Controversies and the History wars', in Russell West-Pavlov and Jennifer Wawrzinek (eds), *Frontier Skirmishes: Literary and Cultural Debates in Australia since 1992* (Heidelberg: Winter, 2010), 34; Henry Reynolds, *Aboriginal Sovereignty: Three Nations, One Australia?* (Crows Nest NSW: Allen & Unwin, 1996).

18 Judith Butler, *Giving an Account of Oneself* (New York: Fordham University Press, 2005).

19 Les Murray, 'The Conquest', *Collected Poems* (London: Minerva, 1992), 47.

for the purposes of analysis, but only to better understand their inextricably tangled co-existence. It follows, therefore, that they must be read together in a manner akin to what Said called 'contrapuntal' reading:[20] as part of vertical sedimentations of cultural bedrock, and as nodes of a horizontal network of spread-out relations spanning the globe.

Searching for a way of theorizing this approach more extensively, I think of Lévi-Strauss's recollections of his early forays into geology as a metaphor for the structuralist undertaking. He describes the experience of 'pursuing, on the slope of a limestone plateau in the Languedoc, the seam between two geological bedrock layers.' This anecdote stands for the search for meaning, tracing 'this pale and blurred line, this often imperceptible difference in the form and consistence of rocky debris' and discovering beneath this 'immense disorder' of 'sudden drops and cliff-faces, scree slopes, scrubby undergrowth, agriculture' a 'master-meaning, hidden from sight, doubtless, but of which each of the others is a partial or deformed transposition.'[21] Appealing as this conceit may be, however, it reduces the immense narrative of sedimented layers of cultural conflict, interaction and transformation to a binary opposition (the two sheets of bedrock meeting along a fault line) which releases a single meaning. Lévi-Strauss's master narrative is not apt to perform the work I want done by this metaphor of contrapuntally interconnected layers of meaning. If we remember that the earth's crust is only a thin outer glacis, the less mobile epidermic surface of a core of turbulent lava flows, then our metaphor must be modified to factor in multiple layers, themselves dynamic, each one mediating between many other, from deep core flows, via the uneven surface and its vegetable outgrowths, to the winds and slipstreams of the atmosphere. Other metaphors may better articulate the ways in which discrepant layers of meaning may overlap and intertwine. Lévi-Strauss's irritated brushing aside of 'sudden drops and cliff-faces, scree slopes, scrubby undergrowth' points, perhaps, to a more promising way to go, a plunge off the beaten track into the bush, down a Heideggerian *Holzweg* which may teach us significantly more about global contrapuntality.[22]

I turn therefore, to an abiding image of Australianness which recurs in many narratives, whether indigenous, settler, immigrant or other, and also joins autochthonous and global strands of narrative to each other: that of the eucalyptus tree. The tree is a hybrid conceit that combines subterranean root systems within the earth, a trunk or trunk system on a horizontal axis (Eliot's 'axle-tree' articulating the respective layers of earth and heavens),[23] and a foliage system. As part of a sylvan community, it lends itself to a complex metaphoricity expressing multiple connective relationships across extended pluridimensional spaces. Like Glissant's mahogany tree in the novel of the same name, 'it reads/deciphers/spells out the forest, whose depths it multiplies everywhere. | A tree is a whole country, and if we ask what this country may be, immediately we plunge into the dark rootedness of time

20 Edward Said, *Culture and Imperialism* (London: Vintage, 1994), 59–61.

21 Claude Lévi-Strauss, *Tristes tropiques* (1955; Paris: UGE 10/18, 1966), 42–43; my translation.

22 Martin Heidegger, *Holzwege*, 5th ed. (Frankfurt/Main: Klostermann, 1972), 3.

23 T. S. Eliot, 'Burnt Norton', *Four Quartets*, in *The Complete Poems and Plays of T. S. Eliot* (London: Faber, 1982), 172.

that we are labouring to clear of brushwood.'[24] The tree is bearer and a disseminator of meaning across time and space, a communicative system which interacts with other communicative systems. It connects various elements and their environments, pervading them with its own networks of intercommunication in a way that embodies interrelationality more aptly than Lévi-Strauss's overly neat geologics.

From Barron Field's classic dismissal of the eucalyptus's 'unpicturesqueness,' 'monotony' and 'harshness' ('I can therefore hold no fellowship with Australian foliage'), via the mute tree of Oodgerroo Noonuccal's poem '?', to the eponymous flora of Murray Bail's *Eucalyptus*,[25] the family of the eucalypts takes on multifarious symbolic valencies for a host of actors within Australian history and literature. But the eucalyptus is also a wanderer, and extends its influence into other geographical, cultural and linguistic domains: 'Their humans, meeting them abroad, | often grab and sniff their hands'.[26] One of the essays in this volume began life as a set of jottings in Cardiff, Wales – there, to my surprise I discovered a large number of eucalyptus trees flourishing in the back yards of the terraced rows of miners' cottages. Since then, I have also met them in Portugal, the south of France, Kenya and South Africa. My brother-in-law grew up with them in his native Argentina.

Whence the global resonance, for me, of a poem by a bilingual Welsh writer, Menna Elfyn, 'Eucalyptus.' The proper noun needs no translation, taxonomic Latin functioning as a quasi-universal language. But the rest of the poem is about the nitty-

24 My translation of Edouard Glissant, *Mahogany* (Paris: Seuil, 1987), 13: '. . . il épelle la forêt, dont il multiplie partout la profondeur. | Un arbre est tout un pays, et si nous demandons quel est ce pays, aussitôt nous plongeons à l'obscur indéracinable du temps, que nous peinons à débroussailler.' See my *North-South/East-West: Global Entanglements in Post-imperial Writing in French and German* (Trier: WVT, 2010), 55–63.

25 Barron Field quoted in Leonie Kramer & Adrian Mitchell (eds), *The Oxford Anthology of Australian Literature* (Melbourne: Oxford University Press 1985), 12–16; Oodgeroo Noonuccal, '?', *My People: A Kath Walker Collection* (Milton QLD: Jacaranda, 1970), 57; Murray Bail, *Eucalyptus* (London: Harvill, 1999).

26 Les Murray, 'Eucalypts in Exile', *Größer im Liegen* (Berlin/Hörby: Edition Rugerup, 2011), 108. I deliberately cite from this bilingual edition with translations by Margit Lehbert.

gritty of the local manifestations of global migrations. The poem's epigraph reads parenthetically:

> (I heard how the scent of the tree filled Baghdad during the Gulf War, its oil being used to cook in the absence of electricity.)
> (Clywais fod arogl yr eucalyptus yn llenwi strydoedd Baghdad yn ystod Rhyfel y Gwlff a bod olew'r goeden yn cael ei ddefnyddio fel tanwydd am nad oedd trydan yn y ddinas)[27]

Elfyn's eucalyptus trees, evoked in English and Welsh, grow in war-torn Iraq, the scent of their oil signalling domesticity. But the volatility of that scented oil allows these eucalyptuses as symbolic beings to escape from any imposed container or constraint. Thus the eucalyptus tree, its unruly tendency to seed far and wide making it an expatriate on every continent, becomes a bearer of rhizomatic rather than arborescent meanings. To the extent that the eucalyptus indexes any version of rootedness, it is its radical tendency to put out large reticular irrigation systems seeking every available source of moisture in the vicinity that characterizes its relationship to place. The eucalyptus spreads its nutritional bases in a tentacular manner below and above ground, bespeaking thereby its implicit desire to communicate with its fellows in native and non-native environments, taking root in other linguistic ground while gesturing incorrigibly towards its Antipodean affiliations.

[27] Menna Elfyn, *Detholiad o Gerddi – Selected Poems 1978–1994* (Llandysul: Gomer, 1995), 48–49.

Those Antipodean affiliations continue to exist in the rich soil of the imagination. When I reminisce of my own childhood, I think of a tall and ancient eucalyptus which grew next to the front gate of a disused rural property in the Grampians/Gariwerd in Western Victoria where our family took its yearly winter holidays. The father of the owners could remember his own father's recollections of indigenous people coming at regular intervals to visit the tree. It was presumably a sacred tree, a node of significance in the enduring intertwining of country, spirit and narrative, its meaning spilling out across the borders of indigenous lore into the oral history of Western District settler families. From there it percolated into the less securely rooted memory of place of an urban Anglo-Celtic family and one of its expatriated members. None the less, the image of that tree remains deeply entrenched, affectively resonant, in my own imagination of place. These two stories, rooted partially but not exclusively in Cardiff and the Victoria Valley, Grampians/Gariwerd, and narrated now in urban Berlin, are vignettes from my idiosyncratic version of a transnational, multilayered, contrapuntally read streaming of an Imaginary Antipodes.

PART ONE

1 'Why, White Man, Why?': White Australia as the Addressee of Apostrophe in Contemporary Aboriginal Writing

Since the 1960s, the most dynamic area of new and experimental writing in Australia in English has been the work produced by indigenous poets, novelists and dramatists. The innovative force of their writing partly resides in the fact that black authors constantly stress the complexity of their relationship with the audience. The poet Lionel Fogarty elaborates some aspects of the difficulty of writing as an indigenous artist in contemporary Australia:

> To write I have to use
> A medium
> That is not mine.
> If I don't succeed, bear with me.
> I see words beyond any acceptable meaning
> And this is how I express my dreaming.[1]

But here Fogarty is disingenuous, for his use of the English language is anything but timorous. The frequently aggressive tones of his poetry are inflected by his awareness that to write as an indigenous poet in Australia is an act of confrontation. In this poem and elsewhere, Fogarty constantly thematizes the context of poetic enunciation and its most basic social configuration, that of the writer-reader relationship. In 'You Who May Read My Words,' he directly addresses his audience, 'You [who] hope that I speak of beauty | And tell of Dreaming . . . You who will laugh or cry | but never set a goal.' Reading Fogarty's turbulent, unpredictable poetry is a disturbing experience, not least because he deliberately sets out to confound reader expectations. Although he politely deflects his comments into the third person, his opening lines show that he is well aware of the wider political ramifications of the confrontation with the white majority audience: 'Everyone wants writings of Aboriginals | Past, Present and Future. | But do they want the | REALITY.'[2] In this opening chapter, I wish to accept Fogarty's challenge to the white reader, exploring this issue by listening to a range of ethnic literary voices. Underlying this reading is the much debated question of how white readers can read and speak about the literature of the indigenous people of Australia, given the violent history which both connects and separates the two peoples.

Who speaks, who listens?

During the two centuries after the white settlement – or invasion – of Australia in 1788, the native inhabitants of the fifth continent suffered from a more or less sys-

1 Lionel Fogarty, 'Tired of Writing', in *Yoogum Yoogum* (Ringwood, VIC: Penguin, 1982), 1.
2 Lionel Fogarty, 'You Who May Read My Words', in *New and Selected Poems: Munaldjali, Mutuerjaraera* (Melbourne: Hyland House. 1992), 142.

tematic process first of genocide and later of institutionalized marginalization. Only in 1967 did the Aboriginal people receive Australian citizenship and recognition of full civic rights; in 1992, two centuries after invasion and occupation, the highest court in Australia confirmed the legal priority of Aboriginal ownership of the land in the historic Mabo decision. Despite these belated reforms, successive federal governments have been hesitant to take action to rectify continuing discrimination. Symptomatic of the generalized reluctance to implement genuine reform was the Howard government's persistent refusal to issue a representative apology to the Aboriginal people for the crimes of the past, rectified only by Rudd's historic apology speech in Parliament on 13 February 2008.

In this context, it is supremely important that white Australians read indigenous writing, for as the Aboriginal activist Marcia Langton has said: 'Australians do not know and relate to Aboriginal people. They relate to stories known by former colonists.'[3] Kevin Gilbert stresses the need to '[r]ewrite our Aboriginal history and remove the distortions and the lies . . . the general public of Australia knows little of our real situation.'[4] Whence the importance of contemporary indigenous writing, as exemplified in the words of Ruby Langford (Gibini):

> My story is about twentieth century Aboriginal Life. About the way we live today. And it's probably the only information a lot of students get that puts the Aboriginal point of view. Because Koori[5] history and culture is almost never taught in schools, and if it is, it is usually as it seen by whites, and not from an Aboriginal perspective.[6]

Yet as soon as soon as the white reader wants to move from a purely passive, receptive stance, to a more active discursive role as a teacher, politically engaged citizen or sympathizer, it becomes difficult to know what position one can responsibly take up. How can I as a white Australian speak about what I have read? Since the earliest days of the white occupation of Australia, the systematic destruction of Aboriginal social structures and the extensive extermination of the indigenous people themselves, white commentary has interpreted Aboriginal culture in a discursive gesture complicit with, indeed essential to the ongoing campaign of marginalization and dispossession of the native inhabitants of the continent. The production of white discourse on the Aboriginal people went hand in hand with the obliteration or suppression of the indigenous peoples' own voices – with the reduction of indigenous discourse to a 'silent Other,' to use Said's terms, rather than a genuine 'interlocutor.'[7] Aboriginal authorship has been elided by anthropologists passing the

3 Quoted in Tom O'Regan, *Australian National Cinema* (London: Routledge, 1996), 277.

4 Kevin Gilbert, 'Black Policies', in Jack Davis and Bob Hodge (eds), *Aboriginal Writing Today*, Papers from the First National Conference on Aboriginal Writers, Perth, Western Australia, 1983 (Canberra: Australian Institute of Aboriginal Studies, 1985), 40.

5 'Koori': a generic term for the indigenous people of South-Eastern Australia. Other terms used are 'Murri' (Queensland and Northern New South Wales), 'Nunga' (Southern Australia) or 'Nyoongah' (Western Australia).

6 Ruby Langford (Ginibi), 'Koori Dubays', in Dale Spender (ed.), *Heroines* (Ringwood, VIC: Penguin, 1991), 129.

7 Edward W. Said, 'Orientalism Reconsidered', in Francis Baker et al. (eds), *Literature, Politics and Theory: Papers from the Essex Conference 1976–84* (London: Methuen, 1986), 215.

indigenous storyteller's name under the anonymous label of the 'native informant' and replacing it with their own. Traditional oral narratives have been recast by white writers in a flat prose which eliminates the context of the narration, its relationship with the land, and reduces indigenous tradition to children's stories reciting 'primitive' platitudes.[8] Aboriginal writers continue to be trammelled by the constraints of Western literary conventions, the price to be paid for gaining possibilities of publication and holding readership.[9]

In the light of this ongoing history of the displacement of Aboriginal voices by the apparatus of white discourse, commenting upon indigenous literature as a white teacher or academic becomes a fraught undertaking. As Kateryna Olijnyk Longley says, '[e]ven the most sympathetic white observers and promoters of Aboriginal culture face the now familiar risk of consolidating the old patterns of domination each time they attempt to act as interpreters of Aboriginal production.'[10] So often the freedom of the (white) reader (and often, by extension, re-writer) of Aboriginal texts has been at the costs of their original authors. How then, can we read indigenous literature and write about it – clearly a necessary educational task – without merely accumulating our own discursive capital, and thereby perpetuating the imbalance of power to speak and be heard which still characterizes modern white Australia its resistance to real change in black-white relations? Stephen Muecke suggests one possible reading position which does not culminate in undermining the artistic autonomy and dignity of indigenous producers: 'Find the place where your discourse is only made possible by its relationship to the other.'[11]

In what follows, I wish to explore in a concrete manner the perspective opened up by Muecke's comment. This will involve pursuing one recurring figure in contemporary Aboriginal literary discourse which does indeed determine, from within its own discursive framework, the conditions of its reception. Specifically, the frequent utilization of second-person address of the public in indigenous texts, already evinced in the opening examples of Fogarty's poetry, quite literally constructs a reading position to be taken up by the white Australian reader. I would argue that this discursive form makes possible a critical reflection on the part of whites which does not lead to mastery of the text, but reflection upon the way in which one relates to the Aboriginal people of whom the poem's speaker is a literary synecdoche – as in Mudrooroo's apostrophe which clearly situates the reader within a geography of silence and complicity: 'On the outskirts of your earhearing, . . . We live unsafe lives in your violence.'[12] To accept that stance is to take up a position made available by the author, and thereby to enter a reader-writer dialogue in which the

8 See Colin Johnson [Mudrooroo Narogin], 'White Forms, Aboriginal Content', *Aboriginal Writing Today*, 21–22.

9 Mudrooroo Narogin, *Writing from the Fringe: A Study of Modern Aboriginal Literature* (Melbourne: Hyland House, 1990), 26–33.

10 Kateryna Olijnyk Longley, 'Autobiographical Storytelling by Australian Aboriginal Women', in Sidonie Smith and Julia Watson (eds), *De/Colonising the Subject: The Politics of Gender in Women's Autobiography* (Minneapolis: University of Minnesota Press, 1992), 370–84, 370.

11 Stephen Muecke, *Textual Spaces: Aboriginality and Cultural Studies* (Kensington, NSW: University of New South Wales Press, 1992), 204.

12 Mudrooroo Narogin, 'On the Outskirts', in *The Garden of Gethsemane: Poems from the Lost Decade* (Melbourne: Hyland House, 1991), 157.

(white) reader does not dictate the terms of the exchange. To accept the reader-role imposed by the black author is one way of allowing a respectful response to Aboriginal discourse, by locating one's own discourse not in a position of appropriation and dominance, but rather, of acknowledgment and listening. Granted, second-person address of the reading public is a time-honoured element of literary rhetorics, and only one aspect of second-person narrative more generally.[13] Granted also, the white public is not the only possible addressee of second-person narrative in Australian indigenous writing. Fellow Aboriginal people may also constitute the 'you' of some texts, as in Kevin Gilbert's poems 'Until You Learn' and 'Shades of Grey' or Lional Fogarty's poem 'Little Murri Be a Murri before an Australian'[14] (or alternatively, both black and white readers may constitute the text's audience[15]). None the less, despite these riders, this mode of literary address is of emblematic significance for white readers. For this form of direct address brings into being a dynamic literary model of a new black-white relationship initiated by the original habitants of the fifth continent.

Addressing the white reader

The opening lines of Oodgeroo Noonuccal's poem 'The Unhappy Race' (from the pioneering 1970 collection *My People*) is exemplary in its implementation of the second-person address to the white reader:

> White fellows, you are the unhappy race.
> You alone have left nature and made civilized laws.
> You have enslaved yourselves as you enslaved the horse and other wild things.
> Why, white man?
> Your police lock up your tribe in houses with bars,
> We see poor women scrubbing the floors of richer women.
> Why, white man, why?
> You laugh at "poor blackfellow", you say we must be like you.
> You say we must leave the old freedom and leisure,
> We must be civilized and work for you.
> Why, white fellow?
> Leave us alone, we don't want your collars and ties,
> We don't need your routines and compulsions.
> We want the old freedom and joy that all things have but you,
> Poor white man of the unhappy race.[16]

[13] For a helpful survey, see Monika Fludernik, 'Introduction: Second-Person Narrative and Related Issues', *Style* 28: 3 (1994), 281–311.

[14] Kevin Gilbert, 'Until You Learn', in *Black from the Edge* (Melbourne: Hyland House, 1994), 34; Lionel Fogarty, 'Little Murri Be a Murri before an Australian', in *New and Selected Poems: Munaldjali, Mutuerjararea* (Melbourne: Hyland House, 1995), 42–43.

[15] See, for an analogous function in the Native American literature, James Ruppert, 'Mediation and Multiple Narrative in Contemporary Native American Fiction', *Texas Studies in Literature and Language* 28 (1986): 209–25; 'Mediation and Multiple Narrative in *Love Medicine*', *North Dakota Quarterly* 59 (1991): 229–41.

[16] Oodgeroo Noonuccal, 'The Unhappy Race', in *My People: A Kath Walker Collection* (Milton, QLD: Jacaranda Press, 1970), 19.

The poem ironically reverses the customary tropes used to describe the Aboriginal people. The 'poor blackfellow' appropriates this appellation and turns it against the white man. Rather than the white man merely being described as an oppressor, he is perceived as enslaving himself. In this way, the indigenous poet assumes the critical, interrogative gaze of the anthropologist, quizzically dissecting the white man's self-oppression, out of which flows his desire to subjugate others. Underlying this inversion of the tropes of oppression, and the reversal of the objectifying anthropological gaze, is the act of directly addressing of the white man. The second-person mode of address thrusts the act of enunciation itself into the foreground. To speak as a black poet, in the discursive environment of late 1960s Australia was itself a gesture of political significance. The act of speaking up is thus emphasized and made into the discursive ground upon which the poem's message rests. A self-assertive appropriation of the power to speak out becomes the basis of communication between white and black. The direct address highlights the way in which the poem defines its very conditions of reception – that of reception of a distinctively indigenous mode of speech, rather than white speech about the 'Aboriginal.'

Crucial in Oodgeroo Noonuccal's poem is the interrogative form, which casts the white reader into question, but also demands a response. The utilization of the interrogative form has two broader implications.

The first is a profound questioning of the agency of the reader. Often, in contemporary indigenous texts, the white reader or spectator (in the case of drama) is confronted with cultural elements such as words in the native language or dance or traditional literary forms which remain opaque. In Jack Davis' *The Dreamers*, for instance, the Dancer's movements and song are only minimally accessible to most white spectators. The script gives a translation of the Dancer's monologue in Act 2, Scene 5, revealing an angry lament: 'Gnullarah dumbart noychwa,' 'My people are dead.' However, as Hodge and Mishra point out, 'Gnullarah' means 'ours' and not 'mine'; furthermore, this possessive pronoun signifies an exclusive, and not an inclusive relationship of belonging, 'a "we" that links the speaker to others as a collective ego but specifically excludes the people spoken to from that identity.'[17] Here, the white spectator is excluded by the cultural resistance of the performance text even as it is addressed to her or him; the reader of the printed script, though partially enlightened by the (approximate) translation, is still not admitted to the indigenous discursive community and its knowledge. Iser, following Ingarden, suggests that the interpretative work of responding to the enigmas thrown up by the text, located in sites of semantic or interpretative uncertainty (what he calls ‚Unbestimmtheitsstellen,'), accords the reader an active role in the process of signification.[18] The presence of enigmas and opacities in Aboriginal texts, however, is

17 See Jack Davis, 'The Dreamers', in *Plays from Black Australia* (Sydney: Currency Press, 1989), 69; Bob Hodge and Vijay Mishra, *Dark Side of the Dream: Australian Literature and the Postcolonial Mind* (Sydney: Allen and Unwin, 1991), 207–8.

18 See Wolfgang Iser, *Die Appellstruktur der Texte: Unbestimmtheit als Wirkungsbedingung literarischer Prosa* (Konstanz: Konstanzer Universitätsreden, 1974), also to be found under the same title in Rainer Warning (ed.), *Rezeptionsästhetik; Theorie und Praxis* (München: Fink, 1993), 228–52; *Der implizite Leser: Kommunikationsformen des Romans von Bunyan bis Beckett*, 3rd ed. (München: Fink, 1994), 67, 70.

not necessarily a signal for the activation of the reader's participation. Such activation assumes hermeneutic capacities on the part of the white reader which in many cases will not and cannot be present. In some situations, a notion of the 'incompetent reader' would seem to be more appropriate than Stanley Fish's idea of the 'competent reader.'[19]

Less jocular versions of this disempowering aspect of the reading experience are also provided by reception theorists. Gadamer speaks of the approach to the text as one where the reader's initial set of assumptions must be modified by experience of 'foreignness' or 'otherness' which inevitably accompany an engagement with the text.[20] Equally, one might invoke a radicalized version of Jauß's notion of the reader's 'horizon of expectations,' which necessarily changes at different historical periods, thus producing a reading experience which may be more or less alienating, more or less thought-provoking.[21] When reading an Aboriginal text, the most appropriate response for a white reader may be to accept partial incomprehension.[22] To acknowledge one's place outside black culture, to acknowledge that understanding is not only dependent upon the volition of the reader but also upon a decision of the owners of the text – even when it has been released into the public domain – would appear an apposite response to indigenous writing. Here the reader-text-author relationship needs to be understood in a larger socio-political framework, and the power of the reader curtailed so as to avoid replicating an ongoing history of expropriations of indigenous cultural self-determination.

A second aspect of the interrogative form of the mode of direct address is important. Oodgeroo Noonuccal's questions are open-ended. To this extent they do not map out concrete discursive strategies for the future, but rather trace the very conditions of possibility of new developments. In her work on second-person narratives, Monika Fludernik has remarked that the performative character of the second-person discourse in literary texts foregrounds the pragmatic act of narration as the source for the narrated story.[23] Out of the *sujet/histoire/*story (depending on whether one employs the terms coined by Shklovsky, Genette, or others) flows the *fabula/discours-récit/*discourse. This creative function of second-person address can be further illuminated by recent advances in reception theory. Iser, in his later research on the act of reading, has reworked Austin's theory of speech acts to take account of non-pragmatic fictional speech (‚entpragmatisierte fiktionale Rede'). Fictional speech acts, he suggests, are speech acts in a vacuum, not inherently

[19] See Stanley Fish, *Is There a Text in this Class? The Authority of Interpretive Communities* (Cambridge, Mass.: Harvard University Press, 1980), 48–49.

[20] See Hans Georg Gadamer, *Wahrheit und Methode: Grundzüge einer philosophischen Hermeneutik,* 2nd ed. (Tübingen: Mohr Siehbeck, 1965), 329.

[21] See for instance Hans Robert Jauß, *Literaturgeschichte als Provokation* (Frankfurt/Main: Suhrkamp, 1970), 175–76. Case studies can be found in Jauß's *Ästhetische Erfahrung und literarische Hermeneutik* (Frankfurt/Main: Suhrkamp, 1982).

[22] Bell Hooks (in *Teaching to Transgress: Education as the Practice of Freedom* [New York: Routledge, 1994], 172) suggests an interesting parallel in the Americna classroom situation. My experience of teaching Australian indigenous texts at university level suggests that when adequately explained and reflected, making space for partial non-comprehension can constitute an appropriate and fruitful performative pedagogical strategy.

[23] Fludernik, 'Introduction: Second-Person Narrative and Related Issues', 288.

attached to any one real discursive situation and thus deprived of an immediate 'perlocutionary' impact. Fictional speech acts are non-situational. Instead, they possess the power to *create a situation* (and thus are 'situation-forming', ,situationsbildend') through the work of a continuous feedback system operating between text and reader.[24]

In his work on direct address in poetry, in its classical rhetorical form of *apostrophe*, Jonathon Culler has suggested that the second-person mode of writing is a linguistic operation which eludes the dichotomies of presence/absence or real/imaginary, occupying instead the space of a fictive event[25] – one whose character is potential, pointing towards the future. This aspect of the mode of literary or dramatic speech examined above corresponds to the prominence of forward-looking constructions of cultural identity in the context of post-colonial writing. This future orientation has been underscored by the British cultural theorist Stuart Hall who has asked:

> Is it only a matter of unearthing that which the colonial experience buried and overlaid, bringing to light the hidden continuities its suppressed? Or is quite a different practice entailed – not the rediscovery but the *production* of identity. Not an identity grounded in the archaeology, but in the *re-telling* of the past?[26]

The power of literary speech acts to bring about a novel situation is given self-reflexive emphasis when that speech act is literally formulated, at the textual level, as a mode of direct verbal address, as in the indigenous address to the white audience. Decisive here is Zima's notion that the formation of cultural identity (both individual and collective) is a process arising out of a communicational context, where identity is forged through an ongoing process of *dialogical* or *polemical* confrontation with other discourses of identity[27] – a process figured indexically in contemporary indigenous writing in Australia through the prominence of second-person address which interpellates, engages and constructs the reader. Here theories of reception can suggest ways of envisaging the act of reading as inherently embedded in a larger context, one which is part of political processes and thus oriented towards future social transformation.

The functions of second-person address of the white reading public in contemporary indigenous literature are very diverse. In what follows I shall examine the use of the second-person mode as an exemplar of the complaint genre, as a mode of accusation, and as an invitation to participate in a process of political change.

24 See Wolfgang Iser, *Der Akt des Lesens: Theorie ästhetischer Wirkung* (München: Fink/UTB, 1976), 87–114.

25 See Jonathon Culler, *The Pursuit of Signs: Semiotics, Literature, Deconstruction* (London: Routledge and Kegan Paul, 1981), 135–54.

26 Stuart Hall, 'Cultural Identity and Diaspora', in Jonathan Rutherford (ed.), *Identity: Community, Culture, Difference* (London: Lawrence and Wishart, 1990), 224.

27 See Peter V. Zima, *Theorie des Subjekts: Subjektivität und Identität zwischen Moderne und Postmoderne* (Tübingen: Francke/UTB, 2000), 11, 15, 376.

Modes of indigenous address

The complaint genre, which looks back to a long history in popular and elite literary production straddling the divide between oral and written cultures, and often foregrounding the enunciating poetic voice,[28] is widespread as a contemporary mode of literary expression among Aboriginal writers. It is to be found in many new hybrid forms of oral narration,[29] and appeared early on in the Aboriginal writing in English which began to emerge in the 1960s and 1970s. Jack Davis' poem 'Desolation' exemplified this complaint genre utilizing the direct address form:

> You have made our land into a desolate place.
> . . .
> *The tribes are all gone,*
> *The boundaries are broken:*
> *Once we had bread here,*
> *You gave us stone.*[30]

A similar example of the complaint genre is to be found in Kevin Gilbert's poem 'People Are Legends' in the volume of the same title: 'Kill the legend | Butcher it | With you acute cynicisms | Your paternal superfluities | With your unwise wisdom.' Gilbert's poem claims that the destruction of a people and the destruction of its legends, its culture, amount to the same thing. Generally, the rhetorical use of the imperative can often constitute a defiant challenge to the addressee to continue a practice implicitly condemned by the speaker. But in the indigenous Australian context, it also represents a rhetorical assumption of an 'imperious' enunciative mode associated with power. This gesture of appropriation reverses the customary vector of speech, speaking forth from the position of the powerless. Thus the imperative second-person address embodies a challenge to power, just as the direct address is a challenge to the one-way flow of objectifying white discourse. This discursive process is echoed later on within the poem, when the same second-person mode is used to hold up a mirror before white subjectivity:

> All this
> And more you must needs do
> In order
> To form a husk of a man
> To the level and in your own image
> Whiteman[31]

28 Danielle Clarke, 'Introduction', in Danielle Clarke and Elizabeth Clarke (eds), *'This Double Voice': Gendered Writing in Early Modern England* (London: Macmillan, 2000), 1–2.

29 See Tim Rowse, *After Mabo: Interpreting Indigenous Traditions* (Melbourne: Melbourne University Press, 1993), 2; Ross Chambers, *Room for Maneuver: Reading (the) Oppositional (in) Narrative* (Chicago: University of Chicago Press, 1991), 16–26.

30 Jack Davis, 'Desolation', in *The First Born and Other Poems* (Sydney: Angus and Robertson, 1970), 36.

31 Kevin Gilbert, 'People *Are* Legends', in *The Blackside: People ARE Legends and other poems* (Melbourne: Hyland House, 1990), 68.

Not only the destruction of Aboriginal culture, but also conversely, its maintenance in the face of all odds, is performed through the mobilization of the direct address mode. On the stage, this is a literal process, as in the last act of Bob Maza's 1988 play *The Keepers*. At the end of the play, the Aboriginal woman Mirnat makes a speech. Through her friendship with the white woman Elizabeth, a friendship strengthened through their shared loss of their husbands and sons in the racial conflicts of the pioneer era, Mirnat has become the director of a home for Aboriginal girls. Upon the jubilee of the home's foundation, which coincides with the celebration of Australian Federation in 1901, she meditates upon her place in white Australia:

> My name is "Mirnat Koonowar", which translated means "black swan of the bullrushes". From that hill over there at that place called Bulli Murra, if you were to cast your eyes around as far as the eyes can see, you will see what is the land of the Boandik. I say "is" because in Boandik law as long as the land is there, so is the law. It's like putting your mark on water: . . . you can put all the lines you want . . . you never change it. It stays the same way. So it is with the land. Man or animal or plant . . . comes and goes. Some foolish men believe they can own the land, but to the Earth Spirit . . . it is like a flea that tries to own the dog. The law of this land, the Boandik law, says that all is there to use. It will feed you, clothe you . . . protect you and it will be your friend if you learn its ways and live with it. If you don't, it will be your enemy . . .This land is alive. It moves, it breathes . . . we know this because we are its keepers.[32]

The direct address mode, which draws attention to the performative aspect of literary writing, is all the more forceful in the context of theatre, where it is spoken to a real audience in a real time and place. It is significant that Maza's play was performed in 1988, the year of (white) Australia's Bicentennial – an event which was largely boycotted by Aboriginal groups. Thus Mirnat's address of the proud colonists of 1901 is addressed to the equally proud Australians of 1988. It is an injunction not to forget the moral imperative of listening to and caring for the land, despite two hundred years of exploitation – and an assertion of the indigenous people's living relationship to a land which has been withheld from them for two centuries. The 1992 Mabo decision confirmed under white law perennial indigenous claims of their unbroken relationship of belonging to the land.

Indigenous self-confidence in the resilience and power for renewal of their cultural traditions has been accompanied not only by 'complaint' modes of discourse, but also by demands for political and social change on the part of white Australia. Such demands for a change of mind motivate an oral narrative told by the Broome storyteller Paddy Roe. An Aboriginal man is imprisoned for marrying a girl who is underage, promised to him under indigenous law. Paddy Roe is called in to mediate between the two parties, explaining the intricacies of indigenous law to the social welfare service, with the result that the offender is released on parole. The mediator

32 Bob Maza, *The Keepers*, in *Plays from Black Australia: Jack Davis, Eva Johnson, Richard Walley, Bob Maza* (Sydney: Currency Press, 1989), 227–28.

vents his irritation upon the white social workers and their inadequate knowledge of black traditional customs:

> oh I got mad too –
> "You people try and dig little bit more deep –
> you bin digging only white soil –
> try and find the black soil inside" (Laughter) –
> YEAH –
> I said to him –[33]

This is a typical example of the referential slippage affecting second-person literary address, where 'you' potentially indicates both a narratee within the text and an actual reader. Not only the social workers in the story, but Stephen Muecke, the interlocutor and 'informed scribe' who has transcribed and published Roe's narratives, and also the reader, are included in Paddy Roe's diatribe against white ignorance and its devastating effects upon black lives.

The active challenge to the white reader to embark upon a disturbing process of reflection is also embodied in the apostrophic form in Jack Davis' poem 'Earth People,' which ironically compares the 'strange habits' of black people in South Africa and Australia: falling off balconies, tumbling out of windows, climbing up walls with pieces of clothing. The poem sarcastically proposes anodyne reasons for this aberrant behaviour ('maybe they don't like tall buildings . . . Or perhaps they don't like symmetrical | precision of iron bars') before tossing the ball back into the reader's court:

> Or perhaps the reason is
> or could it possibly be
> could be?
> No no white man
> you tell me[34]

Kevin Gilbert issues a similar challenge which endows the reader with an uncomfortable self-questioning agency: 'In kingdoms where injustice reigns |. . . and democracy fails | like now – | the choice is yours my friend.'[35]

A similar use of the interrogative apostrophe occurs in Gilbert's 'Mister Man,' written, he explains in the introductory note to the poem, 'after watching a tribal Aboriginal berate Judge Furnell for his facile cleverness and his incomprehension of the affinity of the Aboriginal and his tribal land.' The poem implicitly demands what right a white judge has to arrogate the authority to speak about the land and its original trustees:

33 Paddy Roe and Stephen Muecke, 'Intellectuals, Power and Truth', in Krim Benterrak, Stephen Muecke and Paddy Roe (eds), *Reading the Country: Introduction to Nomadology* (Fremantle: Fremantle Arts Centre Press, 1984), 172.

34 Jack Davies, 'Earth People', in *Black Life: Poems* (St Lucia: University of Queensland Press, 1992), 3.

35 Kevin Gilbert, 'Choice is yours', in *Black from the Edge*, 20.

Mister Man,
Have you stood on this rock
Have you come close to this ghost-gum tree
Have you stood on green fingers of grass
And felt deep their life surge like me?

After rehearsing this rhetorical move several times, there is an abrupt shift in the strategy employed:

Mister man
Have you stood on the shore
Of this land your own soul now rent bare
And discovered the hatred you wrought
The suffering the death you ploughed there.[36]

Gilbert's poem evinces here one of the ambiguities of second-person discourse, in the contiguous uses of two forms of 'you.' The first instance implicitly overlaps with the use of the second-person mode as a designation for the narrating self objectified as a 'protagonist' within its own discourse (as in the frequent colloquial use of 'you' to designate the 'I' of the discourse). Thus, the 'you' is addressed to the white man, but employs the shadowy suggestion of the 'you'-as-self to anchor the accusing questions in the secure ground of the *indigenous speaker's* cultural and spiritual knowledge. This knowledge forms the basis for a comparison of the two cultures and their relative discursive authority. The second instance clearly refers only to the *white man as addressee* of the Aboriginal speaker's tirade.[37] Yet within the context of that questioning tirade, there is a subtler potential function inherent in the protagonist-'you.' The interrogative use of the second-person address has an implicit rhetorical function: 'Can you speak from a position of indigenous knowledge of the land? – If not, then remain silent and cease to pontificate.' However, this rhetorical function remains mute, with the question being maintained as an open-ended form. This 'challenge' mode leaves intact the remote possibility of the white man showing enough humility to learn from his black fellows, and indeed, being able to transfer to the enunciative community implied by the protagonist-'you.'

The same double valency of the 'you' evinced in Paddy Roe's diatribe cited above frequently operates in Sally Morgan's bestselling *My Place* of 1987. The collective autobiographical text recounts the writer's gradual discovery of her indigenous identity, hidden from her by her parents in the fear that the children would be taken away by the state. Child removal was a common practice and widespread of Australian government native policy from the end of the nineteenth century until the 1970s, as the recent government report, *Bringing them Home*, revealed.[38] Many families experienced the repeated removal of 'mixed-blood' children generation after generation, a phenomenon recorded by the life stories of Morgan's

36 Gilbert, 'Mister Man', 8–9.
37 See Fludernik, 'Introduction: Second-Person Narrative and Related Issues', 285.
38 *Bringing them Home*: Report of the National Inquiry into the Separation of the Aboriginal and Torres Strait Islander Children from Their Families (April 1997) http://www.austlii.edu.au/au/special/rsjproject/rsjlibrary/hreoc/stolen/prelim.html. Accessed 26 April 2011.

mother, grandmother and great uncle, which make up the subsequent portions of the text. This practice had devastating effects on the identity of those affected, especially as white fathers' reluctance to admit paternity facilitated the removal of 'mixed' children, as Morgan's grandmother makes clear in the life-narrative included in *My Place*:

> My name is Daisy Corunna . . . My Aboriginal name is Talahue. I can't tell you when I was born, but I feel old. My mother had me on Corunna Downs Station, just out of Marble Bar . . .. Now, some people say my father wasn't Howden Drake-Brockman [the owner of the cattle station where she was born], they say he was this man from Malta. What can I say? . . . Aah, you see, that's the trouble with us blackfellas, we don't know who we belong to, no one'll own up.[39]

The 'you' of this discourse is the granddaughter Sally with her tape recorder, but also, indirectly, the reader of the book. The grandmother's use of the second-person pronoun is another example of referential slippage. This is not a narratological deficit: on the contrary, at work here is not only the clearly accusatory complaint discourse which structures the grandmother's narrative, but also, the tone of conciliatory mediation which underpins Morgan's project in general. The double valency of this use of second-person address engenders a particularly intense form of what Bonheim in another place labels 'conative solicitude,' the capacity to deliberately involve the reader in the narrative.[40] Thus the repeated use of the 'you' in the embedded narratives within Morgan's text support her wider project: to communicate the reality of indigenous experience to her fellow Australians without excessively alienating them, as I argue more detail in the next chapter. The bestseller status of *My Place*, with more than half a million copies sold to date in Australia alone, indicates that this strategy has been successful. The complaint genre is carefully modulated by Morgan into a genre of emotionally based solidarity and affective community.

The optimism underlying Morgan's use of the apostrophic invocation of a white reader can also be found, for instance, in Mudrooroo's 'Song Thirty' from *The Song Cycle of Jacky*, in which the apostrophe is delivered by proxy, spoken through the mouth of a child:

> 'Mummy, Mummy,
> What's a Naboriginal?
> One came to talk to us today –
> What's a Nunkanbah?
> Told us Captain Cook was bad,
> Only came to steal this land –
> Mummy, what's a Nembaluk?
> Said that we had spoilt the ground,
> Said that time would condemn us for our crime –

39 Sally Morgan, *My Place* (Fremantle: Fremantle Arts Centre Press, 1987), 325.

40 Helmut Bonheim, 'Conative Solicitude and the Anaphoric Pronoun in the Canadian Short Story', in Werner Wollte (ed.), *Sprachtheorie und angewandte Linguistik: Festschrift für Alfred Wollmann zum 60. Geburtstag* (Tübingen: Narr, 1982), 77–86.

Mummy, do you know about the Unguru?
Said it was a great big snake;
Said it struck when it was hurt;
Said that it was hurting now –
Mummy, I'm too scared to cry,
I don't want our land to die.'
Jacky smiles, he's getting through.[41]

'Jacky' was a name often used for Aboriginal men treated as infants within the workings of white society. Paradoxically, this modern-day, politically militant Jacky is best able to communicate with white Australia through its children, who are figured as taking to heart the Aboriginal cause. In this image of a new generation of white Australians, Mudrooroo presents the issue of justice for the indigenous people as a question which affects the moral and spiritual well-being of all Australians. In the poem, the children address questions to their parents, questions which, both in their rhetorical form and substance, echo the interrogation of the white reader through the direct address in other poems mentioned above.

Childhood as a place of potential for change also occurs in Jack Davis' play *The Dreamers*. The old and dying Uncle Worru brusquely interrogates a small white boy, Darren, who has come to play with the old man's grandson Shane: 'You *Wetjala* or *Nyoongah*?' – translated: Are you white or Aboriginal? Once again the direct interrogative mode demands that the representative of white Australia take up a stance which is implicitly politicized. The frightened boy does not understand the question, but a few moments later, Worru has softened and is teaching him names of parts of the body in the Nyoogah language, figuring a process of learning about indigenous culture.[42] This is an apposite vignette encapsulating the author-reader relationship invoked by second-person enunciation and the receptive position it offers to the white reader.

A short poem by Oodgeroo Noonuccal, entitled '?' sketches a scenario in which an infuriated speaker imperiously demands a reply from a mute eucalyptus tree. In its stubborn refusal to answer, the tree silently questions the questioner, implying that only when the questioner ceases to rant and begins to listen, will space emerge in which an answer can be heard.[43] The eucalyptus is a ubiquitous image in contemporary Aboriginal poetry, standing for the organic character of indigenous tradition, rooted in the land but capable of growth, renewal, development and interaction with its environment. The implications of Oodgeroo Noonuccal's '?' regarding black culture are clear. If we as white readers, commentators and teachers of indigenous writing wish to participate in the process of cultural renewal initiated by the indigenous writers of Australia, one small way in which we can contribute is to accept the role their texts ascribe to us. This means acknowledging that it is Aboriginal writing which interpellates us, so that only through its construction of us as readers can we speak about indigenous literature. And it means remembering that

41 Mudrooroo Narogin, 'Song Thirty' from *The Song Cycle of Jacky*, *The Garden of Gethsemane*, 111.

42 Jack Davis, *The Dreamers*, 27, 28.

43 Oodgeroo Noonuccal, '?', *My People*, 57.

our stance with regard to indigenous literature – especially as teachers – should never cease to be that of the listener and the learner.

2 Uncovering Collective Crimes: Sally Morgan's *My Place* as Australian Indigenous Detective Narrative

Two men are discovered dead, their bodies eighteen miles apart, on a remote sheep station in drought-stricken outback Australia. The murders have no obvious motivation, and no trace is to be found of their perpetrator. Unable to make any headway with their investigations, the police lay the case to rest until, six months later, the part-Aboriginal Detective Inspector Napoleon Bonaparte, the protagonist of Arthur Upfield's novel *Bony and the Black Virgin*, is called in to reopen the proceedings.[1] Inspector Bony of course successfully solves the mystery of the double murder in *Bony and the Black Virgin*. It is the hero's skill in 'reading the Book of the Bush,' a motive frequently mentioned in the story, which marks him out from other investigators and makes him the super-sleuth that he is. The indigenous people's traditional ability to read the minute details of the land, the marks left by weather, animals and human beings, constitutes Bony's uncanny powers of detection: 'A small problem unworthy of a white man's attention! . . . Meticulous attention to detail, unlimited patience, and unbounded curiosity received their reward from the ancient Spirit of the Land who had tested him . . . History was written on this page of the Book of the Bush' (*Bony and the Black Virgin* 76). This is a white writer speaking – the English-born detective novelist drew upon his experience of working on remote cattle stations in Australia to craft his tales. It is instructive to contrast Upfield's ventriloquism of the black speaker with the chiding tones of a contemporary Aboriginal storyteller: '*You people try and dig little bit more deep – you bin digging only white soil – try and find the black soil inside*'[2] If Upfield's tale purports to describe a detective who brushes away the layers of outback dust to reveal the traces of a crime, the indigenous storyteller would appear to be implying that the white man is not genuinely interested in, nor indeed capable of, uncovering the past and its secrets.

In this chapter I would like to examine two Antipodean variations of the detective narrative, first taking a brief look at this novel by the white Australian writer Upfield, and then moving on to a more sustained reading of a 1987 autobiography by the black Australian Sally Morgan, *My Place*. Common to the two texts is the capacity of the indigenous investigator to read Australian history for traces of crimes hidden by the passage of time. The order in which I will examine these two texts does not indicate a hidden cultural hierarchy, but follows a historical development: for the best part of the two centuries after the white occupation of Australia, white writers described the indigenous peoples whose land they had seized, until the 1970s, when Aboriginal literary voices became more strident and replaced those

1 Arthur Upfield, *Bony and the Black Virgin* (Sydney: Pan Books/Heinemann, 1984). All references in the text.

2 Krim Benterrak, Stephen Muecke and Paddy Roe, *Reading the Country: Introduction to Nomadology* (Fremantle: Fremantle Arts Centre Press, 1984), 168.

which had previously determined their representation in white Australia.[3] Upfield's text figures here as a foil to highlight the full radicalism, but also the limitations, of Morgan's investigative project.

The Western Australian writer and artist Sally Morgan published her family autobiography *My Place* in 1987. Her text was hugely successful, selling over half a million copies in Australia by 2000, and seeing seven reprints under the London Virago imprint with in the first decade or so after publication. For a small country with a population of twenty million, a traditional antipathy towards high cultural forms and an ongoing tradition of racism, sales of this quantity are quite remarkable, all the more so given that indigenous literature does not always belong on the best-seller lists. Part of the reason for this success is perhaps that *My Place* speaks about a much-debated aspect of recent Australian history: that of the 'Stolen Generation,' a term coined to refer to the Aboriginal children forcibly removed from their parents under white government policy until the mid 1970s.

In 1997, *Bringing them Home*, the Australian Government report of a national inquiry into the separation of Aboriginal and Torres Strait Islander children from their families, concluded that between one in three and one in ten indigenous children were forcibly removed from their parents and communities in the period from approximately 1910 until 1970. The children were raised in institutions or given to adoptive families, often subjected to sexual abuse and racial discrimination, and frequently lost contact with their biological parents. Most indigenous families have been affected, in one or more generations, by the forcible removal of one or more children. The long term psychic trauma and social and familial disintegration caused by these government policies are immeasurable, but the report provides hundreds of individual testimonies to the pain and discrimination experienced by indigenous children and their families in the name of 'enlightened' state intervention (*Bringing them Home*). The aim of this policy was ostensibly to provide better living conditions for children than in shattered indigenous society, but effectively drove a wedge, one the one hand, between 'full-blood' Aboriginals, segregated out of sight in conditions of poverty on reserves and marginal settlements, and 'half-castes' who were to be assimilated into white society; and, on the other hand, between older and younger generations, so that the linguistic heritage and traditional knowledge of the indigenous peoples was rapidly lost. The policy also aimed to break up a potential block of collective Aboriginal protest by vitiating the integrity of Aboriginal society. The policy of forced removal needs to be seen in the larger context of the European invasion of Australia and the expulsion of the indigenous people from their lands: the later policy effectively perpetuated the process of cultural destruction initiated by the expropriation of land (the land was the basis for, indeed the embodiment of the economic, social, cultural and religious structures of traditional Aboriginal society, and its reappropriation remains central in Aboriginal activism against all forms of white discrimination). I shall refer consistently to these practices as a form of collective crime, for though child removal was ratified by government legislation, this very legislation deprived indigenous Australians of most basic human rights on

[3] J. J. Healy, *Literature and the Aboriginal in Australia*, 2nd ed. (St Lucia: University of Queensland Press, 1989), xx–xxi.

the basis of skin colour until into the late 1960s – from the right of free movement to the right to a minimum standard of living; from the right to sexual and marital self-determination and the exercise of parental responsibility, to the right to legal appeal against such legislation.[4] The crime mystery scrutinized in this chapter is that of the darker side of white Australia's history, and could be placed under the sign of the storyteller Paddy Roe's injunction: '*You people try and dig little bit more deep – you bin digging only white soil – try and find the black soil inside.*'[5]

Reading between the (colour) lines

Upfield draws upon such commonplaces of Aboriginal culture to create a new sort of detective. By appropriating this aspect of the indigenous people's intimate knowledge of their country, he secured a lucrative place on the detective-fiction market, of which the frequent reprints and worldwide translations of the *Bony* novels are a clear indicator. But it is important that Bony is not merely one of the Aboriginal trackers, blacks co-opted by the white police in colonial Australia for their superior bush knowledge and their skill at finding the traces of criminals on the run, of which the novel makes mention during the preliminary episodes (*Bony and the Black Virgin* 41). Bony is a 'half-caste' Aboriginal and thus differentiated from the 'real' Aboriginal whose skills are used by the white police without their persons being of any interest to the narrative. Rather, it is Bony's partly white identity (accentuated by a markedly English touch betraying the author's compensatory need to justify the choice of his protagonist[6]) which allows him also to belong to the upper echelons of the white Australian police force, and thereby, to take on a mediatory role of discoverer in the narrative process which the text is at pains to underline: 'History was written on this page of the Book of the Bush ... It was not unlike trying to read a serial story backwards from the installment one picks up by chance' (*Bony and the Black Virgin* 176). This, of course, as Tzvetan Todorov points out, is the narrative role of the detective or the concomitant narrator in the crime narrative. In his work on the detective narrative, Todorov adapts the Russian formalist concepts of 'story-line' (*fabula*), meaning the chronological sequence events forming the basis of the narrative, and the 'plot' (*sujet*), signifying the reconfiguration of the story-line within and through the event of narration.[7] In Todorov's formulation, the initially obscure series of events resulting in the crime corresponds to the 'story-line' (*fabula*), and the narrative process of their elucidation is coterminous with the 'plot' (*sujet*).[8] The detective mediates between the reader and the original course of events, working back from the crime as culminating point in what can be compared to the

4 C. D. Rowley, *The Destruction of Aboriginal Society* (Ringwood, Victoria: Penguin, 1972), 183–84.

5 Benterrak, Muecke and Roe, *Reading the Country*, 168.

6 Beryl Langer, 'The Real Thing: Cliff Hardy and Cocacola-Nisation', *SPAN* 31 (1991), 41, note–15.

7 Viktor Shklovsky, *Theory of Prose*, trans. Benjamin Sher (Elmswood Park, IL: Dalkey Archive Press, 1990), 170.

8 Tzvetan Todorov, 'Typologie du roman policier', in *Poétique de la prose suivi de Nouvelles recherches sur le récit* (Paris: Seuil/Points, 1980), 12–13.

fabula-function, so as to reconstruct the pre-history of the crime in a *sujet*-process in which the reader is called to participate. Bony as a reader of the bush partakes both in Aboriginal knowledge of the land, and at the same time, in the fragmentary, accumulating knowledge of the perplexed white reader. He is a mediator between two cultures of reading, one black, one white.

Where Upfield himself stands, as a white with considerable knowledge of black culture, is difficult to say. He makes some gestures towards advocacy for the Aboriginal people, commenting that 'much money is spent on [the Aborigines'] education – and barriers erected to prevent them benefiting from it' (*Bony and the Black Virgin* 107), or deftly reveals the psychological mechanisms of racism: 'So many people fail to see the Aborigines for what they are. To regard them as uncouth savages is such a boost for the ego, and yet, search as you might, you won't find a moron among them' (*Bony and the Black Virgin* 124). Yet at the same time, the reader is confronted with repeated comments which indicate some sort of deeply ingrained and unreflected prejudice, when, for example, we are repeatedly told that for an Aborigine, she [Lottee, the main indigenous character] was good-looking (*Bony and the Black Virgin* 122) – as if Caucasian criteria of physiognomic beauty are held to be a universally valid norm shared by writer and readers, to the exclusion of the indigenous people. The ambiguities of Upfield's position are perhaps understandable. *Bony and the Black Virgin* was published in 1959, less than a decade before the white Australian people voted in a referendum to grant the indigenous population Australian citizenship in 1967. Yet it is worthwhile also bearing in mind that in 1958, the Western Australian Commissioner of Police could publicly justify the use of neck-chains to restrain Aboriginal prisoners, and that less than two decades had passed since the last paramilitary punitive expeditions were sent out against Aboriginals.[9]

I would argue that Upfield's detective novel is very much a product of its time, partly expressing outrage at the condition of the indigenous people in an era which would see the first moves to granting the Aboriginal people basic civil rights, and partly a bearer of ongoing attitudes denigrating the original inhabitants of the fifth continent. It is particularly with regard to Bony's own cultural status that the novel operates a strange sort of double vision made up of insight and wilful blindness combined. Bony says he was found as a child beside his dead mother, who had ostensibly been killed for giving birth to him. The boy was raised on a Mission, thus excluding him from full knowledge of traditional Aboriginal culture (*Bony and the Black Virgin* 66). Here the novel gestures towards a broader practice of removal of 'half-caste' children maintained by the Australian government for three-quarters of the twentieth century. This practice was facilitated by the frequent refusal of the white fathers to acknowledge paternity (together with the absence of black mothers' legal rights to half-caste children). Such paternal disavowal is projected by Bony onto the main suspect for the double murder, Eric Downer: Bony hypothesizes that Eric killed the two victims in order to prevent them publicizing his surreptitious Aboriginal marriage with Lottee, a marriage which his white-man's shame does not allow him to admit to friends and family (*Bony and the Black Virgin* 149–50). Yet it

[9] Rowley, *Destruction of Aboriginal Society*, 199, 204.

is the same Aboriginal mother, we are told, who endows Bony with an acute sense of the limits of his intuitive capacity to read the land and unravel the most difficult of conundrums (*Bony and the Black Virgin* 150). And it is Bony's nostalgic attentiveness to Lottee's voice, 'the mother voice he had never known and always longed to hear' (*Bony and the Black Virgin* 154), as the embodiment of a lost narrative of black-white sexual liaison, which leads him to give epistemological weight to Lottee's alternative account of the murders, thus modifying his original supposition. In the final denouement, we learn that Lottee was raped by a white man after her secret marriage to Eric, killed her rapist and a second white man who subsequently threatened her with rape; Eric was merely instrumental in disposing of the bodies (*Bony and the Black Virgin* 153–54). Moreover, as the title of the novel indicates, the secret marriage does not culminate in sexual union, thus foreclosing the question of 'half-caste' children. In this way, an ostensibly more complex reason than mere racist shame at the sexual entanglement of white man and black woman is given as the motivation for the murders. Both of these issues had literary predecessors, for instance in Xavier Herbert's *Capricornia* (1937).[10] And the massive exploitation of Aboriginal women by white men had a long history which is hinted at by Lottee's (secondary, reactive) violence. Ironically, however, it is Bony's own origins in a crime associated with a black-white sexual union, and his own removal to an orphanage – the shadowy fictional trace of real state practices illegal by international human rights standards – which works to operate the textual shift away from the domain of state policy regarding half-blood children, and towards individual indigenous criminality. Thus a structural, collective crime against the indigenous people is elided in the very act of the solving of the fictional riddle. Upfield may condone Lottee's crime, but he none the less places black violence in the foreground of the narrative, not unlike more recent white novelists such as Keneally and Ireland[11] and in parallel with practices of stereotyping in other European cultures. At the close of the story, Upfield has Lottee commit suicide, thus confirming the criminalization which Upfield's enlightened liberalism does not permit him to utter explicitly, and effectively diverting attention from less visible crimes perpetrated by white society against the indigenous population. It is difficult to know whether this elision, on the part of a well-informed observer, was conscious or not. By way of comparison, Rowley's ground-breaking and devastatingly detailed classic of 1970, *The Destruction of Aboriginal Society*, refers to child removal practices, but, significantly, gives no indication of their endurance over the century, nor of the extent of their implementation.[12]

Through its privileging of black over white crimes, Upfield's narrative itself figures an enduring pattern of Australian 'cultural amnesia,'[13] a cultural amnesia which is addressed in a subsequent text also structured by the detective-story narrative, Sally Morgan's *My Place*. In what follows, I wish to read Morgan's

10 See Bob Hodge and Vijay Mishra, *Dark Side of the Dream: Australian Literature and the Postcolonial Mind* (Sydney: Allen and Unwin, 1991), 56–58.

11 Healy, *Literature and the Aboriginal*, 241–62.

12 Rowley, *Destruction of Aboriginal Society*, 232, 236, 380, 302.

13 Benedict Anderson, *Imagined Communities: Reflections on the Origin and Spread of Nationalism*, 2nd ed. (London: Verso, 1991), 204.

autobiographical account against Upfield, as a text which also places an assimilated Aboriginal 'detective' at the centre of the narrative activity, but which is written by an Aboriginal rather than a white author. Furthermore, in place of a detective fiction, this text relates the detection of non-fictional crimes, though no less shocking. And the perpetrators of the crimes are not black, but rather white, the very protagonists initially suspected but then exonerated in Upfield's narrative. In many respects, Morgan's text reverses the structures of Upfield's detective fiction, signifying a collective return-of-the-repressed in contemporary Australian society, accompanied by all the difficulties and pitfalls that such a process entails.

The narrator-detective as mediator

Morgan's immensely successful autobiography contains the narratives of the author herself, as well as those of her mother, her grandmother and her great uncle.[14] In the opening lines of her grandmother's narrative, Nan, as she is known to her family, introduces herself with the words: 'My name is Daisy Corunna . . . My Aboriginal name is Talahue. I can't tell you when I was born, but I feel old. My mother had me on Corunna Downs Station, just out of Marble Bar . . . Now, some people say my father wasn't Howden Drake-Brockman [the owner of the cattle station], they say he was this man from Malta. What can I say? . . . Aah, you see, that's the trouble with us blackfellas, we don't know who we belong to, no one'll own up' (*My Place* 325). Here the question of white fathers' denial of paternity and the consequences for half-caste offspring opens an elderly Aboriginal woman's account of her life, taking up the very same complex of sexual, social and interracial relationships which Bony initially surmises to be at the centre of the double murders in the *Black Virgin*. Essentially, the same tragic historical entanglements of black and white society are at stake, both on an individual and a collective level, and the same attempt to deny that entanglement, whether by the replacement of one murder narrative by another, or through the policies of removal and assimilation. It is the former technique of narrative repression and elision which is decisively reversed in Sally Morgan's *My Place* through its historiographical project so as to reveal the full extent of the removal policy and its cultural bankruptcy.

Sally's mother, exasperated by her daughter's constant interrogations regarding arcane details of family history, accuses her of behaving like a 'detective' (*My Place* 238). This epithet is more than a mere passing quip, for it points to the very principles upon which the narrative is constructed. Morgan's text is organized as a type of detective story. As mentioned above, Todorov has suggested that the detective story is made up of two narratives: first, an absent story-line, corresponding to the Russian formalist term of *fabula*, culminating in the crime; and second, a process of narration which follows the elucidation of that crime, roughly corresponding to the *sujet*, or the narrative (re)construction of the earlier chain of events making up the crime.[15] The opening section of *My Place*, Morgan's own narrative of her childhood and

14 Sally Morgan, *My Place* (Fremantle: Fremantle Arts Centre Press, 1987). All references in the text.

15 Todorov, 'Typologie du roman policier', 12–13.

youth, constitutes this second strand of the detective-story structure (put more accurately, it is a *fabula* which recounts the preconditions of its own unfolding *sujet*-process). We are told of her growing up in suburban Perth in the belief that she has some sort of Indian ancestry, but the text is strewed with clues that point to a submerged Aboriginal heritage. These clues are clearly planted by the author, but are ostensibly invisible to the protagonist herself and to the uninitiated reader. Thus Sally feels a strange fascination for dark-skinned visiting relatives of her own age from the country, whose language she cannot understand (*My Place* 47), a deep sense of symbiosis with the natural life of the wild swamp biotope behind the South Perth housing estate (*My Place* 59), or, as an artistically gifted youngster, has recourse, when paper and pencils run out, to 'small pieces of charcoal from the fire, and . . . strips off the paperbark tree in our yard' (*My Place* 45) thus alluding to Aboriginal traditions of bark painting. These clues to Sally Morgan's rootedness in an Aboriginal cultural heritage are inserted in the text without comment, and provide the textual dynamic which makes the discovery of Aboriginal identity an inevitable part of the narrator's diegetic undertaking. This process is accelerated as Sally grows older and little by little explicitly reclaims her submerged Aboriginal heritage, a project with culminates in a visit to the traditional tribal lands, and finally in the project of recording and transcribing the reminiscences of her mother, grandmother and great-uncle as representative of three generations of indigenous experience, material which formed the basis of the later sections of *My Place* (at this point, the *fabula* of *sujet*-construction arrives at the moment of its own narration, thus fading into pure *sujet*, foregrounding the process by which indigenous history comes to light and is narrated by an older generation, to the listening younger generation).

However, other clues planted in the text are commented on explicitly by the narrator, but cannot be explained at their respective point of occurrence in the narrative. The very fact that these clues cannot be decoded is signalled as a disturbing hermeneutic problem for the child. 'I was often puzzled by the way Mum and Nan approached anyone in authority; it was as if they were frightened. I knew that couldn't be the reason, why on earth would anyone be frightened of the government?' (*My Place* 96). Or elsewhere, when one summer, the State Housing Commission paints all the houses in the Morgans' street – the renovation 'really panicked Nan . . . I tried to reason with her, but to no avail . . . For her, they were here to check on us, and the possibility of eviction was always there, hanging in the air' (*My Place* 103–4). Likewise, Sally cannot understand Nan's excessive pandering to the rent-collector who comes from the State Housing Commission once a month (*My Place* 104). These explicitly problematized puzzles within the text do not underpin the affirmation of an Aboriginal identity. On the contrary, they are indices of the destruction of Aboriginal identity, of a deeply internalized insecurity. As clues or indices in the etymological sense of the word, they point towards a concrete causal connection. They are mute, as clues inevitably are, for reasons that are intimately attached to the policies maintained by the white government of Australia. The causal motivation for these textual puzzles is condensed in a clue of the first variety mentioned above, a fear experienced on the part of Sally herself about the time her father died, in 1961: 'I felt very strongly about families sticking together. So strongly, in fact, that I had a secret meeting with my brothers and sisters; for some reason, I was frightened we would be put in an orphanage' (*My Place* 50). Here, the adults' strange silences are elucidated, implicitly, by the small girl's own instinctive fear – for at this period, the policy of forcible removal was still being carried out on a large scale all over Australia. It is precisely this threat which the narrator claims to have instinctively sensed. At this stage in the narrative, however, there has been no explicit mention of these governmental policies, and this childish reaction functions as yet another mute clue buried in the text which neither the reader nor the narrator are yet in a position to interpret.

It is only in the later sections of *My Place*, when Sally's mother, grandmother, and the latter's brother take over the narration, that the *fabula*, or chain of historical events taken up and reorganized by Sally's *sujet*-construction, is revealed. The three later narratives represent Sally Morgan's family history, but also furnish the details of a crime committed collectively over generations against the indigenous peoples. What constantly recurs in the narratives of the two preceding generations are accounts of being taken away from parents by the officials of the Native Welfare Department. Sally's grandmother and her brother Arthur record being taken away from their mother (*My Place* 332, 207). In turn, Gladys, Sally's mother, recounts her removal, saying at one point in her account: 'Even when I was sick, I belonged to the Native Health Department. I wasn't even allowed to have the comfort of my own mother' (*My Place* 250). Two generations of Aboriginal experience of forcible removal in turn determines the silence which hangs over the third generation, that of the narrator herself. Sally's mother recounts: 'Bill [her white husband] had only been dead a short while when a Welfare lady came out to visit us. I was really frightened because I thought, if she realized we were Aboriginal, she might have taken the children away . . . It was after the visit from the Welfare lady that Mum and I decided we would definitely never tell the children they were Aboriginal' (*My Place* 304–5). Even Morgan's disturbed and violent father appears to have wielded at times the threat of forcible removal against his wife, despite his own seemingly irrational fear that his children might be 'stolen' when he is absent at the pub (*My Place* 301, 26). The historical fact which thus determines the structure of the narrative from the outset is on occasions also inscribed in the margins of Morgan's text, in the clear register of an objective historical discourse. A footnote draws attention to the 'active policy of miscegenation in Western Australia through the 1930s' which entailed 'the legal removal of "half-caste" Aboriginal children from their mothers' (*My Place* 211). The text also mentions curfews and pass laws for black people (*My Place* 250), the sexual exploitation of black women (*My Place* 336–37), brutal beatings of children in homes (*My Place* 186) and the chaining of Aboriginal labourers or shooting of Aboriginals for sport (*My Place* 181). However, the central structure of the text is determined by the policy of forcible removal of Aboriginal children from their families, and the concomitant suppression of the narrator's Aboriginal identity for fear of the family being broken up. It is the pressure exerted upon Aboriginal people over a century by government policy which motivates the hidden core of a detective story whose mystery is, on the one hand, a hidden indigenous identity, and on the other, a silenced history of cultural and social sabotage systematically undertaken by white government, to a great extent out of sight of the public.

One role of these autobiographical writings is to address a fundamental blind spot in Australian national consciousness. Another Aboriginal woman autobiographer, Ruby Langford (Ginibi), has described her undertaking thus: 'My story is about twentieth century Aboriginal Life. About the way we live today. And it's probably the only information a lot of students get that puts the Aboriginal point of view. Because Koori [Aboriginal] history and culture is almost never taught in schools, and if it is, it is usually as it seen by whites, and not from an Aboriginal perspective.'[16] This point is reinforced by the prominent Aboriginal activist Marcia Langton: 'Australians do not know and relate to Aboriginal people. They relate to stories told by former colonists.'[17] Morgan's narrative fulfils this educative role, negotiating between two Australias and two versions of Australian history.[18] Morgan recounts being sent as a child to negotiate between her war-traumatized and deranged father and her terrified mother: '"He'll listen to you", they said. I don't think he ever did . . . One night, I told Nan I didn't want to go, but she said, "You must, there's no one else"' (*My Place* 41–42). This relationship of mediation between violent white father and Aboriginal mother prefigures the later role of *My Place*, that of constituting an appellative form which bridges the gap between indigenous experience and a white audience. Todorov suggests that the narrator in the detective story is a mediator whose *sujet*-construction work makes the buried crime-*fabula* available not only for himself, but also for the reader.[19] In this respect, Morgan performs the role of detective as mediator as does Upfield's Bony. The go-between status of the part-Aboriginal sleuth, bridging the gap between black and white cultures, is crucial to this mediator role. The mediating function of *My Place* is to make Aboriginal history available for Australians, in particular the history of forcible removal. Thus *My Place* prefigured by a decade the massive accumulation of bare facts and figures in the *Bringing them Home* report, and quite possibly paved the way for the public reception of the information transmitted in a more detailed fashion in the later report. The detective-story structure underlying Morgan's narrative is thus crucial to *My Place*'s status as 'a significant act of intercultural brokerage.'[20]

The work of mediation undertaken by the book can also be seen in its appropriation of the recent history of Aboriginal politics. Sally's own rediscovery of her past goes hand in hand with the discrete marking of notable political events in the emergent activism of indigenous people in Australia. Thus the narrative of Morgan's personal discovery of her Aboriginal identity runs parallel to white Australia's progressive awakening to the presence of an indigenous people demanding public and political recognition. Many of the dates Morgan inserts in her text as chronological

16 Ruby Langford (Ginibi), 'Introductory notes to "Koori Dubays"', in Dale Spender (ed.), *Heroines* (Ringwood, Victoria: Penguin, 1991), 129.

17 Tom O'Regan, *Australian National Cinema* (London: Routledge, 1996), 277.

18 Anne Brewster, 'Aboriginal Women's Autobiography: Alice Nannup's *When the Pelican Laughed*', in Dieter Riemenschneider and Geoffrey V. Davis (eds), *Aratjara: Aboriginal Culture and Literature in Australia* (Amsterdam/Atlanta, GA: Rodopi, 1997), 125.

19 Todorov, 'Typologie du roman policier', 13.

20 Tamsin Donaldson, 'Australian Tales of Mystery and Miscegenation', *Meanjin* 50 (1991), 350.

markers correspond to political milestones outside the narrator's private world, but whose significance is crucial for the public fulfilment of a private quest.

In this regard, Morgan's text is a hybrid form, straddling personal discovery and public emergence. The text is an example of what Todorov has called a gnoseological or epistemological narrative: a narrative which emphasizes less the question, What will happen next? than the question, How do perceptions change in the course of the story?[21] Morgan's story, like all detective narratives, is a narration of epistemological transformation both on the individual and the collective planes. The mediating role of the narrator connects these two functions so as to make indigenous history available in a personalized form for the white Australian reader.

The detective's dilemma

However, if Sally as 'detective' fulfils the role of mediator that Todorov ascribes to the sleuth, she as an Aboriginal person also constitutes one of the victims of the crimes – and the public with whom she communicates must find itself on the side of the perpetrators. The task of mediation is thus complicated by the fact that the text's main readers, white Australians, inevitably read their own indictment, however minimal, in the revelation of white destruction of black familial structures. Inherent to Morgan's project are conflicting components which at once enlighten and alienate.

This central problem is most clearly evident in Morgan's style. Language is a central facet of her undertaking, as is indicated by the narrator's repeated allusions to indigenous languages which remain inaccessible to her as a non-tribal Aborigine (*My Place* 30, 47, 148–49), which in turn is an implicit judgment on the value of the English language. Something which cannot fail to draw the reader's attention about *My Place* is the resolutely colloquial tone of the narrative, its apparent refusal of sophisticated narrative technique, its artless, indeed naive register. Stated bluntly, the book is exceptionally easy to read, which, incidentally, makes it a favourite choice of students. The tone of Morgan's autobiographical account is typically suburban and lower-middle class, ostentatiously Australian with its references to 'chip-heaters' and 'kero,' to the ubiquitous Vegemite sandwich or to goannas in the backyard, and characteristically Antipodean in its bland unawareness of, or indifference to, the utter banality of such details. However, it is the contrast with the occasional footnotes which makes one realize that this style is not (only) the narrator's natural 'tone of writing,' but a careful transposition of a particular Australian social register – the more so that the transcribed autobiographical texts of her mother and grandmother assume yet other registers again (Nan's narrative is strongly marked as Aboriginal English). The everyday Australian register is the central vehicle of the autobiography's communicative function. It allows Morgan to perform two otherwise mutually exclusive functions, on the one hand to speak explicitly as an indigenous person with the moral authority entailed by that status, and on the other hand, to

[21] Tzvetan Todorov, 'Les deux principes du récit', in *La Notion de littérature et autres essais* (Paris: Seuil/Points, 1987), 53–54.

speak implicitly as an average Australian, with another sort of moral authority typical of Antipodean working-class reverse snobbery.

The use of conversational Aussie English is the key to the mediating function served by *My Place*. Morgan's text makes the indigenous tradition and perspectives upon the historical forces responsible for the destruction of that tradition, available to the white Australian readers in a form that can be readily received. As David Napier comments, a given culture can only perceive foreignness – be it ethnic or historical, two pertinent forms of alterity made visible in Morgan's autobiography – if it is encoded in a form 'enough like us, and only enough unlike us, to be heuristically useful.'[22] In their *Dark Side of the Dream*, Hodge and Mishra propound the thesis of schizophrenic/hebephrenic split in Australian culture, according to which Australian culture oscillates between a paranoid alertness to threatening double meanings in public discourse, and a philistine refusal to heed anything but the literal meanings of words. Hodge and Mishra argue that these phenomena are two sides of white Australia's ongoing repression of its colonial past, motivated by a profound but repressed collective guilt regarding the expropriation of Aboriginal land. Thus a hostile sensitivity to perceived double meanings and the radical rejection of deeper meanings can be seen as two (only apparently) contradictory symptoms of national repression of a history of illegitimate confiscation of Aboriginal territory.[23] Both these functions can be identified in Morgan's text, and it is not implausible that the acclaim granted to the book is connected to the fact that her style allows these functions to be reconciled. Australian paranoia is given a safe epistemological space in a language which appeals to the featurelessness of Australian discourse; the mystery-story allows the admission of a second level of meaning, while couching this discovery in an absolutely flat linguistic code. This dialectic is of course central to the detective novel, which alternates between bland surface (whether of persons, events or things) and a murderous depth. This double function mirrors Morgan's double identity as ordinary Australian and indigenous representative. In this way, *My Place* can achieve what could only be gestured at by Upfield, the full revelation of a history of white crimes against the original population of the continent. To this extent, Morgan's text touches upon the seldom asked question of the reader to whom the detective novel is addressed, and of the ways in which the reader is interpellated, manipulated, guided through the process of discovery of the crime.[24] The principal difference between Morgan's 'detective story' and more conventional examples of the genre is that this reader is a collective reader, that of white Australia as a whole. Thereby, the reader is in some way also identified, albeit never explicitly, as carrying some sort of responsibility for the crimes revealed. It is for this reason also that the text is so preoccupied with the establishment of a discursive community: in order not to alienate a public which it inevitably places in the dock. The question is, to what extent the conflicting tasks of Morgan's detective narrative, which combines revelation with accusation, are at loggerheads.

22 David A. Napier, *Foreign Bodies: Performance, Art, and Symbolic Anthropology* (Berkeley: University of California Press, 1992), 140.

23 Hodge/Mishra, *Dark Side of the Dream*, passim.

24 See Michael Dunker, *Beeinflussung und Steuerung des Lesers in der englischsprachigen Detektiv- und Kriminalliteratur* (Frankfurt/Main: Lang, 1991).

The very factors making communication with a white reader possible may well militate against the aim of such communication. The construction of a common discursive ground with white readers has drawn deeply hostile responses from indigenous critics. Sally Morgan has been heavily attacked for speaking as an Aboriginal when, some commentators have claimed, she has merely appropriated an indigenous identity with which she did not grow up, with the Aboriginal poet and literary critic Mudrooroo Narogin taking a particularly uncompromising stance (albeit one since moderated).[25] More problematic, however, is the issue of what Mudrooroo Narogin has termed Morgan's tendency to reach some sort of 'accommodation' with white Australian society.[26] In particular Morgan's diction would appear to be complicit in this process, as it inevitably panders to the white assumption that a text written by a member of a marginalized ethnic group will lack the sophistication of literary technique and will use an 'effortless stream of natural expression from a "speaking" rather than a "writing" subject.'[27] Subhash Jaireth has suggested that the narrative voice of *My Place* speaks directly to a comfortable Australian middle-class sensibility and mode of subjectivity and thereby renounces its own potential for cultural subversion.[28] Morgan's narrative style thus offers itself perfectly to containment and recuperation within white society. The cushioning of the message implemented by the text runs the real risk of its accusatory force being flattened and blunted to such an extent that it loses all efficacy for historical change. In other words, the discursive strategy employed by the text to enable its unpalatable message to be conveyed to collective white Australia, a collective subject adept at forgetting the racial crimes of the past, appears to risk vitiating its own objectives. The detective structure of the text reveals a crime, but in the mode of its revelation to a reading public inevitably compromised by that revelation, implicitly dilutes the force of its message.

In this context of political containment it is worth recalling the stalling of the long-awaited reparation of wrongs done to the indigenous peoples of Australia in the 1990s and early 2000s.[29] Significant in this respect was the Australian government's attempt before the High Court to challenge the historical existence of the Stolen Generation, a revisionist coup which was rejected in decisive terms by the court; the same judge, however, also ruled in 2000 against the first two cases for compensation filed by members of the Stolen Generation. Moreover, as the *Bringing them Home*

25 Brewster, 'Aboriginal Women's Autobiography', 14–15; see also Tejaswini Niranjana, *Siting Translation: History, Post-Structuralism and the Colonial Context* (Berkeley: University of California Press, 1992), 170.

26 Mudrooroo Narogin, *Writing from the Fringe: A Study of Modern Aboriginal Literature* (Melbourne: Hyland House, 1990), 14–15.

27 Pam Gilbert, *Coming Out from Under: Contemporary Australian Women Writers* (London/Sydney: Pandora/Unwin Hyman, 1988), 190; see also Sneja Gunew, 'Women's Experimental Writing' in Anna Couani and Sneja Gunew (eds), *Telling Ways: Australian Women's Experimental Writing* (Adelaide: Australian Feminist Studies, 1988), 5–8; Sneja Gunew, *Framing Marginality: Multicultural Literary Studies* (Melbourne: Melbourne University Press, 1994).

28 Subhash Jaireth, 'The "I" in Sally Morgan's *My Place*: Writing of a monologised self', *Westerly* 40: 3 (Spring 1995), 69–78.

29 For regular updates on current issues see *ATSIC, Aboriginal and Torres Straits Islanders Commission Homepage*. http://www.atsic.gov.au. Accessed 15 April 2011.

report claims, Aboriginal children are still being removed from their families at an unacceptable rate, whether by the child welfare or the juvenile justice systems, or both. This means that a high proportion of the people affected by the past laws, practices and policies of forcible removal continue to have their own children taken from them in turn. A process of second (or subsequent) generation removal has been found to have occurred in more than one in three cases.[30] The larger context in which Morgan's project of detection/accusation is to be situated inevitably modifies the ostensibly optimistic stance of the story, giving its enlightenment values of historiographical education, informed dialogue and communicational community a decidedly ironic edge. The text celebrates the restoration of indigenous community after generations of deliberate dislocation on the part of white policy; and yet, as the text attains canonical status, the crimes it reveals and 'overcomes' by laying them bare, continue to be perpetrated by a white Australia reluctant to embrace profound structural change in its relationship to its indigenous peoples.

If *My Place* is to be read as an ethnic detective story, it may need to be categorized as a postmodern anti-detective narrative, in which the traditional meting out of justice as a result of the detection of the crime can no longer be taken for granted, in keeping with other postmodern narratives which eschew narrative closure and axiological resolution.[31] The dissonance between narrative resolution of crimes against indigenous peoples present in Morgan's text, and the real continuation of a historical process of expropriation and discrimination, is also a common characteristic of indigenous detective fiction from other parts of the English-speaking world.[32] In a genre once noted either for its indifference to socio-political questions or for its ideology of defence of middle-class order against a threat from below[33] this aspect of indigenous detective fiction represents a radical rupture, and demands a rethinking of the very notion of crime narrative. For all its importance as a milestone of contemporary indigenous literature, this profound ambivalence in *My Place*, paradoxically associated with the very terms in which the text endeavours to inform white Australians of their own past, renders Morgan's project deeply disturbing. Even when Morgan's autobiography confronts and revises earlier representations of crimes against the indigenous peoples, to be found for instance in Upfield's *Bony* narrative, such an undertaking appears to be trammelled by the broader social conditions determining the enunciation of indigenous discourses of activism and protest.

30 *Bringing them Home*. Report of the National Inquiry into the Separation of Aboriginal and Torres Strait Islander Children from Their Families (Australian Commonwealth Government) April 1997. http://www.austlii.edu.au/au/special/rsjproject/rsjlibrary/hreoc/stolen/prelim.html, 12. Accessed 24 March 2011.

31 Stefano Tani, *The Doomed Detective: The Contribution of the Detective Novel to Postmodern American and Italian Fiction* (Carbondale and Edwardsville: Southern Illinois University Press, 1984), 39–40.

32 Tim Libretti, 'Lucha Corpi and the Politics of Detective Fiction', in Adrienne Johnson Gosselin (ed.), *Multicultural Detective Fiction: Murder from the 'Other' Side* (New York: Garland, 1999), 62; Michelle Pagni Stewart, '"A Rose by Any Other Name": A Native American Detective Novel by Louis Owens', in Adrienne Johnson Gosselin (ed.), *Multicultural Detective Fiction: Murder from the 'Other' Side* (New York: Garland, 1999), 170.

33 Bernard Benstock, 'The Education of Martin Beck', in *Essays on Detective Fiction* (London: Macmillan, 1983) 189; Stephen Knight, *Form and Ideology in Crime Fiction* (London: Macmillan, 1980), 1–7.

Or, alternatively, to reformulate an issue addressed by John Irwin, the ethnic mystery story, once it has been unravelled, continues to hold the interest of the reader through its synecdochic refiguring of a social dilemma whose urgency as a non-fictional task none the less remains in the form of a 'mystery to a solution,' necessarily beyond the boundaries of the inevitably limited reach of the fictional project.[34]

[34] John T. Irwin, *The Mystery to a Solution: Poe, Borges, and the Analytical Detective Story* (Baltimore: Johns Hopkins University Press, 1994), 2.

3 The Time of Biopolitics in the Settler Colony

Kim Scott's description of the Moore River Native Settlement, also known as Mogumber, in his 1999 novel Benang, suggests implicit analogies with the mid-century concentration camps of the Holocaust. The indigenous detainees are transported there by rail in stock cars, they are welcomed by uniformed overseers armed with whips, they are housed in barracks with barred windows, and a punishment regime of solitary confinement and ritual humiliation operates as a means of coercion. Niches can be found, however, where survival, as in the concentration camps, is possible: the narrator's uncle Jack Chatalong is reunited with his mother Dinah who works in the kitchen at Mogumber.[1]

The analogy between twentieth-century government control of the lives of Australian indigenous people and the biopolitics of Nazism have not gone unnoticed in other quarters. Elizabeth Povinelli describes the equation, made by the Royal Commission's Bringing Them Home report in 1994, of a century of child-removal practices with cultural genocide, as 'an analogy made more compelling by the age of the Aboriginal applicants, many of whom had been taken in the early 1940s.' The impact of that equation was that 'Australians looked at themselves in a ghastly historical mirror and imagined their own Nuremberg. Would fascism be the final metaphor of Australian settler modernity?'[2]

Another view of that settler modernity, originating this time in Germany itself, similarly identified an avatar of Nazism in the Woomera internment centres. Australia was labelled, by a 2002 article in *Die Zeit*, a left-liberal forum for intellectual and political debate, as having reintroduced the camp, the privileged instrument of control of the great totalitarian states, and thereby as having inaugurated the 'the return of the camp system under western democratic auspices.'[3] The disenchanted German view of Australia targets a different aspect of the Nazi spectre: the camp rather than genocide. At the same time, it focuses upon a rather different population, that of the 'aliens' who have often joined indigenous people as the 'Other' of the Australian racist imaginary. Kim Scott's implicit analogy between Mogumber and the concentration camp joins these two ascriptions of a 'haunting' of the settler nation by spectral recurrences, at different times and places, by a biopolitics whose privileged locus was in Germany in the 1940s. The analogy is on occasions made quite explicit: '"They had some good ideas, those Nazis," Ern said, "but they went a bit far"' (*Benang* 154).

Are such ascriptions of a purported Antipodean fascism far-fetched or misleading, or even scandalously false (as, for instance, my outraged Melbourne relatives found when I reported the German media reactions to them soon after the Tampa

1 Kim Scott, *Benang: From the Heart* (Fremantle: Fremantle Arts Centre Press, 1999), 89–94, 99–102. All references in the text.

2 Elizabeth Povinelli, *The Cunning of Recognition: Indigenous Alterities and the Making of Australian Multiculturalism* (Durham NC: Duke University Press, 2002), 38.

3 Richard Herzinger, 'Die Lippen zugenäht'. *Die Zeit*, 31 January 2002. http://www.zeit.de/2002/06/Die_Lippen_zugenaeht. Accessed 27 October 2009.

and Woomera affairs)? On the one hand, the spatial analogies between certain techniques of management of populations – what contemporary critical theory, following Foucault, has come to term 'biopolitics'[4] – cannot be overlooked. Indeed, recent scholarship suggests that the architects of the Nazi police state and its pan-European apparatus may have drawn some important ideas from methods forged in various parts of the British Empire.[5]

However, the temporal differences belie these apparent similarities. Whereas Nazi domination of Germany lasted only a little more than a decade, and in much of occupied Europe less than half that period, in the settler colonies European domination now has a history stretching back several centuries. The processes of colonial domination, superficially similar to those of Nazi biopolitics (the camp, management of indigenous populations, genocide and eugenics) have contributed to the making of contemporary settler states. The history of biopolitics in the settler states (unlike that of post-war Germany's extensive if heavily conflicted attempts to work through the Nazi past and its legacy), is so embedded in the fabric of the contemporary state structures that it cannot be finally dealt with.[6] The very space of the settler state is one that is so complete that even exceptions to its sovereignty – that of indigenous sacred sites, for instance – are predicated upon the totality of Westminster law, despite the apparently countervailing authority of the Mabo decision of 1992; correspondingly, this spatial saturation makes the temporal structure of its constitutive biopolitics, even when their more extreme manifestations are abolished, one that is in fact never-ending.

The provocative analogies between the Australian colonial scenario and Nazi biopolitics are thus both accurate and misleading at the same time. The reasons for this ambivalence in the drawing of analogies are simultaneously spatial and temporal in complex and entangled ways: the uncanny temporal 'resurgence' of the camp diagnosed by *Die Zeit* is temporally inaccurate; if anything, colonial biopolitics (for instance the concentration camps invented by the British in turn-of-the-century South Africa) resurged in mid-century Germany, and not the reverse; and this strange inversion of temporal relationships is related to the manner in which the nation-state space of various settler colonies (Australia, New Zealand, Canada, albeit to varying degrees), is predicated upon the 'logic of extermination' which sought to remove the prior indigenous nations from the domain of their sovereignty.[7] To this extent, any real undoing of these historical processes would entail the

4 Michel Foucault, *History of Sexuality: Vol. 1: An Introduction*, trans. Robert Hurley (London: Vintage, 1990); Michel Foucault, *The Birth of Biopolitics: Lectures at the Collège de France 1978–1979*, trans. Graham Burchell (Basingstoke: Palgrave Macmillan, 2008).

5 See Mark Mazower, *Hitler's Empire: Nazi Rule in Occupied Europe* (London: Allen Lane, 2008); for a contrasing argument, see Shelley Baranowski, *Nazi Empire: German Colonisation and Imperialism from Bismark to Hitler* (Cambridge: Cambridge University Press, 2010).

6 Bain Attwood, 'Historical Controversies and the History Wars in Australia', in Russell West-Pavlov & Jennifer Wawrzinek (eds), *Frontier Skirmishes: Literary and Cultural Debates in Australia after 1992* (Heidelberg: Winter, 2010), 34.

7 See Patrick Wolfe, 'Nation and MiscegeNation: Discursive Continuity in the Post-Mabo Era', *Social Analysis* 36 (October 1994), 93–152.

undoing of the settler state itself, a notion so massive in its implications that it is strictly speaking unimaginable.[8]

This chapter seeks to think through some of the ramifications of this convoluted spatio-temporal complex of issues connected with the ongoing history of biopolitics in the Australian settler state by undertaking a twinned engagement: primarily with the theory of Giorgio Agamben, and secondarily with Kim Scott's novel *Benang*.

Agamben's highly influential theory of the 'state of exception' in his *Homo Sacer* (1995; Engl. transl. 1998)[9] seeks to articulate the anomalous position of those subjects which the state 'bans' from full citizenship, excluding them from the body politic and reducing them to 'bare life,' to instances of biological existence without civic identities. These subjects are paradoxically excluded from the body politic of civic community but none the less included within the zone of its jurisdiction. Unprotected by the status of the full citizenship they have lost, they are utterly exposed to the harshness of a law now unleashed upon them without checks or controls. Agamben's prime examples of these excluded/included subjects without rights but still under the force of the law are the inmates of the Nazi concentration camps, but they could equally well be the indigenous people subject to government legislation of the first half of the twentieth-century Australia.

Correspondingly, I begin with an attempt to frame Agamben's theory of the 'state of exception' within the context of postcolonial studies and, more concretely, of the settler nation-state in its colonial manifestation. Three examples of something akin to Agamben's exclusion/inclusion relationship down the course of Australian history serve to present 'deep structures' of exclusion/inclusion. I discuss the spatial and legislative implications of two significant historical moments: 1788 and 1900 (with 2008 as a third historical juncture overshadowing the chapter in its entirety).

Having demonstrated the significance of this spatio-temporal entanglement in Australian history, I then move on to consider the tensions between the intertwined spatial and temporal narratives of the 'state of exception' within Agamben's theory. I pursue this agenda by scrutinizing the temporal fabric of Agamben's conceptualization of modern biopolitics in *Homo Sacer*. The final destination of Agamben's narrative in *Homo Sacer* and its sequel *State of Exception* (2003; Engl. trans. 2005)[10] are the Nazi concentration camps and the contemporary detention centres at Guantanamo or the refugee deportation cells in international airports. These are instances of the spatial dimension of (civic) exclusion/(juridical) inclusion constituting 'bare life' which is paramount in *Homo Sacer*. Yet such zones of exclusion/inclusion have a history, and this is equally important in Agamben's concept, for this temporal component frames his manifesto and gives it its explicitly political rationale.

In Agamben's exposition, the temporal logic of the 'state of exception' which reduces civic subjects to 'bare life' consists of three aspects: a conceptual level in

8 South Africa presents a complex (but closely related) exception here: see Fanie du Toit & Erik Doxtader (eds), *In the Balance: South Africans Debate Reconciliation* (Johannesburg: Jacana, 2009).

9 Giorgio Agamben, *Homo Sacer: Sovereign Power and Bare Life*, trans. Daniel Heller-Roazen (Stanford, Cal.: Stanford University Press, 1998). All references in the text.

10 Giorgio Agamben, *State of Exception*, trans. Kevin Attell (Chicago: University of Chicago Press, 2005).

which the possibility of the suspension of the law is constitutive of the very moment of the foundation of the law; a chronology of avatars of the 'state of exception' from classical through to contemporary times; and finally, the claim that the 'state of exception' has been regarded as tangential to the polis, rather than recognizing its central and constitutive role; this means that the 'state of exception' has been allowed to proliferate uncontrolled,[11] to the extent that today it has increasingly become a permanent state of affairs (witness global developments since 9/11).

It is this temporal aspect, less prominent in *Homo Sacer*'s argument but ultimately its driving force, which I wish to address in my welding of Agamben's theory to the Australian colonial context. The impossibility of disentangling these three aspects of Agamben's theory, rather than hampering my enquiry, paradoxically allows me finally to think through the temporality of biopolitics in the Australian context, a task I try to make more concrete by offering, at various pivotal moments in my argument, a reading of Kim Scott's *Benang*.

An Antipodean Agamben?

Before moving into the main body of my argument I wish to lay down its main points of reference. To that end it is worth reiterating the main components of Agamben's three-pronged polemic about the temporality of biopolitics. Those three components can be glossed as follows.

First, Agamben explores, at a very abstract level, the possibility built into the law, at some point in the future, to suspend its own system of checks and balances and to declare a 'state of exception.' In this sense, the 'state of exception' in which the exclusion/inclusion position of 'bare life' outside the normal protection the law affords to its subjects is temporalized in the 'potentiality . . . of the law to maintain itself in its own privation, to apply in no longer applying.'[12] Second, on a philosophical-historical plane, Agamben constructs a chronology in which such an act of inclusion/exclusion of 'bare life' founds Western polity: 'Western politics first constitutes itself through an exclusion (which is simultaneously an inclusion) of bare life.'[13] Agamben is at pains to stress that this is not a real historical chronology.[14] Rather, he is talking about a conceptual a priori by virtue of which the law itself is underwritten by no other authority than arbitrary, sovereign gesture – so that the law can equally well be abolished by the same sovereign gesture. In other words, Agamben claims that the sovereign power's capacity to constitute the law at some founding moment of the polity also implies its capacity to subsequently abolish it at moments of crisis by declaring a 'state of exception.' This latent potential for arbitrainess lies dormant in the very fabric of Western polity, but has been forgotten by mainstream political and philosophical thought.

11 For analogies with this 'proliferation' topos, see Bruno Latour, *We have Never Been Modern*, trans. Catherine Porter (Cambridge, MA: Harvard University Press, 1993) and Jean Baudrillard, *La Transparence du Mal: Essai sur les phénomènes extrêmes* (Paris: Galilée, 1990).

12 Agamben, *Homo Sacer*, 28.

13 Agamben, *Homo Sacer*, 7.

14 Agamben, *Homo Sacer*, 105.

Third, emerging out of the previous two points, Agamben tables the semi-psychoanalytical proposition that the forgetting of this archaic origin of Western politics has permitted the 'state of exception' to become ubiquitous in contemporary democracies as a recurring and quasi-permanent phenomenon. Its forgetting means that the 'state of exception' can and does emerge at any place and at any time, with increasing frequency. Indeed, the re-emergence of the 'state of exception' has become so massive that it has gradually coalesced into the norm. An urgent ethical concern about this creeping tendency towards a permanent 'state of exception' is the underlying motivation for Agamben's attempt to provide a genealogy of the 'state of exception' and its subtle expansion to a permanent state of affairs.

The temporal dimension motivating Agamben's meditation, especially the spectral logic of the ignored origins of state forms returning to alienate democracy, is germinal for the Australian context. Certainly the exclusion/inclusion relationship is helpful for describing the fate of Australia's indigenous people for most of the more than two centuries since British occupation. One of *Benang*'s white characters from the 1930s summarizes this structure of exclusion/inclusion: '"An ideal camp," he continued, "is near enough to town to allow the natives to call for rations when they are indigent, to come under surveillance by police and other local protectors, and to provide a ready labour force when necessary. However, it must always be far enough from white habitations to avoid complaints and to discourage unwelcome visits by white men"' (*Benang* 45). In the state of emergency, which temporalizes this inclusion/exclusion structure, maintaining it over a (possibly open-ended) period of time, a more sinister aspect of 'bare life' emerges. The same character posits that the indigenous people '"have no place in the scheme of things, and have simply become a nuisance. Many otherwise gentle folk think and openly say it were better that they were dead, were dead, were dead..."' (*Benang* 45–46). The subjunctive mood, the final repetition and the points of suspension transform what begins as a tendentious and racist opinion, posing as a fact, into dystopic potentiality whose temporality is that of repetition. The 'were,' hovering between fact and imagination, translates the exclusion/inclusion ambiguity of 'bare life,' and the repetition of 'dead' suspends the closure of mortality, opening up a perpetual half-life of mere existence – 'bare life.'

The title of Scott's novel, *Benang*, 'tomorrow' in the Nyoongar language (*Benang* 464), may thus have an unwelcome subtext, one which surely goes against the grain of Scott's resilient politics of indigenous cultural reconstruction: namely, the possibility that the processes of reduction to 'bare life' that it so vigorously combats are by no means eradicated. In the words of Robert van Krieken, discussing successive Australian governments' implementation of 'power over bodies' in the form of policies of assimilation, 'the important analytical question is not "Why did it happen?" but "Why did it stop?". This in turn makes possible another question that we might pose to any practice of assimilation: "Has it stopped?"'[15] Mounting evidence suggests that after the 1960s, far from being dismantled, assimilation as a policy, implemented via child removal, continued. From the 1970s on there was a

15 Robert van Krieken, 'Asimilation and Liberal Government', in Rowse (ed.), *Contesting Assimilation* (Perth: API Network/Curtin University of Technology, 2005), 46.

new wave of child separation through the actions of police, welfare authorities and the juvenile justice system.[16] And certainly, biopolitical intervention into the lives of families and focussed upon children was at the core of the most blatant recent excrescence of the 'state of exception' in Australia: the state of emergency declared in 2008 in Northern Territory.

The temporal structure of biopolitics in Australia, I suggest, is characterized by its disturbing continuities from the earliest days of European settlement up to the present moment. Hegemonic white historiography in its quotidian manifestations generally opts for a convenient segmentation of historical temporality.[17] Thus John Howard could announce to Parliament on 26 August 1999, 'I have frequently said, and I will say it again today, that the present generation of Australians cannot be held accountable . . . for the errors and misdeeds of earlier generations.'[18] This tendency to parcellize historical epochs hermetically sealed off from one another – albeit constitutive of the modern historiographic undertaking in general[19] – is diametrically opposed to the countervailing *longue durée* phenomena I investigate in this chapter. According to the latter perspective, the past is connected to the present – not so much by the reassuring continuities of living tradition as by the nightmarish temporality of a 'state of exception' that refuses to end.

Two versions of an Australian 'state of exception'

It may be worth asking whether the spatial relationship between outside and inside which underlies 'bare life' and the 'state of exception' might need to be remobilized to scrutinize a constitutive exterior silenced by Agamben's own focus upon an occidental history of political thought. In other words, an attempt to meld Agamben's theory of biopolitics with the Australian context necessitates retooling his account, addressing its myopic neglect of the non-European world. Agamben tangentially mentions Schmitt's notion of a New World origin of the line of demarcation in modernity, but demotes the potential colonial topos of the origins of modernity's 'bare life' to a mere metaphor; he also acknowledges the colonial origins of the concentration camp in British South Africa and Spanish Cuba.[20] These brief hints at a postcolonial history of 'bare life' remain metaphorical in the first case and merely suggestive in the second. But the conditions of contemporary (post)colonial states demand that we interrogate critically the notion of the 'state of exception,' as one of its origins may lie there and not just (as in Agamben's analysis) in classical political theory.

16 Anna Haebich, *Broken Circles: Fragmenting Indigenous Families 1800–2000* (Fremantle: Fremantle Arts Centre Press, 2000), 608.

17 Bain Attwood, 'Introduction: The Past as future: Aborigines, Australia and the (dis)course of History', in Atwood (ed.), *In the Age of Mabo: History, Aborigines and Australia* (St. Leonards, NSW: Allen & Unwin, 1996), xx; John Frow, 'A Politics of Stolen Time', in Jon May and Nigel Thrift (eds), *TimeSpace: Geographies of Temporality* (London: Routledge, 2001), 73–88.

18 Quoted in Rosalind Kidd, *Black Lives, Government Lies* (Sydney: UNSW Press, 2000), 4.

19 See Michel de Certeau, *L'Ecriture de l'histoire* (Paris: Gallimard, 1975), 3–23.

20 Agamben, *Homo Sacer*, 36, 166; see also Niall Ferguson, *Empire: How Britain Made the Modern World* (Harmondsworth: Penguin, 2004), 280.

To this end, it may be instructive to focus on several episodes in the history of Australian political existence. The first episode would be at the moment of the First Fleet's arrival at Botany Bay in 1788. In the South Pacific, the British explorer-invaders repeatedly drew lines in the sand when they set foot upon newly 'discovered' territory, to symbolize the act of taking possession. Curiously, this practice did not occur in Australia, with, apparently, one single exception, at the inaugural moment of landing at Botany Bay in January 1788.[21] Among Governor Phillip's first acts upon the beach was '[make] a circle around us. There was little difficulty in making [the local natives] understand that they were not to come within it, and then they sat down very quiet.'[22] Watkin Tench, the chronicler of the 1788 settlement, recorded the drawing of the line on the beach, recognizing its significance as a prototypical frontier: 'The Indians . . . so far acknowledged their authority as to submit that a boundary, during their first interview, might be drawn on the sand, which they attempted not to infringe and appeared to be satisfied with.'[23] The line in the sand drawn at Botany Bay takes on the character of an inaugural gesture in which inside and outside, symbolically, are marked out. This is the gesture of sovereignty whose significance is not substantive (the line in the sand has no real power to effect exclusion) but rather performative. It is a gesture which celebrates its own power to demarcate as a specific instantiation of a global sovereignty. In its very moment of execution, however, it clearly locates the executor on one side of the line, and the excluded on the other, thus founding all future demarcations, from the colonial frontiers to the tacit demarcations of the 1901 Constitution.

A single gesture, according to this anecdote, was needed to instantiate British sovereignty on Australian soil. On the one hand, this demarcation derived itself from extant British claims to sovereignty; on the other hand, it can be seen as a founding inscription which reposed upon no prior authority outside itself, thereby leaving open the future possibility of suspending the law it had created, and thus inaugurating what I wish to posit as a permanent 'state of exception' with regard to the indigenous peoples. This is the gist of what Carl Schmitt identified in colonial foundations:

> What is at issue in the sovereign exception is not so much the control or neutralization of an excess as the creation and definition of the very space in which the juridico-political order can have validity. In this sense, the sovereign exception is the fundamental localization (Ortung), which does not limit itself to distinguishing what is inside from what is outside but instead traces a threshold (the state of exception) between the two, on the basis of which outside and inside, the normal situation and

21 Anja Schwarz, 'Beached: A Postcolonial Reading of the Australian Shore', Unpublished PhD thesis, Free University of Berlin, 2008 [to appear as *Beached: A Postcolonial Reading of the Australian Shore* (Bristol: Intellect, forthcoming 2012)], 178–85.

22 Arthur Phillip, 'Governor Phillip to Lord Sydney. Sydney Cove, New South Wales, May 15th, 1788.' *Historical Records of New South Wales*, Vol 1, Part 2 – 1783–1792 (Sydney: Charles Porter, Government Printer, 1892), 129, quoted in Schwarz, 'Beached', 184.

23 Watkin Tench, 'A Narrative of the Expedition to Botany Bay', in Tim Flannery (ed.), *1788. Comprising A Narrative of the Expedition to Botany Bay, and A Complete Account of the Settlement at Port Jackson* (Melbourne: Text, 1996), 45.

> chaos, enter into those complex topological relations that make the validity of the juridical order possible.
>
> The 'ordering of space' that is, according to Schmitt, constitutive of the sovereign nomos is therefore not only a 'taking of land' (Landesnahme) – the determination of a juridical and a territorial ordering (of an Ordnung and an Ortung) – but above all, a 'taking of the outside,' an exception (Ausnahme).[24]

Schmitt's collocation of the 'taking of land,' an appropriation of the interior, and, simultaneously, as the making possible of its 'exterior,' the opening up of an area of lawlessness, go hand in hand in concrete examples such as the possession and occupation of the Australian continent. The two perspectives also explain in part the well-known nineteenth-century ambiguity in the status of the indigenous people: on the one hand, they were British subjects and were aware of the rights accruing to them as such; on the other hand, in frontier areas, and with the connivance of colonial officials, British law was effectively suspended, and a situation reigned in which, to quote Agamben paraphrasing Arendt, 'the principle that supports totalitarian rule and that common sense obstinately refuses to admit [came] fully to light: this is the principle according to which "everything is possible."'[25]

There is one significant passage where Agamben, following a lead offered by Schmitt, points to the ways in which these demarcations may have been important in the colonial world. Indeed, Agamben's reading of Schmitt suggests, though this was doubtless the intention of neither of these theorists, that the spatio-temporal notion of the 'state of exception' may in fact have had its origins as much in the colonial experience beyond the borders of Europe as in Europe's own antiquity:

> Schmitt shows how the link between localization and ordering constitutive of the nomos of the earth always implies a zone that is excluded from law and that takes the shape of a 'free and juridically empty space' in which sovereign power no longer knows the limits fixed by the nomos as the territorial order. In the classical epoch of the ius publicum Europaeum, this zone corresponded to the New World, which was identified with the state of nature in which everything is possible (Locke: 'In the beginning all the world was America').[26]

For students of Australian colonial history, the notion of 'empty space' may be suggestive of that of terra nullius, while the idea of a 'juridically empty space' may evoke the lawlessness of the colonial frontier. Agamben however skates over this passage, treating it as a historical predecessor of the emergence of the camp in the metropolis:

[24] Agamben, *Homo Sacer*, 19.
[25] Agamben, *Homo Sacer*, 170.
[26] Agamben, *Homo Sacer*, 36.

> Schmitt himself assimilates this zone 'beyond the line' to the 'state of exception', which 'bases itself in an obviously analogous fashion on the idea of delimited, free and empty space' understood as a 'temporary and spatial sphere in which every law is suspended.'[27]

But if we follow Agamben's own logic, namely, that of a forgotten origin whose very forgetting enables its perpetuation as a recurring and now resurgent, indeed virulent phenomenon, then it is useful to take a second look at this historical antecedent in Schmitt. From the point of view of the non-European world, the 'New World' as a genuinely existing space outside the *nomos* (or law) continues to resonate in the collective (un)consciousness of settler colonies in particular. But rather than reducing this to a metaphor for a juridical status, it may be understood as a real situation which has perpetuated itself in parallel to 'states of exception' in other parts of the world. These colonial phenomena resonate so loudly in the settler nation-states because they do so as uncanny, unthought residues which are 'acted out' in endless repetitions rather than being 'worked through'[28] in a political process of real decolonization.

The 1901 Constitution is a case in point for this phenomenon of repetition, and constitutes my second episode from Australian political history. This 'second' act of foundation of the Australian polity was an inaugural moment which to a certain extent repeated the structures of the prior act of demarcation. The 1901 Constitution mentioned the indigenous peoples only twice: once to stipulate that they would not be counted in any census of the population, and once to give priority to the various states' or territories' legislation over Commonwealth legislation in indigenous matters.[29] (Both of these points would be overturned by the 1967 referendum, but even then, as Scott's novel attests, indigenous people would continue to feel themselves 'only tenuously citizens of their own country' [*Benang* 409]). Together, these two measures placed indigenous Australians in a strange position, simultaneously outside the population of citizens but within the scope of legislation. These measures effectively reduced the Australian indigenous population to a manifestation of 'bare life' outside the realm of the 'political life.' Legislation continued to be passed governing their existence (by the States, the Commonwealth having abdicated its responsibility), but indigenous people remained outside of the body politic. In other words, they fell under the 'governmentality' specific to the 'state of exception.'[30] Indigenous people at Federation were confirmed as 'banned' in the sense intended by Agamben:

> He who has been banned is not, in fact, simply set outside the law and made indifferent to it but rather abandoned by it, that is, exposed and threatened on the threshold in which life and law, outside and inside, become indistinguishable. It is literally not

27 Agamben, *Homo Sacer*, 36–37.

28 Dominick LaCapra, *Writing History, Writing Trauma* (Baltimore: Johns Hopkins University Press, 2001), 141–53.

29 Pat Grimshaw, 'Federation as a Turning Point in Australian History,' *Australian Historical Studies*, Special Issue 'Challenging Histories' 118 (2002), 31–32.

30 Agamben, *State of Exception*, 32–40.

> possible to say whether the one who has been abandoned is outside or inside the juridical order.[31]

To the extent that indigenous people were 'abandoned' by the constitution, they were 'delivered over to [their] own separateness and, at the same time, consigned to the mercy of the one who abandons [them]' in an act of 'inclusive exclusion (an exceptio).'[32] In the temporality of this variously manifested 'state of exception,' to adapt Agamben's words, Australian 'politics first constitutes itself through an exclusion (which is simultaneously an inclusion) of bare life.'[33]

Let us return to Phillip's line in the sand. What is curious is that such demarcation practices cease in Australia. Anja Schwarz has suggested that the general absence of lines in the sand in Australian colonial conquest can be ascribed to the global gesture of possession that rendered the Australian continent from the outset British territory and made lines of demarcation superfluous.[34] More significant, perhaps, is the internal temporal logic of this singular line. Rather than reading its singularity backwards to an authorizing global sovereignty, we can read it forwards as a self-authorizing gesture which, in its temporal singularity, renders any spatial reiteration unnecessary. This is so in two senses. First, no spatial reiteration is necessary, for a single demarcation suffices to annex the whole continent. Second, no spatial reiteration is necessary, for that singularity of this inscription, with its once-and-for-all validity, sanctions a state of permanent exclusion. These intertwined aspects of an inaugural sovereign demarcation opening up a space of exception continue to resonate in Australian political being up to the present.

It is for this reason that we need to re-jink Agamben's theory of the 'state of exception' in a number of ways. In a remark highly pertinent to the Australian context, Agamben observes, 'As the absolute space of exception, the camp is topologically different from the simple space of confinement.'[35] Confinement, i.e. the prison, is known in Australia (Port Arthur would be the classic topos). However, the prison was the exception to a convict norm, which treated the entire continent as a space of confinement, and could thus dispense with prisons: 'what happened to felons who were fooled by the absence of walls'? is a question asked by a character in Grenville's *The Secret River* (2005): 'Mostly they vanished forever, absorbed into the formless space.'[36] In Australia the camp is known too: one thinks of the native

31 Agamben, *Homo Sacer*, 28.
32 Agamben, *Homo Sacer*, 110, 7.
33 Agamben. *Homo Sacer*, 7.
34 Schwarz, 'Beached', 158–62, 178–85.
35 Agamben, *Homo Sacer*, 20.
36 Kate Grenville, *The Secret River* (Melbourne: Text), 178; see also Robert Hughes, *The Fatal Shore: A History of the Transportation of Convicts to Australia 1787–1868* (London: Collins Harvill/Pan, 1988), 203–43.

settlements such as Mogumber portrayed in *Benang* (89–94, 99–102), and of the Woomera internment camps for illegal refugees in the 1990s.[37]

Yet both of these examples of prison and camp had been, from the very outset, pre-empted by the continent itself as a camp, for the indigenous peoples: an entire territory which was marked off as a space of exception. Scott imagines his white settlers 'taming, controlling, elevating the whole bloody country so that it might achieve its potential and become part of the civilised world' (*Benang* 194). This, as shown above, exemplifies the rhetoric of eugenic engineering which sees the entire life of the nation as its domain, and in the Australian case, envelops the continent itself. The continent as a whole becomes an all-inclusive space of exclusion for its original owners.

Agamben's times

Agamben constantly stresses the topology of inside and out, of exclusion and inclusion, and their blurring in the 'bare life' and its formalized political equivalent, the 'state of exception' – yet he also wishes to create a chronology in which 'bare life' is fundamental to the very foundation of politics in Western culture: 'Western politics first constitutes itself through an exclusion (which is simultaneously an inclusion) of bare life.'[38] The constant spatio-temporal metaphors in Agamben's work mean that it is not enough to think about synchronic structures of exclusion (such as the concentration camp, the acme of exclusion of the subject from civil existence). The paradoxical relationship of within and without must be thought, simultaneously, as a paradoxical relationship of before and after the founding moment of the polis. This is precisely Agamben's point: the unthinkable 'before the law' which is created by the act of foundation is also the unthought 'after the law' which constantly resurges as an uncanny haunting of the state, a lawlessness at its heart. The unthought origin in a whole series of historical avatars (instantiated variously by the figures of constituting vs. constituted powers, the king's two bodies, the werewolf, the 'banned' outlaw figures of medieval law, and so on) have been elided by modern democracies. Precisely because of this has increasingly emerged within them:

> We must learn to recognize this structure of the ban in the political relations and public spaces in which we still live. . . . if in modernity life is more and more clearly placed in the centre of State politics (which now becomes, in Foucault's terms,

[37] As Agamben points out, the refugee has become, in the century since the First World War, a new avatar of bare life (Agamben, *Homo Sacer*, 126–27, 130–34); the internment camps in central Australia and the excised 'non-immigration' zones declared by the Howard government to deprive illegal immigrants of the right to demand asylum have been read in the light of 'bare life' and the spatial localization of the 'exception' (Nikos Papastergiadis, 'The invasion complex: the abject other and spaces of violence,' *Geografiska Annaler (Series B)*, 88.4 (2006), 434–37; Anja Schwarz and Justine Lloyd, 'The Pacific Solution meets Fortress Europe: Emerging Parallels in Transnational Refugee Regimes,' in Anja Schwarz & Russell West Pavlov (eds), *Polyculturalism and Discourse* (Amsterdam: Rodopi, 2007), 253–57, 270.

[38] Agamben, *Homo Sacer*, 7.

> biopolitics) . . . this is only possible because the relation of ban has constituted the essential structure of sovereign power from the beginning.[39]

Agamben's concern is with '[m]odern democracy's decadence and gradual convergence with totalitarian states in post-democratic spectacular societies.'[40] In the present day, he claims, 'the state of exception comes more and more to the foreground as the fundamental political structure and ultimately begins to become the rule. When our age tried to grant the unlocalizable a permanent and visible location, the result was the concentration camp. The camp – and not the prison – is the space that corresponds to the originary structure of the nomos.'[41] The camp has been superseded, however, by a much more generalizable 'state of exception', in which all citizens are potentially homines sacri, i.e. banned 'bare life' able to be killed with impunity.[42] The sources for this development, he stresses, need to understood as going back to the very roots of Western political thought if their results are to be effectively combated:

> The contiguity between mass democracy and totalitarian states . . . does not have the form of a sudden transformation . . . before impetuously coming to light in our century, the river of biopolitics . . . runs its course in a hidden but continuous fashion.[43]

His notion of biopolitics in its modern manifestation has a history, one whose retrieval from collective amnesia, he implies, is crucial to the elaboration of an appropriate critical response and the proposing of an antidote.

It is not difficult to see how this underlying ethical concern with an increasingly permanent 'state of exception' may be relevant to the Australian context. The significance of the 1992 Mabo decision was that it reversed this chronology of sovereignty, declaring that native title pre-existed European invasion and persists despite it. Native title thus also gained the potential to overturn the continent-wide 'state of exception' by declaring the ubiquity of a prior indigenous ownership (even though it could under some circumstances be extinguished). Prior to the originary act of European sovereignty, there had been what was tantamount to an alternative sovereignty which was acknowledged principally by the strenuous measures undertaken by the judges to prevent its fulfilment.

However, Mabo did not put an end to the 'state of exception': even this tacit acknowledgement of a sovereignty pre-dating the European act of sovereignty could be suspended. Immediately after the 1992 High Court Mabo ruling was translated into legislation in the 1994 Native Title Acts, the Howard government undid these measures via its Ten Point Plan (1997). A decade later, a further reversal of Mabo was revealed, as it became clear that land rights already granted could be revoked: in the state of emergency declared in 2008 in the Northern Territory, five indigenous communities had their native title claims rescinded. The Northern Territory Inter-

39 Agamben, *Homo Sacer*, 111.
40 Agamben, *Homo Sacer*, 10.
41 Agamben, *Homo Sacer*, 20.
42 Agamben, *Homo Sacer*, 115.
43 Agamben, *Homo Sacer*, 121.

vention initiated in 2008 appears to confirm the temporal logic of the 'state of exception.' Once inaugurated as sovereign possibility of suspending the law, there is nothing which can set temporal limits upon the 'state of exception.' The exception can, effectively become the rule.

As Benjamin remarked, 'The tradition of the oppressed teaches us that "the state of emergency" in which we live is not the exception but the rule.'[44] Indeed, the suspension of law announced by the first acts of legislation in Germany in 1933 were never revoked.[45] More recently, the zone outside the law into which detainees in Guantanamo have been cast has been accompanied by legislation which makes 'indefinite detention' possible.[46] Even more recently, the term 'Katrina Time' has been coined to describe the suspension of civil law, of varying, and apparently quite arbitrary durations, in the wake of Hurricane Katrina.[47] It is in the nature of the originary demarcation which marks out the domain of 'bare life,' thus making possible the 'state of exception,' that it perpetuates itself as a 'process that is no process,'[48] that is, as a sort of temporal stasis, albeit in a plethora of forms.

In the Australian context, the Northern Territory Intervention has lapsed, but not been terminated. The legislation for its implementation has been modified (in particular regarding the suspension of the Racial Discrimination Act) but not repealed. At the time of writing, the intervention continued to have the support of the Gillard government, as it had of her predecessor Rudd's.

The time of assimilation

In my argument up until now I have sought to open up the central temporal/spatial ambivalence within Agamben's work so as to make it productive for a specific example of biopolitics, that of Australian state policy with regard to indigenous people. In that policy, the temporal element was and continues to be central to the implementation of a more or less permanent 'state of exception.' In what follows I wish focus in a more specific manner on the Australian context, turning again to a detailed reading of Kim Scott's *Benang*.

After the conflicts of the first contact period and the subsequent period of frontier expansion, indigenous policy went through two phases: first, one in which the rhetoric of the dying race dominated (roughly up until Federation); and second, a period of state intervention and management of indigenous lives (through to the 1960s). Both of these phases of policy were underpinned by a temporal narrative: the first by one of extinction, the second by one of assimilation, or 'biological absorption.'[49]

44 Walter Benjamin, *Illuminations*, ed. Hannah Arendt, trans. Harry Zohn (London: Pimlico, 1999), 248.
45 Agamben, *Homo Sacer*, 167–68.
46 Judith Butler, *Precarious Life: The Powers of Mourning and Violence* (London: Verso, 2004), 50–100.
47 Greg Grandin, 'Katrina Time', *London Review of Books* 33.1 (6 January 2011), 27.
48 Butler, *Precarious Life*, 62.
49 Kim Scott, 'Apologies, Agency and Resilience', in Russell West-Pavlov & Jennifer Wawrzinek (eds), *Frontier Skirmishes: Literary and Cultural Debates in Australia after 1992* (Heidelberg: Winter, 2010), 63.

Scott's *Benang* is a significant text because it positions its own narrative beginnings at the cusp between the first and second phases. The narrator ruminates that 'It was he [his grandfather Ernest Scat] who, if not indeed forming the idea [of assimilation via intermarriage], applied it as Mr Neville was unable to do . . . It was as if he – a little too late to be a pioneer, and not really cut out to tame the land – could still play a role in taming a people into submission' (*Benang* 32). The colonial frontier period is over, but new techniques of control and subjugation (assimilation as a eugenic programme, the attempt to '"absorb them into our population"' [*Benang* 46]) have been projected, which Ernest Scat seeks to convert from theory into practice. His project is truly an exercise in eugenic engineering: 'I made you mine,' he says to his grandson (*Benang* 435).

Scott's novel insists upon the connections between the technologies of extinction and assimilation: 'It's another sort of murdering. What the law was doing. And helping people do. Killing Nyoongars really, making 'em white' (*Benang* 337–38). Likewise, the novel suggests that the two temporalities, that of extinction and that of assimilation, are in fact coterminous. The 'timetable' (*Benang* 23) that Ernest Scat maps out for his progeny involves a waning of indigeneity which is simultaneously a waxing of whiteness. The photo that the narrator discovers in his grandfather's papers of 'Three Generations (Reading from Right to Left)' depicting 'sequences of three or four in which I was always at the end of the line' (*Benang* 26). The double temporality of this notion of assimilation is exemplified in the notion that '[t]he one community's progress is measured by the other's decline. The power of the one community is increased by the feebleness of the other; or better still, by the complete absence of an indigenous community' (*Benang* 207).

Is this an instantiation of Agamben's 'bare life'? In a very literal sense, what Rowley famously termed 'the destruction of Aboriginal society'[50] exemplified the 'reduction of a rich and variously shared place to one fragile, impoverished consciousness' (*Benang* 31), and even more, to a mere existence as subsistence. The turn-of-the-century panorama of environmental depredation and indigenous cultural collapse on the Western Australian goldfields seems to encapsulate 'bare life' in a literal manner: the 'people huddled in groups, dressed in the rags of white people. They held out their hands to strangers, and were herded about like sheep and cattle, though less well fed' (*Benang* 479). This is 'bare life' as a literal manifestation of 'abandonment' (in Agamben's sense) by the polity. What, however, of the intensified 'governmentality' that characterizes the 'state of exception'[51] and which is played out in the legislated management of indigenous lives (typified, for instance, in the 'new bill being proposed which will give us the power to locate natives on certain areas' [*Benang* 206])? Scott has a white character explain two contrasting versions of 'bare life': '"There seems to be a clear choice . . . Let them multiply in wretched camps, let rations cost more, let them be useless and untaught, keep them out of sight; or absorb them into our population"' (*Benang* 46). The manner in which the twentieth-century Australian programmes of assimilation exemplified the management of 'bare life' in the latter mode become clear as soon as one compares

50 C. D. Rowley, *The Destruction of Aboriginal Society* (Ringwood VIC: Penguin, 1972).
51 Agamben, *State of Exception*, 32–40.

the concepts of 'racial hygiene' elaborated in German from shortly after the First World War and converted into legislation immediately after the National Socialist seizure of power.[52] The theorists of 'racial hygiene' were concerned with the 'life of the people.'[53] The 'life of the people' referred both to the civic life of the polity, which had to be enhanced by a biopolitics, and the 'bare life' which it captured with a view to such enhancement. The 'life of the people' included the population as a synchronic whole, but also as a diachronic process as targeted for instance in notions of 'biological heredity.'[54] Identical temporal notions were being promulgated in the Australian press at the same time. Scott's opening epigraphs quote The West Australian of 22 July 1933: '*the half-caste . . . is merely a passing phase, an incident in history, an interesting event in what we call "progress", a natural transmutation in what we know as cultural evolution. He will solve himself and disappear*' (*Benang* 5, italics in original). The last version of 'bare life' treats it as a eugenic experiment, framed by a temporality of improvement and progress, which is simultaneously one of disappearance. To the extent, however, that it constitutes a continuation as much as a rupture with regard to prior policies, it raises the larger question of the global temporalities of various forms of assimilation, and their possible place within a history of biopolitics which is by no means over.

Scott's protagonist, in a deeply ambivalent formulation, casts himself as 'the successful end of a long line of failures. Or is it the other way round' (*Benang* 10). It is unclear whether Scott positions his narrative at the close of a 'failed,' and thus terminated project of assimilation, or whether, by virtue of his dubious 'success' he may be the latest scion of a eugenics whose temporality he paradoxically embodies. Contrary to the ultimately optimistic tenor of Scott's literary project, his subtext may interrogate the very idea of a conclusion in the realm of biopolitics, implying that we are in the midst of a long-running, ongoing war of attrition against indigenous culture and its peoples. Tim Rowse, asking the question 'when (and if) [assimilation] stopped,'[55] contrasts white assumptions about the feasibility of 'pos[ing] questions such as: When did "assimilation" start and end?' with indigenous perspectives on the temporality of assimilation:

> For them, . . . 'assimilation' was coterminous with colonisation: it began in 1788 and it continued as a persistent pressure on Indigenous people to internalise an alien perspective on who they were and what their advancement amounted to. . . . For them, the most important fact about 'assimilation' was its pervasive constancy as a pressure in their lives and heads.'[56]

Scott's *Benang* oscillates between the two positions, narrating the temporal closure of biopolitics but by the same token performatively undercutting its own narrative of endings.

52 Agamben, *Homo Sacer*, 148–49.

53 Verschuer writing in 1936, quoted in Agamben, *Homo Sacer*, 147.

54 Agamben, *Homo Sacer*, 148.

55 Tim Rowse, 'Introduction: Contesting assimilation', in Tim Rowse (ed.), *Contesting Assimilation* (Perth: API Network/Curtin University of Technology, 2005), 2.

56 Rowse, 'Contesting assimilation', 1.

The temporalities of *Benang*

Given the persistence with which the 'state of exception' recurs in Australian politics, bearing out the colonial 'haunting' which Gunew detects in putatively post-colonial nations,[57] it is worth asking to what extent Scott's Benang, crucially concerned as it is with the temporal politics of 'bare life' and assimilation, plausibly offers alternatives to these powerful regimes of time. The fragmented narrative structure of the novel is patently conceived in part as a reflection of cultural disintegration, but in part as a performative attempt to undermine the linear genealogies of the sort constructed by the narrator's grandfather. The narrator himself ruminates upon this wilful subversion of linearity, reflection that to 'the extent to which I had freed myself from the timetable set for me' (Benang 19). In one instance of a frequently reiterated metanarrative topos, the narrator comments, 'Once again, I am confusing things, not following an appropriate sequence' (Benang 97). The vector of temporal progress posited by eugenics is explicitly turned about in Scott's narrative: 'Raised to carry on one heritage, and ignore another, I found myself wishing to reverse that upbringing' (*Benang* 19).

The novel freely concedes the difficulty of this temporal project. As the narrator admits, 'Of course it is impossible to completely retrace the process' (*Benang* 28). More disturbingly, is it possible that the strategy of temporal reversal, of going back to retrieve a lost culture ('"I tell you you gotta go right back"' [*Benang* 164]), may simply situate Scott's project, despite its overtly contestatory agenda, within the purview of the eugenics and its temporal vectors? The rhetoric of eugenics sets up a binary opposition between progress (the 'clever progressive men of the time,' 'Seeking a future, aiming at me') and regress ('throwbacks,' 'atavism' [*Benang* 48]). Strategies of historical reversal seeking to undo the cultural destruction effected by assimilation thus operate within the same linear logic of social Darwinism. Merely recoding movement backwards as positive rather than negative does little to shift the broader framework in which much indigenous cultural activism is conceptualized. Scott has acknowledged the problematic character of making the colonial archive – that is, the documentation of a temporalizing and temporalized eugenic project – so central to his own undertaking: 'It's impossible to get a story of such a relationship with country that's from the archival histories.'[58] This impossibility reposes upon the very temporality which underlies the concept of the archive. Positing history as that which is recorded in writing, it by definition excludes all forms of history (oral, plastic, place-based) which are not encoded in written language, and consigns them to the bin of 'pre-literate societies' or 'people without history.'[59] Kim Scott himself has said of the archives he used when researching Benang, 'I worked out where my family moved around and then I read the police station books. The letters and their

[57] Sneja Gunew, *Haunted Nations: The Colonial Dimensions of Multiculturalisms* (London: Routledge, 2004).

[58] Kim Scott, 'Apologies, Agency and Resilience', 68.

[59] Eric Wolf, *Europe and the People Without History* (Berkeley: University of California Press, 1982).

names are there, but their voices aren't there.'[60] Archive-time is thus in principle an instrument of temporal exclusion, though the subaltern actions it occludes are never entirely sealed off from elite structures.[61] Clearly indigenous peoples in Australia have been intervening into archival history almost from the first European arrivals in the form of petitions, letters, etc.,[62] thus blurring the fallaciously hard boundaries between archival history and subaltern history. Yet by and large, archival time ignores the possibility of any other temporalities.

Whether this actually poses a genuine problem for a cultural politics motivated by the pragmatic demands of everyday welfare and community enhancement, or whether this is merely a point of intellectual concern of little relevance outside academia, is a moot point. However, if one takes seriously the profound effects of the linear structures of biopolitics and its vectors of progress and elimination, then this problem at least deserves attention.

From this point of view it is surely of significance that the underlying spiritual values and cosmological beliefs informing the indigenous ethos of place in part at least elude the trap of linear temporal vectors:

> Here.
> Here.
> Here. (*Benang* 189)

These deictic markers[63] create their own sequence, one which is distinctly atemporal. Analogously, Scott's narrator repeatedly shifts the focus of his story from events to places: 'But now – having written such a very little of my people, both before and behind me – I would show you a place' (*Benang* 451). Scott's story is a performative re-invention of a heritage which is both lost and intuitively rediscovered. Yet this heritage is primordially and intimately anchored in the land: it is entangled in a politics of temporality, but seeks ways of eluding that politics based upon 'my awareness of my historical *place*' (*Benang* 29; emphasis added). In Scott's reading, 'the land holds all things . . . from which we may later select, amplify, and consider the resonances' (*Benang* 43). Here the land itself is an archive readable within what might be described as the 'block-time'[64] of indigenous tradition: the 'site-based story' 'challenges the idea of "assimilation" at the same time as it offers a different perspective altogether.'[65] This is a principle which countermands the time of the white archive, supplementing the narrative's effort to rescue alterna-

60 Victoria Laurie, 'Reclaiming the voices: Kim Scott discusses his new novel *Benang*', *Weekend Australian*, 14 August 1999.

61 Ranajit Guha (ed.), 'On Some Aspects of the Historiography of Colonial India', in *Selected Subaltern Studies* (New York: Oxford University Press, 1988), 37–44.

62 Penny van Toorn, *Writing Never Arrives Naked: Early Aboriginal Cultures of Writing in Australia* (Canberra: Aboriginal Studies Press, 2006).

63 See my *Spaces of Fiction/Fictions of Space: Postcolonial Place and Literary DeiXis* (Basingstoke: Palgrave Macmillan, 2010), 37–57, 184–205.

64 Mark Currie, *About Time: Narrative, Fiction and the Philosophy of Time* (Edinburgh: Edinburgh University Press, 2007), 15–20.

65 Scott, 'Apologies, Agency and Resilience', 63.

tive histories from the racist rhetoric of 1930s eugenics by means of (merely) another temporality.

Thus, to the extent that the land itself is the ground of indigenous heritage, it offers a counterweight to European biopolitics, an alternative genealogy which has its own atemporality of the natural environment. That atemporality may be one of Abiding Events (the ancestors residing in place), embodied in the land, which collectively form an Abiding Law.[66] It is the land which constitutes its own sovereign temporality, of which human actors are a residue, 'manifestations of the spirit of place impossible to conquer.'[67] From such a perspective, it is possible that the duality of 'bare life' vs. civic life ('zoē'/'bios') which Agamben traces down through the Western political tradition may be tangential to the indigenous world. Here, the land itself perhaps bodies forth a different meaning of 'bios,' a life and a history which encompasses mineral, vegetable, animal and human life and their respective temporalities in quite different ways to the European tradition: 'I am part of a much older story, one of a perpetual billowing from the sea, with its rhythm of return, return, and remain. . . . We are still here, Benang' (*Benang* 495).

In his work not only as a creative artist, but also as an academic and activist, Kim Scott's projects strive for the revitalization of indigenous culture, the retrieval of language and narratives. Yet such programmes are always threatened with suspension – by funding cuts or shifts in government policy. The state of exception, even on a small scale, can re-emerge at any moment. However, Agamben's theory of the 'state of exception' may be excessively fixated on the state and the sovereign, leaving too little space for a multiplicity of other actors contesting that power in its interstices;[68] possibly it is also excessively focussed on human actors, whether victims or oppressors, albeit inevitably the central figures of a humanistic politics to which most of us subscribe. Perhaps, however, and this may be another message of *Benang*, there is an atemporality of the land which is prior to any sovereign division of the rights to live of 'bare life' or civic life – one offering an alternative paradigm with the potential to inform and inflect anew contemporary cultural politics, whether indigenous or other, in Australia today.

66 Tony Swain, *A Place for Strangers: Towards a History of Australian Aboriginal Being* (Cambridge: Cambridge University Press, 1993), 22.

67 Kim Scott, *That Deadman Dance* (Sydney: Picador, 2010), 398.

68 Nikos Papastergiadis, 'The invasion complex: the abject other and spaces of violence', *Geografiska Annaler (Series B)*, 88.4 (2006), 439.

PART TWO

4 'White Aboriginals': White Australian Literary Responses to the Challenge of Indigenous Histories

White Australia has been, for much of its two centuries of existence, a society which has repressed the territorial expropriation and genocide upon which it was founded. In his 1968 ABC Boyer Lectures, the anthropologist W. E. H. Stanner spoke of 'the great Australian silence' – 'a cult of disremembering' – 'a cult of forgetfulness practised on a national scale.'[1] This phenomenon of collective amnesia held sway into the 1980s, but has increasingly been exposed to the corrosive effects of indigenous political activism. Important milestones in the recent history of indigenous political visibility were the submission of the Bark petition to Federal Parliament in Canberra in 1963 by the Yolgnu people of Arnhem land; the Wave Hill protests in 1965 which culminated in the granting of wage parity for indigenous workers, and also contributed to the 1967 referendum granting indigenous people Australian citizenship; the Tent Embassy, which indigenous activists planted on the lawns of Parliament House in 1972; the vociferous indigenous contestation of two hundred years of white occupation on the occasion of the 1988 celebrations; and of course Eddy Mabo's lobbying and successive appeals, which led to the historic Mabo decision handed down by the High Court in 1992, and resulted in the Native Title legislation. These dates mark progressive stages in the relentless elimination of white Australian amnesia over the past third of a century.

A similar phenomenon has occurred in white Australian literature, with an impressive upsurge of indigenous writing evinced since the 1960s. Symptomatic of this shift in the constitution of Australian literature was J. J. Healy's registration of a paradigm change from white writing about indigenous people to indigenous codification of black experience in white Australia. Paradoxically, at the very moment when Australian literature graduated from non-existence within the academy, via a place within 'Commonwealth literature,' to the status of 'postcolonial literature,' it also found itself in the position of 'occupier' literature, colonizer writing.[2]

Of all the events mentioned above, the most significant was without a doubt the Mabo decision of 1992, which confirmed the existence across two hundred years of white expropriation of indigenous ownership of the land. To take the Freudian title of a book by Ken Gelder and Jane Jacobs, Mabo made Australia an 'uncanny' place. The home of the European settlers abruptly became unsettling, '*unheimlich*,' the familiar suddenly became the unfamiliar, the majority became a moral minority, the erstwhile marginal suddenly became central and primordial.[3] The uncanny process epitomized in Mabo had already been gathering momentum for more than twenty

1 W. E. H. Stanner, *After the Dreaming: The 1968 Boyer Lectures* (Sydney: Australian Broadcasting Commission, 1969), 25.

2 J. J. Healy, *Literature and the Aborigine in Australia*, 2nd ed. (St Lucia: University of Queensland Press, 1989), xx.

3 Ken Gelder and Jane M. Jacobs, *Uncanny Australia: Sacredness and Identity in Postcolonial Australia* (Melbourne: Melbourne University Press, 1998).

years, and white Australia has been reacting to that process in a variety of different ways ever since.

States of unsettlement

In this chapter, I attempt to trace white literary responses to the seismic upheavals in the white Australian consciousness over the past three decades by examining a literary topos which I call the 'white Aboriginal' narrative: stories of white persons, escaped convicts or shipwrecked travellers who were taken in by indigenous tribes during the colonial epoch. This topos reworks historical narratives about figures such as the convict escapee William Buckley, the shipwrecked Eliza Fraser, or alternatively, the mythical white woman who was said to be held captive in the 1840s by the native peoples in Gippsland.

I adopt the term 'white Aboriginal' for strategic reasons, in explicit contrast to the earlier term 'white Blackfellow' coined by Barrett to describe transcultural actors in the early contact period, and employed by more recent writers such as Julie Carr.[4] The term 'white Aborigine' was derived from Norman Mailer's 'white Negro' epithet and achieved prominence in Australian debates on 'cultural convergence' in the 1980s. Meaghan Morris saw in Mick 'Crocodile' Dundee the exemplification of the 'white Aborigine,' 'one of the privileged figures of postmodern rhetoric in Australian art writing' of the early 1980s.[5] The Australian-Lithuanian artist Imants Tillers wrote that the notion of cultural convergence 'is attractive . . . because it offers a painless way to expiate our collective guilt . . . while simultaneously suggesting an easy solution to the more mundane but nevertheless pressing problem of finding a uniquely Australian content to our art in an international climate sympathetic to the notion of "regional" art.'[6] His paintings 'White Aborigines' (1983) and 'I am Aboriginal' (1988) aroused considerable controversy.[7] Ian MacLean objects that Tillers appears to collapse Aboriginality into a (post)modern diaspora: 'Here, the only place Aborigines have is as part of the modern diaspora, that is, as wanderers in a *terra nullius*. . . . The effect was to de-Aboriginalise and de-essentialise Aboriginal art.'[8] More recently, the term 'white Aboriginals' has emerged as a specifically indigenous term of abuse, referring to indigenous people who profit from their pale skin as a means to social privilege in discriminatory white Australia. Thus the term can be seen as a site of contemporary cultural contestation, one that is

4 Charles Barrett, *White Blackfellows: The Strange Adventures of Europeans Who Lived among the Savages* (Melbourne: Hallcraft, 1948); Julie Carr, 'The White Blackfellow', *Island Magazine* 56 (Spring 1993), 71–72.

5 Meaghan Morris, *The Pirate's Fiancée: Feminism, Reading, Postmodernism* (London: Verso, 1988), 260, 286n.

6 Imants Tillers, 'Locality fails', *Art & Text* 6 (1982), 53.

7 See Wystan Curnow, *Imants Tillers and the 'Book of Power'* (North Ryde, NSW: Craftsman House, 1998), 25 Fig. 8, and 91 Fig. 23.

8 Ian McLean, *White Aborigines: Identity Politics in Australian Art* (Cambridge: Cambridge University Press, 1998), 116–17.

highly apposite to the discursive negotiations with political and cultural change discussed in this chapter.[9]

In this chapter, I read five avatars of the 'white Aboriginal' figure, to be found in Patrick White's *A Fringe of Leaves* (1976), Rodney Hall's *The Second Bridegroom* (1991), David Malouf's *Remembering Babylon* (published, significantly, a year after Mabo, in 1993), Liam Davison's *The White Woman* (1994) and Stephen Gray's *The Artist is a Thief* (2001).[10] With one exception, these narratives deal with the interface of white and black societies during the first contact phase. Such stories offer a powerful metaphor of the ways in which the two societies interacted with each other in a safely distant past, and thus a way of working through white Australia's contemporary relationship to a people whom it has recently discovered not to be despised guests, but rather, maligned hosts. Perhaps Malouf's figure of the transcultural Gemmy, drawn in Jeff Fisher's 1993 dustcover illustration balancing on a post-and-rail fence, his body shaded in tones of black, grey and white, is the most captivating embodiment of the white Aboriginal figure. This 'unsettled fellow' (*Remembering Babylon* 7) who unsettles the Scots settlers in frontier Queensland, powerfully exemplifies the capacity of indigenous visibility in white Australia to disturb the nation's self-image. I suggest that narratives of 'white Aboriginals' are ways of trying to situate white Australia in relation to, and indeed, in many cases, to participate in and recuperate, increasingly powerful discourses of Aboriginality.

Mediation or mirroring?

It is significant that for the Nobel-Prize Winner Patrick White, the issue of white-black relations addressed through the figure of the 'white Aboriginal' is subsidiary to another aspect of Australian cultural consciousness – and thus, not surprisingly, is neglected within the programme set by his novel *A Fringe of Leaves*. White's 1976 historical narrative sets out to lay bare one of the principal areas of amnesia in Australian cultural consciousness: the barbaric penal origins of the nation and the malaise it continues to create in contemporary society.[11] On the way, White also gives a version of that other forgotten origin, the violent confrontation with Australia's prior inhabitants. White's protagonist Ellen Roxburgh, modelled on Eliza Frazer, is made to cross the border into primitivism in order to lay bare the harshness of colonial Australian society. It is her sojourn with an indigenous tribe persistently characterized in terms of hunger, dirt and brutality which is made to contrast with

[9] I wish to thank my artist brother Edmund West for telling me about Imants Tillers during a gallery-crawl down Flinders Lane, and Stephen Gray, of the Law Faculty of Northern Territory University, for providing a plethora of helpful information not immediately available in Germany.

[10] References in the text are to the following editions: Patrick White, *A Fringe of Leaves* (Harmondsworth: Penguin, 1983); Rodney Hall, *The Second Bridegroom* (London: Faber & Faber, 1991); David Malouf, *Remembering Babylon* (London: Vintage, 1994); Liam Davison, *The White Woman* (St Lucia: University of Queensland Press, 1994); Stephen Gray, *The Artist is a Thief* (Sydney: Angus & Robertson, 2001).

[11] See Kay Schaffer, *In the Wake of First Contact: The Eliza Fraser Stories* (Cambridge: Cambridge University Press, 1995), 159; Robert Hughes, *The Fatal Shore: A History of the Transportation of Convicts to Australia 1787–1868* (London: Pan/Collins, 1988).

the no less barbarous penal regime. Similarly, Jack Chance, the escaped convict who rescues Ellen from the tribe and leads her back to white settlement, returns to indigenous tribal society because he (rightly) fears the dreadful punishments that will be meted out to him as an escapee. 'They've murdered Mr Roxburgh,' she says, speaking of the natives, and then continues, 'but will the whites – kill Jack?' (*A Fringe of Leaves* 306). It is Mrs Roxburgh's experiences of native 'savagery' which permit her to transfer the white attitude towards 'savage' black spearings to the workings of European 'justice.'

White is clearly not interested in creating a narrative of cross-cultural communication in the early contact period. The indigenous people among whom Ellen spends her period in the bush are never endowed with a language worthy of White's attention, thus remaining outside the realm of genuine transcultural interaction. Ellen herself claims to have not been in the tribe long enough to learn the language (*A Fringe of Leaves* 328), thus figuring it purely as an absence within the European consciousness. Ellen's lack of linguistic competence means that for the reader, black society remains below the threshold of recognisable civic organization. This 'white Aboriginal' does not offer the reader possible perspectives upon white-black interaction; its function is entirely subordinated to white Australia's gaze upon its history – understood exclusively white.

Only via the escaped convict Jack Chance, now an adopted member of an indigenous tribe, is any indication of social coherence in black society visible – and paradoxically, only via the *transcultural* mediation of the convict is a truly critical glimpse of white society available. Jack's account of the spearing of Mr Roxburgh furnishes one of the few occasions when we are offered a view of things from the black side of the fence: 'I heard tell . . . among the blacks. They was provoked, though, by the whites' (*A Fringe of Leaves* 262). Significantly, Jack decides against re-integration to white society, disappearing back into the scrub once Ellen reaches civilization (*A Fringe of Leaves* 299). Thus the only mediator between the cultures which the book allows to appear is neutralized by the narrative, thereby figuratively ostending its own inability to transcend the ethnocentric point of view it embodies. Jack Chance thus stands for a 'chance' which White neglects through the nature of his novelistic project. For White, black tribal society merely functions as a counterfoil to white colonial barbarism. Thus it must remain separate, in stark contradiction to the real historical dynamics of early black-white interaction, so as not to lose its contrastive function.

What happens more frequently, however, is an odd shift of point of view, which far from righting the distorting ideology of barbaric 'civilization,' inverts the historical situation of whites and blacks in post-invasion Australia. Ellen becomes a slave within the indigenous tribe. Her exhaustion and despair result in a 'habitual state of mind, dull indifference' (*A Fringe of Leaves* 251) which mirrors the passive indifference and apathy resorted to by the indigenous people as a protective strategy after two hundred years of oppression. At the same time, however, Ellen attains a special status within the tribe. In her everyday functions she is a slave, exploited and maltreated, but she also possesses a paradoxical symbolic status. 'The Blacks were for the most part lost in open mouthed wonder as they examined the exhibit from every angle' (*A Fringe of Leaves* 249). Here the indigenous people are figured as partaking in the musealization of the exoticized 'Other.' To this extent Ellen's situation also mimes that of the indigenous people in white Australian society, subjected to everyday exploitation and marginalization, but also celebrated as icons of essential Australianness, just as their cultural productions are reified and expropriated as images and artefacts for the tourist industry. In one very significant passage, White reveals the motivation behind his strange reversals of white and black social status:

> *Their faces were her glass*, in which she and they were temporarily united, either in mooning relationship or mystical fantasy. What the blacks could not endure, it seemed, was the ghost of a woman they had found haunting the beach. They may have felt that, were the ghost exorcized, they might contemplate with equanimity the supernatural come amongst them in their own flesh. (*A Fringe of Leaves* 239; emphasis added)

In this narrative, the black people function as a mirror for white society. The mirror reflects an image of the observer, but it also inverts reality and gives an illusory image. These narratives of 'marginality' serve White's superannuated 'avant-garde' project, based upon a modernist 'alienation effect.'[12] The glimpse of black society and culture thus afforded is instrumentalized in service of a critique of white society. In this way, White's narrative also elides the 'ghost' of a black society with which genuine interaction was in some instances possible[13] – an interaction towards which narratives of 'white Aboriginals' could perhaps have pointed, but one which was perhaps as yet barely available to the white Australian cultural imagination of the mid 1970s.

Forging the new place

Fifteen years later, Rodney Hall would repeat White's scenario of the marginalized white member of a black tribe with his renegade convict character FJ in *The Second Bridegroom*. This time, however, a genuine coexistence of the white interloper and the black tribal members seems to be possible. The convict's marginal position is not that of a slave, as in White's Ellen Roxburgh, but is limited by his respect for the taboos and limits set on him by the indigenous group itself.

FJ is shown the tribe's sacred sites, their water holes and their food sources, perhaps in accordance with the obligation upon the custodians of a country to introduce newcomers to the country. Jimmy Mangayarri, of the Yarralin people, comments on the ritual of introduction, in which the visitor is 'watered' so that the country now knows the person's smell and will not harm him: 'Dreams can smell other people. After you water him, that Dream knows him.'[14] Deborah Bird Rose suggests that this ritual 'also marks the strangers as people who, while no longer at risk simply by being there, are dependent. In acknowledging their status as strang-

12 See Simon During, *Patrick White* (Melbourne: Oxford University Press, 1996).

13 See James Boyce, 'Journeying home: A new look at the British invasion of Van Diemen's Land: 1803–1823', *Island Magazine* 66 (Autumn 1996), 38–63.

14 Jimmy Mangayarri, quoted in Deborah Bird Rose, *Dingo Makes Us Human: Life and Land in an Aboriginal Australian Culture* (Cambridge: Cambridge University Press, 1992), 109.

ers, they assent to these facts: that others are the owners, that their own knowledge is limited, and that the country has no real responsibility for them.'[15] It is thus highly significant that FJ accepts that he cannot move of his own accord, nor search for food. 'Not for the world would I trespass beyond the limits they set me. To my surprise, I realize now that I showed their taboos more respect than the taboos of my own folk' (*The Second Bridegroom* 40). Here the figure of chiasmus does offer an alternative image of black-white history – one where the power differential which guaranteed white superiority is inverted, so as to allow indigenous people to maintain their legitimate position of owners of the land, thus forcing their protégé to respect their space and customs.

Of particular interest in Hall's narrative is the protagonist's awareness of the epistemic violence potentially inherent in language, and his care not to impose alien paradigms upon the new land: 'When I could . . . I promised not to try reading the messages I heard and smelled and touched, tasted and saw. I would respect them as having no use. None of them would be the same tomorrow' (*The Second Bridegroom* 21). Such ideals are not always feasible, and he does resort to calling his protectors 'Men' as being 'cleaner than clumsy dodges with roundabout words, which would lead with an even greater plague of English spreading in a world which English has no right to. . . . Order is a way of trapping anything wild, tricking us into the game of thinking we understand. . . . So each of my saviours was a man – and I prayed I would not be forcing them into a frame too rigid if I thought of them in secret as Men' (*The Second Bridegroom* 41–42). This humble stance allows him to remain receptive for the land around him, which gradually takes on a meaning not previously available. He continues to refer to the bush as chaos, thereby contrasting it with the repressive order of transplanted white civilization. Chaos, he claims, is not subjected to the strictures of a foreign linguistic regime, and thus unfolds itself for the receptive newcomer. Here Hall appears to sketch a potential model for mutually respectful and careful negotiation between black and white Australia.

However, no verbal communication comes to pass in Hall's novel: 'although I gave signals upon which they might sometimes act there was no give-and-take between us. What I did, they observed. What they did, I observed' (*The Second Bridegroom* 86). This may be a reluctant admission that reconciliation along the line of a fusion of cultures is not possible at the current time, as many commentators believe today.

Halfway through the text, after a frontier skirmish, the Men simply disappear from sight, never to be seen again. In the second half of the book, the land is strangely depopulated; it has become the empty land which the whites claim to have 'discovered.' Now endowed with indigenous knowledge, the white narrator tries to pass on to his beloved, Mrs Atholl, his new view of the now 'empty land.' Knowledge has been passed on, to the advantage of white society, but no real integration has actually occurred, and indigenous society has noiselessly disappeared from the historical stage.

Hall's text is superficially more aware of the imperial character of exogenic sign systems than White's text, and affords the indigenous people a more generous

[15] Rose, *Dingo Makes Us Human*, 109.

hearing. None the less, it marginalizes them from its landscape as they were historically marginalized from the Australian landscape, pushed back into more and more remote enclaves by the advance of settlement and armed expulsion. Yet the terms of exchange merely mirror the expropriation of indigenous knowledge upon which white settlement and the elaboration of European society has always depended, but which it has never acknowledged.

The reasons for the disappearance of the indigenous people are never given in Hall's text. To that extent, the text appears to participate in white Australia's 'forgetting of its forgetting,' performing an erasure which elides its own action. One is reminded of what appears to be a similar case of disavowal in White's *Tree of Man*:

> It's not known how or why the district in which the Parkers lived got its name, but it was about the time of the floods that the official voice began to refer to it as Durilgai. And this meant 'fruitful', a friend of Mr Armstrong's who was a professor, or something, said. But the people who lived in that district were disinclined to use their name, anyway for a long time, as if something was expected of them that they could not, or did not care to, fulfil.[16]

Only the vaguely sensed breach of contractual obligation aroused by the resurfacing of an elided indigenous trace points towards some sort of responsibility created by the re-emergence of the place name.

It is significant that Hall's entire narrative is written in the second person: the writer addresses a loved woman, to whom he wishes to convey his new knowledge. The text is addressed to white Australia, from the borders between the old and new lands. It is not a communication between black and white, for this interaction has melted away by the time of FJ's writing. It is hardly surprising, then, that his narrative deals with the white relationship to the enigmatic continent, and not with the original inhabitants of that continent. Paul Carter has commented on the way in which white discourses of the dilemma of the land function as a symptom whose latent content is the genocide committed against indigenous peoples. With the marginalization and eradication of the indigenous people, their relationship to the land was lost, so that the link had to be onerously re-established by the white settlers.[17] As in White's novel, the transcultural figure of the 'white Aboriginal' serves less the cause of black-white reconciliation than the legitimization of white Australia's purchase on expropriated land.

A particularly important strand of metaphors within the novel is that of forgery. FJ is transported to Australia for the forgery of a Caxton text, a fraud so expertly executed that he is initially charged with the 'theft of a national treasure' (*The Second Bridegroom* 101). Elsewhere he claims that the white settlement of Australia tries to make the southern continent a cheap forgery of Europe (*The Second Bridegroom* 103, 194) – and it is precisely for this reason that the narrator so passionately tries to convey his newfound knowledge of Australia to his female 'patron,' in the hope that the land will be allowed to persist in all its alien and irreducible beauty. But we need to ask to what extent his account of Australia, in so far

16 Patrick White, *The Tree of Man* (1956; Ringwood: Penguin, 1961/1965), 99.

17 Paul Carter, *The Road to Botany Bay* (London: Faber & Faber, 1988), 343.

as it excludes the original owners, in fact registers the theft of an indigenous 'treasure,' the land itself, passed off as 'legitimate' expropriation. The narrator conveys an entirely positive value upon the work of forgery, emphasizing the forger's love for the original, his dedication to something that is unique, and thus only then worth replication (*The Second Bridegroom* 159, 185). This is 'legitimate' forgery, justified theft. The book declares FJ's love for Australia, but it is a love which uses and then displaces indigenous presence in its narrative sequence. Hall's marginalization of the land's copyright owners suggests that in the long term, the text is actually complicit with the theft of their inalienable property perpetrated by white Australians for the past two centuries. What becomes of the 'white Aboriginal' motif after 1992 and the definitive naming of that expropriation in the High Court's Mabo decision?

Speaking for the Other

As the first of the five 'white Aboriginal' narratives examined in this chapter to be written in the aftermath of the Mabo decision, Malouf's 1993 novel *Remembering Babylon* could justly be expected to engage with the issues of reconciliation and reparation raised by the High Court's historic stance. The story of the half-white, half-black Gemmy's appearance in a small Queensland frontier settlement, his adoption by a family of Scots settlers, his eventual exclusion, his return to his earlier tribal belonging, and his final death in a 'dispersal' cannot but bear an exemplary significance. The sheer technical perfection of Malouf's writing contributed to the symbolic weight attributed to the novel. Not without good reason, Malouf's luminous novel was hailed almost unanimously by critics (with the exception of Germaine Greer) as a brilliantly inspired tribute to the ideals of reconciliation.[18]

It is likely that Malouf is well aware of the 'white Aboriginal' tradition within which he wrote. Malouf's Gemmy has a curious predecessor in White's *Fringe of Leaves*, in which Jemmy, one of the native station hands, makes an appearance at the window at Mrs Oakes' farm, frightening Ellen Roxburgh, who fears that the blacks have come to recapture her (*Fringe of Leaves* 305). Certainly Malouf would appear to be acutely sensitive to White's authority, and also of some sort of 'anxiety of influence' at work in that burdensome heritage, as his prudent public critiques of White and his thematizing of the issue in *Child's Play* (1982) indicate.[19]

But to what extent does Gemmy the ship's boy constitute a genuine transcultural actor? With Malouf's novel, there occurs a decisive transformation of the 'white Aboriginal' narrative. This time, the transcultural actor is genuinely integrated into a tribe. Malouf tracks the process of Gemmy's insertion into a new culture after being shipwrecked off the Queensland coast. He goes so far as to record in poetic detail the learning of the indigenous language (*Remembering Babylon* 27), rather than

[18] For an overview of the debate unleashed by Greer's critique, see Julie Carr, *The Captive White Woman of Gipps Land: In Pursuit of the Legend* (Melbourne: Melbourne University Press, 2001), 280 n74, and Suvendrini Perera, 'Unspeakable Bodies: Representing the Aboriginal in Australian Critical Discourse', *Meridian* 13: 1 (1994), 15–16.

[19] David Malouf, interview with Ray Willbanks, 'A Conversation with David Malouf', *Antipodes* 4:1 (Spring 1990), 16; *Child's Play*, with *Eustace* and *The Prowler* (Ringwood, VIC: Penguin, 1983).

simply noting the loss of the old one, as White and Hall do. Malouf works to portray his version of an indigenous concept of the natural world and lived environment, and focuses intensively upon the protagonist's place between two languages. Conversely, however, Gemmy's identity subsequent to his return to the white settlement remains that of the barely integrated indigenous person on the margins of white society. Predictably, that society does not accept him as white, and ejects him violently after a brief sojourn.

If there is a transcultural character in the novels examined in this chapter who really embodies the cultural impact of Mabo, it is Gemmy. He incorporates the uncanny – the eruption of unfamiliarity in the midst of the familiar – which was unleashed by the rediscovered persistence of native title. Neither White's Ellen Roxburgh nor Hall's FJ ever really integrate to tribal society. Gemmy, by contrast, does enter indigenous society, and never really comes back. Mrs McIvor wrangles with her neighbours: 'They were forgetting, she told them frostily. Gemmy was white' (*Remembering Babylon* 78) – but for the Scots settlers, he remains a synecdoche of the blacks (*Remembering Babylon* 42), as he does, I suggest, for Malouf. Whence the power and at the same time, the risk inherent in *Remembering Babylon* – a deep ambivalence which I shall attempt to elucidate in what follows.

Gemmy is hailed in Mr Frazer's euphoric writing as a hybrid, a transcultural being. '*Our poor friend Gemmy is a forerunner. He is no longer a white man, or a European, whatever his birth, but a true child of the place as it will be one day . . . in allowing himself to be at home here, he has crossed the boundaries of his given nature*' (*Remembering Babylon* 132). Mr Frazer's immensely appealing perspective upon cultural fusion culminates, however, in an apolitical focus upon the white relationship to the land and the hope of benefit from black knowledge of the land, without acknowledging the process of expropriation which has accompanied the establishment of white tropes of space: 'We have been wrong to see this land as hostile and infelicitous . . . It is habitable already. . . .We must humble ourselves and learn from them [the indigenous people]' (*Remembering Babylon* 129–30). The violence of conquest is belatedly acknowledged at the end of the novel when Lachlan searches for Gemmy's grave at the site of a 'dispersal,' but this note of disharmony is swiftly erased by the transcendent, totalizing tones of the novel's conclusion: 'all the outline of the vast continent appears, in touch now with its other life' (*Remembering Babylon* 200). The suspicion that this utopian moment of union does not operate an *acknowledgement* of 'the other life' so much as its *assimilation*, hardens upon examining Malouf's narrative technique in more detail.

In *Remembering Babylon*, Malouf makes extensive use of Free Indirect Discourse (FID) and related narrative devices in order to represent the thoughts of his character Gemmy, in particular, and the indigenous cultural universe, in general. FID works to facilitate reader empathy with characters by blurring the boundaries between characters' thoughts or statements and narrative enunciation.[20] To this extent it could be said to perform the work of 'transcultural border-crossing' which is the novel's principle theme. At the same time, however, it creates ineradicable

[20] See Monika Fludernik, *The Fictions of Language and the Languages of Fiction: The Linguistic Representation of Speech and Consciousness* (London: Routledge, 1993), 72–82.

political problems. When Malouf tells us that Gemmy's stammer 'belonged to someone *he thought* was lost,' or that there was 'so much dislocation between what *he meant* to convey and the few words he could recover of his original tongue' (*Remembering Babylon* 14, 16; emphasis added), the reader is confronted with the problem of knowing who determines what Gemmy thought or meant: is it Gemmy himself or his Scots settler interlocutors or the Maloufian narrator? The narratological aporias of Malouf's technique become acutely apparent in a character who can barely speak English, yet is fluent in FID (for instance 22–23).[21]

While offering advantages of readerly identification, FID runs the strong risk of overbalancing into discursive annexation – that is, of arrogating the right to read someone else's thoughts, of invading their private world. To think oneself into others' skin is of course one of the most primordial tasks of the novelist. Indeed, the impulse to create organic fictional subjectivities has been selected as one of the defining characteristics of Malouf's literary oeuvre.[22] But this undertaking is extremely problematic in the context of the long expropriation of black knowledge and discourse by white anthropologists and writers. In a highly pertinent anecdote, Espeth Probyn tells how her white Canadian grandmother 'liked to inhabit the skins of others' through her poetic imagination – a statement that is greeted with ironic scepticism by her Koori interlocutor.[23] The problem of cultural expropriation is highlighted by Joseph Wambugu Githaiga:

> The protection of indigenous folklore and knowledge has become a pressing issue both within Australia and abroad. This has been due to the development of a lucrative international trade in indigenous heritage, which has seen most of the economic benefits diverted to non-indigenous persons and institutions. . . . For indigenous people the graver and more reprehensible consequence of the commercialisation of their heritage is the denigration of their cultures through the use of heritage in culturally inappropriate ways.[24]

It is only necessary to move from the level of the individual character Gemmy to that of indigenous cultural attitudes in general – as in the descriptions of the cultural universe in which the young boy Gemmy grows up, or the mystical communion of Gemmy and his fellow tribespeople (26, 117–18) – to establish the deeply problematic nature of Malouf's 'reconciliation' project. Upon closer examination of Malouf's use of FID and similar narrative devices, one is tempted to read the characterization Mr Frazer, engaged in taking down Gemmy's account, as a dis-

[21] A similar aporia is to be found in W. E. H. Stanner's otherwise acutely (self-)critical *After the Dreaming:* 'On the outskirts of the settlements there were a few groups of "myalls" (bush natives), who were as wild as hawks, timid and daring by turns, with scarcely a word of English, and in two minds what to do: drawn towards the settlement . . . but unreconciled to the prospect of a sedentary life' (12).

[22] See for instance the title of Philip Neilsen's *Imagined Lives: A Study of David Malouf* (St Lucia: University of Queensland Press, 1990).

[23] Elspeth Probyn, 'Eating Skin', in Sara Ahmed and Jackie Stacey (eds), *Thinking Through the Skin* (London: Routledge, 2001), 89–90.

[24] Joseph Wambugu Githaiga, 'Intellectual Property Law and the Protection of Indigenous Folklore and Knowledge', *E Law - Murdoch University Electronic Journal of Law* 5: 2 (June 1998), 3.

placed description of Malouf's own undertaking: 'It was Mr Frazer's belief that the sympathy he felt for the man, which was very strong, gave him an infallible insight into what he was trying to get out' (*Remembering Babylon* 17). Good will, indeed love for the object, may not be sufficient justification, in the Australian context, for cultural forgery and appropriation. The epistemological annexation evinced in Malouf's novel is of no small significance, given the prominence of its author, and the exemplary status attributed to the text a year after Mabo.

Malouf is infinitely more ambitious than White and Hall in what he attempts, but thereby strays into the risky area of 'speaking for' Gemmy and 'his people' (64), and by extension, for Australia's indigenous population in general – at a time when a large number indigenous writers are using the public platform clearly available to them, thus making white incursion into this discursive space both superfluous and presumptuous. Malouf's description of Gemmy as an 'in-between character who would have been in contact with that culture and would be able to stand for that culture but wouldn't speak directly for it,' and his curious claim that 'His silence is their silence. He stands as an emblematic figure' appear less than credible in this context.[25]

Certainly there is reason to believe that such experiments are technically not entirely successful. To whom are we to attribute a disturbing statement in FID such as the following: 'Till they arrived no other lives had been lived here' (*Remembering Babylon* 110): is this the settler-wife Ellen McIvor's thought, or the text's conviction, and how are we to decide? – as we must, given the inflammatory nature of such an utterance. It may well be that Malouf's relatively traditional narrative style, with its fairly unified narrative voice and plot structure, is inadequate to deal with the discursive rifts and conflicts he is speaking of. Possibly, a more radically disruptive or disrupted structure would be necessary to indicate genuine respect for indigenous discourse. Helen Gilbert's verdict on Malouf's *Blood Relations* equally well summarizes the dilemma evinced by *Remembering Babylon*: 'So, despite Malouf's desire to "let an Aboriginal voice take control of a major stage" in Australia, language remains a strategy of containment in the play, no doubt partly because of the playwright's limitations as an articulator of Aboriginal speech registers.'[26] In this context, it is difficult to avoid the impression that Malouf's ventriloquizing of indigenous discourse, embodied in the 'inbetween creature' Gemmy (*Remembering Babylon* 28), serves not to create reconciliatory reader-character relations – but rather, that Gemmy's hybrid status serves as the basis for a white bridgehead into the territory of indigenous discourse.

Exemplary here is Malouf's usage of 'you' in some sections of *Remembering Babylon*: 'Could *you* lose it? Not just language, but *it*. *It*. | For the fact was, when *you* looked at him sometimes he was not white. His skin might be but not his features' (*Remembering Babylon* 40; emphasis in bold type added). In FID, with its implicit phatic appeal to the reader, 'you' means 'one,' but is also subject to the

[25] David Malouf in an interview with Nikos Papastergiadis, *Dialogues in the Diasporas: Essays and Conversations on Cultural Identity* (London: Rivers Oram Press, 1998), 85.

[26] Helen Gilbert, *Sightlines: Race, Gender and Nation in Contemporary Australian Theatre* (Ann Arbor: University of Michigan Press, 1998), 42; the embedded quotation is from Jane Heath, 'Malouf: Relatively Speaking', *Weekend Australian*, 18–19 July 1987, 11.

'referential slither' affecting the use of 'you' in second person narratives,[27] and by extension, in FID narration. Thus Malouf's narrative discourse appears to address the white Australian audience which is the ultimate descendant of the novel's Scots settlers in Central Queensland. For them, Gemmy is and remains 'other' and disturbing because he presents the possibility, for instance, of what their own children could become. In the context of post-Mabo 'uncanny Australia,' the loss affects less the whiteness of skin than the very sense of national identity based upon a 'sense of place' previously unquestioned.

A striking transition from third-person narration to the ambiguous use of 'you' in one of the descriptions of Gemmy's life with the tribe is even more revealing:

> Watching out for it, and for himself, *he* got into his mouth as much of its fat and flesh as *he* could manage, its names too, its breath. What kept *you* alive here was the one and the other, and they were inseparable: the creature with its pale ears raised and stiffened, sitting up alert in its life as *you* were in *yours*, and its name on *your* tongue. When it kicked its feet and gushed blood it did not go out of the world but had its life now in *you*, and could go in and out of *your* mouth for ever, breath on breath, and was not lost, any more than the water *you* stooped to drink would cease to run because *you* gulped in down in greedy mouthfuls, then pissed it out. (*Remembering Babylon* 26; emphasis added)

The 'you,' and the possessive 'your' in particular (reinforced by the thematics of naming and eating as modes of appropriation), offers the white reader the illusion of participation in indigenous culture, of 'crossing the line,' and thus of mastering the uncannily shifting border which has been unsettling Australian cultural identity since Mabo. In this way the novel both addresses white anxieties and offers mechanisms of recuperation in which new forms of cultural appropriation compensate for a rising sense of 'dispossession.' Certainly this is a broader trend perceived by indigenous people in Australia. In empirical research carried out by Heather Goodall on post-Mabo historical consciousness, it transpired that 'virtually none of the indigenous respondents were interested in moving towards a . . . narrative of "Australian" history to which all could lay claim.' Rather, the notion that 'non-indigenous Australians could lay claim to the millennia of indigenous ownership of and traditional knowledge about the continent' was regarded by indigenous respondents as 'a way for invading newcomers to stake a claim to "belonging."'[28]

Remembering Babylon thus appears, among other functions, to be an attempt to restabilize unsettled cultural boundaries, to quell the uncanny unleashed since Mabo. Indeed, this is the implicit verdict delivered by two novels which appeared after *Remembering Babylon* and place the 'white Aboriginal' topos in unrelentingly critical light.

27 The term is that of Helmut Bonheim, 'Narration in the second person', *Recherches anglaises et américaines* 16 (1983), 76; see also Monika Fludernik (ed.), *Second-Person Narratives*, Special issue of *Style* 28:3 (1994).

28 Heather Goodall, 'Too Early Yet or Not Soon Enough?: Reflections on Sharing Histories as Process', in Kate Darian Smith (ed.), *Challenging Histories: Reflections on Australian History* (Special Issue of Australian Historical Studies 118 [2002]), 11.

The white Aboriginal as mirage and myth

Liam Davison's *The White Woman* (1994) casts into question the three preceding 'white Aboriginal' novels by concentrating upon this topos as a purely discursive phenomenon. Davison's ironic novel never allows us to meet this 'historical' avatar of the white Aboriginal. The nineteenth-century white woman of the title, ostensibly kidnapped by the indigenous tribes of as-yet-unsettled South-Eastern Victoria, remains a mirage or will-o'-the-wisp which permanently recedes before the search party's gaze. In this way, the author underlines the illusory character of the white woman, emphasizing her function as a screen for white projections and as justification for the brutal subjection of native Gippsland. The narrator indirectly comments upon the other 'White Aboriginal' narratives and their persistent recasting of early colonial history: 'You have to give it [the past] shape. And even then, when you think you've got it nailed – the right events in the clearest possible order – it squirms into the present and changes things. It should be settled but it isn't. Don't I still see her? Still hear her voice?' (*The White Woman* 3). In this narrative, there is no idealized transcultural actor to be found, but rather, white discourses which legitimize the exploration/appropriation of as-yet-unconquered tracts areas of Gippsland, the massacre of indigenous groups, and the self-justification of search-party members only too aware of their complicity in the atrocities committed by the local settlers.[29] The projection of the fictive white-woman image, with its brutally effective militaristic-imperialistic outcome, is the discursive correlative of Malouf's FID as a 'merely novelistic' occupation of indigenous cultural territory.

Davison constantly stresses the involvement of the press in the search party's expedition, and the moulding of public expectations around a fiction of white-black interaction. His use of second-person narration, a technique shared with Hall, foregrounds the fact that, in the words of the semiotician Peirce, signification is always signification for someone, 'stands to somebody for something . . . addresses somebody.'[30] Davison's narrative devices suggest that whatever original experiences of cross-cultural exchange may have occurred at the time (experiences which are in any case never retrievable in their pristine, pre-discursive originality[31]), the white narratives which have recycled those experiences have only served white ends. The sheer non-existence of the white woman lays bare the exclusively ideological, manipulative interests served by the storytelling. Her permanently receding image generates ever new and fresh discursive structures, of which Davison's novel is avowedly a further instance – but one that ostentatiously betrays the cause.

29 Some of the historical background to Davison's novel is documented in Peter D. Gardner, *Gippsland Massacres: The Destruction of the Kurnai Tribes 1800–1860*, 2nd ed. (Ensay, VIC: Ngarak Press, 1993).

30 Charles Sanders Peirce, *Collected Papers*, ed. Charles Hartshorne and Paul Weiss (Cambridge, Mass.: Harvard University Press, 1974), I/II: 135.

31 See Chris Healy, *From the Ruins of Colonialism: History as Social Memory* (Cambridge: Cambridge University Press, 1997), 159–89.

White Aboriginals, white thieves

In our last exemplar of the 'white Aboriginal' narrative, Stephen Gray's *The Artist is a Thief* (2001), the transcultural actor himself figures as forger and thief. The world-famous indigenous painter Margaret Thatcher Gandarrwuy exhibits a painting which is discovered to have been vandalized, the canvas slashed and the words 'The artist is a thief' scrawled across it. It transpires that Margaret Thatcher Gandarrwuy has been losing her sight, and that her white manager, Guy Randhawa, who identifies himself as a 'truly . . . Aboriginal' in the last pages of the novel (*The Artist is a Thief* 275), has taken over her work and her persona (his name is an anagram of hers – 274). When he appropriates motifs taken from the ancestral territory of another member of the community, the offended party takes action, acting as the responsible custodian of a specific cultural heritage. 'It was his country on the painting. Nobody should have been allowed to paint that without his permission. To him that was theft – or worse than theft, desecration. The colours weren't even right, or the stories. . . . It was a white person. No Aboriginal person would have painted such a thing' (*The Artist is a Thief* 249). The vandal's defacement of the painting is a way of 'stealing back' what has been illicitly taken by the self-styled 'white Aboriginal.'

In Gray's novel, the 'white Aboriginal' discourse frees itself from complicity in cultural theft by consigning that function to the transcultural character himself. But this self-liberation is simultaneously an unequivocal condemnation of cultural theft masquerading as cultural fusion. Gray distances himself from all forms of cultural expropriation: his protagonist, the young financial advisor Jean-Loup Wild, sent up from Melbourne to audit an indigenous art centre's book-keeping, is made acutely aware of the limits of his knowledge of indigenous culture and the boundaries which he cannot overstep; Gray is careful only to use indigenous names which do not infringe upon traditional customs ([vii]); and the sources of his fiction are acknowledged in detail ([v-vi], *The Artist is a Thief* 281–82). To that extent, the author rigorously follows the interrogations he has articulated elsewhere in a theoretical context:

> how far should indigenous or non-indigenous authors – either painters or writers – go when 'speaking about' Aboriginal people today? At a certain point it is clear that permissible reference or depiction becomes impermissible, and unethical, appropriation. For writers, that points exists somewhere along a spectrum between an author who depicts an Aboriginal presence as a minor character in a novel, to a major character or a narrator, to an author who herself trades upon her Aboriginal experience and 'street cred', or even claims to be Aboriginal herself.[32]

In his fiction, Gray picks up the issues of forgery raised by Hall's fiction and those of narrative perspective raised by Malouf's text, so as to implicitly point out the pitfalls of 'white Aboriginal' narratives.

32 Stephen Gray, 'In Black or White, or Beyond the Pale?: The "Authenticity" Debate and Protection for Aboriginal Culture, Pointing the Literary Bone', *Australian Feminist Law Journal* 15 (December 2001), 105–6. I am grateful to Stephen Gray for sending me a copy of this article.

A bankrupt topos?

The figure of the 'white Aboriginal' offers, at first glance, the possibility of exploring potential forms of cross-cultural communication or cultural hybridization in Australian society. At closer examination, however, 'white Aboriginal' narratives can be seen to be engaged in ongoing forms of expropriation, particularly as regards the availability of indigenous cultural resources for unsanctioned white consumption. Thus politically enlightened motivation on the part of these novelists does not preclude the participation of their texts in discursive formations which perpetuate long-lasting structures of cultural annexation. Several indices for this diagnosis can be found.

First, these stories appear to be told primarily for the benefit of white Australia, in order to assuage white anxieties about the shifting political, territorial and discursive hegemonies within Australian culture. Liam Davison articulates explicitly the sense that 'white Aboriginal' narratives may primarily be addressed to white sensibilities. He deconstructs the performative effects of 'white Aboriginal' narratives by enacting the collision of phatic reader-address with the naked admission of cultural self-legitimization: 'It was us, you see? It was exactly what we wanted. . . . [O]ur own stories came spinning back on us the way we'd always told them, as if they knew all along it was our own voices we wanted so much to hear' (*The White Woman* 138–39). Here Davison delivers an ironical commentary on all the preceding 'white Aboriginal' narratives. Far from projecting a potential site of black-white communication, they merely reflect white aspirations to annex the indigenous discursive territory abruptly out of white control since Mabo.

Secondly, discourses of reconciliation which may survive the subjection of the 'white Aboriginal' narrative to this sort of ideology critique are none the less hampered by the fact that they proceed from privileged white speakers. There is no reason to assume that the forms of reconciliation proposed by dominant white society should be inherently attractive to other groups still experiencing discrimination. A manifesto issued by the activist Robert Eggington on behalf of the Nyoongah people explicitly addresses this question: 'We oppose Nyoongah Culture being exploited and used to create a false Illusions of Reconciliation.'[33] Offering 'false Illusions of Reconciliation' would appear to be one of the unavowed functions of the 'white Aboriginal' topos. Such reconciliation, akin to the 'normalization' proposed to the German Jewish community by the conservative German establishment in the 1980s, tends to be a 'generous' offer made to victims by perpetrators, on terms dictated by the latter party. 'In the media,' comments Heather Goodall, 'the phrase most often heard has been reconciliation for Aborigines, as if this were a new welfare "hand-out" to be magnanimously granted to Aborigines or withheld if they did not appear grateful enough.'[34]

[33] Robert Eggington, 'Jangga Meenya Bomunggur (The Smell of the White Man is Killing Us)', in Anne Brewster, Angeline O'Neill, Rosemary van den Berg (eds), *Those who Remain Will Always Remember: An Anthology of Aboriginal Writing* (Fremantle: Fremantle Arts Centre Press, 2000), 134.

[34] Heather Goodall, 'Too Early Yet or Not Soon Enough?', 8.

Discourses of 'cultural convergence' or 'hybridity,' of which the 'white Aboriginal' topos is one prominent avatar, are similarly problematic. Suvendrini Perera comments on white notions of hybridity and their 'settling' effects in terms which are pertinent to the 'white Aboriginal' figure of the transcultural actor: 'With its reliance on the willed combination of two prior, given components, hybridity seems an easy answer to the troubled questions of identity posed by settler societies, and one that erases the complexities of the process for its indigenous subjects.'[35]

In the light of these considerations, one could well conclude that under the present circumstances, the 'white Aboriginal' topos is too politically and morally compromised to provide a creative model for future black-white relations in Australia. In this context, it would appear impossible to endorse the positive reception of such narratives given by critics such as Julie Carr.[36] A more productive alternative than the formulation of white versions of reconciliation might be the analysis, by white cultural critics, of ongoing white discursive practices of cultural annexation. The present chapter hopes to make a contribution to that critical project.

[35] Suvendrini Perera, 'Unspeakable Bodies', 19.
[36] Carr, *The Captive White Woman of Gipps Land*, 242–46.

5 Fencing In the Frontier

Australia is a nation whose borders are coextensive with its gigantic continental coastline, thereby naturalizing them to the point of invisibility. Borders are something that Australians, if they are not immigrants, have never had to live with. But is Australia a borderless nation, just as it has always liked to think of itself as the classless society? Significantly, if the great southern land doesn't have much in the way of borders, it certainly makes up for it in fences. Indeed, they form one of the archetypical icons of the Australian landscape. For some writers, they may even function as an icon of nationhood itself. David Day's *Claiming a Continent*,[1] which is among the more recent popular histories to foreground the conflictual nature of the process of nation-formation on the fifth continent, uses the fence-line as a metonymy of the act of claiming or taking possession.

My interest in the fence arises out of the notion that it offers the closest equivalent to the frontier in Australia – a word which evokes something akin to the American frontiers of the Wild West. However, whereas the Wild West could be mythologized in countless narratives in literature and film extending up to the present day, the frontier in Australia has quite different, less easily assimilable resonances. Fences, by contrast, may be a frequent icon of Australianness, albeit a discrete one, because they mark a clear line in the otherwise tangled scrub of the historical landscape.

This chapter approaches and scrutinizes the fence-line in three stages. First I briefly summarize the broader background of what came to be known as the 'history wars.' Then I go on to focus upon one small episode in those intellectual controversies, namely about fences and their role in settler indigenous conflicts. Finally, I turn to recent literary avatars of the colonial fence to investigate the ways literary texts confront the notion of the frontier.

Historical wars – History wars

Australia's frontier of progressive settlement was often violent, but the conflicts, indeed the protracted engagements which on some occasions did ensue – for instance in parts of Queensland – could never be mythologized as proper wars because the enemy was not, in the eyes of the settlers, worthy of the name. The Australian frontier conflicts were frequently low intensity skirmishes, occasionally massacres, but more often outbreaks of violence interspersing the constant interaction of settlers and stubbornly residual, if dwindling, indigenous populations. It appears that the settlers may even have resented those indigenous people who resisted their slow by steady encroachment upon the continent's rich once hunting, now grazing lands – resented them because they did not offer the sort of opposition affording the settlers a noble self-image as warriors – but rather, the creeping shame of ignoble poisonings, murders, ambushes, and mistreatment. The frontier conflicts did not take

1 David Day, *Claiming a Continent: A New History of Australia* (Sydney: Harper Perennial, 2005).

the form of 'public violence against a respected foe, but more frequently a drama of betrayal, fear and disdain. A proper war would have dignified [the frontier] violence, brought it out in the open and allowed [the settlers] the romance of heroes and campaigns.'[2]

It is hardly surprising, then, that popular Australian mythology silenced the frontier skirmishes which endured down the nineteenth century, endowing the explorer narratives with the heroism which the settlers' more significant campaign of occupation could never attain. Most nineteenth and twentieth century histories of white Australia after 1788 constructed an account of plucky settlers battling not the recalcitrant natives but nature itself – the barren and hostile continent which they forced to yield up the fertility of modern rural Australia. It was only in the 1970s that radical historians such as Henry Reynolds began to investigate the historical records more closely to offer a revisionary account of the conquest of the fifth continent – one that documented the lacunary and contradictory memories of the violent settlement of the country. Reynolds' *The Other Side of the Frontier* (1981, 1982) inaugurated a spate of revisionary frontier historiography which fundamentally altered the picture white Australia had of its own origins. It suggested that the process of settlement was one which had been much less peaceful, more tarnished with bloodletting than previously acknowledged, and that the indigenous casualties of white expansion reached into the tens of thousands. The cause of the revisionary historians was not helped, however, by the work of some popular historians who skewed the picture to much towards the more spectacular instances of violence, such as massacres, and the notion of a linear, oppositional frontier, and obscured the fact that much of the violence went hand in hand with patterns of often intimate co-existence. Roger Millis' *Waterloo Creek* (1992), for instance, was criticized for foregrounding naked violence at the expense of the more complex relationships, often intertwined with sexual intimacy and forms of co-occupation.[3]

The backlash came at the beginning of the 1990s with the conservative historian Geoffrey Blainey lambasting what he called the black armband view of history[4] – a term which was later adopted in Parliament by the conservative Prime Minister John Howard. There ensued a public debate about the nature of Australia's history and about the role and responsibilities of historians which subsequently became known as the history wars.[5] Conservative commentators used the magazine *Quadrant* and the major conservative daily newspaper *The Australian* as platforms to launch an attack on ostensibly biased left-wing historians who had created a biased orthodoxy which besmirched the real achievements of white Australia. Their sloppy and ideologically driven historiography had supposedly skewed the facts and created negative and self-hating notion of Australian history since 1788. This conservative

2 Tom Griffiths, 'Past Silences: Aboriginals and Convicts in Our History Making', in Penny Russell and Richard White (eds), *Pastiche I: Reflections on Nineteenth Century Australia* (Sydney: Allen & Unwin, 1994), 11.

3 Tom Griffiths, 'The Language of Conflict', in Bain Attwood and S. G. Foster (eds), *Frontier Conflict: The Australian Experience* (Canberra: National Museum of Australia, 2003), 144.

4 Geoffrey Blainey, 'Drawing up a balance sheet of our history', *Quadrant* 37: 7–8 (July–August 1993): 10–15.

5 Stuart Macintyre and Anna Clark, *The History Wars* (Carlton VIC: Melbourne University Press, 2003).

backlash reached its apotheosis in the weighty volume published by Keith Windschuttle in 2002, *The Fabrication of Aboriginal History: Van Diemen's Land 1803–1847*.[6]

Windschuttle claimed that leftwing historians had ignored the facts and had exaggerated the level of settler violence in colonial Van Diemen's Land; far more deaths had been caused by indigenous raids and killings than the other way around. He insisted upon a rigorous implementation of historical methodology, modelled upon courtroom evidence, with a rejection of all hearsay or conjecture.[7] The fact that much of the evidence for frontier violence had been deliberately suppressed or distorted, documents destroyed, and local oral narratives radically transformed in the process of their retelling over generations, was ignored by Windschuttle. Military historians pointed out that if one was to regard the frontier conflicts as low intensity warfare, which in some cases they were, then it as unrealistic to expect accurate casualty figures as in any other war context.[8] Windschuttle's accusations of sloppy methodology appealed to popular notions of history as a chronological sequence of verifiable facts rather than contesting narratives with conflicting agendas. Their popular appeal served furthermore as a moral basis for discrediting those of the 'chattering classes' who wished to belittle the achievements of settlers, pioneers, bushmen, farmers, or pastoralists, by portraying them as brutal colonizers.

The history wars gained considerable airing in a public sphere that was and is generally hostile to intellectual enquiry and to professions not directly productive of wealth or material objects. They foreshadowed a period of governmental interference into public bodies, ranging from the cutting of funding for public multicultural broadcasting or indigenous cultural organizations and communities, to the culling of funded research not deemed to be in the so-called 'national interest' – such as critical intellectual projects from the humanities.

Reading the fence

One of Windschuttle's privileged targets was the frontier historian Henry Reynolds. In his *Fabrication*, Windschuttle takes Reynolds to task for referring to 'miles of fencing' cordoning off settler farming land and inhibiting the passage of indigenous people across what had once been their hunting territories and their traditional sacred sites.[9] The fences Reynolds claimed to find in early nineteenth-century Tasmania, Windschuttle scoffed, had not been, indeed could not have been built at that early stage in Tasmania's colonial history, for a number of reasons. Wire or barbed-wire fences were an invention of the late nineteenth century. Their predecessors, the post-and-rail fences constructed out of the wood cleared on the land subsequently cordoned off, were labour intensive and slow to construct. Equally slow to erect were the hawthorn hedges the early settlers brought with them from England

6 Keith Windschuttle, *The Fabrication of Aboriginal History: Volume One: Van Diemen's Land 1803–1847* (Sydney: Macleay Press, 2002).
7 Windschuttle, *The Fabrication of Aboriginal History*, 165.
8 John Connor, *The Australian Frontier Wars 1788–1838* (Sydney: UNSW Press, 2002).
9 Windschuttle, *The Fabrication of Aboriginal History*, 78–79.

and planted across the countryside. Fencing was thus a slow, expensive and labour-robbing undertaking.[10]

In this sense, Windschuttle was right. One of Windschuttle's principal opponents in this area, the Tasmanian historian James Boyce, concurs with him in this respect. Much of the subsistence farming done by early Van Diemonians involved a fairly low level of investment matching the return necessary for local needs, and thus often farmed unploughed, uncleared, unmanured, and unfenced land. A Commissioner Bigge observed in the second decade of the century, 'the cultivated lands of each farm are entirely open, and except upon an estate of Col. Davey and Mr Lord, I did not observe a single fence.' Another observer lamented that 'the beautiful appearance of a hedge … is unknown in Van Diemen's Land.'[11] Fencing progressed so slowly that in the late 1820s, action was demanded, with one commentator demanding, 'so long as the colony remains a common, and it is at the option of every one whether he chooses to fence or not, how can any man count upon being repaid for his labours by agriculture, or how is the breed of sheep to be improved?' In 1835 Governor Arthur legislated with the Fencing Act, which forced neighbours to cover half the cost of fencing – explicitly in order to curtail cattle theft and bring ill-disciplined farmers and wandering drovers to order.[12]

Windschuttle's foray into the fascinating details of fencing history is designed to lay bare the sloppiness and historical inaccuracy of radical historians, and thus to delegitimize their portrait of early colonial frontier conflict. But it also assumes that fences, by blocking indigenous access to what had once been their property, caused conflicts. As there were few fences during this early phase of colonization, he implicitly suggests, any conflicts which arose must have been instigated by the indigenous people and not by the settlers. Where there are fences, there is encroachment, ergo, where there are no fences, there is no encroachment, and thus no conflict generated by settler expansion.

A patent rebuttal of this argument was mounted by Boyce in his keynote contribution to Robert Manne's *Whitewash* collection.[13] Boyce begins from the manifold and variegated forms of co-existence which structured indigenous-settler relations during the earliest colonial period, and which he has explored in the more recent milestone history of Van Diemen's Land. Early settler land usage for hunting, cattle for domestic meat production and unsupervised sheep grazing allowed a considerable degree of intermeshing with indigenous hunting and mobility.[14] This initial balance would progressively disappear as more white settlers arrived, and the emphasis of settler agriculture shifted towards the wool export industry. Boyce concurs in some respects:

> It is true that fences were rare until well into the 1830s. However, the implications of this are the reverse of what *Fabrication* suggests. … What Windschuttle misses is that

10 Windschuttle, *The Fabrication of Aboriginal History*, 77–82.

11 James Boyce, *Van Diemen's Land* (Melbourne: Black Inc, 2008), 107.

12 Boyce, *Van Diemen's Land*, 181–82.

13 James Boyce, 'Fantasy Island', in Robert Manne (ed.), *Whitewash: On Keith Windschuttle's Fabrication of Aboriginal History* (Melbourne: Black Inc, 2003), 17–78.

14 Boyce, *Van Diemen's Land*, 63–83.

> the lack of fences now exacerbates the conflict between this form of land use [the export wool trade as opposed to earlier predominant domestic meat consumption] and continuing Aboriginal occupation. The need to separate the flock, graze the land more intensively and maintain a much greater level of supervision and control was in direct conflict with Aboriginal hunting and land-management techniques, which used both dogs and fire. ... Aborigines were thus moved on to protect the unfenced flocks and associated investments, and, as all the best land was similarly taken up, force was increasingly required to achieve this. ...[15]

Boyce concludes, returning to fences and their absence: 'The unwillingness or incapacity to make the significant capital investment required to build fences thus added to, not mitigated, the potential for violent conflict.'[16] In direct contradiction to Windschuttle, Boyce notes that the absence of fences did not index the absence of settler-indigenous conflict, but on the contrary, exacerbated that conflict. The fence does not inaugurate conflict. Rather, it indicated the end of a transitional and conflict-ridden process of encroachment. The fence marked the completion of possession. Boyce shows that the forms of encroachment were changing, and that the absence of signs of encroachment did not mean that encroachment was not happening. He notes that the dramatic increase in Aboriginal resistance after 1824 and the parallel lack of fencing can be seen to be closely linked, 'once they are seen in the context of the changing economic and social realities of Van Diemen's Land.'[17]

Thus, when Windschuttle scoffs at radical historians who mention fences as privileging 'theory over evidence'[18] he is actually describing his own elevation of a simplistic theory of fencing over the facts of complex and changing land usage. Windschuttle's own belief that fences signify encroachment and the absences of fences signifying the absence of encroachment is a simplifying binary with no basis in the historical complexities of colonial interaction between settlers and indigenous people. His theory rides roughshod over the complexities of spatio-historical fact. Windschuttle offers an idealist view of fencing/non-fencing which is analogue to his idealist demand that the proprieties of legal procedure and forensic evidence be applied to the historiography of frontier conflict. These in turn are part of a larger epistemology of certainty which evinces nostalgia for settled relationships and clear genealogies simply not in keeping with the realities of a postcolonial, migrant nation whose identities can never be anything but hybrid and in flux.

Windschuttle's assumption that where no fences existed, no settler encroachment occurred tends to erase many aspects of possible histories of interaction before the moment of fencing. Windschuttle's chronology curiously mirrors *terra nullius*, positing a land as void of prior settler incursions as it was ostensibly void of prior indigenous owners. Windschuttle's conception of fencing creates a version of the land in which a largely unmarked space is marked by the fence-line, converting nature into culture. This nature, however, had always already been cultivated, and the incursions of settlers were one of a long history of interactions between inhabi-

15 Boyce, 'Fantasy Island', 55–56.
16 Boyce, 'Fantasy Island', 5.
17 Boyce, 'Fantasy Island', 57.
18 Windschuttle, *The Fabrication of Aboriginal History*, 82.

tants and the land. This did not make the settlers' impact upon indigenous space any less violent, but it suggests that one should see the fences as one event within a succession of variegated instances conflicted negotiations of space. In Windschuttle's reading, the fence becomes another of the founding sites of settler heritage – one sullied by the regrettable violence it accompanied – but no different to the others, usually more noble, by which national narratives were framed.

Finally, the fence operates not just as an element in Windschuttle's simplified version of colonial cross-cultural interaction, but as a signifier of dichotomized historiographical argumentation – cutting through the complexities to reach clear conclusions. The fences dispute can function as a synecdoche, a vignette, of the larger conflict between those who argue for a conflicted and violent history of expropriation, and those who argue for a peaceful and therefore legitimate settlement. The fence is both an element in the historical 'story,' and a component in the metahistorical or historiographical 'plot' – both as focus of metahistorical dispute, but also as the site upon which two camps face up over an intellectual line of demarcation.

It is for this reason that it may be salutary to look at some explicitly fictional historical narratives, as an alternative to the historical fictions proposed by the likes of Windschuttle. I suggest that they offer more complex pictures of the fence, one which, paradoxically, may more accurately index the functions of fencing in a colonial and postcolonial landscape.

Fictional fences

In 1993, the prominent Australian writer David Malouf published a novel entitled *Remembering Babylon*, already commented upon in the previous chapter Jeff Fisher's cover image of the first 1993 hardback edition featured a figure in three shades of grey balanced unsteadily on a colonial-style post-and-rail fence against an orange background. Significantly, the image disappeared from subsequent editions of the book, especially the large print-run paperback published by Vintage. Perhaps the image was too pregnant with problematic connotations to be welcome in a publishing world more interested mass-marketability than uncomfortable historical truths.

The cover image refers to the inaugural scene in Malouf's novel where the protagonist, a ship's boy named Jemmy who has grown up among the Queensland natives after a shipwreck, first re-enters European civilization. He springs onto the rough-hewn fence which marks the boundaries of a bush settlement in Northern Queensland, totters for a moment, and then tumbles over into this outpost of European society The post-and-rail 'boundary fence' marks the frontier, the interface between the advancing front of white colonization, and the retreating line of still intact indigenous society, rooted in respect and responsibility for the land. It is significant that Jemmy's incoherent cry, as he balances on this tangible manifestation of the frontier, is 'Do not shoot! I am a B-b-british object!'[19] For a Scots settler child

[19] David Malouf, *Remembering Babylon* (New York: Vintage, 1994), 3. Further references in the text.

has raised a stick in imitation of his parents' rifle at the terrifying prospect of what they take to be a native attack 'A black! That was the boy's first thought. We're being raided by blacks. After so many false alarms it had come' (*Remembering Babylon* 2). Malouf alludes indirectly to the brutal character of the colonization process, but only via the projective mechanism ('But it wasn't a raid, and there was just one of them,' the text admits – *Remembering Babylon* 2) of the natives' reported attacks on settlers. At the end of the novel, we learn that Jemmy, who has returned to his tribe, has probably died in a ' "dispersal" ' (*Remembering Babylon* 196) – a euphemistic description, implicitly marked as such by Malouf's own inverted commas, of a strategically planned massacre of an indigenous groups gathering for a corroboree. The inaugural post-and-rail fence is the anodyne textual marker, a spatial index, of the forgotten frontier of erstwhile colonial Australia.

The figure on the fence is 'flamelike' and 'flickering,' 'a shape more like a watery, heat-struck mirage than a thing of substance' (*Remembering Babylon* 2). It is matched by the later indexing of the continent as totality: 'in a line of running fire all the outline of the vast continent appears, in touch now with its other life' (*Remembering Babylon* 200). It seems that the inaugural frontier fence is merely the counterpart of the concluding totality which rounds off the novel. Gemmy, as a token half-white indigenous representative, for all that the text proclaims him to be a spokesman for a future hybrid race ('a forerunner … a true child of the place as it will be one day' [*Remembering Babylon* 132]), is merely the vehicle for a settler narrative of nationhood. Thus Malouf's story assiduously displaces the other historical fence narrative which it indexes just enough to establish its moral credentials and assuage the guilty conscience of its readers. I would suggest that Malouf's fence acts as a simplifying marker of ahistorical inauguration not dissimilar to Windschuttle's fences – erasing complex and unsettling non-originary genealogies of settler-indigenous interaction. However, the novel is entirely dependent upon the hybrid genealogies it foregrounds and then displaces, thereby unwittingly pointing up the significance of 'its other life' (*Remembering Babylon* 200).

By contrast, Kate Grenville's more recent *The Secret River* (2005) approaches fences from a slightly less ingenuous angle. Like Malouf's *Remembering Babylon*, Grenville's pioneer tale is a white settler myth of founding gestures, and like Malouf's novel, has become a bestseller. I am interested in the moment when the settler Thornhill decides to fence his property on the Hawksbury river in the midst of a scare about a native attack. In order to determine where exactly the fences are to be placed, the settler tentatively takes on the role of the attacker.

> He determined to clear a space around the hut. But how wide would such a moat have to be? He cut down a stalk from one of the grass-trees and felt something of a fool, standing with his spear in his hand and everyone watching. Sal had a look on his face he could not read as she stood in the door of the hut.[20]

The settler's pre-emptive mimicry of a native strike anticipates upon the more radical form of mimicry which follows. Thornhill's attempt to ascertain the right posi-

[20] Grenville, Kate, *The Secret River* (Melbourne: Text, 2005), 248. Further references in the text.

tion for a border involves him in an act of performative cross-cultural mimicry, but it also reveals his son's more complex hybrid identity. Whoever can throw a spear with this degree of skill has spent a considerable amount of time with the indigenous people, and has already absorbed significant elements of their culture. The settler family has a border-crosser in their midst. If the settler community marks out its space by the erection of fences, thereby inaugurating encroachment – this is Windschuttle's assumption – the very processes of marking suggest that the land to be marked is not unmarked, but rather, already marked in complex and intermeshing ways. The marking out of the border is posited upon the simplification, the polarization and the reduction of cultural contacts long since in place, just as it is posited upon the destruction of the environment:

> He paced out the distance the spear had gone, added another few yards, and then got to work. Every tree – apart from the one on which Sal marked the weeks – was hacked at with the axe until it fell. Every bush was grubbed out, every loose rock was rolled away and the whole lot fenced. As far as this bumpy land could be, a protective circle around the hut was flattened. Nothing remained that any man could hide behind. (*The Secret River* 248)

Grenville's text epitomizes the settler notion that the bush must be tamed, beaten into submission. It must be radically curtailed so as to make it susceptible of possession:

> He had made something of this place. He had cut down trees, got rid of bushes, chopped out the tussocks that were big enough for snakes to make a home in. With each day that passed, a little more progress could be measured: one more tree cut down, one more yard of bushes cleared, another length of fence. (*The Secret River* 250)

The fence can be read as marking clearly the borders of encroachment and clarifying both the interactions and the conflicts of early settler-indigenous action. The fence, rendered permanent at the end of the novel by Thornhill's thick-walled stone mansion with its surrounding garden walls, is a figure of Grenville's own narration. It acknowledges white encroachment and its violence, but implies that white guilt can be expunged by an act of restitutive memory. Once the violent past has been admitted, it is dealt with. Relocating the fence as a memorial, according to this ritual, allows the wrongs associated with it to be ignored. Fences are monumentalized in art in a gesture that reveals the cementing of white possession in the very act of admission the injustice of the origins of possession. Grenville's text thus performs an act very similar to that of Prime Minister Kevin Rudd's historic 2008 apology to the indigenous peoples.[21] It called for a resolute turning towards the future, thus implying that a formal apology could close off the past: 'as many Aboriginal people know, [the apology] does not recognize the depth of their historical

21 Kevin Rudd, *Apology to Australia's Indigenous Peoples*, Speech in House of Representatives, Parliament House, Canberra (13 February 2008). http://www.pm.gov.au/media/speech/2008/speech_0073.cfm. Accessed 26 January 2009.

trauma or give them a national memorial. It is meant to validate enough of their suffering to enable the celebratory memory of the Australian past to progress with less dissent in the future.'[22]

It is thus no chance that Thornhill's spear-throwing son Dick retreats from his hybrid position and ends his days caring for the blind and broken Blackwood, a settler who had lived with an indigenous woman and been lynched by his white neighbours when trying to avert a massacre. Dick, as token border-crosser, can only form a community with other defeated border-crossers (*The Secret River* 326). None the less, the novel has at least gestured towards the forms of co-existence which burgeoning white settlement appears to have stifled. Such modes of co-existence form a prehistory preceding the putatively inaugural gestures of fencing. Those modes of interaction may be only faintly legible in the archives making up Australian cultural memory, but they can be deciphered just enough to allow possible alternative models for our own age.

Before I turn to a more distinctly critical perspective on the fence, I wish briefly to mention a hybrid text in which an escaped convict, FJ, sees the settlers' fences 'from the other side.' In Hall's *The Second Bridegroom* (1991) which narrates the experiences of a renegade convict who lives for a period with an indigenous tribe, the fence marks the beginning of the end of his nomadic bush idyll:

> Then we came to the fence. Imagine it. The fence baffled me as if I had never seen one before. Most likely I cried out. The Men would certainly have no name for this thing so I gave it the name I had brought with me. Fence. But what would happen now that the world of dreams – where fences belonged – began to trespass on the existing world?
>
> My subtle hand touched the hewn rail. . . . Like a blind man's fingers checking a forgotten face my hand checked the fence. The post was a crude job, squared with an adze. So it came about that the word adze required the object adze. My fingers said yes to the adze and yes to the fence. But not me. I felt a sudden flood of anger because our way was barred. Oh, we could easy climb over or duck between the rails, but what sort of answer was that? [23]

The text takes care to reference the elements of the fence and the tools needed to construct it, as well as meditating upon the relationship between words and things, and the relative substantiality and insubstantiality respectively of indigenous and settler worlds. Yet these realities of incursion and encroachment are not presented as beginning with the fence as a marker of space. There are other markers which precede the fence within the text and disqualify the fence as an inaugural gesture. Hall takes care to have the fence episode buttressed by an earlier episode of boundary-drawing:

> So I stood, confronted by the old lack. The fence brought the whole horror home again. . . . The fence marked a boundary across changed land. Grass inside the fence,

[22] Tony Barta, 'Sorry, and not sorry, in Australia: How the Apology to the Stolen Generations Buried a History of Genocide', *Journal of Genocide Research* 10:2 (June 2008), 210.

[23] Rodney Hall, *The Second Bridegroom* (London: Faber & Faber, 1992), 85–86. Further references in the text.

> though it looked like grass outside, was not the same: that grass was Property, as this was Nature. (*The Second Bridegroom* 85–6)

The fence has its prehistory, 'the old lack,' the class struggle of propertied against unpropertied brought from England to Australia with the convict system. FJ escapes from its ubiquitous influence by escaping to a more 'real' life with the indigenous peoples, only to land up in the nightmare of property once again.

The other side of the fence

I turn finally to indigenous perspectives upon fencing. How has indigenous writing re-inscribed the historical process by which 'ghosts [white settlers] roamed [indigenous] land and marked it out as their own?'[24] It is worth examining closely the rabbit-proof fence which makes up the central icon of the film of the same name.[25] That fence postdates the first contact fences by decades. It was erected to rein in the rabbits overrunning the grasslands in Western Australia, and bisected the continent from north to south. It is evidence of an attempt to simplify an ecological problem which had already reached continental proportions. Ironically, the base camps set up for the fence builders and the later maintenance teams acted as magnets for the indigenous groups in the remote areas. Increasingly deprived of their traditional lands, rapidly losing their basis for sustenance, and exposed to the violence of settlers, indigenous groups from remote areas migrated towards the base camps and formed new nuclei at nodes along the great north-south fence. Paradoxically, the fence as a great bisector actually generated hybrid societies as the fencing workers coupled with the indigenous people. The mixed-background children of these unions would subsequently become the target of the child removal practices so graphically documented in the film – and in the thousand-page report entitled *Bringing them Home*, which formed the narrative impetus and archival background for the film (*Bringing them Home*).

In Noyce's film, the three indigenous girls tramp their way home, using the fence as their navigation instrument, appropriating its demarcating linearity to surmount the social demarcation which has taken them away from their families to the orphanage far in the south. Just as indigenous people used the corridors between the borders of tribal areas as routes to traverse the country, so too the children convert the white fence into a long corridor of return home to the Jigalong depot. Doris Pilkington-Garimara's *Follow the Rabbit-Proof Fence*, upon which the film was based, explicates these complexities:

> From when she was young, Molly had learned that the fence was an important landmark for the Mardudjura people of the Western Desert who migrated south from the remote regions. They knew that once they reached Billanooka Station, it was simply a matter of following the rabbit-proof fence to their final destination, the

24 Colin Johnson, *Doctor Wooreddy's Prescription for Enduring the End of the World* (Melbourne: Hyland House, 1983), 10–11.

25 *Rabbit-Proof Fence*, dir. Phillip Noyce, Miramax 2001. Outside Australia, the film was screened under the more accessible title *Long Walk Home*.

> Jigalong government depot; the desert outpost of the white man. The fence cut through the country from south to north. It was a typical response of the white people to a problem of their own making. Building a fence to keep the rabbits out proved to be a futile attempt by the government of the day.
>
> For the three runaways, the fence was a symbol of love, home and security.[26]

The film version of *Rabbit-Proof Fence* has been criticized for directing attention away from the frontier conflict issue, towards that of the Stolen generation issue[27] – an issue more easily digestable for majority Australia, more easily assimilated to a mainstream family narrative, and more easily universalized to generate empathy.[28] A films such as Rolf de Heer's *The Tracker* (2002), which directly addressed questions of frontier violence, has received much less publicity. Yet the frontier is visible in *Rabbit-Proof Fence* – in the stark visual form of the fence itself, virtually ubiquitous throughout the central sections of the film. It is not visible so much as a frontier between black and white as an axis along which the path of escape is conducted.

This is significant, because it breaks down the polarized versions of the frontier dependent upon dichotomizing massacre narratives, that were becoming widespread by the end of the 1980s, in favour of the more diffuse and very intimate zones of contact which often connected black and white as much as they divided them. It is not by chance that the fence is multiple, with branch lines and spurs: one of these spurs allows the girls to elude the government search parties advancing towards each from north and south to intercept them. The fence itself is hybrid, dividing according to its own specifically fuzzy logic. The ubiquitous icon of the wire fence, crossing the beautiful desert landscape, transfers the diachronic, indeed generational hybridity of settler-indigenous interaction onto the synchronic spatial axis of visual representation. For all its stark linear symbolism, then, the rabbit-proof fence indexes the intermixing of settler and indigenous societies that has been occurring from the earliest contact, and which fences have only ever followed upon as a reactive and secondary phenomenon.

Contemporary fences

A recent poem by Anthony Lawrence, 'Fencing,' returns to the motif of the fence in its modern-day avatar, the high-tensile wire fence. The poem begins in a purely hypothetical mode, meditating upon the treachery of fencing wire:

> High tensile wire, when strained,
> is a volatile thing.
> I'd been warned how the wire can break,

[26] Doris Pilkington/Nugi Garimara, *Follow the Rabbit-Proof Fence* (St Lucia, QLD: University of Queensland Press, 1996), 109.

[27] Felicity Collins and Therese Davis, *Australian Cinema after Mabo* (Cambridge: Cambridge University Press, 2004).

[28] Tony Hughes d'Aeth, 'Which Rabbit-Proof Fence? Empathy, Assimilation, Hollywood', Australian Humanities Review 27 (September 2002). http://www.australianhumanitiesreview.org/archive/Issue-September-2002/hughesdaeth.html. Accessed 27 October 2009.

> whipping back through the eyes
> of the fence posts, leaving your fingers
> flexing at your feet, or worse,
> your throat smiling redly from ear to ear.
> You hear stories.

What is enacted here is a self-reflexive transfer of the early conflicts which gathered around the fence, abstracted from the landscape and its inhabitants, and projected back onto the fence and its settler owner-builder. The fence is treacherous – not the natives, not the squatter, not the landscape itself. Then the diction changes abruptly, as the overstrained wire snaps:

> Then I heard it: a loud ping like a struck tuning fork.
> I leapt away from the fence as the wire
> ripped past me – silver, on fire
> with my name cut into its tail.[29]

The circuit of self-reflexivity is completed. The solipsism of the settler mentality collapses under its own weight. 'Fencing' here is a brutal duel, in which the occupier's weapon becomes his own nemesis. The high-tensile successor of the erstwhile barriers around white settlements, now criss-crossing the entire continent in straight lines, no longer does its work of disciplining the country, but wields language, the owner's name, against him.

The fence is ostensibly that device by which unmarked space becomes marked, by which identity, and in this European idiom, possession is asserted. The examples above have shown that such simplistic, originary concepts of the fence are fallacious and ideologically charged. More accurately, the fence was the mode of concrete, material inscription of the cadastre grid employed to appropriate and overwrite the older network of tribal tracks and boundaries by white pastoralists. Fencing and naming-possessing go hand in hand. In this poem, the fence in turn re-writes the 'name' of the pastoralist. The poem suggests that the fence itself, strained to breaking point in the process of holding in check for more than a century the conquered country, has becomes charged with the accumulated force of only-half-told frontier narratives: 'You hear stories.'[30] One day the strung-out linearity of the fence snaps, and the history of the land since white settlement comes dangerously close to branding those who tacitly owe their existence to it.

Malouf's, Hall's, Grenville's and Lawrence's images of the fence are literary figures of the line that marked the frontier between white and black in colonial Australia and the manner in which it persists in contemporary Australia. Its complexities are deepened by the indigenous perspective on the fence to be found in Pilkington-Garimara's account of the fence in its contemporary resonances. One last index of

29 Anthony Lawrence, *Skinned by Light: Poems 1989–2002* (St Lucia, QLD: University of Queensland Press, 2002), 17.

30 For commentary on such local massacre narratives see Ross Gibson, *Seven Versions of an Australian Badland* (St Lucia, QLD: University of Queensland Press, 2002); Katrina Schlunke, *Bluff Rock: Autobiography of a Massacre* (Fremantle WA: Curtin University Books/Fremantle Arts Centre Press, 2005).

this persistence of the past bears mentioning. A 2004 photograph by Rosemary Laing, ironically entitled 'Welcome to Australia,' shows the razor-wire compound of the Woomera internment centre in outback South Australia set up by the conservative Howard government for so-called illegal refugees. The photograph is taken at one of the right-angle corners of the compound, with two fences receding, perfectly symmetrically, to the horizon line on the right and left sides of the photograph. The still dawn/dusk atmosphere of the photograph, unpeopled, belies the controversial history of the camp. Conditions in the Woomera camp were so bad that a significant number of suicide attempts, hunger strikes and breakouts occurred, gaining international attention and outrage. The government refused access to the UN and the Red Cross, but finally bowed to international pressure and closed the camp in 2003, though internment centres still exist in the major cities. Laing's ironical word of welcome presents the fence as the perennial inaugural experience of Australia.

Fences have a long history of inscription upon the Australian landscape and in Australian fictions. They proliferated in the apparent absence of other forms of boundary marking. In the South Pacific, the British explorer-invaders repeatedly drew lines in the sand when they set foot upon newly 'discovered' territory, to symbolize the act of taking possession. This ceased in Australia, apparently with a single exception, at the inaugural moment of landing at Botany Bay in January 1788 (see chapter 3 above for a discussion of this episode). As already mentioned above, Anja Schwarz has suggested, building upon Agamben, that the general absence of lines in the sand in Australian colonial conquest can be ascribed to the global gesture of possession that rendered the Australian continent from the outset British territory and made lines of demarcation superfluous.[31] When, on very single occasions where lines appear in the sand, they are in a sense retrograde, marking out old and new masters, ancient peoples and modernity. They merely signify the work of conquest which has already been achieved. To this extent they resemble the business of fence-building in colonial Van Diemen's Land. They do not inaugurate conquest, but seal it as a fait accompli. The natives have already been relegated to the past, and foreclosed from colonial history.

Following Agamben, Schwarz claims that it is the erasure of more obvious borders in the colonial context which allows the establishment of a new and invisible frontier – that of the distinction between human and non-human. The indigenous people are cast into a zone of the non-human no longer worthy of human treatment.[32] Doubtless this is an accurate genealogy of the limbo into which colonized indigenous peoples all across the colonial world were thrust – one outside the borders of the civil society. Certainly it has been confirmed by the work of theorists such as Mbembe describing the African context of 'commandement.'[33] The notion of the erasure of borders and the concomitant creation of a zone of the non-human does, however, obscure the continued working of frontiers in the Australian context

[31] Anja Schwarz, 'Beached: A Postcolonial Reading of the Australian Shore', unpublished PhD thesis, Free University of Berlin, 2008, 158–62, 178–85.

[32] This relegation to a non-human, merely bodily existence, was formalized definitively upon Federation in 1901. From that date to through to the 1967 referendum, the indigenous peoples were simply no longer be included by the censuses which counted the Australian population.

[33] Achille Mbembe, *On the Postcolony* (Berkeley: University of California Press, 2001), 24–65.

– in particular, as we have seen, that of the increasingly ubiquitous fence which imposes its grid patterns upon the landscape, making its an 'espace strié' à la Deleuze and Guattari. Far from being elided by postcolonial theory, the fence must be historicized as a phenomenon of '*longue durée*' – reaching back to the English enclosures which drove the future immigrants into petty crime and thence via the hulks and transportation to New South Wales[34] only to reproduce the enclosing phenomena as perpetrators rather than victims – to the razor-wire fences of the Woomera internment camp in the 1990s.

[34] Craig Robertson, *Buckley's Hope: A Novel* (Melbourne: Scribe, 1997), 3–4.

6 Invasion and Pathology: Australia, Mabo, McGahan and Malouf

In an infamous image of Australia, A. D. Hope imagined the continent as a body, weakened by 'five cities, like five teeming sores': 'Each drains her: a vast parasite robber-state | Where second-hand Europeans pullulate | Timidly on the edge of alien shores.'[1] This image of suppuration and pullulation might seem to go to the limits of the abject. However, it has been given a more aggressive turn in a recent image of bodily pathology which makes the brain a synecdoche of the Australian continent:

> The disease was called a cholesteatoma.
>
> According to the specialists, it was a tumour that grew in the lining of the middle ear. It usually began when some minor injury created a perforation in the ear drum. Foreign tissue from the outer ear was then able to invade the middle ear cavity, where it could latch on and develop into an abnormal growth.

This gruesome description is one of the final sentences of the semi-popular Australian novelist Andrew McGahan's bestselling *The White Earth* of 2003.[2] In this novel, the young boy's disease can be read as an apocalyptic allegory of the white invasion of Australia.

The figure of the body here is a mortiferous one. Phil Cloran observes that through McGahan's 'fascination with the entrances and exits of the body, the integrity of nerves and skin, [he] has continued to use abject and morbid tropes to explore the inner shame and self-disgust of the Australian psyche.' He sees here 'a familiar device in McGahan's work: whether it is through disease, alcohol abuse, wild hormones, high temperatures, physical duress or some other hallucinatory catalyst, the result is that normal social rules are relaxed or forgotten and a new awareness of something hideous and primal emerges.'[3] McGahan's appropriation of the figure of the brain is literally perverted, obscene. What can be instantly read out of this pathological neural scenario is a spatial vector of invasion and destruction which models the white occupation of the Australian continent since 1788.

McGahan's elaborate description of young William's ear infection in its advanced stage, already corroding the skull and eating into the brain tissue, occurs at the very close of his novel *The White Earth*. The disease has its own narrative history which can be read as a corporeal allegory of the history of the white settlement in Australia: 'Foreign tissue from the outer ear was then able to invade the middle ear cavity, where it could latch on and develop into an abnormal growth' (*White Earth* 374). The allegory continues as a displaced description of white European Australia – in itself neither good nor bad, but in the context of first contact and then

1 A. D. Hope, *Australia* (1939).

2 Andrew McGahan, *The White Earth* (Crows Nest, NSW: Allen & Unwin, 2004), 373. Further references in the text.

3 Phil Cloran, Review of Andrew McGahan, *The White Earth*, *API Review of Books* 25 (July 2004). http://www.api-network.com/cgi-bin/reviews/jrbview.cgi?n=1741141478. Accessed 12 December 2005.

progressive expansion into the continent, bringing about the end of the prior human, cultural and environmental equilibrium:

> This tumour itself was not malign, said the doctors, but as it grew it distorted the cavity, shed dead skin, harboured bacteria and, worst of all, released an enzyme that ate away at the bone. The cavity would thus fill with necrotic tissue, some of which would leak back through the perforation of the drum, resulting in a foul-smelling discharge. (*White Earth* 374)

The disease has what eighteenth-century medicine called its specific 'semiotics' – the array of symptoms that the physician would read like the signs of a coherent language. The semiotics of corruption are perfectly evident, and, once read and interpreted correctly, can lead to healing. But has white Australia read the signs of corruption attendant upon its invasion of the body of the land? This is the question which McGahan's allegory implicitly poses:

> The odour was what usually alerted the patient to seek treatment. In William's case, though, the tumour had been left to rage unchecked, eating its way from the ear right through the bone of his skull. Abscesses had then formed on his brain.
>
> The surgeons were confident, however. They had relieved the pressure in his skull cavity, and excised the tumour. (*White Earth* 373–74)

Like William, the reader needs a while to read correctly, and to interpret fully. McGahan's elaborate description of young William's ear infection in its advanced stage, already corroding the skull and eating into the brain tissue, occurs at the very close of McGahan's *The White Earth*. Throughout the text the reader is merely struck by an array of physical symptoms plaguing the lad: earache, dizziness, a rotten smell. But they only begin to make sense once the narrative has been comprehended as a whole.

Mabo and the shape of the nation

What do they stand for? McGahan uses the figure of the brain to sketch the changing symbolic contours of the Australian nation in the early 1990s. He responds to the deep transformations of national consciousness resulting from the 1992 Mabo decision – a High Court decision which declared that, contrary to prior legal convention, white possession of Australia was not legitimized by the putative absence of inhabitants when the Europeans arrived (*terra nullius*). Rather, it affirmed the ongoing and unbroken existence of indigenous ownership of the continent (native title) before and after the British invasion of 1788. Rather than the deictic arrogance of the *terra nullius* doctrine, which asserted by a unilateral verbal proclamation the possession of a continent, Mabo allowed indigenous title, based upon a reciprocal relationship between place, human society and narrative, to become visible after two centuries of elision. In McGahan's allegory, the High Court lawyers had 'relieved the pressure in his skull cavity' – though perhaps not entirely successfully 'excised the tumour' (*White Earth* 373–74).

Mabo had legislative consequences (the Native Title legislation from 1993 onwards) and ownership consequences (the accelerated return of indigenous land to traditional owners) – with subsequent backlash measures designed to roll back the newly enacted legislation (in the Ten Point Plan of 1997, and, for instance, government measures, in some cases, to rescind land rights altogether in 2008 in the context of the Northern Territory Intervention, analysed at length in chapter 3 above).. The short-lived political process triggered by Mabo was curtailed by the profound fact that white Australia does not need indigenous Australia. White Australia is in no way dependent upon black Australia, except for the utility of indigenous iconicity which has always been and continues to be exploited at a symbolic level (including the economic gains of the tourist industry, with gigantic sums being trawled from the symbolism of culture and landscape, and of the immense international popularity of indigenous art). A deeper socio-political transformation of white Australia in the face of Mabo is not necessary. Indigenous leaders such as Noel Pearson recognized the unlikelihood of a permanent political movement in majority white Australia, and in consequence shifted away from a rhetoric of rights (within which Mabo must be situated) to one of earning benefits only accruing to the truly deserving. Such modifications dovetailed neatly with the neo-liberal rhetoric of a level playing field (the notion that all Australians are the same and no one deserves assistance more than anyone else). In terms of indigenous policy, this resulted in the prevalence of new neo-liberal strategies such as the individual brokering of benefits to indigenous communities (which in turn heralded the individual negotiation of workplace contracts introduced by Howard's government in late 2005). There was, thus, an absence of real change brought about by Mabo at a material level. Mabo as a potential paradigm shift entailing an official apology and a re-asssessemnt of the fundamental bases of Australian identiries was countered by Howard's programme of 'practical reconciliation'. Those policies proclaimed their disdain for symbolic gestures such as apologies, in favour of pragmatic action, but failed signally to achieve real improvements in the living standards of indigenous Australians.[4]

Symbolically, then, and only symbolically, Mabo had the potential to delegitimize the very bases upon which white Australian identity, always precarious, attempted to justify its appropriation of the continent, resulting, under the aegis of post-Mabo right-wing rhetoric, in a symptomatic reiteration of Australian goodness.[5] Yet in structural terms, this moment of caesura represented the 'Aufhebung' of a previously existing barrier: an erasure which maintains that which is allegedly erased ('Aufheben', paradoxically, can mean 'to abolish' but also 'to preserve'). On the one hand, the *terra nullius* doctrine, whose legitimizing effect Mabo demolished, had previously worked to maintain the 'repression' of the historical facts of white invasion and frontier expropriation. The 1992 lifting of this barrier allowed the suppressed element to flow back into the national consciousness. The extant nation-state, posited upon the barring of that which constituted its identity, found itself pervaded by a disturbing form of alterity. On the other hand, 'Aufhebung' (with its

4 See Bob Hodge and John O'Carroll, *Borderwork in Multicultural Australia* (Crows Nest NSW: Allen & Unwin, 2006), 113.

5 Ghassan Hage, *Against Paranoid Nationalism: Searching for Hope in a Shrinking Society* (Annadale, NSW: Pluto/London: Merlin, 2003), 90–91.

double meaning of 'lifting,' but also 'preservation') is also to be understood in the context of Mabo in the paradoxical sense of the shadowy persistence of the ostensibly erased barrier. From 1993 onwards, the rights of pastoralists – in many cases the direct descendants of the original expropriators of indigenous land – were assiduously protected by the post-Mabo legislation. It was as if, despite Mabo, *terra nullius* retained its repressive validity precisely in those places where it had been most violently asserted.

The consequences for the 'shape of the nation' resulting from Mabo bear close scrutiny. Mabo did not change the outer contours of the nation (though these were constantly altered in the wake of the Howard government's policy on so-called illegal refugee containment, with possible landing places being 'excised' from the national immigration zone). Conversely, however, Mabo underpinned the white template of the nation with a black template, thus doubling received Westminster legal relationships of land ownership with a much older, archaic palimpsestic set of corresponding relationships of land curatorship. This doubling can be understood as implacably opposed to, but deeply entwined in the doubling of an 'Aufhebung' of *terra nullius* which both erased and reinforced it

Thus Mabo changed the 'texture' of every centimetre of the Australian contour. Mabo made white Australia irreversibly 'different' to itself. But at the same time, to employ a chiastic inversion, Australia once again became, from the point of view of indigenous Australians, what it had always been, thus revealing a deeper sameness. Chiasmus, as always, is a profoundly ambiguous figure, inverting but preserving a set of hierarchical relations. It is this ambiguity which lies at the heart not of a putative 'aftershock' resulting from Mabo[6] but far more of white Australia's deep-seated and enduring indifference to that moment of symbolic caesura.

The brain as synecdoche

Images of the brain, as will become evident in my reading of McGahan's text, are central to his fictional dramatization of the debates around Mabo and its consequences for the sense of what it means to stand on Australian ground. McGahan has up until now written bestselling fiction with a decided grunge tenor, and has been hailed as graduating to serious literary status with the publication of *White Earth*. The themes he deals with may justify such judgements, but the form and style of the novel remain stubbornly popular. This, far from being a disadvantage for literary analysis, may ensure a wide public exposure to the issue he debates in fictive form. For McGahan's novel remains, to date, almost the only popular piece of cultural production work to address explicitly Mabo. It is as if, almost two decades after that momentous symbolic event, the potential of that event has yet to strike home.

Indeed, this belated, still deferred recognition, is a central structural principle in McGahan's text. His elaborate description of young William's ear infection in its final stage, already corroding the skull and eating into the brain tissue, occurs at the very close of *The White Earth*. Throughout the text the reader is merely struck by an

6 Felicity Collins & Therese Davis, *Australian Cinema after Mabo* (Cambridge: Cambridge University Press, 2004), 78.

array of physical symptoms plaguing the lad: earache, dizziness, a rotten smell. But they only begin to make sense once the narrative has been comprehended as a whole. And they only gain their symbolic significance in the light of the Mabo decision whose resonance fills the last pages of the novel.

Symptoms, of course, are partial signs which stand for a larger entity, the illness as a whole, and as indexical signs they thus entertain a relationship to the disease which is not dissimilar to synecdoche. Once the symptoms are explained by the provision of a diagnosis in the closing pages of the novel, the reader is enabled, if not obliged, to re-read the text in the light of its narratives of Mabo and questions of land rights, interpreting the final morbid vignette according to an allegorical mode which makes white Australia a parasitical presence corrupting the body of the continent.

The reading process is a figure of the revisionist process of understanding Australian history as it has been interpreted in the final decades of the twentieth century. Reading itself thus becomes a 'back-tracking' process which Davis and Collins, employing a significant spatial metaphor, see as a generic phenomenon in Australian culture since Mabo.[7] The hermeneutic theory of reading suggests that all reading proceeds by means of an oscillation between part and whole so as to construct an overarching unity in the 'organic' work of art. This process is destabilized in the avant-garde artwork, where the constituent parts become autonomous with regard to the whole, so that the reader, rather than constructing the coherence of a 'work,' is obliged to reflect upon the code which makes the work readable (or unreadable).[8] Something akin to this encounter with 'difficult' art happens in the reading of cerebral illness in McGahan's novel, which in turn mimics the hermeneutic understanding of part (national subject) and whole (national history and national space) that Mabo disrupts. In this spatializion of historical understanding the movement from part to whole, as a hermeneutic reassessment of national identity, is enacted in its constituent conceptual steps.

It is perhaps for this reason that ear and brain go hand in hand in McGahan's morbid allegory. William's skull is eroded via a punctured eardrum. From then on he is subject to spatial and narrative confusion, the two hallmarks of the putative national 'shock' attendant on the historical and territorial paradigm shift caused by the Mabo decision. Bewildered by the adults' contradictory opinions, the hapless adolescent tries to parry with his PC cousin's arguments with slogans told him by his ultra-conservative landowner uncle:

> 'The blacks are gone. You just want to rewrite history. . . . Australia is our place now! You can't make us give it back!' . . . But he felt so dizzy and hot, and Ruth was studying him now with distaste. (*White Earth* 284–85)

7 Collins & Davis, *Australian Cinema after Mabo*, 3, 7.

8 Peter Bürger, *Theorie der Avantgarde* (Frankfurt/Main: Suhrkamp, 1974), 107–11; *Theory of the Avant-Garde*, trans. Michael Shaw (Minneapolis: University of Minnessota Press, 1989), 80–82; Hans-Georg Gadamer, *Wahrheit und Methode: Grundzüge einer philosophischen Hermeneutik*, 3rd ed. (1960; Tübingen: J. C. B. Mohr/Paul Siebeck, 1965), 250–90; *Truth and Method*, trans. W. Glen-Doepel, 2nd ed. (London: Continuum, 1989), 265–306.

The boy's dizziness is a symptomatic sign of the spatial disorientation triggered by the momentous shifts in the national landscape, the ground of national identity:

> His ear throbbed and the sun hurt his eyes. He lifted his gaze and stared out over the plains. Everywhere he looked there was haze and smoke, vague shifting shapes that could have been anything. . . . Nothing was solid, not the land, and even less so its history. He had been told so many stories – but which ones was he to believe? (*White Earth* 284–85)

The ear is an organ of balance and an organ of acoustic perception. It functions almost synaesthetically, so to speak, mixing aurality with other modes of perception. Aural disturbance is translated directly into two other paradigms: those of space and of temporality; or, more concretely, of synchronic territorial possession and linear, diachronic narrative. William's confusion is double. He is plagued by a spatial disorientation indexed by blurred vision and dizziness. And he becomes increasingly bewildered about narratives, the multiplicity of conflicting stories he is told by his elders. William's double perceptual pathology is evidence of larger shifts in the way Australian history is experienced. As the narrative progresses, the apparently separate realms of local geography and history merge. Increasingly, space, far from being a neutral given, comes to be seen as being determined by the linear temporality of narratives. The stability of geography is predicated upon the linear preservation of narratives over the generations, a process once invisible but now laid bare. William's cousin invokes the power of narratives to influence the shape of space in land rights legal proceedings, recasting ownership relations after two centuries of indigenous dispossession:

> 'No criminal court maybe. But a Native Title tribunal? That's a different thing altogether. Old letters, old journals, old stories – that's exactly the sort of evidence they're going to have to accept. If we're talking about Aboriginal history, what else is there? And those old women haven't forgotten. They know that those men and boys never came back. They know what must have happened.' (*White Earth* 354–55)

What the boy hears from his cousin about history and its persistence against willed amnesia has immediate spatial repercussions: 'William felt an abrupt shifting of the ground' (*White Earth* 335).

The ear has one further function, that of connecting the inside and outside worlds, processes of perception and the empirical realities they putatively grasp at. All the organs of perception, from the eyes to the skins, fulfil this role, of course, but in the ear, as a canal, this function is spatialized. The channel or corridor formed by the ear enables us to visualize the synecdochic relationship between the individual and collective, between the self and the community. What of synecdoche, however, when the very corporeal image which concretizes it is diseased?

Corruption, revelation, recuperation

As a spatial figure of the nation, the infected brain of McGahan's young protagonist can carry many meanings. One possible tenor to be attached to this corporeal vehicle is that of the continent that it inhabits, invaded and corrupted by the intrusion of white civilization. The figure of the brain can be read as an allegory of the manner in which white settlement turns into a malignant tumour destroying the land and the erstwhile indigenous culture which developed there. This imagery can be extended even further, so as to have the brain stand for the body politic as a whole, morally corrupted and weakened by the injustice which it has committed, and plagued by its festering past.

In one significant passage, William's PC cousin Ruth, like himself capable of smelling the putrid odour emanating from his ear canal, searches for its source. William is wearing an old hat which, it transpires, is part of his great uncle's Queensland Mounted Police uniform – and thus a metonymy of the massacres perpetrated against the indigenous peoples of North Queensland during the colonial frontier wars. One of the Gothic ghosts of the hallucination episodes says to William as he wanders through the bush wearing the cap, 'You bear the mark, boy' (*White Earth* 317). Ruth, as sensitive to the putrescent odour as William is, attempts, in a highly allegorical episode, to localize it:

> 'Is it just me' she asked, after a time, 'or is something dead in here?'
> William said nothing, his eyes wide.
> 'What is that smell?' she repeated.
> 'You can smell something?' William asked.
> 'I'm not sure ... I thought there was something ... or is it just this thing?'

Ruth thinks 'this thing,' the hat, smells, whereas in fact it is the pus in William's ear:

> William rolled over. His cousin was holding his captain's hat, and sniffing it curiously.
> 'Is it? No ...'
> She sniffed the air again . . .
> But he examined the hat closely. Had this been the source all along? And indeed, the material was pungent with age . . . but it wasn't the rotten smell. That was something much stronger, and it seemed to come from everywhere and nowhere.

The 'everywhere and nowhere' precisely captures the ambivalence of a form of historical corruption which has contaminated the entirety of the body politic, but at the same time is curiously elusive because it has been forgotten, and its forgetting forgotten. Unearthing these repressed connections is a matter of some difficulty:

> 'Where on earth did you get it?' his cousin asked, watching him.
> 'I found it,' William said. 'I thought it was from the army. But Uncle John said it's only an old police hat.'
> 'It's old all right.'
> 'He said it was his father's.'
> That caught her attention. She peered at the cap again.

At this moment, the text has Ruth half-explicitly make the connection – what stinks is the festering past:

> 'I didn't know my grandfather was ever a policeman.' She touched the brim. 'So that's a police badge? …. QMP,' she read. 'Queensland something Police? Queensland Mounted Police?' She shook her head and pushed back her grey hair. Her eyes were dry now. 'Maybe I'll ask my father about it, next time I see him.' (*White Earth* 286–87)

Here two metonymies collide: the ear as the metonymy of the conscious, responsible body politic, and the cap as the metonymy of the institutionalized and socially active body politic. By mistakenly identifying the smell with the metonymy of socially irresponsible action, Ruth sets up an oscillation between the social action and the social corruption of the nation. Thus the two metonymical relationships between ear and body and hat and body, themselves metonymies for the macrocosmic body politic, are complemented by a third, triangulating metonymy (hat and head), one which dissociates and then re-associates the two sources of the scent of corruption: 'take this fucking thing off your head,' Ruth later snaps at the boy (*White Earth* 320). This third vector of metonymic association is not static, but like the hat itself, mobile. It thus figures a process which occurs as connections are made, abandoned, and then remade.

These oscillations are only stilled when the evidence of the brutal past finally, in the penultimate chapter, comes to light. In a belated avatar of his earlier activities as a paramilitary Mounted Policeman, William's uncle's father murdered a group of indigenous people returning to their sacred sites. The bones of the victims have been hidden in a cave below the water level of a billabong, but have now become visible as a drought dries up the water hole. In a last effort to destroy this evidence of family misdeeds, William's uncle attempts to incinerate the bones, just as his father had incinerated the bodies of his victims. Together, uncle and nephew probe the darkness of the cave in search of the past: 'White bone shone in the beam. . . . The rank smell of rotting had returned, as if the cave was filled with it, even though he knew that the bones were dry as the dust' (*White Earth* 363). Here the text is on the verge of finally confirming the link between the two instances of corruption, via the crossed figure of chiasmus. The blood shed decades ago, and then pushed out of sight into the darkness of the cave, contrasts with the blood pouring out of William's ear, extruding the undeniable evidence of infection. The bones emerge from their subterranean, indeed submarine hiding place, into the light: and the boy's ear canal and cerebral bone housing, perforated by the mother's angry blow months before, are pierced by the corrosive work of infection. These crossed vectors of extrusive and intrusive blood, on the one hand, and bone on the other, are matched by the central inversion enacted here: the white bones are those of black victims; their whiteness points to the displaced guilt of the white perpetrators. Chiasmus and inversion here function as figures of the 'righting' of a deceptive, inverted semiotic which has distorted the truth for over a century.

The oscillation of the earlier metonymies is now banished, and is replaced by a fully revealed correspondence, soon to be completed by the closing description of William's disease. Chiasmus, it appears, anchors metonymy in a more stable relationship of reference than is customary. By virtue of its looser, 'associative' relationship between vehicle and tenor, metonymy suffers chronically from a lack of the 'originality and expressive power of metaphor'[9] because 'instead of forging new links or uncovering new resemblances [it is] motivated by relationships of spatial juxtaposition.'[10] Synecdoche, as a form of metonymy, also suffers from this debility. Because the relationship between part and whole is spatial in character rather than more closely iconic, it can easily be disputed. And when synecdoche enters the public realm, as historical synecdoche has in Australia during the 'history wars' of the 1990s, its looseness of connection can easily be cast into question.

Thus the conservative historian Windschuttle could attack radical revisionist historians, from Henry Reynolds onwards, on the basis of shoddy scholarship: they had extrapolated, he claimed, from a paucity of evidence, to a generalized but spurious claim for genocide. Windschuttle demanded a more rigorous matching of evidence and conclusions of the sort one might find in a court of law: 'for a claim of killing to be credible it needs either first-hand reports from eyewitnesses, second-hand reports from those with direct contact to the participants, or accounts by those who saw the bodies afterwards. These reports should be reasonably contemporary with events and provide specific details like names, dates, places and numbers.'[11] His demand for a 'forensic' historicism, however, ignored the reality of the archive-based historiography of the colonial frontier: the conflicts of contemporary (sometimes, but not always, 'eyewitness') reports, the use of euphemism in police memos, the destruction of evidence by police and settlers from colonial times up until recent days, and the collective amnesia approved by local communities eager to cleanse the stain of frontier violence. The frontier 'was a shifting, complex and violent site, where the usual practices of British law and order were not consistently applied. In this context, the metaphor of historical research as a courtroom setting does not hold. Windschuttle's forensic approach is an inappropriate tool for understanding the colonial frontier.'[12] In a situation which military historians themselves qualify as often reaching the sustained levels of war, accurate casualty counts are even less reasonable an expectation.[13] The reign of metaphor, in the context of frontier history, is tenuous to say the least, and to demand its application is to banish, conveniently, the only evidence available.

Deborah Bird Rose, commenting on the colonial frontiers conflicts, notes that 'It is clear that settlers actively constructed silences through a variety of practices. With time, however, silences have come to tell an ambiguous story: does silence cover and conceal the knowledge of deeds, or does it mean that nothing happened?'[14] To demand metaphor where only metonymy can function is merely to install another

9 Stephen Ullmann, *Language and Style* (Oxford: Blackwell, 1964), 177–78.

10 Jonathan Culler, *The Pursuit of Signs: Semiotics, Literature, Deconstruction* (London: Routledge & Kegan Paul, 1981), 190.

11 Keith Windschuttle, *The Fabrication of Aboriginal History. Volume 1: Van Diemen's Land 1803–1847* (Sydney: Macleay Press, 2002), 165.

12 Lyndall Ryan, 'Waterloo Creek, Northern New South Wales, 1838', in Bain Attwood and S. G. Foster (eds), *Frontier Conflict: The Australian Experience* (Canberra: National Museum of Australia, 2003), 43.

13 John Connor, *The Australian Frontier Wars 1788–1838* (Sydney: University of New South Wales Press, 2002), xi-xii.

14 Deborah Bird Rose, 'Oral Histories and Knowledge', in Attwood and Fosters (eds), *Frontier Conflict: The Australian Experience*, 129–30.

version of synecdoche: the absence of local proof vindicates the nation's amnesia. Thus, in another novel which deals with similar massacres, Davison's *The White Woman*, a collection of bones discovered in a hollow tree in Gippsland, a remote area of colonial Victoria, is declared to be the remains of a pioneer woman ostensibly kidnapped by the natives[15] – whereas, in actual fact, the flimsiness of forensic evidence allows this claim to mask its direct contrary: the evidence of indigenous people massacred by the settlers and the native police. A claim for metaphor ('No room for doubt' – *The White Woman* 3–4) masks a more incriminating synecdoche. Bone can be made to speak in a plethora of ways, a dizzying potential McGahan tries to stem by doubling synecdoche so as to anchor an accusatory deixis.

Generational space

A final aspect of the cerebral synecdoche in McGahan is its place in a chain of generational causalities. The brain stands for society as a whole, which is constituted by the coexistence of several generations at the one time.

The punctured eardrum and subsequent infection, tumour and erosion of the skull are caused by a blow to the ear dealt William by his mother on the day of his father's death (*White Earth* 4). The boy is a witness to what he takes to be an atomic mushroom cloud, but which then transpires to be the fireball from an explosion in the petrol tank of his father's harvester. The blow to the ear is given as a punishment for having seen the explosion and having failed to act. The putative mushroom cloud stands at the opening of this novel for the impact of Mabo, only half acknowledged in white Australian society. McGahan's *White Earth* is the first work of fiction in Australia to deal explicitly with Mabo. That collective disavowal of Mabo in white Australia is figured by the text's own explanation that the mushroom cloud arises from the exploding petrol tank. But the disavowal is also enacted within the plot, because it is the boy who is punished for having seen the explosion and not acting – whereas in fact it is his mother, as the subsequent action reveals, who fails to come to the rescue of her son in moments of distress. The diseased brain is thus an index (a sign linked by causality to its referent according to Peirce's famous formulation) of the 'bad mother(land)' which Ghassan Hage, building upon Klein's theories of the 'bad breast,' has identified with the contemporary nation-state as it increasingly defaults upon its responsibilities for the welfare of its citizens. Under contemporary regimes of neo-liberalism in Western nations, the social welfare state is being constantly eroded, leaving the lower and lower-middle classes increasingly vulnerable and resentful of the benefits and privileges they have lost, but reluctant to acknowledge that the once-nurturing state is abandoning them. In such a climate, it is the other (refugees, indigenous people and other minorities asserting their rights) who are identified as the culprits. This is a ploy often mobilized by the very right-wing governments which are cutting social services to their own citizens (*Against Paranoid Nationalism* 31–41). McGahan's image of the sick brain can thus be understood as an implicit re-apportioning of guilt to the weak but vindictive

[15] Liam Davison, *The White Woman* (St Lucia, QLD: University of Queensland Press, 1994), 3–4.

mother(land), incapable of protecting the next generation of citizens, and blaming them for its own failures.

William's father, as romantically unpractical as his mother is malingering and weak, dies, and the place of the father is taken up by uncle John, the owner of Kuran Downs and founder of a right-wing league militating against the impending Mabo decision and Native Title legislation. It is Uncle John's father Daniel who, as an erstwhile member of the brutal Queensland Mounted Police, also perpetrates a later atrocity. The evidence of this act is hidden in the waterhole and now comes to light in the days of drought. Throughout the narrative, Uncle John reiterates one of the central topoi of the Anglo-Australian right-wing, namely that the absence of the indigenous people from the land confers rights of possession upon those who came after them: 'The Aborigines are gone. And that's the point. This is my property now. . . . We must be prepared to defend what we own' (*White Earth* 209). This white supremacist argumentation elides the causes of that absence, naturalizing what was in fact a brutal process of paramilitary expulsion in which John's own father, in the context of the novel, had a hand. That process of expulsion, however, is latently acknowledged by a second trope which pleads innocence for the events of the past, claiming that one is not responsible for the sins one's ancestors may have committed. The argument for non-responsibility, resting upon the absence of influence one has upon past actors and their actions, remains silent upon the fact that the present generation is more than willing to enjoy the material benefits of those actions. To that extent the present generation is materially implicated in a process of active dispossession (as a verb whose subject was the white invader of earlier generations) which has become enshrined as a state of dispossession (a noun which is a predicate of the indigenous people of today). McGahan rebuts this argument with a narrative device: he has Uncle John discover his own direct causal implication in the belated massacre perpetrated by his father:

> And the incident had happened when John was only a child. An innocent, wailing in fear.
> And that was like another gulf opening beneath him. For if his own cries had initiated the slaughter, then he was his own prime cause, the unwitting mover of his own downfall. . . . And then the ground was falling away yet again, he was in an abyss of memory . . . He was smelling smoke and crying and he was only a little boy, clutched tight in his mother's arms . . . (*White Earth* 349–50)

The novel dramatizes an unresolvable paradox between innocence and culpability, and in this way expertly concretizes the dilemma at the heart of white Australia's ambivalence about its responsibility for the past – the genocidal past upon which the contemporary nation reposes in its smug wellbeing.

The relationship between uncle and nephew is a pedagogical one. Uncle John tries to train William to 'listen' to the land. His intention is that William will grow up into an inheritor of his property, a 'white Aborigine' with a sense of belonging strong enough to defend the land from the predatory grasping of 'minorities,' 'elites' and indigenous groups (*White Earth* 136): the land ' ". . . wants *you*. . . . You can't lie to me, Will. You feel this country calling. I know you do" ' (*White Earth* 296). He sends the boy out on a lone expedition which takes on the appearance of a rite of passage. Ironically, in a series of Gothic episodes, the boy accedes during this expedition to a knowledge which exceeds that of the uncle – namely, knowledge of the bones hidden in the dry billabong. At this point William does indeed insert himself into the genealogy which the uncle wants to forge – but ironically, with precisely the reverse effects to those which the old man desires. For William discovers the evidence of the massacre perpetrated by the great uncle, and prompts the uncle to remember his own infantile role in triggering the murders. But to the extent that William is the missing link in an intergenerational triangle, reversing amnesia and restoring the earlier connection between John McIvor and his father Daniel McIvor, his own place in that geological lineage becomes ambivalent.

William ruptures the apparently pathological generativity which links the older and younger members of the family. The outcome of William's disease, and indeed, of the tainted ownership of the land, is left in suspense at the end of the novel. Uncle John tries to argue that because the indigenous people died out, or moved away, they abandoned the land. For him, indigenous history is closed off, concluded. His daughter Ruth contradicts this closure of history:

> 'Oh yes, it's a nice legal trick. But in this case they kept coming back, didn't they? Year after year. Until your father killed them.' . . .
> 'It doesn't matter why they stopped. They stopped. It's over.'
> 'It isn't. This law is brand new, it has to be interpreted by judges.'
> (*White Earth* 354–55)

Healing or permanent disability; maintenance of the family possession of the Kuran property or ceding of ownership to the original Kuran people – these are alternatives which the text's closing pages leave undecided. The young William prises open the father-son dyad of Daniel McIvor and John McIvor, and creates a space in which events may subsequently follow many possible paths. The ground upon which one stands, in this context, will always be someone else's. This 'dispossession' is an index of loss, and only to that extent, of novelty and renewal.

The significance of McGahan's project, with its disjunctive conclusion, can be best appreciated in comparison with another post-Mabo assessment of land and nationhood, one mentioned above on several occasions: Malouf's *Remembering Babylon* of 1993.[16] Malouf's opens with the hybrid youth, Gemmy, balancing on a fence rail between black and white culture before toppling over into the white settlement. Malouf assimilates that border to a great divide between known, settled land, and 'unknown country,' 'impenetrably dark,' 'illimitable night' (*Remembering Babylon* 8). By elevating the other side of the border to the power of 'Absolute Dark' (*Remembering Babylon* 3), Malouf subscribes to a colonial trope consecrated but also ironized since Conrad's *Heart of Darkness*. By so doing, he erases the historical frontier of territorial conquest and indigenous resistance: 'On the one hand, this locale might stand for the point from which a properly Australian identity springs. On the other hand, it is the site of violent dispossession. . . . From the first pages of *Remembering Babylon* it is evident that the book sets out to re-member the

16 David Malouf, *Remembering Babylon* (1993; New York: Vintage, 1994). Further references in the text.

former rather than the latter.'[17] The concluding mention of the 'dispersal' in which Gemmy possibly dies (*Remembering Babylon* 196) is encoded in the euphemism in a manner similar to 'disavowal' (the intellectual admission of repression which none the less does not reverse its erasures). Already muted in this manner, the mention of violence is belated enough not to disturb the calculated mitigation of the brutal processes of colonial conquest.

It is highly significant that Malouf's novel concludes during the First World War – an iconic moment of national self-definition of the Australian nation-state in the wake of Federation in 1901. Malouf uses in relation to Gemmy the periphrasis for death in battle – 'fell' – at which price mature nationhood is ostensibly attained: Gemmy 'fell' from the fence into civilization, just and Willie, Lachlan Beattie's grandson, 'fell' in no-man's-land of the Flanders trenches (it was Lachlan who, half a century earlier, armed with a stick-rifle, had 'captured' the half-native as he crossed the border back into settled territory (*Remembering Babylon* 190, 192). Malouf inadvertently admits the warlike character of colonial settlement in the same moment as he sterilizes it for the purposes assimilation to a white-Anglo narrative of emergent settler nationhood and its (European) baptism of fire (the First World War functions similarly in Malouf's *Fly Away Peter*, as does the Second World War in *The Great World*[18]).

What can be achieved by this assertion of continuity of generations of settlers across the internal Australian conflicts of the frontier wars to the external global conflicts of the European war, is the assertion of a putatively seamless process of nation-formation. This diachronic process then culminates logically in the equally flawless synchronic apotheosis of nationhood whose geographical integrity completes the novel: 'the light, running in fast now, reaches the edge of the shore … and in a line of running fire all the outline of the vast continent appears, in touch now with its other life' (*Remembering Babylon* 200). It is precisely this sort of wholeness and closure which *The White Earth* denies, dislocating the ground upon which the nation is built, allowing the 'other life' to prise open the spurious unity of the settler nation and its mendacious stories of origin.

17 Peter Otto, 'Forgetting Colonialism', *Meanjin* 52: 3 (1993), 545.

18 David Malouf, *Fly Away Peter* (London: Chatto & Windus, 1982); *The Great World* (London: Chatto & Windus, 1990).

PART THREE

7 Exile as Origin: Definitions of Australian Identities in Malouf's *12 Edmondstone Street*

At the conclusion of his successor volume to *Orientalism*, entitled *Culture and Imperialism*, Edward Said suggested that 'it is possible to regard the modern intellectual as first distilling then articulating the predicaments that disfigure modernity – mass deportation, . . . population transfer . . . and forced immigrations.'[1] Thomas Keller concurs with this judgement, noting the increasing prominence of a class of intellectuals, 'die ihre Arbeit mit Fremderfahrung verknüpfen und die eigene Identität als fremd wahrnehmen . . . Die Zunahme der Mobilität und der Migration und die Anthropologisierung der eigenen Kultur vervielfältigen . . . vor allem in jüngster Zeit interkulturelle Aspekte von Leben.'[2] Said's perhaps myopic focus on intellectuals as the epitome of exiles neglects the majority of contemporary refugees or labour migrants and has been justly criticized. But his focus upon the expatriate intellectual is perhaps primarily a rhetorical move which prefaces the social responsibility accruing to the diasporic or exilic intellectual.

This responsibility has been highlighted in an Antipodean context by Paul Carter. Carter, like Said himself a migrant whose writing on the poetics of exploration have been highly influential in recent years in the English-speaking world is more inclusive when he states, 'Living in a new country is not an eccentricity: it is the contemporary condition.' Carter's statement gains its full import when put in its context of utterance: namely, the author's concern over newly emergent forms of nationalism in an Australia which seems eager today to renegue on the multicultural tolerance and relatively successful co-existence of diverse ethnic groups of the 1970s and 1980s. Noting this new conservativism only shortly after Australia's 1988 bicentennial, he observed: 'In this situation it becomes more than ever urgent to develop a framework of thinking that makes the migrant central, not ancillary, to historical processes. We need to disarm the genealogical rhetoric of blood, property and frontiers and to substitute for it a lateral account of social relations, one that stresses the contingency of all definitions of self and other, and the necessity always to tread lightly.' Carter's considerations remain no less relevant than when there were written. It appears increasingly important to offer other versions of Australian identity, as Carter suggests, ones based not upon an organic tradition whose authoritarian character legitimizes the violent gestures of exclusion, but one open-ended enough to leave room for cultural plurality and ethnic tolerance: 'We live as others allow us to live, creating meeting places as we go along. Such places may not be monumental, they may be nothing more than encounters, spatial events that leave behind them less litter than a campsite, yet they can form the basis of a social fabric, one that does not suppress the contingency of its community but makes its migratory

1 Edward Said, *Culture and Imperialism* (London: Vintage, 1994), 402–3.

2 Thomas Keller, 'Einleitung: Ein Leben in und zwischen verschiedenen Kulturen führen', in Bernd Thum and Thomas Keller (eds), *Interkulturelle Lebensläufe* (Tübingen: Stauffenberg, 1998), 1.

haphazardness the material out of which it weaves its identity.'[3] This chapter attempts to address the issue of a nomadic poetics of the variety evoked by Carter. It focuses upon one possible form given to such a poetics, that of autobiography. If, as Anna Johnston claims, 'Autobiography is a genre central to the constructions of nations,' going on to illustrate this using two recent Australian autobiographies, A. B. Facey's *A Fortunate Life* and Merv Lilley's *Gatton Man* whose tenor is nationalist rather than pluralist,[4] it may none the less be possible to harness the symbolic force of the autobiography so as to help craft and strengthen the plural cultural fabric of migrant nations such as Australia. In order to interrogate the the potential inherent in autobiography as a form of cultural agency offering models of social existence based upon tolerance and pluralism, this chapter returns once again to the work of David Malouf, whose writing is iconic for white Australian identity. The chapter examines in detail how such autobiographical writing of inter- or multicultural 'meeting places . . . . encounters, spatial events' may be manifest in a writer whose trademark has been the creation of 'imaginary lives'.

Indeed, the title of one of Malouf's earliest novels, *An Imaginary Life* (1978) (which came three years after his debut Malouf such as *Johnno* of 1975), alludes implicitly to the conjunction between Australian identities, questions of exile and immigration, and the genre of autobiography.[5] Less obviously focussed upon questions of cross-cultural identity, the later autobiographical text, *12 Edmondstone Street*, speaks of a childhood in Brisbane, albeit as the son of first- and second-generation migrant parents.[6] It is a text which bears a very specific place name, and explores the genesis of personal places, yet always under the sign of exile and marginality. The aporias created by the apparent tension between roots and nomadism become, in Malouf's poetic exploration of what Bachelard has called 'notre premier univers,' the basis of a generous openness to cultural plurality.[7]

The failures of autobiography

David Malouf's autobiographical essay opens with an apparent paradox. It is an account of place as the ground of the writer's self, yet this primordial site of selfhood has been lost: 'The house I lived in as a child is no longer there' (*12 Edmondstone Street* 3). Doubtless, recollections of the past thrive on the demise of their object; if this inaugural site of childhood experience were present in all its original freshness, the autobiographical enterprise would become redundant. Yet at the same time, the very condition of autobiographical writing – in the case of

3 Paul Carter, *Living in a New Country: History, Travelling and Language* (London: Faber, 1992), 7–8.

4 Anna Johnston, 'Australian Autobiography and the Politics of Narrating Post-Colonial Space', *Westerly* 41:2 (Winter 1996), 75.

5 David Malouf, *Johnno* (St Lucia: University of Queensland Press, 1975); *An Imaginary Life* (London: Chatto & Windus, 1978); on the latter novel see in particular Irina Grigorescu Pana, *The Tomis* Complex*: Exile and Eros in Australian Literature* (Berne, Frankfurt/Main: Peter Lang, 1996), 155–76.

6 David Malouf, *12 Edmondstone Street* (Harmondsworth: Penguin, 1986). All references in the text.

7 Gaston Bachelard, *La Poétique de l'espace* (1957; Paris: PUF/Quadrige, 1994), 24.

Malouf's *12 Edmondstone Street*, the inaccessibility of past places – dooms the genre to failure: Malouf's opening words only perpetuate the absence of that which he aims to recall. At the very moment of announcing the autobiographical project, the author apparently vitiates the possibility of his undertaking. Place can never be recuperated; all autobiography, with what Joy Hooton calls its 'tantalising and treacherous promises to invest . . . places. . . . with a life that defeats the erosions of time,' is an illusory project.[8] Autobiography is no more than the declaration of an irrevocable experience of exile.

This apparent paradox is particularly poignant in the context of Australian (auto)biographical writing, whether non-fiction or fiction, much of which recounts the loss of a motherland and the wearisome process of acquiring an Australian identity, often doomed to failure: Henry Handel Richardson's Richard Mahony, who never truly belongs to his 'ultima thule', is a typical example.[9] Malouf's foregrounding of the problem of exile, in his introductory comments questioning the mode of writing itself, forms an oblique reflection upon the frequently reiterated sense of cultural and geographical exile which has characterized generations of Australian artists and writers. 'It has taken us a very long time – only in the last couple of decades have Australians stopped thinking of themselves as being at the edge of everything' says Malouf in an interview with Ray Willbanks.[10] I wish to argue in this chapter that Malouf, far from perpetuating this Eurocentric syndrome of cultural alienation, or conversely, celebrating a newly forged brash 'Australocentric' identity based on the comforting cohesion of an island nation,[11] works with the notion of exile as indicating a suggestive version of Antipodean identities, ones in closer accord with the multiple realities of Australian destinies. Indeed, it is the very business of autobiographical recall – or its impossibility – which Malouf wields in order to propose alternatives to these hegemonic versions of an Australian identity. In this chapter I will attempt to show how Malouf, in *12 Edmondstone Street*, presents exile as the very ground of linguistic innovation and artistic redemption; the loss of the past, through the absence of a single spatial origin to be recuperated by the text, offers a model of identity based on communication and community.

Hints of experiences of exile pervade the entire first part of Malouf's autobiographical essay. Hardly a single member of the family is immune from the corrosive effects of cultural displacement, from Malouf's grandfather and both his parents, through to the author himself and his sister.

David Malouf's grandfather came to Australia from Lebanon in the 1880s, although, the author remarks sardonically, Australia, still a parcel of minor British colonies, had not yet been brought into existence by Federation, and Lebanon was no more than ideal in the mind of a few patriots (*12 Edmondstone Street* 132). Malouf doubles the instability of expatriation by making both the places of departure and arrival equally uncertain, subject to historical changes of identity wrought by political upheavals. Furthermore, the grandfather's choice of Australia as a land of

8 Joy Hooton, 'First Person Narratives', *Overland* 103 (July 1986), 60.

9 Henry Handel Richardson, *The Fortunes of Richard Mahony* (London: Heinemann, 1930).

10 Ray Willbanks, 'A Conversation with David Malouf', *Antipodes* 4:1 (Spring 1990), 14.

11 David Malouf, 'A Spirit of Play - The Making of the Australian Consciousness' (Australian Broadcasting Corporation 1998 Boyer Lectures), Lecture 1, broadcast on 15 November 1998.

asylum was arbitrary. The beginning of Malouf's family story is thus entirely aleatory; the disturbance implicit in the movement of exile contaminates the choice of the new land and the geographical boundaries constituting that land. This contingency of the family's Australian origins is perpetuated by the grandfather's apparent failure to achieve integration into Australian society, remaining an alien in his refusal to learn the language, to have himself naturalized, or to go out to work.

The primary rupture of exile and geographical displacement spreads further within the family as the three unmarried daughters abandon the Maronite faith for Catholicism. A deeper schism within the family is caused by the only son, David Malouf's father: 'My father too had betrayed him [the grandfather]; or had, in his quiet way, adapted himself so completely to this new place that there was no link between them' (*12 Edmondstone Street* 7). Adaptation, here, paradoxically signifies an inverted form of exile. Significantly, Malouf's father has 'buried' his first language: 'He must, I understood later, have grown up speaking Arab as well as he spoke Australian; his parents spoke little else. But I never heard him utter a word of it or give any indication that he understood' (*12 Edmondstone Street* 133). The father appears to have eradicated a whole layer of experience, erased it from consciousness; the reasons for this paternal suppression of childhood multiculturalism are indicated by Malouf's use of the all-pervading image of the house as a complex signifier of early experiences. 'Like most people in those days, my father was ashamed of our house . . . Weatherboard was too close to beginnings . . . Weatherboard houses can be lifted if necessary, loaded on to the back of a lorry and set down again two suburbs or a thousand miles away' (*12 Edmondstone Street* 10). Malouf's father, it seems, rejects the contingencies of his own life, the existence of apparently unmotivated and irreconcilable alternatives, the mobility surrounding his early years. He represses the evidence of an 'other' language and of paternal origins elsewhere than Australia, in order to construct an authentic and seamless Australian identity, one not threatened by the accidents of emigration. Curiously, this rejection of exile itself merely breeds further exile; for Malouf's father is estranged from his forbears, from the fabric of his own childhood and from the language of which that fabric was woven. A second generation of less evident, but no less potent exile, models Malouf's account of his own origins.

On his mother's side a further example of exile is in play. Malouf's mother left England before the First World War, and is described in the autobiography as harbouring, for many years, a nostalgic yearning for Edwardian England, and attempting to preserve vestiges of that bygone era in subtropical suburban Brisbane. She imposes upon her children codes of behaviour and in particular of speech radically at odds with the place in which they grow up. 'Forbidden to use local slang, or to speak or act "Australian", we grew up as in a foreign land, where everything local, everything outside the house that was closest and most ordinary, had about it the glow of the exotic.' The hypercorrected English upbringing to which Malouf and his sister are subjected produces a variety of domestic exile in which the son, not unlike the father, strives for an exaggerated version of 'Australianness': '"Gimme," I would snarl when my sister and I were out of earshot . . .; or, with shocking self-consciousness, "Him and me done it this arvo. I betcha we did" ' (*12 Edmondstone Street* 33). This heteroglot self-consciousness arising out of an experience of 'inner exile' endows the boy with a particular sensitivity to linguistic registers, and a heightened awareness of his own place within language. Listening to his grandfather's tales, 'at the edge of the circle, with my chin resting on the bent cane of a chair, I would get so lost in the telling that I almost understood: not the words but the tune' (*12 Edmondstone Street* 5). Two generations and two languages separate the grandfather and grandson, giving the boy a sense of living on an 'edge' at once social and linguistic – to the extent that his own sense of self becomes uncertain: 'At the edge of the circle . . . I would get lost. . . .' Exile, in the last analysis, seeps into the self, dividing it from any sense of wholeness or totality.

Home *as* away

Now it becomes clear why the first, programmatic page of *12 Edmondstone Street* claims such difficulty in the task of locating the house of the title. Malouf's autobiography offers an account of houses as the 'grounds of our first experiences' (*12 Edmondstone Street* 8). But the child's link to the family home is tenuous, marked by geographical exclusion, for Malouf and his sister are 'cast out' onto the veranda every evening at bed time, 'abandoned, shut out, not only from the continuing life of the house . . ., but from the house itself, that secure enclosure' (*12 Edmondstone Street* 21, 20). This intimate and primary experience of exile, this regular sense of places of origin as unstable, holds good for a more generalized notion of collective Australian identity. Through three generations of Malouf's family (in many ways typically Australian, as members of a nation constituted since 1788 of immigrants; though this is precisely what late 1990s One nation party leader Hanson's rhetoric, with its strident refusal of an immigrant heritage – 'To hell with that, I was born here' – wished to disavow[12]), the primary ground of experience is multiple and disparate. Origins, here, are irredeemably multiple – Malouf is careful to assert the plural in his terminology, speaking of the '*grounds* of our first experiences' – and above all, heterogeneous, indeed schizoid.

Significantly, the children, scrounging about under the house, discover assorted objects which 'suggest that habitation here might go back centuries. History tells us, of course, that it does not (we discount the abos), but I don't believe it. History belongs to the world of light' (*12 Edmondstone Street* 44). The house, with its wide verandas and vernacular building material becomes a generic representation of Australian society, apparently open and confidently established, but unaware of its own repressed past; the sombre underside of Australian history, the annihilation of the prior inhabitants of the continent, undermines the new society's claims to represent the sum total of Australian experience. The notion of alienation, installed in Australia itself, increasingly obliges the reader to acknowledge that the nation is a multiple, split entity, to a large extent foreign to itself.

The last section of the autobiography, 'The Kyogle Line,' stresses the fragmentary character of Australia, as the main routes of communication, with their differing

12 Tony Clifton, 'Talking Trash', *Newsweek* [Australian edition] (5 October 1998), 32. See also Jennifer Rutherford, *The Gauche Intruder: Freud, Lacan and the White Australian Imaginary* (Carlton VIC: Melbourne University Press, 2000).

railway gauges, force interstate travellers to break their journey as they pass from one ex-colony into another. Australia is an ensemble of disparate 'countries': the alien New South Wales line intrudes into Queensland, establishing a Brisbane bridgehead at Kyogle Station, from which travellers departed 'on a line that was foreign from the moment you embarked on it' (*12 Edmondstone Street* 125). In interviews, Malouf constantly stresses 'how different we might be as Australians according to the different parts of the continent we've grown up in'; 'Once we would have been able to say to ourselves, "I am an Australian. I know how Australians think everywhere." That is no longer true. [Different cities] . . . have very different modes of being and behaviour.'[13] Australia itself is envisaged as radically discontinuous, in its history and in its present configuration; for Malouf, exile is the experience out of which modern Australia is born, and is also the name for its own relationship to itself.

The fragmentary character of Australian destinies as presented in *12 Edmondstone Street* is, however, also a function of the autobiographical project itself. Brisbane is a historical entity particularly resistant to unitary recuperation, a task not made easier by the pitfalls of the literary process: Maurice Blanchot, for instance, has described the radically destructive character of the literary signifier, whose very existence advertises the absence of that which it signifies, as '[denying] the substance of what it represents.'[14] Words can destroy, as Malouf recognizes in his description of the single curse uttered by the pregnant woman who takes refuge on the Maloufs' veranda: her unfamiliar epithet 'punches . . . a hole in the clear fabric of things' (*12 Edmondstone Street* 16). The autobiographical act, constructed out of literary signifiers, shatters the remembered real rather than recalling it to full presence. Like Benjamin's materialist history, autobiography 'takes cognizance of [the past] in order to blast a specific period out of the homogenous course of history.'[15]

The project of literary recuperation of the real is declared doubtful from the very first line of Malouf's autobiography, even before the announcement of the absence of the Edmondstone Street house: 'Memory plays strange tricks on us' (*12 Edmondstone Street* 3). The strange trick of memory referred to is the author's inability to recall the new bathroom door built by his father during wartime renovations which divided the dwelling into several self-contained parts so that rooms could be rented out to boarders. 'The fact is that however hard I try, I cannot find this new door or remember where it was' (*12 Edmondstone Street* 11). Equally, halfway through the essay, Malouf acknowledges that he has passed over the Front Room in his reconstruction of the house, omitting this less attractive sector of childhood existence, and a little further on, that he has left out the principal reason for speaking of the Front Room: once again, memory has played tricks upon him, one of his 'remembered' senses 'has declined to work,' forgetting the odour of the turds he

13 Richard Kelly Tipping, 'An Interview with David Malouf', *Southerly* 3 (September 1989), 500; 1983 interview with David Kerr, quoted in Kerr, 'Uniting the Hemispheres: David Malouf's Fiction', *The Commonwealth Review* III: 2 (1991–92), 61.

14 Maurice Blanchot, *The Gaze of Odysseus and Other Literary Essays*, ed. P. Adams Sitney (Barry Town, NY: Station Hill, 1981), 30.

15 Walter Benjamin, *Illuminations*, trans. Harry Zohn (London: Pimlico, 1999), 254.

once deposited in the corner (*12 Edmondstone Street* 48, 53). Literary language reworks its raw material, 'turning' it into something else (whence the 'tropic' character of literary language) just as the grandfather 'turn[s] a bit of suburban South Brisbane into a Mediterranean garden' (*12 Edmondstone Street* 5); inevitably, in this linguistic process of transformation, the real object is lost: what is ostensibly a process of recall merely deepens an exile already felt acutely.

Felix culpa

But Malouf has commented extensively upon the 'redemptive' character of his literary enterprise, claiming that literary repetition and writerly memory allow objects, characters or situations to be seen anew and thus redeemed.[16] Similarly, Blanchot, although underlining the destructive character of the literary act, none the less conceives this as the first part of a dialectical movement, ceding that 'a word may give me its meaning, but first it suppresses it'; less negatively, he claims that, 'in order to write, the writer must destroy language in its present form and create it in another.'[17] Malouf's incapacity to recall the new bathroom door signalling the division of the original house appears in this light not only as a loss, but also as a gain for his project: 'I hang on hard to this failure of memory, this impossibility, because it allows me, almost by accident, to keep my larger memory whole. So long as that door remains blank, and our handyman, Old Jack, has not yet taken his hammer to the wall, I can keep our first house undivided, as it was in my earliest experience of it' (*12 Edmondstone Street* 11–12). The loss of memory is inverted to become a means of recovery, of the restoration of a house, still entire before a moment of severance. The linguistic process of writing the past, apparently subverted by the loss of memory, is in reality facilitated by its own impotence to overcome that loss: 'it is this *whole* house I want to go back to and explore' (*12 Edmondstone Street* 12; my emphasis). The curious ambivalence of the word, both destructive *and* creative at once, is embodied in the shocking expression uttered by the pregnant woman on the Maloufs' veranda, a word so new that it effectively inaugurates a future speech, enabling the author to '[see] a whole new generation, a different world' (*12 Edmondstone Street* 16). This creative capacity does not erase the impossibility of recalling the past, but obliges Malouf, as he says in an interview, to 'make' a new Brisbane from scratch, as it were; in another interview, with Paul Carter, he acknowledges that the absent past is never available for reappropriation, but can be 'rescued' only at the creative moment of writing.[18] Apparently, exile is the only possible mode of relationship to the places of the past, and it is the role of language to occupy this place of exile, taking this experience of alienation as the very material of its word-turning activity. In what follows, I will explore the ways in which Malouf's autobiographical enterprise takes exile as the ground of its creative and redemptive process, to make it a place of 'meetings.'

16 Barbara Williams and Shelagh Rogers, 'Two Interviews with David Malouf', *Australian and New Zealand Studies in Canada* 5 (Spring 1991), 85.

17 Maurice Blanchot, 'Literature and the Right to Death', 42, 34.

18 Richard Kelly Tipping, 'An Interview with David Malouf', 499; Paul Carter and David Malouf, 'Spatial History', *Textual Practice* 3:2 (1989), 179.

The journey described in 'The Kyogle Line,' beginning at a South Brisbane railway station which already belongs to another state (the gauge of its tracks being wider than those of Queensland railways), culminates in an epiphanic intensification of the 'intrusive' alterity already prefigured in the opening paragraphs of this section of Malouf's reminiscences. The heterogeneity of Australia's political geography comes to have more intimate consequences for the young Malouf travelling south out of Queensland for the first time, on a train which, it eventually transpires, carries several Japanese prisoners of war. As Malouf and his father gaze at the cowering prisoners, they are initially assimilated into a group identity constituted by a collective rejection of a common enemy; but as the inquisitive crowd thins and the verbal abuse gives way to silence, however, they find themselves alone, stripped of the protections of an assumed collective consciousness, and delivered up to the awareness of their own solitude: 'The experience was an isolating one,' driving home a sense of a 'distance between people that had nothing to do with actual space, or the fact that you were breathing, out here in the still night of Australia, the same air' (*12 Edmondstone Street* 131). The young Malouf discovers alienation, the fact of his own 'otherness,' as a direct consequence of being faced with the 'foreignness' of the POWs. As the train travels on into New South Wales, Malouf is aware of 'that darker wagon with the Japs' included within the collective social world of the travellers. The presence of this 'Otherness' as an integral part of an 'Us' provokes, initially, 'silence,' and subsequently, 'some sort of inner argument or dialogue that was in a language that I couldn't catch' (*12 Edmondstone Street* 134). One language, that of a socially imposed collective identity cemented by the propaganda-stereotypes of war, peters out, to be replaced by another interior language, incomprehensible and multiple, conflicting and argumentative. The young boy watches in vain, during the night journey, for some sign of difference that will tell him he has crossed the 'threshold' (to take a term dear to the terrorist narrator of Malouf's *Child's Play*[19]) separating Queensland from New South Wales – but in fact, the change of 'states' is inward, though its consequences no less spatial, leading as they do, to the unknown, to exile: 'It was, to me, as if I had all the time been on a different train from the one I thought. Which would take me more than the sixteen hours the timetable announced and bring me at last to a different, unnameable destination' (*12 Edmondstone Street* 134).

Exile implies a border-crossing, experienced here not as a loss, but as a turbulent transformation. Border-crossings are like the folds or creases dividing the neighbouring topological structures described by René Thom's catastrophe theory, where one space butts up against another: turbulence, rupture and the alteration of the fabric of one topographical structure accompany the transition to the contiguous space.[20] Such border-crossings are present everywhere in Malouf's autobiographical text. In the section entitled 'A Foot in the Stream' Malouf is a tourist in India where

19 David Malouf, *Child's Play*, with *Eustace* and *The Prowler* (Ringwood VIC: Penguin, 1983), 1.

20 Two accessible accounts of Thom's catastrophe theory can be found in *Paraboles et catastrophes: Entretiens sur les mathématiques, les sciences et la philosophie* (Paris: Flamarion, Coll. 'Champs', 1983) and *Prédire n'est pas expliquer: Entretiens avec Emile Noël* (Paris: Editions Eshel, 1991).

'animals, not all of them entirely tamed, move in and out of the lives of men.' Here the 'absolute distinction [the hierarchy of humans over animals] on which our superiority and power is based' has no validity, allowing repeated, daily intermingling between the two orders (*12 Edmondstone Street* 119). This tourist perception echoes a childhood discovery described in *12 Edmondstone Street*: banished to the bathroom for scrapping with his sister, the boy comes across a strange, crudely printed volume describing hybrid creatures such as a sheep-child or a dog-boy. The boy is fascinated by these perverse combinations: 'I think them wonderful. They give me such a marvellous sense of possibilities' (*12 Edmondstone Street* 60). This sense of possibility leads the boy to scrutinize his own naked body in the mirror. This apparent narcissism is not the reunion with the invisible friend and lost twin symbolized by the 'brass jardinière' (*12 Edmondstone Street* 42), but an inquisitive gaze directed upon a self seen, as it were, with an other's eyes – a self questioned rather than merely confirmed in its sameness.

Caught by his puritanical parents in this moment of naked self-appraisal of a no longer familiar body, the child is punished by being sent into 'exile in the yard' – where he goes to help his grandpa, another expatriate, stake Mediterranean tomato plants (*12 Edmondstone Street* 60–61). Like the Ovid of *An Imaginary Life*, exiled for writing his perverse 'Metamorphoses,' the young David, metamorphosing himself into a possible Other, confronts himself across the border between what is, and what might be. He has become an inward exile; it is only a step towards other, outward versions of the same departure. This early instance of alienation from oneself, far from being a moment of loss, inaugurates a process culminating in the later 'inner argument or dialogue' (*12 Edmondstone Street* 134) and prefigures Malouf's references, in other contexts, to the necessity he feels of leaving behind prior versions of himself.[21] In a discussion with Paul Carter, Malouf has commented the dialogic possibilities of such borders or thresholds:

> You also make the point that the frontier is really a place where communication takes place, that a frontier is a place where dialogue occurs – that's quite different notion from the notion of frontier we are used to . . . [the] boundary becomes . . . a point at which . . . two things can meet one another and some kind of interaction can take place – and that's the sense in which you mean 'communication'.[22]

The innovative, creative process brought about by border-crossings is also evident in the transformation, during the course of *12 Edmondstone Street*, of the weatherboard house. Initially it is experienced by the child as a place of insecurity, in which the veranda sleep-out opens onto a threatening fernery which burglars can enter by the side door. But the experience of the burglar, and the boy's frightened discovery that descriptive language can by no means control the elusive reality of a housebreaker (*12 Edmondstone Street* 28), obliges him to find another, identificatory form of representation to deal with an incursion impinging upon his own bodily sense of security. The child identifies completely with the imagined burglar, crossing the

21 Ray Willbanks, 'A Conversation with David Malouf', 13; Barbara Williams and Shelagh Rogers, 'Two Interviews with David Malouf', 88.

22 Paul Carter and David Malouf, 'Spatial History', 181–82.

boundary between his own self and that of the intruder, becoming *someone else*. Malouf is a 'night wanderer, a rebel nomad' (*12 Edmondstone Street* 20), as he crosses the borders of identity, moving about the darkened house along the imagined tracks of the burglar (*12 Edmondstone Street* 28–29). As he travels between his 'favourite camping places' the house is no longer, as Deleuze and Guatarri would say, an *espace strié* (ruled, delimited, bounded space), but rather, a series of interflowing areas to be traversed at will: *espaces lisses* (smooth spaces) to be 'explored in travelling along them' without 'calculation,'[23] spaces to be welded together by disregarding limits – as the child David does for the merely nominal frontier tacitly dividing family space from that of the friend and helper Cassie, discovering that symbolic limits are precisely that, and nothing else (*12 Edmondstone Street* 18–19).

Exilic Australia

This weatherboard house functions as a place of nomadic encounters, of dialogue with the world, its verandas giving onto the street on one side, and onto the bush with its unknown darkness on the other, an image of the self, social and libidinal at once: 'Airy, open, often with no doors between the rooms, they are on such easy terms with the breezes, with the thick foliage they break into at window level, with the lives of possums and flying-foxes, that living in them, barefoot for the most part, is like living in a reorganised forest' (*12 Edmondstone Street* 10). The house's porous boundary, its veranda, becomes, as a place of dialogue between mutually foreign spaces, a paradigm of artistic creation – in its figuring of the spatial interlinkings of disparate worlds (and words) making up the creativity of literary language, and in its image of the diachronic process of departure and arrival, of loss and rediscovery, which the process of verbal metaphorization enacts in the obliteration of prior meaning by new accretions of sense. Malouf says of his childhood sleep-out of the veranda: 'Perhaps it is the daily experience of being cast out and then let in again that has made the house and all its rooms so precious to me. Each morning I step across the threshold and there it is, a world recovered, restored' (*12 Edmondstone Street* 21). Malouf accepts the moment of exile not as loss, but as the opportunity, or as the opportune necessity, to take the old and to make it new.

The weatherboard house, with its surrounding veranda, is a loose synecdoche, in this text, of the eastern seaboard of Australia, open to the ocean on one side and closed in by the inland deserts or the escarpments of the Great Divide on the other.[24] Centred as it is on a South Brisbane dwelling, Malouf's autobiography contains a parable for Australian identity in general – if such a unitary identity were indeed possible. For in declaring exile the basis of any sense of place and concomitant sense of self, it becomes impossible to formulate *an* Australian identity. According to Sneja Gunew, the immigrant voices within Australian writing, a tradition to which Malouf's fiction clearly belongs, 'draw attention to heterogeneity rather than

23 Gilles Deleuze and Félix Guattari, 'Traité de nomadologie: La machine de guerre' in *Capitalisme et schizophrénie: Mille Plateaux* (Paris: Minuit, 1980), 459–60. My paraphrase.

24 See Philip Drew, *The Coast Dwellers* (Ringwood: Penguin, 1994); Martin Leer, 'Sheer Edge: Geography and the Imagination in David Malouf', *Australian Literary Studies* 12:1 (May 1985), 4.

homogeneity as do their histories.'[25] Malouf explicitly resists the notion of a single, closed, homogenous Antipodean identity ('I hate nice, neat closed things'[26]), declaring that the concept of a 'national identity' is a fiction created by a desire for 'very, very simple concepts' inadequate to deal with the reality of 'lots and lots of little regional identities and tribes and loyalties . . . all crossing one another's territories, quite amicably most of the time.'[27]

Australia, in Malouf's vision, is a constant intermeshing, historically and spatially, of multiple exiles and homelands. The early years of (white) Australia, as James Boyce has shown in his work on the early years of settlement in Tasmania, were characterized by a constant process of exile and of dispossession of an imported culture in order to meet the unfamiliar land and its inhabitants in fruitful – if, admittedly, often short-lived – dialogue and community.[28] It seems that for Malouf, exile is the only means of coming home: he discovers, in his Tuscan village, that 'we're all Italians here,' finding a quirky sense of belonging at the very moment of being stripped of his Australian identity by his landlady Agatina (*12 Edmondstone Street* 78). With the filmmaker Richard Kelly Tipping, he constructs a fictional, filmic circuit of the village, made up however of a disconcertingly random and fragmentary series of shots, an accurate representation of the exiles of a lifetime: 'the geography of my walk puzzles me' (*12 Edmondstone Street* 91). Nevertheless, eventually '[we] make our way back towards the house. So my walk is circular after all, I *do* get home' (*12 Edmondstone Street* 93). Exile appears to be the very material out of which a sense of place is knit – as Paul Carter also suggested in the long quotation opening this chapter. The possibility of expatriation as the very ground of subjectivity, and of writing as a necessary means of (re)creating identities, is what Malouf honours in his autobiographical celebration of the places of the past. To what extent Australians today are prepared to take up such a challenge, accepting the risks inherent in such an appraisal of their heritage, and abandoning the search for illusory constructs of national identity – these are the implicit questions posed by Malouf's evocation of the no-longer-extant weatherboard house in South Brisbane.

25 Sneja Gunew, 'Constructing Australian Subjects: Critics, Writers, Multicultural Writers', in Peter Quartermaine (ed.), *Diversity Itself: Essays in Australian Arts and Culture* (Exeter: University of Exeter, 1986), 53.

26 Ray Willbanks, 'A Conversation with David Malouf', 16.

27 Richard Kelly Tipping, 'An Interview with David Malouf', 495.

28 James Boyce, 'Journeying home: A new look at the British invasion of Van Diemen's Land: 1803–1823', *Island Magazine* 66 (Autumn 1996), 38–63; *Van Diemen's Land* (Melbourne: Black Inc, 2008), 15–141.

8 The Absence of Hungary: Notes on a Didactic Autobiography by David Martin

The autobiographical act as we traditionally know it opens with a narrator looking back upon the time and place of her or his birth. The sequential structure of this typically chronological narrative form, which offers an iconic representation of lived experience in the linearity of a syntactic construct,[1] necessarily fixes the emergence of the speaking subject at the origin (both temporal and spatial) of the narrative chain, in a place and date of birth.

Fox on My Door, an autobiography for younger readers written by the Hungarian-born Australian author David Martin, at once confirms the linear metaphor structuring many autobiographical texts, with its subtitle *A Journey through my Life*, and simultaneously flagrantly infringes this very same convention.[2]

David Martin was born in 1915 in Budapest into an assimilated Jewish family (whose Hungarian lineage he traces back at least four generations in the later autobiography, *My Strange Friend*[3]) as Ludwig Detsinyi; he later changed his name by deed poll. His parents came to Berlin at the end of the First World War; he himself subsequently left Germany in the early 1930s. After some time in Holland, Hungary and Palestine, he served in the Spanish Civil War in the International Brigade in 1937–38. In 1938 he settled in London, where he worked as a newspaper and radio journalist, and married an English writer and teacher, Richenda Powell, in 1941. After a period as a journalist in India in 1948–49, he visited Australia and decided to stay.

Hungarian migration to Australia can be traced back as far as the 1830s, reaching a temporary peak during the 1850s when the exile of political activists from the 1848–49 revolution coincided with the discovery of gold in New South Wales and in Northern Victoria (the area where David Martin later settled); subsequently, numerous free immigrants came to Australia in the years leading up to the First World War. After the First World War there was some immigration as a result of the political unrest following the cessation of hostilities (it was at this date that Martin's family went to Berlin). In the 1930s and in the late 1940s there was a steady trickle of Jewish refugees from Hungary. Martin himself can be counted a member of this group of migrants only in a limited sense, as he had by then given up his Hungarian nationality and came to Australia on a British passport, but other members of his wider family appear to have arrived in Australia during this period. The post-war years saw considerable migration following the establishment of communist government and in particular after the events of 1956. In addition, many members of the Hungarian community in Australia were born outside Hungary, or came to Aus-

1 See Karin Wenz, *Raum, Raumsprache und Sprachräume: Zur Textsemiotik der Raumbeschreibung* (Tübingen: Gunter Narr, 1997), 29.

2 David Martin, *Fox on My Door: A Journey through my Life* (Melbourne: Collins Dove, 1987). All references in the text.

3 David Martin, *My Strange Friend: An Autobiography* (Chippendale, NSW: Picador, 1991), 8. All references in the text.

tralia via intermediate countries; it is to this somewhat nebulous group – in terms of census information – that Martin belongs.[4]

Already before arrival in Australia, David Martin had published several collections of verse and two novels (*Tiger Bay*, 1946; *The Stones of Bombay*, 1949). In the 1960s he published *The Young Wife* (1962), *The Hero of Two* (1965), *The King Between* (1966) and the significantly titled novel *Where a Man Belongs* (1969). In the 1970s he established a reputation as a children's writer, beginning with *Hughie* (1971). Martin's writing was notable for its preoccupation with the hard realities of social existence; he was active in left politics for his entire adult life.

The narrative that I have constructed here moves, faithful to generic expectations, forward towards the present, predicated upon a chain of events which, according to a reverse logic, can be traced back to the subject's birth. But it is precisely this countervailing vector which Martin's autobiography refuses, for the simply reason that it hollows out its own constitutive moment and place of origin.

Fox on My Door confounds expectations of an autobiographical narrative by opening far away from David Martin's native Budapest and by refusing the habitual retrospective gaze towards the moment of his own birth. Rather, this autobiographical work firmly states its implantation in the author's adopted land, and his concentration upon the future instead of the past. The opening chapter is situated in the writer's study in a house on the edges of rural Beechworth, a small town on the erstwhile goldfields of Northern Victoria; in the midst of his labours, the writer is interrupted by his two boisterous grandchildren knocking on his door much akin to Coleridge's maligned person from Porlock.

These implicitly negative gestures embody a movement away from the native land and towards the future which is programmatic for David Martin's conception of his activity as a writer. The places of the past are returned to in this autobiography only to generate an ongoing movement of exile; and crucial moments of development of selfhood are only evoked to be promptly deflated in favour of an orientation towards others. David Martin's attempt to suggest a model of didactic autobiographical literature, a literary precursor of an as-yet-unwritten 'philosophy of emigration'[5] reposes upon two key elements: the one geographical, and intimately linked to a Hungary which is most notable for its absence in the narrative; the other subjective, and typified by a younger generation which interrupts the writer in his work of writing. But though the performative aspect of the inaugural gesture of denial is positive in simply placing another generation and another land in the inaugural scenes of the autobiography, the fundamental negativity of such a gesture generates considerable problems at the level of the epistemological foundations of this didactic undertaking.

4 See Egon Frank Kunz, 'The Settlers: Hungarians', in James Jupp (ed.), *The Australian People* (Melbourne: Angus & Robertson, 1988), 536–41.

5 See Vilém Flusser, *Von der Freiheit des Migranten: Einsprüche gegen den Nationalismus* (Bensheim: Bollmann Verlag, 1994), 34. See also my *North-South/East-West: Global Entanglements in Post-Imperial Writing in French and German* (Trier: WVT, 2010), 148–64.

Mobility as pedagogical principle

Permanent mobility is the dominant theme in this account of a writer's existence, not merely in as the structural principle behind the events related, but also in the effect aimed at by the writer: 'Sophie, Toby, listen to your grandfather,' intones the narrator in a remarkably explicit embodiment of the pedagogic role: 'Can you hear the train? Why sit still in one spot if you do not have to?' (*Fox on My Door* 27). The prominence persistently accorded to grandchildren from the very outset, in the autobiography's dramatization of its own production, confirms 'affiliation,' that ersatz form of connection which, according to Edward Said,[6] emerges in the wake of the erosion of 'filiation' as a mode of cultural inheritance. For martin, 'affiliation' functions as the larger ethical framework, albeit one which is without a secure foundation, in which the book is written as well as its very principle of generation. Mobility, not stability, is something that is passed on from generation to generation, as Martin reveals in his account of childhood rehearsals of the everyday exile performed by his own parents: 'before my nose reached to the top of the diningroom table I put my father's bowler hat on, took his stick and an empty suitcase and started out for the nearest station' (*Fox on My Door* 21). The latent conflict between, on the one hand, a principle of intergenerational imitation, and on the other, a principle of departure and mobility, is manifest in the narrative's incipit: the absence of Hungary figures as a rupture of connections and is doubled by the narrator's turning away from his own birth; but this displacement of the narrator's own birth is immediately compensated in the first scene by an account of the birth of the grandson who perpetuates the family lineage and subsequently generates and founds narrativity in his role as the youthful recipient of storytelling.

The dilemma evident here is that of founding a highly assertive narrative pedagogy upon an absence. The question raised is that of the place from which one speaks. Discursive authority is often embodied in and derived from a specific place, be it a speaker's dais or pulpit, the situation of a reputed publishing house (London, Oxford, Paris . . .) or the proximity of a reporter to the events conveyed (the scene of the crime, for instance). In the so-called postmodern age, however, such authority is undermined by the multiplicity of possible places from which one can speak, and the concomitant revelation of the arbitrary and relative character of sites of discursive authority. Postmodern analyses of the connections between discourse and power tend to discredit discourses of authority. In such a context, how can one speak didactically without falling over into an authoritarian discourse? How can a libertarian pedagogy speak against totalitarian politics and the modes of thought which foster the emergence of such politics and perpetuate their existence, without itself mirroring that absolutism in its own discourse? (Or alternatively, how can one espouse tolerance without depriving one's own words of all significant force?)

David Martin indicates his awareness of this dilemma by making mention in his text, in stark contrast to authoritarian injunctions to his grandchildren, of his wife's criticisms of the 'pompous sermons' which bedevil early drafts of his work before the conjugal editor has taken her merciless red pen to them (*Fox on My Door* 112).

6 Edward W. Said, *The World, the Text and the Critic* (London: Faber, 1984), 16–17.

Likewise, the author's grandchildren vigorously resists their grandfather's assumption of elderly wisdom: his granddaughter Sophie 'gives me a sideways, slightly haughty look. "I know that already," the look says. I watch her stalking round my study, trying to hide how fussed I feel . . . She honours me with another one of those looks. It clearly says, "Don't patronise me, old man" ' (*Fox on My Door* 45). Such episodes dramatize the tensions at the heart of a libertarian pedagogics, one which is implicitly self-questioning at the very moment of making claims for didactic authority.

Addressing this dilemma is all the more pertinent given the immense didactic power possessed by autobiographical modes of writing in Martin's country of adoption. Many Australian autobiographies elide the reality of plural experiences of expatriation or exile and the fundamentally heterogeneous character of 'Australia' as a nation.[7] In marked contrast, another (immigrant) Australian, Paul Carter, has called for a new 'framework of thinking that makes the migrant central . . . to historical processes. We need to disarm the genealogical rhetoric of blood, property and frontiers and to substitute for it . . . one that does not suppress the contingency of its community but makes its migratory haphazardness the material out of which it weaves its identity.'[8] In displacing Hungary as the originary place of autobiographical narration, David Martin, like Malouf, both announces such a project of propagation of mobility as a mode of tolerance, and, paradoxically, undermines the very basis for the selfsame didactic ethics of literary production. Yet this, far from being a contradiction or a weakness, may be precisely the aim of such autobiographical writing: its didacticism may reside in its performative crafting of an ungrounded ethics of mobility whose legitimization rests in its 'doing' rather than its 'being'.

(Un)Doing selfhood

As suggested at the beginning of this chapter, David Martin's autobiography consistently works to displace the habitual narcissism of masculine autobiographies. The chapter entitled 'Photo of a young soldier' (Ch. 8), which recounts David Martin's experiences as a volunteer in the Spanish Civil War, continues this programme of iconoclasm directed at the self by addressing a quintessential image of heroic masculinity:

> In my study there is a photograph of a soldier with thick, rimless glasses. It stands on a shelf to the left of the window which is blocked by the air-conditioner on which my stockwhip rests. His obvious short-sightedness gives the man an unmilitary air, so much so that even Toby sometimes says he does not look at all like a fighting man.
>
> But it is me. (*Fox on My Door* 67)

The narrator constantly stresses his myopia as a strategy of self-deprecation: the allusion to the stockwhip refers to a chapter, significantly entitled 'Shortsighted with

7 Anna Johnston, 'Australian Autobiography and the Politics of Narrating Post-Colonial Space', *Westerly* 41:2 (Winter 1996), 75.

8 Paul Carter, *Living in a New Country: History, Travelling and Language* (London: Faber, 1992), 7–8.

a stockwhip' (*Fox on My Door* Ch. 7) in which the hero, attempting to crack a drover's stockwhip, only succeeds in bloodying his own face and smashing his spectacles; in a parody of the circularity of narcissistic self-reflection, the tool of hypermasculine performance turns back upon its myopic performer, depriving him of the very faculty of self-adoration. And indeed, it is these spectacles which prevented the David Martin from taking up the heroic military role that such a photo might be thought to embody: incapable of shooting straight, he is barred from becoming 'a fighting man' in Spain and is delegated to the medical corps.

Rather than the repetition and 'fixing' of subjectivity Lacan detected in narcissistic self-mirroring, David Martin's autobiography constantly stresses the arbitrary, mobile character of individual identity. The narrator is aware that writing, with its almost simultaneous concomitant of re-reading the image of the self laid down on paper, tends to constitute the writer's ego in a self-confirming mode of existence, as indicated by the grandson's comment on the author's cramped cohabitation with a study full of his own books: 'Your David Martin Memorial Museum?' the boy enquires acerbically (*Fox on My Door* 4).

Contrary to this process, David Martin's autobiography labours to keep such smug self-importance in check. The Spanish Civil War chapter records the narrator's survival, but gives that intact existence a paradoxical final twist: 'And I? I am still here. Yet I am one of the few people alive who have read their own death notice' (*Fox on My Door* 72). But the episode inaugurated by this statement, far from confirming the durability of the self, as it would initially appear ('And I? I am still here'), tends to show to what extent the self is an arbitrary being. The International Brigade medic David Martin lays his overcoat over a shivering soldier suffering from a stomach wound. When the anonymous soldier subsequently dies, the identity conferred upon him is the narrator's: 'For some reason he had no identity disc or document and my own was found in the pocket of the coat which arrived with him on the stretcher' (*Fox on My Door* 73). David Martin is consequently declared dead, and his demise announced in the Haifa newspaper read by his girlfriend on a Kibbutz in Palestine. A person's identity, it would appear, is the product of discourse, external and arbitrary – and here, easily transferable. Any essential identity a subject might posses is subordinated to a linguistically (and thus socially) produced 'subject position' into which the subject is slotted: 'Apparently they had buried him [the wounded soldier] under my name,' explains Martin in a wonderfully lapidary sentence (*Fox on My Door* 73). Subjective identity is not essential, but is principally derived from an instance outside the self, be it name-bearing paternity or language itself. Autobiographical writing functions here, as Blanchot has suggested, as a way of dissolving the self. The act of writing highlights language, through which the subject comes to being, so as to reveal, by performative means, the constructedness of individual subjectivity, and to foreground its insubstantial nature.[9]

Typically, the book opens with a paradox: namely, that children interrupt writing but that they reactivate it and provide its rationale, a paradox prominently dramatized in the inaugural gesture of *mise-en-abyme* already mentioned above. The

[9] See Maurice Blanchot, 'Le journal intime et le récit', in *Le Livre à venir* (Paris: Gallimard/ Folio essais, 1986), 252–59.

opening chapter tells of the narrator's difficulty in concentrating upon his work with his two boisterous grandchildren playing outside his study, and eventually bursting into the writer's intimate space. 'All right for Sophie, I suppose,' he complains, 'but Toby really should know better. Did he not tell me himself that that he too wants to be a writer? Writers should be left alone' (*Fox on My Door* 3). The narrator appeals to the mirror-image of himself – the grandson as disciple following in the grandfather's artistic footsteps – as a defence against that selfsame youthful agent of disturbance. In this way the grandson's disruptive assertion of himself as an independent presence is assimilated to the writer's aspirations to peaceful isolation. Fortunately for this narrative initiated by the episode of disturbance, however, which otherwise would have been cut short – transgression being the trigger of the narrative process, as Lotman has pointed out[10] – the small boy does penetrate his grandfather's study, and succeeds in persuading him to tell a story, that of his own (Toby's) birth (*Fox on My Door* 5–7). The dramatized frame-narrative and the secondary narrative contained within it both portray the irruption of a younger generation into the life of their elders, thus providing the stuff of narration. Without this doubly dramatized transgression of the space of writing, there would be nothing to write about.

Storytelling is predicated upon the interruption of isolation. It is based on the interruption of one's communication with a reflection of oneself which merely confirms and perpetuates that existence in isolation. It is the mobility of the two children which triggers the creative process of storytelling – and which gives that storytelling its ethical rationale. One is reminded of Christa Wolf's description of her children as 'ferment and fundament' of her life as a writer.[11] Writing only finds its true vocation, so to speak, when interrupted, when alienated from itself. Writing which is devoted to itself, which is not confronted with an other outside it, with the world which challenges it, and which it can never do justice to or fully account for, has lost its reason for being. It is the mobility of the younger generation which mobilizes and orients writing, in this inaugural and thus programmatic chapter of Martin's autobiography. It is the paradox of the interruption of writing which becomes the reactivation of writing, driving writing out of the stasis and closure of the writer's customary 'place.'

Writing degree zero?

Such paradoxes not only generate Martin's writing, but are the principle surface feature of the episodic accounts which make up his autobiography. The paradoxical character of these stories often springs from their stark simplicity: there is no moral to be drawn from the tale, and the reader is left baffled by anecdotes from everyday life which are merely odd. They are, to steal a phrase from Thomas Bernhard, 'accessible to the point of inaccessibility.'[12] The action is simple, as befits a

10 Jurij M. Lotman, *Die Struktur des künstlerischen Textes*, trans. Rainer Grübel, Walter Kroll and Hans Eberhard Seidel (Frankfurt/Main: Suhrkamp, 1973), 354ff.

11 Christa Wolf, *Im Dialog: Aktuelle Texte* (Frankfurt/Main: Luchterhand Literaturverlag, 1990), 154.

12 Thomas Bernhard, 'Ein junger Schriftsteller', in Wolfgang Schneider (ed.), *Männerbilder: Ein Lesebuch* (Frankfurt/Main: Suhrkamp, 1998), 87.

children's story, but strangely, by virtue of that very simplicity, defies easy translation into some sort of edifying message. Puzzling clarity, as so often, is the overall impression left by a story about David Martin's search, as a tourist in Salonika, for a penknife with which to peel apples. Having only minimal Greek, he communicates his request in the first shop at which he enquires by means of sign language. The shopkeeper, although himself having no such items in his stock, directs him to another shop nearby where the narrator repeats his performance. Once again his mime is fruitless. It is only when he has exhausted all gestural resources, that he realizes that the first shopkeeper is standing at the window, watching the mute performance. Only then does the first shopkeeper reveal his good command of American English: 'You should be on the stage. You would make your fortune. Forgive me, I couldn't help it. That apple, that knife! It's the funniest thing I saw since I came back from the States' (*Fox on My Door* 36) – upon which the first shopkeeper conveys David Martin's wish to the second. He duly receives the sought-for penknife – and a set of worry beads (*komboloi*) in memory of the occasion.

Here the narrator finds himself the victim of a deception of the variety suffered in an earlier episode by Ruth, the erstwhile girlfriend of the narrator's twin brother Rudi. The latter had employed Ludi (David Martin) as an identical replacement for himself, having tired of Ruth's company (*Fox on My Door* Ch. 2). Like Ruth, the narrator is also taken in by withheld information. Ludi had concealed his real identity, just as the first shopkeeper had concealed his English competence. Both Ruth and the narrator are thus caught up in a fiction of which they themselves are unaware; both perform upon a stage, believing that it is reality. Whereas Ruth quite understandably reacts with anger, the narrator of the Salonika episode realizes that he has benefited from the experience: he has obtained his penknife and a set of worry beads and afforded pleasure to the wily spectator. (Ruth, significantly, does not perceive the change of partner as a possible enrichment of her experience.)

This simple tale, however, is preceded by a prior episode apparently unconnected with its sequel, in which the traveller has his worn shoes repaired by an old man who also communicates in vivacious sign language. The narrator, indeed, anticipates the reader's puzzlement: 'What has my shoemaker in Salonika to do with the *komboloi* in my study, the string of beads Sophie is taking to Richenda? Patience: we shall come to it directly' (*Fox on My Door* 33). He does not, however, subsequently answer this query. Rather, the answer is contained in the first part of the story: 'The old fellow was a born mime' (*Fox on My Door* 37). Mimicry unifies the two parts of the story, as an activity which is passed on from one character to another, both as communication and entertainment. But mimicry, bodily imitation, is also one of the most fundamental forms of learning: we learn by imitating what we see around us. Mimicry involves a high degree of identification with an other whose actions the self scrutinizes and internalizes.

But such identification with the image of an other is exactly what Martin's self-deprecating mode of autobiographical contests. Thus it is important that this identificatory form of learning incorporates an element of freedom always available to the recipient of narration. It is significant that there is a temporal and spatial interval between the two parts of the story; what is 'learnt' from the shoemaker is tested elsewhere in the town and with other people. It is also significant that the author writes, regarding the worry beads which symbolize this experience in Salonika:

> He taught me how to play with [the worry beads], but for *komboloi* to do the nerves good, each owner must develop his own tricks . . . I know that Sophie likes my *komboloi* and I have been wondering if I should let her have them. But I don't think I will. I have heard from other Greeks that you may give a new set of beads to anyone, but never one which you have already used. That would mean passing on your own worries, and who wants to do a thing like that to their one and only granddaughter? (*Fox on My Door* 37)

The worry beads are a reminder of an experience of learning by imitation which incorporates an interval between model and repetition. This is the mode of learning which David Martin performs in his stories, with their insistent dramatization of the didactic relationship: the stories always embody a paradox, such that their stark simplicity forces the listener or reader to reach a conclusion independently. Just as used beads ought not to be passed on to another person, so as not to impose the cares associated with them, so a tale which already includes its own interpretation ought not to be imposed upon the young listener, excluding space for them to work towards their own understanding of the narrative.

This is the role played by the disconcertingly simple surface of the tale, and by the lack of connection between its two constituent episodes. No predetermined interpretative position is offered to the reader. David Martin's paradoxical tales oblige the listener to examine them from several points of view, often conflicting, before coming to some sort of conclusion, if at all. They embody the intellectual virtues learnt by the émigré or exile, who Kristeva contrasts with

> his distainful hosts who lack the *distance* – possessed by him – to see himself and them. The foreigner is fortified by this interval which prises him away from others and from himself and gives him the elevated sentiment not of possessing the truth, but of relativising the world and himself where others are caught in the ruts of monovalency.[13]

Martin's tales teach intellectual mobility, the mental equivalent of the author's own incessant travelling and his nomadic spirit of adventure: 'When I travel, I travel light. I never know in the morning where I shall sleep at night. I put my pack – not a very big one – on my back and trust to fate, so long as my nose is pointed in the right direction' (*Fox on My Door* 28). The functioning of David Martin's anecdotes can be helpfully illuminated by a comment by Meaghan Morris:

> I take anecdotes, or yarns, to be primarily referential. They are oriented futuristically towards the construction of a precise, local and *social* discursive context, of which the anecdote then functions as a *mise en abyme*. That is to say, *anecdotes are for me not*

[13] Julia Kristeva, *Etrangers à nous-mêmes* (Paris: Fayard, 1988), 16. My translation.

> *expressions of personal experience but allegorical expositions of a model of the way the world can be said to be working.*[14]

The world view which David Martin's anecdotes create, in so far as they encourage the reader to formulate a position in response to the paradoxical situations narrated, is one which values a permanently enquiring, questioning spirit, a mode of intellectual mobility. 'Art is large and it enlarges you and me. To a shrunk-up world its vistas are shocking,' comments Jeanette Winterson;[15] art is produced by and produces mobility. Thus Martin, introducing a grotesque gigantic Santa Claus suspended in the summer heat from a wheat silo in Port Pirie, South Australia, writes: 'What I could do, I suppose, is talk about him, this Dinkum Aussie Yuletide Daddy, and see where it, or he, might take us. Because he must lead us *somewhere*. I will not accept that it ended up exactly where it started, twenty or thirty metres up in the December air' (*Fox on My Door* 80). This sight of this huge Christmas mannequin in turn motivates Martin to undertake a journey from Melbourne to Sydney along the Hume Highway, in order 'to take a fresh look at my adopted country and its strange customs, so that I could learn to feel at home in it once more' (*Fox on My Door* 81). It is mobility, precisely, which produces the possibility of identification and belonging. The overland journey produces unexpected results: in Albury, on the Victoria-New South Wales border, Martin learns about the earlier Sikh immigrants in north-eastern Victoria, information which in turn germinates into a project for a novel. The necessity of field research in turn breeds the idea of a trip to India, and a visit to the Sydney manager of Air India: 'I explained my idea and that my book might make some young Australians sufficiently interested in his country to want to visit it' (*Fox on My Door* 82). The poles of exile and belonging are themselves produced within a constant oscillation between places. The generative term in this dialectical process is mobility, both geographical and intellectual.

The basis of Martin's pedagogic project, then, appears to be the rejection of prefabricated models of thought to be imposed upon the pupil by the schoolmaster. The youthful David Martin was very nearly expelled from his boarding school in Germany in the early 1930s for writing an essay against an authoritarian education:

> Teachers, I pointed out, love what they call "helping to form character" . . . In a boarding school they can mould and knead character all day long, from first bell to lights-out. But it was, I reasoned, revolting for any person to want to muck around with the character of any other person, large or small . . . Leave the poor blighters to themselves, don't twist and trim them, let them grow up to make their own characters . . . The school claimed it could model snotty-nosed brats into patriotic sons of the fatherland, and I, a Jewish boy, had spat on it like a boy-scout on his toggle. (*My Strange Friend* 52)

14 Quoted by Victor Burgin, *In/Different Spaces: Place and Memory in Visual Culture* (Berkeley: University of California Press, 1996), xi–xi. Burgin's emphasis.

15 Jeanette Winterson, *Art Objects: Essays on Ecstsay and Effrontery* (London: Vintage, 1996), 66.

Yet such an anti-authoritarian approach to education throws up the dilemma of the authoritarian basis in any educative project. Not to acknowledge and to wield some degree of authority as an educator is simply to hand over that authority to some other social instance or influence. Some form of didactic power must be exerted if education is to function, as Martin admits: 'I am still not sure that this character-forming rigmarole is such a great invention, but how do you get around it?' (*Fox on My Door* 52). Martin's text does, however, suggest some ways of confronting this dilemma.

I am not I

This autobiography constantly foregrounds images and mirrors in order to contest the hegemony of identification with such images. A crucial early experience appears to have been that of being the younger of a pair of identical twins, the follower rather than the leader, constantly caught within the proximity of his own echo (*Fox on My Door* 12). As *My Strange Friend* says, 'Twins have unnumbered experiences in common. . . . There is nothing mysterious, but it can make them wonder whether they are not going to remain for ever two halves of one whole, and since this is how they appear in the eyes of those who watch them the feeling becomes strong' (*My Strange Friend* 21). One early episode concerns learning to 'tell oneself apart,' thus throwing off the oppressive regime of imposed as well as inherited twinhood. This is the episode mentioned above in which the elder Rudi employs his brother Ludi (the narrator) to take up his place in an adolescent relationship with a girlfriend of whom the elder twin has already tired. For Ludi, the experiment offers the chance of intimacy with a woman, but one of a dubious character because it is based upon the brothers' identical appearance. 'Rudi fitted me out in his clothes, and so effectively that even our mirror could not have distinguished Ludwig from Rudolph' (*Fox on My Door* 15). For Ruth, the implicit mirroring of love is abruptly shattered by the discovery that the boy she believes she loves has been absent and thus no longer enables her narcissistic self-reflection; and more devastatingly, that he has been replaced by someone else, demonstrating that romantic attachment is, to some extent at least, arbitrary and interchangeable. The wounded and furious girlfriend gives Ludi a resounding slap on the cheek as a parting gesture mirroring her own experience of Rudi's implicit contempt (*Fox on My Door* 14–18). Mirror images can be exploited, and can wound others; the deceptive game involved in the brothers' exploitation of their mirroring of themselves also reveals the perils experienced by the lover in mirroring one self in the gaze of the loved other. Yet the mirror image equally allows a broadening of horizons: both Ludi and Ruth gain new experiences through this experiment, albeit with radically varying degrees of free will. The condition of such experience, however, is the deconstruction of the mirror subsequent to its exploitation: while Ruth senses a difference on their first date, she has got used to her changed friend on the second, saying, 'today you are my own sweet Rudi,' to which Ludi replies: 'But I am not, you see . . . I am not I' (*Fox on My Door* 18). Here the narrator discovers the arbitrariness in subjectivity, at the very moment of embracing the experience afforded by that subjectivity. 'I' is merely a grammatical function which can be occupied by any number of real speakers, the

'I' of the utterance (énoncé) is not essentially identical with the 'I' of enunciation.[16] Mirrors, here, appear as a tool for experience, if only they can also be escaped from. Significantly, the same expression occurs in *My Strange Friend*, about the time Ludi left school: 'Who was I? To many things at once . . . One thing was clear. I was not I. "Ludi, what do you want from life?" No one asked that question. Had somebody done so I could only have muttered, "Freedom. To be out of this goddam straightjacket" ' (*My Strange Friend*, 45). It is Ludi's sense of his self's non-coincidence with itself which acts as trigger for his quitting Hitler's Germany in 1933, the first of many departures to come, an opportunity gladly seized.

In Lacanian terms, flight from the illusory and megalomaniac reflections of self in the order of the Imaginary is not afforded by the undifferentiated and subject-dissolving Real so much as by the realm of the Symbolic, where systems of signification are lived as pragmatic necessities within social existence, but seen for what they are: mere symbolic representations, otherwise insubstantial, without whose help, however, social exchange could not be carried out. We cannot get by without signs, but need to be aware of their constructed, arbitrary character. The fixity of a didactic master and a stable enunciative subject, even in a pedadogic project such as that of David Martin, in which a permanent questioning and erosion of predetermined points of view is espoused, can be seen as similar to the existential necessity of the Symbolic order within Lacan's triadic modes of representation. Some degree of authority is necessary to any pedagogic enterprise, even when the assumption of a didactic stance contradicts the freedom of thought which that pedagogic project aspires to communicate.

Such contradictions are rife in intercultural education: Annedore Prengel, for instance, articulates the dilemma of a predominantly cultural-relativist orientation in intercultural education which also acknowledges the pragmatic validity of the stance take by an assimilative approach (migrants from other cultures are to be taught competence in the culture of the host country rather than encouraging the maintenance of their distinctive cultures), thus responding to the pragmatic need for host-culture competence if the immigrants are to prosper in their adopted country.[17] Sometimes, there appears to be an ethical imperative for limiting the totalizing aspirations of calls for discursive relativity. Significantly, David Martin says of his Teutonic schoolmasters: 'I have no enmity towards teachers. I owe too much to too many of them . . . And even the sad-sack whose trouser fly we gawked at, he too has my gratitude. That I can write this book in English I owe mainly to him' (*Fox on My Door* 49–50).

This autobiography's ethics of departure and exile espouses not a total departure, but a permanent occupation of the border between usage of discursive fixity and the dissolution of such fixity. The boy David Martin, leaving Berlin for Holland with his parents, is fascinated by the distinction between participation in a place in society (and, by implication, in its discursive conventions) and distance from that place: 'But I am also trying to catch the instant when the wheels will begin turning and

16 See, for example, Emile Benveniste, *Problèmes de linguistique générale* (Paris: Gallimard, 1966), 251–57; Jacques Lacan, 'Subversion du sujet et dialectique du désir', in *Ecrits II* (Paris: Seuil/Points, 1971), 159.

17 Annedore Prengel, *Pädagogik der Vielfalt* (Opladen: Leske & Budrich, 1993), 76.

nothing can stop us any more . . . We are moving and I have missed the precious moment' (*Fox on My Door* 24–25).

The absence of Hungary

What then, is the place – or rather the non-place – of Hungary in this didactic autobiographical project? It is disconcerting, for the reader who knows that David Martin was born in Budapest, or who is familiar with the space devoted to the writer's family origins in the *My Strange Friend*, to discover that there is hardly a single reference to the writer's birthplace in *Fox on My Door*. Martin enthuses over childhood travels: 'At last comes the night of going away . . . The journey starts in streets whose emptiness is like a secret' (*Fox on My Door* 22). This emptiness, this darkness, are images for the absence in the text which is Budapest, the first place left behind, obscured by a narrative of subsequent exilic departures for which it none the less constitutes the powerful but invisible motor. Martin's homeland barely rates a mention, except during the Spanish Civil War, that gathering of exiles par excellence, where Martin meets a Hungarian officer in the International Brigade, 'the handsomest devil of a Captain: black moustache, fiery eyes, curly hair' (*Fox on My Door* 76) – thus the very antithesis of the self-deprecating narrator. Hungarian, one might surmise, is what the narrator is not. It is significant that where *My Strange Friend*, for instance, describes the year the narrator, on his way to Palestine, spent 'in and around Budapest, the city of my birth' (a description repeated on the occasion of the writer's 1968 trip to Budapest) and recovered his Hungarian nationality (*My Strange Friend* 75–76, 280), *Fox on My Door* erases this place of origin. Foucault once commented that the search for origins is

> an attempt to catch the exact essence of things, . . . and their carefully protected identities, because this search assumes the existence of immobile forms that precede the external world of accident and succession. . . . What is found at the historical beginning of things is not the inviolable identity of their origin; it is the dissension of other things. It is disparity.[18]

Perhaps it is because of Martin's vigorous resistance to smug reflections of his own person, his awareness of the mobility of forms of subjectivity and their implication in the disturbances of history, that he is disinclined to anchor his own personality in an initial, and thus henceforth determining, but above all legitimizing, place. The absence of Budapest, where David Martin was born, is not simply an index of the early age at which he left the city with his family: for though he concedes in *My Strange Friend* that 'German, not Hungarian, is my mother tongue,' he nevertheless adds that 'I am pleased that something of Hungary remains in my background' by virtue of the Hungarian relatives on his father's side, a 'branch of the family which

[18] Michel Foucault, 'Nietzsche, Genealogy, History', in Donald F. Bouchard (ed.), *Language, Counter-Memory, Practice: Selected Essays and Interviews*, trans. Donald F. Bouchard and Sherry Simon (Ithaca: Cornell University Press, 1977), 142 ('Nietzsche, la généalogie, l'histoire', in Daniel Defert and François Ewald (eds), *Dits et écrits 1954–1988* (Paris: Gallimard, 1994), Vol. 2: 1970–1975, 138.

has produced artists and professional people, [to which] I feel close . . . I am not only my parents' child, I am the flesh of men and women stretching back into the dimmest past'; moreover, these connections extend into Martin's Australian present: regarding the 1956 events in Hungary, Martin speaks of 'our woes,' and Budapest relatives now living in Sydney maintain 'last links with my Hungarian past' (*A Fox on My Door* 9, 10, 248, 81). Rather, this absence functions to make every subsequent departure recorded in the novel a perpetuation of a process of exile in a life without an originary birthplace. In other words, the place of origin can only figure in this narrative as an absence, freeing the conception of identity and relationship presented in the narrative from the constrictions usually imposed by a site of identity. Mobility, in David Martin's autobiographical narrative, has been always already at work in the mobility of selfhood. In this way, the rationalizations with which rigid identities and exclusions are habitually conferred legitimacy are whisked away and replaced by a nomadism become the norm of existence – as a brutal fact of twentieth-century history, as a realistic appraisal of the production of subjectivity, and as a mode of thought to be appropriated in service of peaceful existence between human peoples.

Yet there is another, contrary trace of Hungary in the autobiography. David Martin's birthplace and a family link to that place, and the language spoken there, are discretely manifested in a photo of Grandmother Joszi included in the volume's endpapers – and simultaneously in a more prominent position, but stripped of accompanying commentary, as the central figure in a constellation of six photos on the dustcover, directly above a drawing of the eponymous fox/door-knocker symbolizing Martin's individualism and outsider persona. Significantly, the narrator tells us that it was Grandmother Joszi who encouraged the aspiring writer to persevere in his chosen vocation, and who may have been the recipient of his first poem (*A Fox on My Door* 46, 58). The photos thus offer an icon of a grandparent-grandchildren relationship and a tradition of creative thought passed on from generation to generation, motivating the autobiography's own didactic impulse. This photo, with its cardboard frame bearing an inscription in Hungarian (in the endpapers), figures the fixed place and imposed linguistic systems which David Martin contests as a coercive and limiting mode of thought, but which he nevertheless recognizes as essential to even the most liberatory pedagogic project. Some sort of a fixed basis for action is gestured at by the framing inscription informing the onlooker of the name of the Budapest 'Cabinet Portrait' where the photo was taken; the Hungarian inscription is representative of the inaugural gifts of language, nationality and familial identity later to be recast by the writing self ('David Martin is the name I adopted much later,' the narrator tells us, 'when I became a writer' – 16) and symbolizes the unavoidable limitations within which and starting from which human freedom must necessarily be exercised. Hungary, then, is not entirely absent from this autobiography: it is contained in the margins of the book, almost outside the text, and thus almost completely mute, but providing the preconditions for an education in exilic creative freedom. In this sense, then, the presence and absence of Hungary in this chronicle of a 'journey through [the writer's] life,' is expressive of the didactic burden that autobiography is made to bear in Martin's version of that genre, and of the dilemma thrown up by his project: on the one hand, the political imperative to educate a younger generation in the skills of striking out alone, away from the beaten track of coercive common sense in a process of intellectual nomadism; and on the other, the stable staking-out of clearly defined ethical territory entailed by the very same didactic project.

9 'Multiple Exposures': Spatial Dilemmas of Postmodern Artistic Identity in the Fiction of Janette Turner Hospital

At a reading in Cardiff in Wales in 1997, I asked David Malouf whether he believed Australian culture included a specific experience of space. In reply he mentioned instead an experience of time: that of being woken in the deep of night by callers telephoning from European daytime. Malouf's reply, far from avoiding the question, directly addresses the question of contemporary Australian experiences of space, indeed of postcolonial 'liminal' or 'peripheral' spaces more generally, by placing the issue in a global context. Australia, rather than being the land in which any news from Europe is already six months old upon arrival, as one character observes in Malouf's most recent tale of the early years of white settlement, is intimately linked to the rest of the world.[1] The 'tyranny of distance' is eradicated by the communications technology of the satellite telephone link, only to be replaced by the temporal confusion revealed in the inevitable bewildered enquiry upon picking up the receiver: 'What time is it there?' Australia's place within shrinking planetary dimensions produces temporal rifts of an unexpected sort.

This is an exemplary experience of what David Harvey has called postmodernist capitalism's 'universal fragmented space' in which heterogenous places are brought into hitherto unparalleled spatial proximity through the combined influence of telecommunications, modern transport, the flow of global capital and dispersal of the various elements of mechanisms of production.[2] The sense of fragmentation inherent in this new universality is pervasive: Fredric Jameson speaks of a loss of the capacity for 'cognitive mapping,' that is, of the capacity of our minds to map the global, multinational, communication networks in which we find ourselves caught up as individual subjects, only vaguely sensed as 'this latest evolutionary mutation of late capitalism towards "something else" which is no longer family or neighbourhood, city or state, nor even nation, but as abstract and nonsituated as the placelessness of a room in an international chain of hotels or the anonymous space of airport terminals that all run together in your mind.'[3] Similarly, in series of recent publications, Paul Virilio has described a culture in which dramatically increased mobility of transport, linked with a revolution in the media by virtue of which the technology of representation operates at constantly increasing speed, such that distances are cancelled out, place erased. This process is characterized not only by communicational possibilities opened up by the ubiquity of Internet connections, but also the coercive potential inherent in military technology and surveillance.[4] Likewise,

1 David Malouf, *The Conversations at Curlew Creek* (London: Chatto and Windus, 1997), 204.

2 David Harvey, *The Condition of Postmodernity: An Enquiry into the Origins of Cultural Change* (Oxford: Basil Blackwell, 1989), 239. See in particular Ch. 17, 'Time-Space compression and the postmodern condition'.

3 Fredric Jameson, *Postmodernism, or, The Cultural Logic of Late Capitalism* (London/New York: Verso, 1992), 44, 116.

4 Paul Virilio, *Vitesse et politique: Essai de dromologie* (Paris: Galilée, 1977); *Esthétique de la disparition* (1980; Paris: Livre de poche/Biblio essais, 1994); *L'Espace critique* (Paris: Christian Bourgeois, 1984).

Ulrich Beck has drawn attention to the increasing heterogeneity of the 'transnational' communities created in the wake of revolutions in transport and communication, the resistance of localities to total assimilation in global entities such as multinational concerns; dense networks of international contacts also ensure that received notions of identity, meaning and values are levered open by contact with other cultures (something that every expatriate has experienced in trying to negotiate the pitfalls of intercultural codes, even between the various linguistic communities of the English-speaking world).[5]

It is increasingly urgent to deal with textual, and in particular literary manifestations of postmodern shifts of spatial sense, in which experiences of postmodern disorientation are articulated and perhaps replied to. Such a task has been undertaken, for example, for the British context by Elmar Schenkel in his readings of contemporary regional British poetry. In the Australian context, similar reappraisals of spatial parameters have appeared in recent years, including such work as Paddy Roe's and Stephen Muecke's transcriptions of Aboriginal stories, which aim to reassert the presence of 'the black soil beneath the white,' Paul Carter's identification of early explorers' creative, dialogical naming of the Australian landscape rather than merely imposing foreign patterns of perception, or Philip Drew's privileging of the periphery of Australia as opposed to the traditional gaze directed towards the centre of the continent.[6]

In the fiction of the contemporary Australian-Canadian novelist Janette Turner Hospital, this process of disorientation and re-orientation is foregrounded under the sign of difference and plurality, going beyond the traditional geographical parameters of the nation-state, as already heralded by theoretical studies such as those of Ulrich Beck. Three of Janette Turner Hospital's novels, *Charades* (1988), *The Last Magician* (1992) and *Oyster* (1996), deal explicitly with the tension between shrinkage of spatial dimensions and the accompanying disruption of previously accustomed modes of presence and fixity which is a hallmark of modern global society; in particular, her work dramatizes versions of Australian identity based on scattered domiciles and divided cultural loyalties.[7] Her early novels, she has said, are 'about people constantly obsessed with places other than where they are at the moment . . . Even on a pragmatic level, when one has family in Australia, one is always aware of the two different time schemes: here and there. It affects my perception of things all the time.'[8]

5 See for instance Ulrich Beck, *Was ist Globalisierung?* (Frankfurt/Main: Suhrkamp, 1997).

6 Elmar Schenkel, *Sense of Place: Regionalität und Raumbewußtsein in der neueren britischen Lyrik* (Tübingen: Niemeyer, 1993); Stephen Muecke with Paddy Roe and Krim Benterrak, *Reading the Country: Introduction to Nomadology* (Fremantle: Fremantle Arts Centre Press, 1984), quotation from dust cover; Paul Carter, *The Road to Botany Bay: An Essay in Spatial History* (London: Faber, 1988). See also *The Lie of the Land* (London: Faber, 1996) and *Living in a New Country: History, Travelling and Language* (London: Faber, 1992); Philip Drew, *The Coast Dwellers: A Radical Reappraisal of Australian Identity* (Ringwood: Penguin, 1994).

7 All references to *Charades*, *The Last Magician* and *Oyster* are to the Virago (London) paperback editions of the texts and are signalled in the text by the abbreviations 'C', 'LM' and 'O' respectively.

8 Diana Brydon, 'The Stone's Memory: An Interview with Janette Turner Hospital', *Commonwealth Novel in English* (Spring 1991), 21.

In this chapter, I show that Hospital's novels are structured by an apparently unresolvable tension between spatial plurality, on the one hand, and a strong hermeneutic drive which assumes the possibility of a singular place of knowledge and narration, on the other. This contradiction is transformed into an ongoing process of production of identity and knowledge by an operation of spatialized interpretation. Hospital's fiction thus implies a version of 'Australian' identities which emerges out of a dialogue between 'Australia' and a transgression of geographical and national boundaries.

The links between global mobility, shifting or uncertain subjective identity, and the production of vertiginous semiotic ambiguity are dramatized by all of Janette Turner Hospital's novels. Many of her protagonists are Australians who live abroad in exile from their home (typically Queensland), living on the borders between several cultures (like Hospital herself, who divides her time between Canada, the USA and Australia, and who is as often featured on Canadian literature courses as Australian[9]). *Borderline* (1985), for instance, recounts the enigmatic encounter of an American gallery owner, a Canadian insurance salesman and a Salvadorean refugee at a border crossing; a collection of stories entitled *Dislocations* (1986) aptly describes the central problem which her fiction addresses: that of subjectivities and signifying systems both made and unmade by the acceleration of transport and communication and the extension of global economies in the contemporary world. *Charades*, *The Last Magician* and *Oyster*, however, as Turner Hospital's most recent books, are the texts which most prominently foreground these issues. *Oyster*, as a case in point, boldly proclaims that 'The writing of this novel was done in four different countries' – Australia, the UK, France and Canada (*Oyster* [v]). The overlap, manifest in this statement, between the spatial mobility of the writer, with its corresponding complications of national or cultural identity, and the multiple places of writing and pluralized narrative vantage points implied by that geographical multiplicity, is the theoretical nexus upon which this chapter is based.

These questions can of course be placed in the context of debates touching upon the rapidly changing spatial paradigms of Australian identities, particularly regarding relationships with trading partners and international neighbours in the Pacific region and the issue of Aboriginal land claims. Jurij Lotman has asserted that a narrative event is generated by a character's transgression of the boundaries of a semantic field, an observation which may be particularly pertinent in relation to Turner Hospital.[10] She articulates approximately the same thought in *Oyster*: 'The arrival of any foreigner changes the map' – with the significant addition: 'and foreigners spell the beginning of the end' (*Oyster* 11). Turner Hospital's narratives signal attempts to rearticulate space, to re-plot the reference points of increasingly mobile (inter)national identities which disturb the spatial certainties of an earlier era.

9 Turner Hospital is qualified as a 'Canadian' writer by Silvia Albertazzi, 'Beautiful Travellers: Some Notes on Postmodern Fiction', *Commonwealth Essays and Studies* 11:2 (Spring 1989), 53–62 and Graham Huggan, 'Orientalism Reconfirmed? Stereotypes of East-West Encounters in Janette Turner Hospital's *The Ivory Swing* and Yvon Rivard's *Les Silences du corbeau*', *Canadian Literature* 16:2 (1991), 182–96.

10 Jurij M. Lotman, *Die Struktur des künstlerischen Textes*, trans. Rainer Grübel, Walter Kroll and Hans-Eberhard Seidel (Frankfurt/Main: Suhrkamp, 1973), 350–58.

Significantly, Australia is always open to the outside world in these novels, always linked to other places whence the characters come or where they yearn to be. Her narratives register often disturbing and unwelcome changes in the topography of Australian identity. Both *Charades* and *The Last Magician* evoke the Anglocentric, xenophobic Australia of the 1950s and 1960, where 'all good little Australians' in the world of academia and letters would be 'rewarded with Oxford,' and when the schoolboy Charlie Chang's confident announcement, 'I was born in North Queensland, Mr Brady. I'm a true blue Aussie" could earn him the teacher's retort, 'Because a man's born in a stable, that doesn't make him a horse' (*Charades* 139/*The Last Magician* 43). In *Oyster*, shortly before the approaching millennium, the graziers and Outback town-dwellers of Outer Maroo are instilled with a siege mentality which harks back to the times before Feminism, Republicanism, Aboriginal land rights and the coming of 'foreigners.' Janette Turner Hospital's fiction signals the demise of a form of Australian identity based upon a determination to 'bash the difference out' (*The Last Magician* 77) – but whose decline is not without numerous rearguard skirmishes and a degree of resistance: in the Outback town at the end of the 1990s, a Greek-Australian visitor realizes that: 'It's *difference* that Australians hate . . . Melbourne or Athens, they're much the same to people out here' (*Oyster* 118). The multinational, multicultural composition of Hospital's narratives constitutes a sharp rejoinder to this aggressive parochialism. That Hospital's fiction appears to be reaching an increasingly large public and gaining the attention of the literary press more and more often indicates that her writing is not only energetic and entertaining, but that it does indeed address existential questions with which the contemporary reading public closely identifies. There have been some scattered critical reactions to Hospital's fiction, but none so far has touched upon the pressing question of the shifting map of Australian consciousness – perhaps in itself evidence of what Ulrich Beck has labelled a certain 'perplexity' in the face of global postmodernity, a perplexity shared by Australians no less than other inhabitants of the globe.[11] The present chapter aims to redress this curious absence by attempting to analyse the clear spatial and geographic import of Hospital's novelistic project.

Spatial confusion

It is clear that shifts in spatial references points, whether geographic, subjective or linguistic, generate confusion and insecurity. In Hospital's fiction, the paradigmatic expression of this confusion is that of losing one's way. Her recent novel, *Oyster*, can be seen to determine this theme retrospectively when the narrator Jess, a surveyor in an earlier life, describes the confusion of the motorist searching for Outer Maroo:

> somewhere far ahead, according to his map, are the dotted lines of the South Australian and Northern Territory borders, but he can see no sign of these poignant ideas of order. They leave no trace on the land . . . The translation of these markings from

[11] Ulrich Beck, *Risikogesellschaft. Auf dem Weg in eine andere Moderne* (Frankfurt/Main: Suhrkamp, 1986), 12.

> map to landscape is a psychic skill, in the exercise of which earnest map-readers may go astray and may wander into Outer Maroo.

Significantly, the *only* travellers who find the Outback opal town are those who have lost their way (*Oyster* 5, 6). The narrator of *The Last Magician* has recourse to Dante's *oscura selva* to describe her disorientation: 'In the middle of the journey, I came to myself in a dark wood where the straight way was lost. | No. That is not the way to put it. In the middle of darkness, I came to the black fact that there was *no* straight way – no way on, no way out' (*The Last Magician* 3). Reading Janette Turner Hospital's decidedly postmodernist fiction, which scrambles dream and reality, swaps various time planes and rocks from one fictional place to another, the reader gains the impression of total abandon of stable narrative orientation, of generalized spatial confusion.

But a modicum of order can be introduced into the experience of disorientation which characterizes these novels. One can make a distinction between spatial confusion caused by perception of contradictory aspects of reality, and spatial confusion produced by the contradictory character of artistic *representations* of that reality. The frequent feeling of *vertigo* which so often assails Hospital's characters, designating the intensely physical experience of a loss of fixed spatial coordinates, stems from two quite distinct sources.

The first variety of vertigo is precipitated by her characters' abrupt awareness of the contiguity of radically incompatible or conflicting social spheres, contradictory worlds which nevertheless share common borders. Charade mentions to Professor Koenig his deranged ex-wife, a permanently traumatized victim of the concentration camps, and immediately provokes an attack of giddiness in her interlocutor: 'The room spins . . . Nothing can be counted on to stay in its proper place' (*Charades* 5). This loss of coordinates gives physical form to Koenig's conviction of never being able to 'attain' his wife, who is caught in a separate nightmare world of her own where the constantly renewed fear of Nazi deportation never recedes into the past (*Charades* 206–7, 210). The photographer Charlie Chang descends into the quarry, a massive open-cut pit which plunges hundreds of meters deep beneath the impoverished inner-city Sydney suburb of Redfern, and extends into a complex of underground tunnels and passages running under the city. He is overcome by 'dizziness. He has to crawl back, he has to lean against the cliff face' (*The Last Magician* 93). The quarry gives concrete form to the social injustice of an Australian society of the near future, and at the same time, the threat which this underworld presents to the privileged ruling classes. Charlie's vertigo is not dissimilar to that of the schoolgirl Lucia confronted for the first time ever with the evidence of a world of poverty radically different from that of her own privileged private school. Lucia wonders later: 'how would she explain that day . . . when she suddenly saw that there were parallel worlds, that you could cross a line, that you could fall through a hairline crack and cartwheel giddily down and round and down in slow motion . . ..?' (*The Last Magician* 37–38). In each of these cases, disturbance of spatial reference points is motivated by the sudden consciousness of economic exploitation and oppression, always expressed, in Hospital's fiction, in terms of troubling spatial rifts and shifts.

A second form of vertigo is provoked by the work of art. In *Charades*, disorderly verbal narratives convey the chaotic form in which events are perceived and registered in human memory. Young Charade, listening to her Aunt Kay's erratic account of the improbable sighting of Charade's long since vanished father, cries, '"Wait, that's a switchback jump. I can't . . . How did we get to Toronto?" . . . "Aunt Kay, don't do this to me. We're in the refectory with my father, and then suddenly you're – "' (*Charades* 156–57). Charade's own lacunary syntax points up the inability of verbal language to deal with the acceleration of the narrative and the consequent spatial rifts that are thus opened up. Lucy, an older Lucia, experiences a new form of vertigo upon seeing one of Charlie Chang's postmodern art-house films, a 'mutational collage' of Queensland rainforest, Salgado photos of Mexican open-cut mines and paintings from the Vatican. The voice-over commentary shocks her:

> It is unmistakeably Charlie's voice. It reaches me from outside of time, it echoes, it causes vertigo and pain . . . The lens catches the braided water where it twists into a whorl around two boulders. I am looking into the eye of the whirlpool . . . Now, as though swaying or drunk, I seem to lose my footing or perspective . . . very clever, Charlie, though you're making me lose my sense of balance. (*The Last Magician* 58)

Charlie's film juxtaposes places geographically separate, and peoples them with persons long since vanished, persons who never met in reality; the connections made deeply disturb Lucy's sense of order and reality. The narrator of *Oyster* is aware of the same potential of narrative topsy-turvy, warning the reader that

> the facts may seem to float loose in a sequence of their own devising, much as a bunch of helium-filled balloons, their strings all reached from the same hand at the same moment in time . . . will certainly not reach you in a cluster . . . Some will veer north or south and never reach you at all. Some will spin on contrary winds and come back to you, days later, from further on. (*Oyster* 6–7)

In this most recent novel it is not only the characters who are confronted with bewildering narratives; the reader, too, is explicitly identified as being caught in the same dilemma. In Hospital's fictions we are rapidly shuttled back and forth between Sydney, Brisbane, London, Toronto and Boston at different periods of time, with little guidance through the labyrinth. *The Last Magician*, for example, includes at least four or five separate time layers, situated in different places, which the fragmented narrative structure renders only partially distinguishable. L2 literature students report utter bewilderment when confronted with Turner Hospital's juggling of place and time; many aspects of the narrative structure only become clear for them through discussion, or at a second reading.

This distinction between two forms of vertigo might appear fallacious, resting as it does upon the assumption that there is some sort of clearly marked distance between experienced reality and the representative power of art, whereas the very concept of vertigo – arising in the examples above out of fragmentation of unified places or juxtaposition of discrete places – logically abolishes the very basis for such a distinction. Yet at the same time, the very idea of vertigo as an aberrant experience suggests that the *desire* for spatial order is deep-seated, rooted in a physical sense of orientation long before becoming affective or psychological. That characters such as Charade express dismay at the odd twists and turns of her Aunt Kate's story, that the narrator of *Oyster* believes it necessary to warn the reader of impending narrative dispersion, speak for the strong urge, in Hospital's narratives, to put things in their right place, to understand the world.

The hermeneutic drive

The forms of vertigo provoked by spatial dislocation in these novels presume a spatial order in representations of the world, but paradoxically, testify to the illusory character of that order; the moment of giddiness arises from the discovery that assumptions of spatial fixity (Charade's unified private-school world, Charlie's aboveground sense of orientation) are inadequate versions of reality because partial, in the double sense of *biased* and *incomplete*. Jess, for instance, claims that linear narrative is based on an occlusion of the narrator's viewpoint; if a different viewpoint is chosen, the linear progression which will emerge will be very different: 'I do know that time does not run in a straight line, and never has. It is a capillary system, mapped outwards from whichever pulse point the observer occupies . . . To put this another way, stepping into a story or constructing a map are much the same thing' (*Oyster* 47). As John Berger has said, 'It is scarcely possible any longer to tell a straight story unfolding in time. And this is because we are too aware of what is continually traversing the storyline *laterally*.'[12] This collapsing of linear narratives into dispersed localized places where versions of reality are constructed perhaps accounts for the frequent switching between first-, second- and third-person narrative in Hospital's fictions. The characters' (and perhaps readers') feeling of vertigo arises out of confrontation with the constructed nature of accounts of reality; the sense of giddiness associated with the dislocations of the work of art arise from the fact that it too disturbs the same (fallacious) sense of things staying 'in their proper place' (*The Last Magician* 10). Yet the idea that apparent linear order is a mere facade to be torn away to reveal an underlying spatial dispersion none the less implies the assumption that this underlying disorder also has a governing logic, if one not immediately apparent. The inadequacy of maps to describe the situation of Outer Maroo (the dislocation which upsets the representational order of map-making) actually transpires to be motivated by an illegal economic order: Outer Maroo has been erased from the maps so that outsiders will not investigate the shady opal deals taking place there *(Oyster* 64). It is for this reason, then, that Hospital's novels are inhabited by a powerful hermeneutic drive despite their apparent vitiation of such a paradigm.

The quest which drives the plots of Hospital's fictions ('I'm looking for someone' Charade announces to Koenig at their first meeting [*Charades* 4]; Lucy is searching for Gabriel, Catherine for Charlie, Charlie for Cat, Mercy goes searching for Brian, Sarah and Nick are searching for their children Amy and Angelo respec-

12 Quoted in Edward W. Soja, *Postmodern Geographies: The Reassertion of Space in Critical Social Theory* (London: Verso, 1989), 22.

tively – and the author too describes herself as an 'urgent quester'[13]) is a search for a single, stable place. Xavier Pons has pointed out the unicity inherent in Charades' parents' names: Verity and Truman.[14] She is determined to discover the origin of her own existence. Lucy is tormented by the problem of determining an originary chronological site where a linear narrative can be anchored and thus made to offer up a logical explanation of subsequent events: 'I cannot start there' she says, thinking of Cedar Creek Falls, where Cat's bones were discovered (*The Last Magician* 3). The same search for origins drives Gabriel's similarly spatialized investigation of the underside of Sydney wealth and power. It is the haunting enigma of his parents' estrangement which propels a second version of quest in Hospital's fiction, the question of 'how to read meaning in appearances,' which Deborah Bowen sees as the author's 'fundamental concern.'[15] Gabriel's effort to uncover the reality behind appearances leads him into a wider-ranging interrogation of 'something lurking *beneath* his father's dogma: heresy perhaps; a countertruth; a lie' (*The Last Magician* 265–66; my emphasis). The vertical metaphors of interpretative depth are ubiquitous: 'Gabriel mapped the quarry,' 'the city's *underside*,' the literal underside of the illegal operations of the likes of Judge Robinson Gray, just as the underground opal mines of Oyster's Reef are the literal underside of Andrew Godwin's and Dukke Prophet's shady financial dealing with American hamburger concerns, Singapore jewel wholesalers and arms traders in *Oyster* (*The Last Magician* 265, 199; my emphasis). Finally, the search for chronological origins or the reality behind appearances takes on an ethical as well as an interpretative character: says Lucy, 'You do actually meet people who make you want to keep on looking' – 'Looking for what?' – 'Oh you know, *goodness*, *meaning*, crap like that. One throw in a hundred' (*The Last Magician* 33). This assertion of 'redemptive' meaning, as Charlotte Clutterbuck has noticed, is the apex of the paradoxical prominence of search in narratives which otherwise display purely contingent, constantly shifting spatial parameters.[16]

It should be stressed that these narratives do not dispute the reality of the historical events which generate their narratives or their narration. In *Charades*, the disappearance of Verity Ashkenazy's parents in the concentration camps, which indirectly leads to Charade being abandoned by her parents Verity and Nicholas; in *The Last Magician*, the death of Willy, the rape of Cat and Charlie and Catherine after Cat's trial, and the subsequent presumed murder of Cat; in *Oyster*, the arrival of Oyster in Outer Maroo and the destruction of his religious clan – these are the traumatic events out of which the narratives flow, and without which narrative would not be initiated. But their traumatic force, generating pain and guilt, is such that they can never be related with any semblance of factual objectivity. Such events can only

13 Christine Hamelin, '"Novelist as Urgent Quester": An Interview with Janette Turner Hospital', *Australian and New Zealand Studies in Canada* 9 (June 1993), 106.

14 Xavier Pons, 'History and Her Story: The Deconstruction and Reconstruction of the Past in Janette Turner Hospital's *Charades*', *Caliban* 29 (1992), 146.

15 Deborah Bowen, 'Borderline Magic: Janette Turner Hospital and Transfiguration by Photography', *Studies in Canadian Literature/Etudes en littérature canadienne* 16:2 (1991), 184.

16 Charlotte Clutterbuck, 'A Shared Depository of Wisdom: Connection and Redemption in *The Tiger in the Tiger Pit* and *Possession*', *Southerly* 52:3 (June 1993), 121.

ever be told from several mutually exclusive narrative vantage points, and often at several removes: how does one reconcile the views of a vanished Nicolas Truman proffered by Bea, who has remained in Queensland, and Kay who fled to Canada? Lucy's intention to 'follow a thin thread of truth through a dark wood' (*The Last Magician* 131) is patently undermined by the dislocations of the narrative we receive through her voice.

Thus the hermeneutic urge has an extraordinarily problematic position in the fiction of Janette Turner Hospital. It presupposes the capacity of narrative to offer up identity, truth, unambiguous chains of causal connection, and distinct separation of time and place at which and in which events 'take place.' But this urge is embedded in a narrative whose voices are multiple, dispersed, contradictory, and which never tire of pointing this out to the reader. To foreground such narrative relativity and plurality clearly strips away the facade of fallacious objectivity, but it may also vitiate the possibility of any reliable place from which a critique of illusion and ideology may be launched. Kate Temby claims of *The Last Magician*, 'the novel's self-conscious questioning and metafictional narrative form subvert the possibility of its providing a comprehensive or effective critique of oppressive power structures'[17] – it could be said that the same impotence to establish a stable place from which to interpret the world also trammels Turner Hospital's narrative project. However, it may be well be that this selfsame erosion of singular spatiality in her fiction also furnishes a new and unexpected variety of truth guarantee. The resolution of this contradiction can perhaps be achieved, though never completely, her texts suggest, by playing off the spatial disruptions of narrative art against the spatial disruptions of social reality.

Spatial interpretation

Most forms of identity are structured by an exclusive either/or: A = non-B. Janette Turner Hospital resists such dualistic constructions of truth. Professor Koenig, for instance, is fascinated by the idea that two mutually contradictory theories can both be right, and consequently comes to the paradoxical conclusion that he never was, on the one hand, married to his elusive ex-wife, and on the hand, will never cease to be married to her (*Charades* 94, 210); likewise, Bea say to Charades, at the end of the novel, 'Verity's your mother. But me and Nicholas made you, that's the truth' (*Charades* 285). The wealthy citizens of Sydney delude themselves that their comfortable neighbourhoods are safely sealed off from the threatening world of the quarry, and implement such wishful thinking by a ruthless politics of 'triage.' But in reality, Lucy claims, 'The quarry is leaking into the city, and the city is slipping quarrywards. Everyone knows this, but everyone denies it.' Dualistic social order is based upon the officially sanctioned violence of 'containment'; the mutual contamination of these two opposed terms cannot, however, be halted (*The Last Magician* 89–90). These versions of truth based on binary oppositions are replaced in Turner Hospital's fiction by less reductive triangular structures.

[17] Kate Temby, 'Gender, power and postmodernism in *The Last Magician*', *Westerly* 40:3 (Spring 1995), 47.

It is significant that in *Charades* and *The Last Magician*, the attempt to ascertain truth is always mediated across several generations. It is Charade who interrogates Bea and Aunt Kate to find out about the slightly older Verity and Nicholas; it is Lucy who recounts Charlie's version of the experiences with Cat, Catherine and Robbie Gray. By extension, the novels' own *mise-en-abyme* of the functioning of the work of art is based on the same mediating instance separating (and/or linking) 'truth' and the artist. Charade's quest for her own truth is carried out by filtering her questions across others' reactions. She uses Koenig as a sounding board to try out her various hypothetical narratives of her own origin; and it is Aunt Kay's returning the young visitor's gaze with a fleeting look of recognition ('the way she looked at me, the shock in her eyes') which Charades reads, arriving at the crucial third version of her own origin (*Charades* 272). The interpretive path is not dual, proceeding from subject to object, but triple, rather like the working of Jess's surveying instruments which emit high-pitched signals, in turn bounced off the faraway geographical feature and returned to the receiver (*Oyster* 158). Charlie's obsessive photography also expands the dual subject-object gaze into a third dimension as the original moment of perception is re-run and subjected to scrutiny: Charlie claims to take photos 'So I'll see what I've seen' (*The Last Magician* 36). Lucy's narrative opens with a similar example of self-reflection: 'In the middle of the journey, I came to myself in a dark wood where the straight way was lost . . . *Ah, how hard a thing it is to tell of that wood*' (*The Last Magician* 3). Her self-recognition, her self-recollection is provoked by the mediating influence of Charlie's film, and reinforced by the emphatic secondary mediation of Dante's epic, and by more discrete mediation of her own problematic attempt at narrative. Whether the doubling of the self by virtue of the mediating instance (listener in the case of narrative, or photograph in the case of visual art) the same effect ensues: with the creation of self-reflexivity, distance, a new form of self-knowledge is produced.

Not only self-knowledge, but also knowledge of others, can be gained in this way. Both Charlie in *The Last Magician* and Jess in *Oyster* are taciturn characters whose reserve provokes others to 'colonise silence with their unburdenings' ('Silence, Charlie said, seduces'), 'a wall or a boulder, or perhaps as a rock cavern in the breakaways, hollow, receptive, capable of the infinite absorption of sound, a black hole that gave nothing back' (*The Last Magician* 83, *Oyster* 165). Faced with an apparently impassive silence, the garrulous reveal themselves. The listener is at once intercalary surface (like Koenig for Charades) and careful observer. A more active form of production of knowledge, and another clear example of triangular structures of knowledge, is that utilized by Charlie with his enigmatic Chinese riddles, or equally, his photographic collages. These conundrums oblige the hearers or spectators to create a meaning out of the rebus with which they are confronted, a meaning is of their own making. The riddle-teller or artist can then read off the meaning produced out of the interaction between art, spectator and artist-observer. Charlie's photo montages offer various potential meanings which are not directly stated, but which the spectator must assemble her- or himself: 'There is no order, no sequence . . . The sequence is determined by the viewer, a magician of sorts, who must shuffle the crossed destinies and read the cards. Meaning is in the eye of the beholder . . .' (*The Last Magician* 243). Accordingly, Robinson Gray tacitly admits guilt when confronted by Lucy's juxtaposition of photos of Gabriel, of Sheba with Cat's hair clip, and of herself at Cedar Creek Falls. 'So you know,' says Gray, producing, by his own implicit confession, the potential knowledge to be gained from the photos' mute contiguity and suggestion of causal connection (*The Last Magician* 233, 339). The references to Hamlet in this novel are no coincidence, pointing as they do towards an age-old dramatizing of indices of guilt (*The Last Magician* 32, 71). Here again, the production of knowledge is a ternary process.[18]

Charlie's collage art produces knowledge by a process of combination and juxtaposition (one thinks of Nietzsche's 'Denken ist ein Herausheben'[19]). The description of Charlie's flat might equally well apply to the artworks it contains: 'Space. That is what the apartment celebrates: the mysterious quality of space, and the way it draws attention to single objects placed judiciously within it, and the way these isolated objects, in turn, give space a form' (*The Last Magician* 46). Both the relations within the artwork, and between artwork and spectator are productive of knowledge. Here, knowledge is not an inert pre-existent entity to be absorbed in the way one might learn facts or dates or vocabulary, but is produced in ways that cannot be predicted or controlled by contingent interactions and relationships. Charlie's collages exemplify a form of spatial knowledge based on relations of contiguity, rather than the relations of identity inherent in putatively 'objective' knowledge.[20] The collage method is thus entirely contextual, both in the possible relations asserted by the mute juxtaposition of images, and in the specific, local place of production of knowledge. Robinson Gray's 'So you know' proves nothing, is not a form of objective knowledge; it is subjective, or better, intersubjective. It is no coincidence that Turner Hospital cites Werner Heisenberg – 'What we observe is not nature itself, but nature exposed to our method of questioning' (*Charades* 288) – for the mode of triadic knowledge which her fiction dramatizes is productive, local, contingent and always inherently social. Janette Turner Hospital's fictional artworks offer a riposte to the pessimism of a critic such as Peter Zima, who claims that Brechtian *Verfremdung*, as an exemplary form of the cognitive-critical role played by art in the era of modernism, has today lost the stable site from which it could unmask ideology. All that is left to art is to cater to aesthetic enjoyment or to figure as 'provocation with-

18 There are many instances of such ternary processes of production of identity or meaning in contemporary social sciences: Lacan's theory of the constitution of the psyche through the social mediation of language, Anzieu's conception of the production of subjectivity through interpersonal epidermic contact; Girard's notion of mimetic desire; Peirce's triadic semiotic structure of object-sign-interpretant; Antony Pym's theory of third-party translators. These theorists are often in disagreement (see for example Didier Anzieu on Lacan, *Une Peau pour la pensée: Entretiens avec Gilbert Tarrab* [Paris: Clancier-Guérard, 1986]), but they all stress the socially mediated production of identity and meaning.

19 Günter Wohlfart (ed.), *Nietzsche – Die nachgelassenen Fragmente: Eine Auswahl* (Stuttgart: Reclam, 1996), 30.

20 See Allan Pred, 'Re-Presenting the Extended Present Moment of Danger: A Meditation on Hypermodernity, Identity and the Montage Form', in Georges Benko and Ulf Strohmeyer (eds), *Space and Social Theory: Interpreting Modernity and Postmodernity* (Oxford: Blackwell, 1997), 117–40. Particularly interesting in this context is Paul Carter's 'Post-Colonial Collage: Aspects of a Migrant Aesthetic', in *Living in a New Country: History, Travelling and Language*, 186–98.

out truth content.'[21] Hospital's fiction points to a way out of this bleak alternative. Accepting that there is no 'outside' of textuality, or of the power mechanisms of late capitalism, for that matter, Janette Turner Hospital creates a new form of the 'critical distance' upon which, according to Fredric Jameson, left cultural politics has traditionally depended and which seems to have been abolished in the cultural space of postmodernism.[22] Hospital herself comments upon the situation of her narrators *in media res*, or as Lucy says, 'the way the teller inserts herself into the tale' (*The Last Magician* 71).[23] She renews aesthetic critical distance by installing a refraction of disparate vantage points within the shifting and multiple outlooks of contemporary culture. It is a mode of knowledge which, like her novels, offers no final answers, no dialectical closure or resolution of contradictions, but rather an open-ended dialogue and experimentation: a mode of knowledge which is thus resolutely postmodern, following Hutcheon's anti-dialectical characterization of the concept.[24] As Lucy says, 'All I can do is feel my way, advancing, retreating, positing theories, testing, rejecting, going in circles and always covering new ground. Everything I say is provisional . . . I spin my webbed translations as I go' (*The Last Magician* 85).[25]

It is significant that there are no examples of triadic artistic productivity in *Oyster*. Rather, the triadic structure has been shifted out of the narrated tale into the act of narration itself. Turner Hospital's use of second-person narrative directly addresses the reader as a member of the narrator-narration-narratee triad: 'I want you to understand why the telling is complicated . . . Time is a trickster, and so is space, but the air . . . is a conjurer who likes to juggle both space and time: the things themselves, as well as your perception of the two. | You probably know this' (*Oyster* 7). This second-person mode of address implicitly raises the question of the productive relationship created in the act of reading a novel by Janette Turner Hospital. Significantly, the process of 'triangulation' is mentioned explicitly by the erstwhile surveyor Jess as a repressive mechanism, when remarking upon the fact that the members of Oyster's sect always come to town in groups of three: 'The triangle is the most stable of forms, they said, and points in all directions to God. | Triangulation, I told them, is a slow and most painful form of death' (*Oyster* 84). Two issues are raised by the contrast between these contrasting modes of 'triangulation.' The first concerns the types of knowledge produced. Sectarian triangulation is structured so as to defend dogmas rather than to place them under a critical light. Hospital, in contrast, resists that notion that her novels should overtly preach a political credo: 'I am not writing propaganda, or didactic art. I simply want to stir my readers to feel that they do have to reach a political stance, but I'm not in

21 Peter V. Zima, *Modern/Postmoderne: Gesellschaft, Philosophie, Literatur* (Tübingen/Basel: Francke/UTB, 1997), 255.

22 Fredric Jameson, *Postmodernism*, 48. See also Ross Chambers, *Room for Maneuver: Reading (the) Oppositional (in) Narrative* (Chicago: Chicago University Press, 1991), xi–xx.

23 Janette Turner Hospital, 'Letter to a New York Editor', *Meanjin* 47:3 (Spring 1988), 562.

24 Linda Hutcheon, *A Poetics of Postmodernism: History, Theory, Fiction* (London: Routledge, 1988), x.

25 See also the excellent article by David Callahan, 'Acting in the Public Sphere and the Politics of Memory in Janette Turner Hospital', *Tulsa Studies in Women's Literature*, 15:1 (1996), in particular 74–76, 79–80.

the business of telling them what that is.'[26] Triangulation as it is dramatized and practised in Turner Hospital's novels ought to function as an unstable, provocative, non-coercive form of enlivening knowledge. The second issue concerns the type of community produced by triadic relationships. *Oyster*'s sectarian threesomes are designed to exert surveillance and to prevent deviation from the norm; the closure of these coercive triplets is, in fact, closely related to the claustrophobia of Outer Maroo with its rejection of novelty, change and foreigners – a form of social introversion which proves to be self-destructive in the last analysis. The reading triad, on the other hand, leaves the position of the reader open to all and sundry, and makes available a stance allowing both passionate involvement and critical distance.[27] Thus the triadic structure combining the ostensibly mutually exclusive terms of belonging and exile, of objectivity and subjectivity, of assent and dissent, can be seen also to offer a tentative model for (inter-) or (trans)national identities.[28] Turner Hospital's fiction provides a partial response to contemporary questions of who we are and where we belong. Her 'spatial collage' enacts a 'reverse explosion' (*Charades* 279), through which a spatialized identity begins to cohere, but as an ongoing construction which is never complete, constantly displaying a tension between closure and openness. This is not necessarily a self-vitiating structure, but can exist as a dialogue, where pluralism guarantees that identity does not harden into dogmatism, and where identity guarantees that pluralism does not topple over into lack of ethical direction or axiological content.[29]

To David Malouf's simile of confusing telephone conversations in which time and space are simultaneously telescoped and fragmented, Janette Turner replies with the concept of 'multiple exposure.' Felicity in *Borderline* describes, in a way which prefigures Charlie Chang of *The Last Magician*, 'her night-time collages, a multiple exposure, a Perugino superimposed on a Bosch or a Munch.' An apparently singular visual artefact encompasses pluralized temporal and spatial relationships which are at once radically incommensurate and productive of meaning when taken up by an observer. Felicity's life itself has been a 'multiple-exposure life' and the reader senses that this is the way in which Turner Hospital conceives her own nomadic existence, the creative process by which her novels are written, and the model she proposes for modes of social interaction in the new local-global society in which we now live.[30]

[26] Christine Hamelin, '"Novelist as Urgent Quester"': An Interview with Janette Turner Hospital', 107.

[27] See Julian Cowley, '"Violent Times': Janette Turner Hospital's Art of Memory and the History of the Present', in Sarah Sceats and Gail Cunningham (eds), *Image and Power: Women and Fiction in the Twentieth Century* (London: Longman, 1996), 178–79, 181–82.

[28] See Beck, *Was ist Globalisierung?*, 55–61, 127–35.

[29] See Peter V. Zima, *Moderne/Postmoderne*, 367–401.

[30] Turner Hospital, *Borderline* (London: Virago, 1990), 35, 16.

10 Double-Crossing One Nation: Contemporary Asian-Australian Narratives

Australia is one of the few nations of the world to be endowed with the dubious blessing of a coastline which is coextensive with the boundaries of its nationhood. The equivalence of geographical and political borders has allowed Australia all too easily to believe in the givenness of its own social/racial boundaries, and has reinforced an Anglocentric tendency to indulge in fantasies of social homogeneity from the very beginnings of European settlement of the fifth continent.[1] These fantasies were reinforced by the legal doctrine of *terra nullius* which legitimized the European annexation of the land at the cost, genocidal in its dimensions as is now increasingly clear, of the indigenous inhabitants of the country. They have also been underpinned by the policy of a white Australia which has dictated Australia's image of itself since graduation to nation-statehood in 1901, with the exception of a brief 'multicultural' interlude between the mid 1960s and the mid 1990s. This fantasy of unicity was made explicit by the name of Pauline Hanson's rightwing One Nation Party which dominated public debate for several years in the late 1990s, or John Howard's 'One Australia' election policies in the same period.

It is a unicity and simplicity which is patently mendacious and always has been. Even Australia has always had a geography more complex than its coast – as was evinced by the Howard government's efforts to redefine the linear borders of the country by 'excising' anomalies such as offshore territories and islands from the 'immigration zone' so as to eliminate them as potential immigration footholds for asylum seekers. The social unicity of Australia is a myth equally flimsy. Even the originary, founding moment of the First Fleet's arrival at Botany Bay in 1788 saw a motley crew of convicts, including a five-percent contingent of non-white felons, many of them re-transported ex-slaves, establishing the nascent colony.[2] The perennial heterogeneity of Australian society has almost continuously suffered repression in the public domain: 'the tendency has been that instead of defining itself, and realizing itself as a continually changing society, [Australia] has nostalgically yearned for stasis, drawing on a large number of myths which, while uniting segments of its population, retard its overall ability to absorb newness and deal adequately with others.'[3]

In this chapter I examine the writing of Australia by Asian Australians as one of several recent attempts to break down illusions of unicity and redefine Australia as a society with blurred boundaries, inhabited by a diversity of cultures, and by the

1 See Ien Ang, 'Racial/Spatial Anxiety: "Asia" in the psychogeography of Australian whiteness', in Ghassan Hage and Roanna Couch (eds), *The Future of Australian Multiculturalism: Reflections of the Twenetieth Anniversary of Jean Martin's 'The Migrant Presence'* (Sydney: The Research Institute for Humanities and Social Sciences, 1999), 189–204.

2 Hsu-Ming Teo, 'Future Fusions and a Taste for the Past: Literature, History and the Imagination of Australianness', in Kate Darian Smith (ed.), *Challenging Histories: Reflections on Australian History*, Special issue of *Australian Historical Studies* 118 (2002), 132.

3 Brian Castro, *Looking for Estrellita* (St Lucia, QLD: University of Queensland Press, 1999), 145.

same token, possessing strong allegiances beyond its putative cultural-coastal perimeters. The import of such a cultural project is not to be underestimated. White Australia has never been chary of declaring its cultural allegiances to far-off Britain, or more recently, its political allegiances to far-off America. However, Australia has traditionally maintained a cultural *cordon sanitaire* with regard to its genuine neighbours along the South-East Asian and Pacific seaboard. Asia is the 'proximate other' related via a 'perverse dynamic'[4] to whom real geographical and regional links have existed since time immemorial. Such connections have been present from the Makasarese visitors with whom the Northern Australian indigenous peoples traded,[5] via the Chinese goldminers of the 1850s and their descendents (typically market gardeners) in the successive decades, to the large Asian-Australian population of the present day. In 1991, 4.9 per cent of the Australian population had been born in an Asian country; in 1996, the figure was estimated at 6.2 per cent; the 2006 census found that 8 per cent of the population was of Asian descent.[6] But public discourse has generally forgotten or ignored these ongoing contacts just as it continues to evince unease with the current changes in Australian society.

Australia in Asia, Asia in Australia

In the mid 1960s, Donald Horne had to remind Australians which part of the world their nation was actually situated in:

> It is usually said that Australia is a part of European civilization transplanted to the big south land and it now finds itself in the alien world of Asia. What can be said at once is that Australians do not yet seem to know where they are . . . It may be worthwhile remembering exactly where Australia is. It lies south of Indonesia and the rest of South-East Asia – Malaysia, the Philippines, Vietnam, Laos, Cambodia, Thailand, Burma, a subcontinent containing almost as many people as there are in Africa. Dominating this sub-continent are the sub-continents of India and China, with more than a third of the world's population . . . This is the strategic world of Australia.[7]

By the early 1990s, under the leadership of a Prime Minister such as Paul Keating, the motif of Australia's strong connections with Asian had become common currency – clearly part of a pragmatic strategic trade policy, as Horne's statement thirty years earlier had already stressed. It is perhaps for this reason that this sense of being part of Asia was so fleeting, with John Howard in his 1996 maiden speech as Prime

4 Jonathan Dollimore, *Sexual Dissidence: Augustine to Wilde, Freud to Foucault* (Oxford: Oxford University Press, 1991), 33–35.

5 See Regina Ganter, *Mixed-Relations: Asian-Aboriginal Contact in North Australia* (Crawley WA: University of Western Australia Press, 2006).

6 Ien Ang, 'Asians in Australia: A Contradiction in Terms?', in John Docker and Gerhard Fischer (eds), *Race, Colour and Identity in Australia and New Zealand* (Sydney: University of New South Wales Press, 2000), 116; Australian Bureau of Statistics: http://www.census data.abs.gov.au. Accessed 24 April 2011.

7 Donald Horne, *The Lucky Country: Australia in the Sixties* (Ringwood, VIC: Penguin, 1964), 81.

Minister claiming that Australia was being 'swamped by Asians.' Several months later he told the Indonesian Prime Minister Suharto that 'Australia does not claim to be Asian,' and the Australian public again some time after that 'Australia does not need to choose between its [Anglo-Celtic] history and its [Pacific Basin] geography.' Even the opposition leader Kim Beazley confirmed that 'Mr Howard should dispense with the message of his recent Asian trip that Australians were not Asians . . . Nobody ever claimed that we were.'[8] Only with the later arrival in office of Kevin Rudd would Australia actually see a Prime Minister fluent in a major Asian language.

Asia is the inveterate Other of white Australia, then as now, as has become patently clear at the turn of the century. The threatening otherness of Asia is a component of cultural identity embedded so deeply in the depths of Anglo-Australia's fantasmic sense of selfhood that it is difficult to deal with the real presence of Asian Australians in the fabric of everyday contemporary Australian society. Castro remarks on

> the huge reality of Asians in Australia and their virtual non-existence in this country's cultural consciousness. The heritage of Australian film and television occupies a museum-space where Asians are depicted as never having left the Burma Railway or the Killing Fields. As the gratuitous Other, they have no narrative position. They do not feature as part of everyday Australian life or of the sanctified Australian Family. They are either silent, or they make strange noises.[9]

In a similar vein, Ien Ang points out that

> there is still hardly any public recognition in Australia of Asian Australians as subjects of representation, as intellectuals, artists, or writers vigorously intervening in, and making inroads into the dominant culture, as active makers of culture in their own right, whether confined within their particular migrant communities or, more ambitiously, in dynamic exchange and interaction with their 'non-Asian' partners, co-workers, colleagues, and co-citizens. There is even less recognition of the complex set of transnational relations and cross-cultural social formations of Asian Australians, connections that may be social, political and economic and which may span several continents and dramatically impact upon everyday experiences of Asians living in Australia and, in turn, on Australian culture more generally.[10]

Khoo concurs in claiming that 'The citizenship of Chinese Australians . . . is, demonstrably, not a "natural" (white) right,' explaining that '[i]n contemporary society, Chinese-Australian citizens still struggle with being "visibly different" while remaining hegemonically "invisible" and mostly inaudible when it comes to

8 Fiona Nicoll, *From Diggers to Drag Queens: Reconfigurations of Australian Identity* (Annadale, NSW: Pluto Press, 2001), 136–37, 144.

9 Castro, *Looking for Estrellit*, 213.

10 Ien Ang, 'Introduction: Alter/Asian Cultural Interventions for 21st Century Australia', in Ien Ang, Sharon Chalmers, Lisa Las and Mandy Thomas (eds), *Alter/Asians: Asian-Australian Identities in Art, Media and Popular Culture*. (Annadale, NSW: Pluto Press, 2000), xv–xvi.

influencing or implementing specific educational, social or governmental changes.'[11]

These trends are reflected in the domain of culture narratives and 'storytelling.' Jon Stratton observes that 'while Australia has had a non-discriminatory migration policy since the early 1970s, it is only in the 1990s . . . that any Asian people have been narrativised as part of Australian society.'[12] Brian Castro dryly comments that 'Two hundred years of white settlement in proximity with Asia has produced few Australian writers capable of writing with any inside knowledge of an Asian country, let alone writing in an Asian language. . . . Asia has yet to visit the psyche of most Australian writers.'[13]

Whence the importance of cultural, especially literary interventions which seek to erode the notion of culture and cultural allegiance as a singular phenomenon. For it is only as such narratives of singular cultural belonging diminish in significance that the hegemony of Anglo-normality will lose its iron grip and that stigmatization attached to 'otherness' will diminish. This is not something which is desired by the majority of Australians today, it would seem, if the support for the stricter draconian immigration policies is any indicator. It is also not clear whether fictional re-castings of unitary white culture can compete in a significant way with the hegemony of talkback radio and the tabloid press. Castro remarks without illusions, 'Relatively few people have read my work and it is certainly not mainstream . . . As a writer I am very much in the minority anyway.'[14] But such riders do not change one white the ethical necessity of 'writing back' against the one-nation, one-culture mentality. This, I argue in what follows, is the task implicitly undertaken by several Asian-Australian novelists over the past two decades. Brian Castro typifies this attitude when he says:

> As a migrant, as a citizen of this country, I do feel a responsibility for promoting difference. There is a real need to take a good hard look at Australia's future. If it cannot interact with Asia (and no nation can interact with another if it only trades at a distance and refuses cultural gestures and exchanges of populations) then it will waste a lot of its resources maintaining itself like an outstation of Antarctica. The thing is, change is rapid and unexpected. How quickly did Hong Kong hotel menus change from Australian beef to New Zealand lamb! Almost overnight. Hong Kong visitors to New Zealand now do not require visas. Unfortunately culture is not as visible or marketable as beef or lamb. It requires years to establish and false moves made by the current Australian government will reverberate for decades to come. Yes, there is a crying need to foster alternative cultures now.[15]

11 Tseen Khoo, 'Re-Siting Australian Identity', in Wenche Ommundsen (ed.), *Bastard Moon: Essays on Chinese-Australian Writing* [special issue of *Otherland Literary Journal* 7 (July 2001), 98, 105

12 Jon Stratton, *Race Daze: Australia in Identity Crisis* (Annadale, NSW: Pluto Press, 1998), 17.

13 Castro, *Looking for Estrellita*, 152, 164.

14 Ouyang Yu, 'An Interview with Brian Castro', *Bastard Moon: Essays on Chinese-Australian Writing*, Special Issue of *Otherland Literary Journal* 7 (July 2001), 78.

15 Yu, *An Interview with Brian Castro*, 80.

Doubling, chiasmus, tripling

In this chapter I read three novels, published at roughly ten-year intervals from the 1980s to the turn of the century: Brian Castro's *Birds of Passage* (1983), often hailed as the first Asian-Australian novel, Yasmine Gooneratne's *A Change of Skies* (1991) and Hsu-Ming Teo's *Love and Vertigo* (2000). In each text I pursue topoi of double textuality, double history and double culture. Doubleness stands in these texts for cultural multiplicity. In contemporary Australia, a country where one in six marriages is inter-ethnic, 'double' cultural allegiance is increasingly obsolescent, as partners whose identity is already 'hyphenated' marry others with a similarly hybrid background. In a study of language and ethnicity in Australia, Allan and Carmen Luke note that

> less than a third of the partners we interviewed [from 55 inter-ethnic couples] could be identified as from a single racial/geographic point of origin (for example, Chinese, Japanese, Filipino). The majority were diasporic Asians of already hyphenated self-identification that mixed the census category of place of birth with an ascribed ethnicity/race: as, for instance, Timorese-Chinese, PNG-born Chinese, Anglo-Indians, Fiji-Indians and so forth.[16]

Clearly, doubleness is no longer an adequate descriptive category for taking account of the cultural allegiances of Australian citizens at the present time. It has already been overtaken by more diverse complexes of cultural hybridization. Indeed, with its suggestions of symmetry and dualism it may be deceptively simplistic and 'balanced,' whereas the meeting places of diverse cultures are generally sites of turbulence and transformation. The significance of doubleness is thus symbolic, indexing a radical overhaul of monocultural norms. Such ambivalences are teased out by Brian Castro in his response to a question by Ouyang Yu:

> Yu: 'One of the recurring themes in your novels, it seems to me, is the <u>duality or the doubleness</u> of human nature. Is this something that you as a migrant of mixed and multiple ethnic background feel particularly strongly about?'
> Castro: 'Yes. . . . I am privileged in that I grew up in Hong Kong and there were <u>three different cultures</u> within my own family. <u>Doubleness and doubling</u> back are also a kind of *mode d'emploi* in the writing of my novels and also in the key to their reading.'[17]

In Castro's work, like that of other Asian-Australian writers, doubleness emblematizes the moment of going beyond a monolingual and monocultural Australian identity. Teo also stresses the 'two or more' of symbolic doubleness: 'the issues of trauma, dislocation and encounters with racism still crop up, but these are almost incidental to the main story. Today's writers tend to treat migration as a

16 Allan Luke and Carmen Luke, 'The Difference Language Makes: The Discourses on Language of Inter-Ethnic Asian-Australian Families', in Ien Ang, Sharon Chalmers, Lisa Law and Mandy Thomas (eds), *Alter/Asians: Asian-Australian Identities in Art, Media and Popular Culture* (Annadale, NSW: Pluto Press, 2000), 43–44.

17 Yu, *An Interview with Brian Castro*, 74–75. Italics in original, underlining mine.

structural device linking two or more sets of stories, two or more sets of histories which are anchored firmly and finally in the Australian present.'[18] Let us now go on to see what fictional interventions may correspond to such programmatic statements.

It is because I am interested in 'doubling' as an inaugural, rather than a conclusive phenomenon, that I move, in each of my readings of three representative Asian-Australian novels, from the figure of doubling to the rhetorical figure of chiasmus and its implementation as a figure of narrative strategies.[19] In each case, I attempt to complicate doubling with particular reference to the manner in which that doubling is activated by the (implied) reader in chiasmus.

Chiasmus is a figure of 'crossing,' etymologically derived from the form of the Greek letter 'chi,' X. In its standard definition, it repeats two elements of a sentence in reverse order, with a correspondence in meaning, sometimes with a direct repetition of words: 'Love's fire heats water, water kills not love.'[20] It can be understood as a figure which doubles doubleness, linking the two versions of doubleness with an imperceptible moment of crossing. It is thus a figure for the contamination of sameness by difference, despite the attenuation of difference by residual sameness. It is, moreover, a spatial figure for the ways in which places and identities may be linked across a border which none the less defines their difference. Chiasmus may appear to be a figure of closure, merely shuffling, as it does, several pairs within a very limited range of permutations and combinations. But the fact that chiasmus is subject to reader activation, and that its activation may trigger similar operations outside the text of which it is a part – that is to say, beyond its own borders – opens up possibilities of multiplication which are no longer as docile as the figure itself may suggest.

This productivity is in fact inherent in the very figure of chiasmus which entails two elements linked by a third operation of inversion. This third operation brings chiasmus into being, generates the second element by exchanging the order of the preceding terms, but also suggests that the doubling of doubleness need not be final, but that it could itself be re-doubled in turn. Chiasmus is only a figure of closure if the activity of the reader across the text-reader boundary is ignored, that is, if the text is reified into a frozen artefact. If, however, the text consciously gestures towards its own 'exterior,' as the texts I read below ostentatiously do, then chiasmus must be understood as a figure which plots the progress of social hybridity, confusing text and recipient, writer and reader, inside and out, self and other, us and them – revealing the 'Asia' always already acronymically latent in 'Australia.'

Castro

Brian Castro's *Birds of Passage* (1983) is commonly acknowledged as the first Asian-Australian novel. It thus undertook pioneering symbolic work after more than a decade of substantial Asian immigration to Australia. Its very title, referring to the

18 Teo, *Future Fusions*, 136.

19 See Richard Aczel, 'Rhetorical Figures as Narrative Strategies in English Renaissance Prose Fiction', in Bernhard Reitz and Sigrid Reuwerts (eds), *Anglistentag 1999 Mainz: Proceedings* (Trier: WVT, 1999), 451–61.

20 Shakespeare, Sonnet 154.

denigrative epithet which attributed to the Chinese immigrants to Australia a putative 'impermanency,' engages with the contemporary reality of Australia. No less than in previous centuries, Asian-Australians tend to be perceived as 'sojourners' whose principal allegiance is to their 'home' culture – immigrants likely to 'betray,' sooner or later, their 'host country.' Castro's novel counters such notions of core and periphery, notions still underlying the state-sponsored conception of multiculturalism in place from the early 1970s to the mid 1990s. In place of those 'ethnocentric' visions, *Birds of Passage* installs a stereoscopic vision anchored in the narratives of the contemporary Chinese-Australian Seamus O'Young and his historical predecessor and alter ego Chinese goldminer, an immigrant to Australia in the 1850s. This is of course an instance of the 'doubling back' which Castro mentions in his interview with Ouyang Yu. The novel alternates between the stories of the two characters, culminating with a final section written in the mode of magical realism, in which the two characters and their voices merge into one.

Seamus, an orphan adopted by a kindly elderly couple in rural Australia, gradually discovers his Chinese ancestry and embarks upon a process of 'becoming' Chinese. This process is a textual equivalent, cast under the rhetorical trope of chiasmus, of the struggle of Chinese immigrants to Australia to 'become Australian.' Seamus himself embodies this chiastic intertwining, given expression in a humorous incident during the young man's typically Australian travels in Europe:

> Seamus O'Young. It's not my real name. I'm not Irish. I am in fact an ABC; that is, an Australian-born Chinese. Yes and no. I find your questions infuriating. People are always very curious about nationality. They will go to great lengths to pigeonhole someone. They think this knowledge gives them power.
> I remember entering the UK at Folkstone on the car-ferry. The customs officer looked at for a long time while holding my passport. In the next queue a black girl was shouting and screaming.
> 'You are blood-minded', she shrieked.
> The customs man turned towards the shouting. Then he said to me, 'So you're one of these bloody Chinese-born Australians.'
> Before I was able to correct him, he waved me through with his head turned. Behind, the shouting intensified.[21]

The reversed epithet is integrated into the narrative as a comic appropriation for the novel's project, which interweaves the Chinese- and Australian-based storylines, having them overlap, significantly, at the moment of border-crossing between past and present. The UK customs and passport control serves as a median point between Ireland (Seamus is linked to Shan by being the descendant of an illegitimate son of an Irish goldfields prostitute, Mary O'Young), Australia and China.

This interweaving entails a fictional project of historiography. Seamus discovers, behind the mirror of his adoptive parents' country shack, the yellowing pages of a Chinese goldminer's diary – that of Lo Yun Shan, who writes down his experiences of immigration, goldfields racism, and eventual liaison with the Irish Mary who will

21 Brian Castro, *Birds of Passage* (St. Leonards, NSW: Allen & Unwin, 1983), 8. Further references in the text.

bear his son. The pages he discovers behind the broken mirror are ostensibly those diary-sections of the novel that we are reading. Seamus describes this textual strategy in speaking of his own reading habits and the moment when he discovers Shan's manuscript:

> It was the way I had always read, with three or four books open. I jump from one book to another. After a while, the passages from different books interconnect. I have then a good picture of several interlinked worlds as I read, the momentum generated by each carrying me through them. . . . I got up from my books, went to the mirror above the old dresser, saw myself in it . . .
> I pushed the dresser towards the window and pulled back the curtains. I tilted the mirror again. Without the wall to limit the angle of the tilt, the mirror was suddenly released from its hinges and felt to the floor . . . The mirror lay in three large pieces on the wooden floor. I saw myself standing in three places above it.
> As I picked up the pieces I noticed the wooden backing of the mirror was cracked. Inserted between it and the glass were hundreds of pieces of fine yellow paper which came apart in my hands as I picked at them . . . When I held them up to the light I was able to see a kind of calligraphy, looking like Chinese or Japanese script . . . (*Birds of Passage* 53)

The cracked mirror is a not infrequent topos in contemporary Australian fiction, as in Flanagan's *Death of a River Guide*, where the protagonist Aljaz is invited to look into his father's old shaving mirror, and discovers there his own indigenous ancestry: 'This is an Abo.'[22] In Castro's novel, the shattered mirror in which Seamus discovers his own Chinese-Australian identity is doubled by the fictional text through which we too are invited to participate in an extant Chinese-Australian cultural lineage. Shan's text is addressed to a reader – literally (*Birds of Passage* 57) – which is at once Seamus (at the level of the 'storyline') and the Australian reader of the text (at the level of the 'narrative discourse'). In reading that text, Seamus takes up the position of interlocutor with regard to his own 'ancestor': 'You have begun to learn English, and I Chinese' (*Birds of Passage* 62). Seamus reads Shan's notes written on the 1850s goldfield and relives his progressive psychic disintegration under the pressure of anti-Chinese racism and violence and incipient madness. Shan's text thus generates Seamus, through his reading and translation of the prior text, in a newfound identity as an inheritor of a Chinese migrant legacy in Australia.

Seamus increasingly enters the imaginative world of his goldminer predecessor, until the moment in the last scene where Shan, searching for his son, meets Seamus:

> 'Shan!' He [Seamus] shouted.
> The visitant bolted into the bush. He had seen his reader: a wriggling, white-haired man spawned by the future on a river bank.
> . . .
> He awoke and remembered a dream. He had seen his reader lying there on the rocks, and had experienced a moment of panic. The feeling was still there. It was a vision of the future . . . It wasn't fanciful. It was a primitive, savage and desperately guilt-ridden vision of his own illegitimate progeny . . . He would have to take on alone the

22 Richard Flanagan, *Death of a River Guide* (Ringwood, VIC: Penguin, 1996), 250.

> full responsibility for his lineage, shoulder the burden of being its author. It was a matter of record. (*Birds of Passage* 144, 151)

Shan generates his own progeny, which the text equates with his future reader, Seamus, who meets him as the two levels of the text intersect. The point of meeting is, as it were, the intersection where the two axes of a chiastic cross(ing) meeting briefly before following their separate paths once again.

By having the fictive writer of an 'Ur-text' and its reader meet, Castro thus includes a figure of the writer-reader encounter which happens at the moment we open his text. For Seamus, the reader of Shan's diaries, is also the 'writer' of the text we read. Thus Castro writes a fictive textual 'precedent' for today's Asian Australia, one upon which it can found its own narratives. Within that fictive text, the immigrant Chinese goldminer writes the future history of Asian Australia from the other direction. This chiasmus of textual vectors forges a loop into which every reader of the text can step, to become a reader-writer (it is no chance that Barthes appears as a character in the novel [*Birds of Passage* 71]) of Asian Australia's symbolic self-textualization.

Gooneratne

Yasmine Gooneratne's *A Change of Skies* (1991) also works with the trope of a double textuality. One of its two protagonists, a Sri Lankan academic working in an Australian university, edits and publishes the diaries of his grandfather, a Sri Lankan aristocrat who makes a 'grand tour' to Australia in the 1880s. The novel is regularly interspersed with extracts from *Lifeline: The Journal of an Asian Grandee in Australia 1882–1887*. The diary tracks experiences of the young Edward, who leaves Sri Lanka after a being jilted in love and falling out with his tyrannical father, works as a cane-cutter and then as a drover, before returning to the family estates. The grandson and editor, Bharat, later Barry, leaves a Sri Lanka gradually sliding towards civil war for a period as a Visiting Professor of Linguistics at a fictive Australian university. Subsequently, he decides to stay on, first as a teacher of ESL, and later as a restaurant owner together with his wife Navaranjini, aka Jean.

Another example of textual doubling similar to that employed by Castro is in the parchment manuscript version of one of the birth tales of the Buddha which Bharat and Navaranjini discover under the floor of their house in suburban Sydney when carrying out renovations.[23] Only a few pages before, Edward has recounted how the Sri Lankan cane-cutter immigrants in North Queensland preserve Buddhist religious texts in the ventilated space under their huts (*A Change of Skies* 73). As in Castro, both these instances of textual doubling suggest a textual, historiographical precedent for the Asian presence in Australia, an archival foundation upon which a sense of 'belonging' can be constructed. The fictional textual lineage evoked by these writers is designed to serve as an internal echo of the text's pragmatic function within the contemporary Australian context of its production and transmission: that

[23] Yasmine Gooneratne, *A Change of Skies* (Sydney: Pan Macmillan Picador, 1991), 87. Further references in the text.

is, as a generator of complex and positive discourses of Asian-Australian-ness which can counteract the racist discourses of which the texts are all too aware. These two are present within the text: Edward's ship carrying a load of Sri Lankan indentured labourers is welcomed at Mackay by stone-throwing residents fearful of an Asian invasion (*A Change of Skies* 71–72), and Bharat and Navaranjini are welcomed, as the taxi bringing them from the airport turns into their street, by a spray-can graffiti slogan screaming 'Asians Out' (*A Change of Skies* 69).

However, this text, though eminently readable in contrast to Castro's Antipodean postmodernism, is more complex in its self-reflexivity. For Barry also begins work on an unfinished *Guide for Asian migrants to Australia*; and his wife composes a bestselling 'fusion' cookery book entitled *Something Rich and Strange* (building on an archive of culinary metaphors for multiculturalism dating from the 1980s,[24] and anticipating, with this 'fusing' of Shakespearean epithet and exotic culinary creation, Teo's employment of the semi-literary figure of 'fusion' cuisine in her non-fictional criticism on Asian-Australian writing[25]). Thus Gooneratne's text does not merely layer the present text with its predecessors, as does Castro's, but also includes two offshoots into the future: one unfinished (as if no Guide for Asian Immigrants could totalize their experiences and prepare for all eventualities) and one completed, but with potentially infinite appropriations and activations in the public sphere (the cookery book as the epitome of the text in its openness to reader participation, indeed, consumption).

If we imagine Gooneratne's loose, disparate fiction as being flanked by two textual predecessors (actually, they are 'internal' to the text, but at the same time project a fictive 'exteriority' of their own, a Möbius-strip effect to which I will return later) and by two textual successors, we can imagine them as forming a chiastic structure which embody both the 'taste for the past' and the 'future fusions' envisaged in the title of Teo's article:

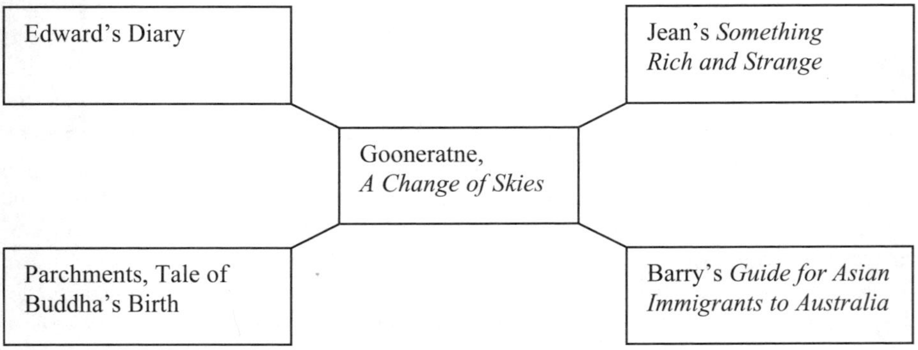

24 See Nicoll, *From Diggers to Drag Queens*, 135–37.
25 Teo, *Future Fusions*, 127–28.

Thus Gooneratne's text positions itself as the intersection between textual vectors of cultural transmission which traverse it on their trajectory from an Asian Australia in the past towards an Asian Australia in the future.

Teo

Hsu-Ming Teo's *Love and Vertigo* (2000) recounts, similarly to these other Asian-Australian narratives, two parallel stories: on the one hand, the story of a young Chinese-Malaysian Singaporean woman, Pandora who is born during the Japanese occupation, grows up in the erstwhile British colony benefiting from an English education at an Anglican girls' school, and eventually marries the wealthy young dental surgeon Jonah Tay. With their small children they move to Kuala Lumpur, and some years after the anti-Chinese race riots of 1969, emigrate to Australia. Pandora, already disillusioned with her marriage, never really settles in Australia, and at the end of her story (the beginning of the narrative) returns to Singapore where she commits suicide by jumping from the roof of a block of flats. The second narrative strand is that of the daughter, Grace Tay, who is conceived just before the family leaves Singapore but grows up in an Australia where multiculturalism has become government policy but has not yet filtered down to the Sydney primary school playground where she and her brother are abused as 'chinks' and 'slit-eyes.' Grace's own adolescent search for a sense of belonging within Australia is intimately entangled with an attempt to elucidate her mother's transition from Singaporean to Australia. The mother struggles to find a narrative to make sense of life in a brutally patriarchal family, and settles upon the metaphysical love poetry of Renaissance England. This hopelessly idealistic narrative of romantic union cannot bridge any of the gaping chasms between herself and her husband, or herself and the suburban culture of her adoptive Australia. Pandora remains a permanent exile within her family and within Australia, for lack of a narrative which will articulate her own position within the social Symbolic. Pandora returns to Singapore, goes in search of her childhood and its locations, and fails. Aphasia is the final manifestation, at the end of her last Singapore visit, of this absence of a life-narrative: 'Eventually she was brought back . . . distraught and barely intelligible, her speech reduced to a stuttering patois in which English, Malay and Teochew nouns had been erased from her vocabulary to be replaced by the word "thing."'[26] In these last, abortive attempts to re-traverse the trajectory of her own life, this constitutive absence of narratives ('There were no bedtime stories. Ours was not a story-telling household' [*Love and Vertigo* 152]) finally takes its toll.

The task of the novel is to find a mode of storytelling which is situated somewhere between the perilous extremes of the (Petrarchan) 'love' and the (suicidal) 'vertigo' of the title. By reconstructing the mother's story, the daughter also constructs her own narrative. Once again, Asian-Australian narratives constitute themselves by appropriating a prior narrative – if necessary, one which they themselves create and project behind themselves. In attempting to find a mediating code which

[26] Hsu-Ming Teo, *Love and Vertigo* (Crows Nest, NSW: Allen & Unwin, 2000), 276. Further references in the text.

steers between the illusory Imaginary of Renaissance love lyrics (I have recourse to Lacanian categories of psycho-social linguistic modes) and the terrifying, suicidal Real of the meaningless void, the narrator weaves a double story which typifies the Symbolic – the realm of language in which our meaning is always 'given': 'given' in that it precedes us, is awarded by the culture into which we are jettisoned – but also 'given' in so far as meaning is as much a gift and a resource as an alienating loss. The exile or immigrant narrative, more than any other, is one which underlines how deeply we are indebted to language for our place in the world. When that link to language is loosened, our identity wavers. On the borders of several languages, the immigrant possesses an identity which flickers and oscillates – a source of concern, indeed threat, at times, but also of visionary innovation.

Confronted with the stillborn narrative of her mother's life, Grace Tay retraces her mother's last journey to Singapore, where she attempts to reconstruct, with the help of her relatives' accounts, the unnarrated maternal history which is also that of her own origin too: 'How was it that you could pour yourself into the careless hands of strangers so that everything I have learned about you since was gleaned from the reminiscences of people I hardly know?' (*Love and Vertigo* 283). The figure which best describes this undertaking is that of chiasmus, albeit a disjointed chiasmus in this case. The trajectories of the two women (Singapore-Sydney-Singapore and Sydney-Singapore-Sydney respectively), make up the temporally and spatially disarticulated axes of two narratives which, in another configuration, would form a chiasmus:

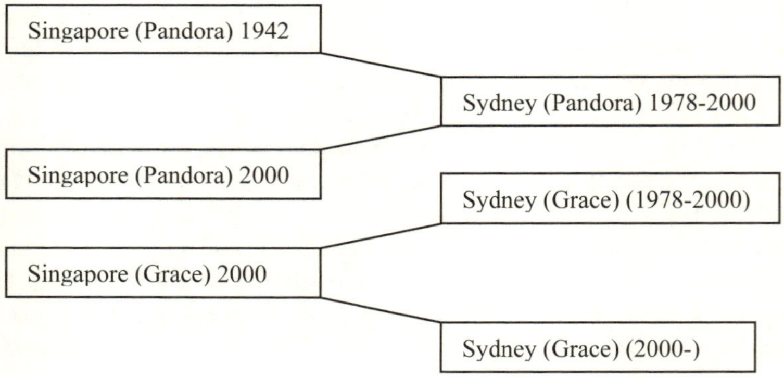

Crossing is, indeed, the very sign under which the narrative, in its framing-discourse mode, is articulated: 'I begin on the eve of my mother's wake, four days after she jumped. I cross a continent and two time zones to land at Changi Airport, Singapore' (*Love and Vertigo* 1). Teo's narrative, then, is about crossings: the crossings which guarantee new hybrid narratives of Asian-Australian identity. Such crossings, as the very topographies of narration sketched in graphic form above show, are incomplete, still in the process of being made. This is indicated in a similar manner in a brief episode relating the playground game of 'elastics,' a game involving jumping over crossed elastic bands to the rhythm of the following ditty:

> *'England, Ireland, Scotland, Wales. Inside, outside, inside, scales . . .*
> How odd to have been rehearsing in a sunny Sydney schoolyard the names of the countries of the United Kingdom thousands of miles away.
> *Inside, outside, crisscross, inside out.* (Love and Vertigo 158–59)

The game is one to which Grace, as playground pariah, is only reluctantly admitted. But the '*Inside, outside, crisscross, inside out*,' once integrated to her narrative, like that of her mother, abruptly appears inside the discourse of outsideness – thereby crisscrossing the boundaries between opposing discourses, between exile and integration.

Between the *stories* (or *fabula*) in the past (Pandora's untold life-history, the schoolground ditties of exclusion) and the *narrative discourse* (or *sujet*) of the (reading) present (Grace's reconstruction of her mother's life, her own recounting of schoolground rituals) the relationships are complex and disturbed. The relationships between *story* and *discourse* in these transcultural fictions are always disjunctive, exilic, and yet *by the same token*, inextricably entangled in the manner in which a Möbius strip entangles its interior and exterior surfaces: '*Inside, outside, crisscross, inside out*.' The figure of exile is itself related to hybridity in a manner which one suspects possibly look very much like chiasmus: these texts are examples of what Roger Bromley calls 'diasporic cultural fictions' – fictions which are, to use his chiastic turn of phrase, 'for the most part, constructed around figures who look in from the outside while looking out from the inside.'[27]

These three Asian-Australian narratives implement doubleness with the help of the figure of chiasmus so as to generate ever-increasing layers of complexity. Doubleness is doubled in these narratives with a view to creating complexity – the hallmark of life, both biological and social.

Let us listen, at the close of this meditation, to another, less literary but no less complex Asian-Australian narrative of the present day, from the mouth of 20-year-old Haline from Western Sydney:

> It's really hard to define myself in that way, because I'm in Australia right now, I was born in France, my parents were both born in Cambodia, but their background was Chinese, but they were in Vietnam and they spoke Chinese and Vietnamese. My mum speaks eight languages and my dad about six. So it's really hard to say, 'Oh, I have an Asian background, I was born in France and living in Australia.' You know, I get this identity crisis, you know you've got people saying, 'Well, what nationality are you?' So I think I'd say it's just an amalgam of everything put together. I do get little bits here and there. I do find that I'm Asian, I do have that cultural thing because of family, from my parents and things like that. But I do have the Australian in me as well, but I think I have some of the French thing as well from growing up there, so yeah.[28]

27 Roger Bromley, *Narratives for a New Belonging: Diasporic Cultural Fictions* (Edinburgh: Edinburg University Press, 2000), 5.

28 Melissa Butcher and Mandy Thomas, 'Being In-Between', in *Ingenious: Emerging Youth Cultures in Urban Australia* (Sydney: Pluto Press, 2003), 31–46.

The notion of the 'hyphenated identities' is barely adequate to describe this life narrative. The doubling of doubling would appear a more recondite figure to take account of such cultural complexity. For those who look back nostalgically to the days of a monocultural white Australia which demanded few skills for the negotiation of (increasingly variegated) cultural allegiances, such intricacy of selfhood is disconcerting. But it is in the nature of history to complicate matters, and the task of culture is to provide adequate models of the complexity of human existence. William Paulson remarks that the

> making, reception and use of cultural works is . . . a complex, indirect and often subtle way of sending a feedback signal to the ongoing processes in which history is made. It is a way of adding to the richness of human activity . . . the complexity of feedback must be commensurate with that of the system being controlled . . . [according to] the principle of requisite diversity . . . literature contributes significantly to the requisite diversity of cultural systems both via its voicing of the past . . . and by virtue of its fictive and poetic qualities.[29]

Fictions such as those we have read above must be adequate to the world's complexity; adequate in that they make sense of complexity – but also in that they do not make *too much sense*, attaining thereby coherence only at the price of sacrificing their own intricacy. Such narrative complication is essential, for it gives us the conceptual tools we need to meet complexity without succumbing to the primitive desire to erase its manifestations. Storytelling, in the contemporary Australian context, is a vital means of maintaining the complexity of manifestly variegated and transcultural social systems: 'The process of cultural transmission will contribute continuously towards the creation of a complexity of Australian cultures, of an ever increasing variety of Australian ways of living,' writes Richard Waterhouse.[30] Recent Asian-Australian fictions such as those analysed in this piece model cultural complexity (in these examples, with the help of chiastic structures) in such a way as to preserve a culture of heterogeneity in a climate which is increasingly hostile to everything that is refractory to reductionism.

29 William Paulson, *Literary Culture in a World Transformed: A Future for the Humanities* (Ithaca, NY: Cornell University Press, 2001), 120–21.

30 Richard Waterhouse, 'Cultural Transmissions', in Hsu-Ming Teo and Richard White (eds), *Cultural History in Australia* (Sydney: University of New South Wales Press, 2003), 126.

PART FOUR

NEVER MIND IF YOU
DON'T SPEAK ITALIAN
WE SPEAK A GOOD
BROKEN ENGLISH

11 'This is a Man's Country': Masculinity and Australian National Identity in *Crocodile Dundee*

In 1994 the Australian brewery Foster's launched an advertising campaign marketing Foster's Lager ('Australia's Famous Beer') with the title 'How to Speak Australian.' All the advertising clips in the series featured stereotypical images of Australia and Australians, so as to present this mark of beer and its consumption as a way of participating, albeit from afar, in that Antipodean lifestyle. The campaign was originally introduced onto the US market, and was subsequently extended for use on markets throughout Europe, Asia, the Middle East and the Pacific.[1] The aim of the advertising series was to facilitate the extension of this already dominant brand of Australian beer on worldwide markets by associating it with particular notions of the Australian character. Significantly, such notions were from the outset connected with quite distinct representations of masculinity and femininity.

One of the earliest and most striking clips in the 'How to Speak Australian' series featured two scenes in an outback pub. In the first scene, two brawny Australians are sitting at the bar. One of them, at the far end of the bar, picks up a boomerang and sends it looping through the air to the other end of the bar where his mate is sitting. The boomerang hits the second bloke on the back of the head; he reaches up and switches the channel of the television anchored in the wall, to a programme showing a game of Australian Rules football. A subtitle appears at the bottom of the frame: 'Remote Control.' The second scene shows the pub from the outside. The Western-style saloon doors suddenly swing open as a man comes flying through them to land on his face on the dirt outside. Equally abruptly, a tall and attractive woman steps through the doors, flinging the ejected fellow's Akubra bush hat after him. Again, a subtitle appears at the bottom of the screen: 'No.' The clip finishes with a view of a bottle of Foster's Lager, and the inscription: 'Australian for Beer: Foster's Lager – Australia's Famous Beer.'

The advertising series focuses on the transmission of the Foster's image across the world, in the forms of 'translation' of exotic Australian practices which ostensibly need to be explained to a puzzled overseas public. These translation operations culminate in an image of the alcoholic beverage, itself also translated as 'Australian for Beer: Foster's Lager.' But the humorous distance between image and explanation also underlines the difference which apparently contributes to the market success of Foster's: it is the fact of its difficult translatability which makes it desirable as a metonym of the inaccessible and thus attractive southern continent. The content of the mute vignettes also figures this process of translation, for both thematize communication. The distance and difference figured in the advertising clip is also that which constitutes the gender identity of Australian masculinity. The wordless communication of the two men at the bar is a figure of the silence of men and between men, which, appropriately, needs to be translated into verbal form. In the second clip, the women's 'No,' expressed in equally wordless form, suggests the

1 http://www.fosters.com.au/ftb_advert.asp. Accessed 31 July 1999.

exhaustion of verbal means of conveying the woman's unwillingness to cede to the unwelcome attentions of the man, and her final recourse to physical violence to get the message across. Thus what the clip transmits to the world are images of a raw, masculine outback society in which language appears almost to have withered away. The function of translation in this context is to compensate for the gendered absence of speech.

The gendered images of communication in the outback in the context of a Foster's advertising campaign were partly derived from a massively successful predecessor in which the Foster's logo was also prominently visible. In the openings scenes of Peter Faiman's 1986 film *Crocodile Dundee*, featuring Paul Hogan (as Mick 'Crocodile' Dundee) and Linda Kozlowski (as American journalist Sue Charlton), a typical outback pub is also the scene of sub-verbal masculine communication, rough humour and physical violence as one drinker attempts to make a pass at Sue. Here, too, a brash outback woman appears in the person of Ida the barmaid, and a hat is also tossed out the door as a senseless kangaroo hunter is carried away after being knocked out by Mick Dundee. In alluding to the opening scenes of *Crocodile Dundee*, the Foster's advertising clip acknowledges its debts to the earlier text, whose worldwide success paved the way for the subsequent international reach and explicit cross-cultural orientation of the advertising campaign. Conversely, the advertising clip also draws attention to the prominence of gender features in the earlier film's propagation of images of Australia. In this chapter I wish to explore the ways in which *Crocodile Dundee* structures its pictures of Australian national identity in gender terms.

It is precisely the success of *Crocodile Dundee* which makes it worth examining in more detail, for it appears to have had a long-lasting effect on the manner in which Australia is perceived all around the world. *Crocodile Dundee* was the most successful film Australian film to date, making more money in Australia than any film ever before, being the most successful film internationally in its year of release and the most successful foreign film ever on the US market, staying in the American cinemas for weeks on end and making $174.6 million dollars in its American release.[2] Given the durability of the impression made by the film and its remarkable global resonance, it would appear that there is some call for an analysis of the way in which a particularly potent image of the Australian nation has been presented in terms of masculine gender. In this chapter I will concentrate on three aspects in particular of this gendering of national identity, all of which are highlighted by the Foster's advertisement. The first aspect is that of the paring-down of speech. The laconic men of the pub are bearers of verbal reserve as one of the central characteristics of Australian masculinity as presented in *Crocodile Dundee*. Reserve, and its concomitant rhetorical figure of litotes, it transpires, is the instrument with the help of which masculinity is constructed in relation to but also in defiance of its constitutive Other. But this reserve is predicated upon a second aspect of the film highlighted by the advertisement, namely, that of the inextricable entanglement of masculinity with the Other in (ostensible) opposition to which it is constituted.

2 Meaghan Morris, *The Pirate's Fiancée: Feminism, Reading, Postmodernism* (London: Verso, 1988), 242; Tom O'Regan, *Australian National Cinema* (London: Routledge, 1996), 83.

Thirdly, the relation of pub scene and Foster's beer is one of chiastic inversion: whereas the *Crocodile Dundee* film scene takes place in an Australian country pub, with ubiquitous Foster's advertising posters constantly visible in the background of the frame as a marginal allusion, the Foster's advertising clips are framed by the 'Australia's Famous Beer' slogan and logo and employ the pub scene as the background material which alludes to the film as intertextual predecessor. Chiasmus underlies the entire structure of the film as the rhetorical turn which best figures the reciprocal imbrication of the respective components of a binary opposition. Translation, foregrounded by the Foster's advertising campaign, represents another chiastic relationship constantly thematized in *Crocodile Dundee*: 'walkabout' and 'tucker' need to be translated for Sue, whilst Mick is confronted with New York parlance when talking with the Italo-American taxi driver and the black drinking companion in a downtown bar, and has to have the word (and the concept) 'shrink' translated for him at a well-to-do NY reception. The culmination of this aspect of the film is the symmetrical exchange of the other nationality's respective greetings carried out by Mick and the New York hotel doorman: 'Have a nice day' – 'No worries, mate.' Language, and its various modes of deployment as expansive or restrictive, as imperial or modest, whether linked to power or powerlessness, whether co-operative or offensive ('bad language,' for instance, is the pretext Mick gives for knocking out the obese kangaroo hunter in the Walkabout Creek pub during his inaugural foxtrot with Sue, and later, the new York pimp who interrupts his well-meaning though naive conversation with two prostitutes) constitutes the underlying tenor of the film. Here, masculinity is predicated upon language. How that language-based manliness functions, as a figure of unavoidably fraught gender relationships, is one of the principle problems addressed in *Crocodile Dundee*.

In turn, these interconnections of masculine gender and language, understood as a network of articulations of differences, are bound up in the constitution of national identity. The background to the gendered configurations of *Crocodile Dundee* is the history of Australian involvement with US foreign politics since Prime Minister John Curtin's historic announcement of December 1941, when the Australian government decided to relinquish its traditional loyalty to Britain and transfer its military allegiance to the US, perceived as a world power whose strategic interests in the Pacific area were more likely to be compatible with those of Australia than faraway, beleaguered Britain. Since the end of the Second World War, Australia has sealed a military pact with the US (ANZUS), and offered its support in Korea, Vietnam and the Gulf alongside the American forces. In 1999, it transpired that the fifty-year policy of military service to the US in the confident expectation of a pay-off in terms of reciprocated assistance in time of need was fundamentally flawed when Australia, intervening in the East Timor crisis, was infuriated at the lukewarm American support. At the same time, Australia found itself accused by South-East Asian neighbours as mimicking the US as world policeman, a situation not without a degree of comic irony as the action revealed Australia's utter military unpreparedness for such a mission. This unpreparedness was itself the spin-off of years of reduced defence spending motivated by the assumption that the brunt of military activity would be born by the senior partner in the alliance – an outcome which, ironically, some political commentators had predicted well before.[3] What was particularly striking in the television reports on the Australian military presence in East Timor was the clearly gendered character of representations of the operation: shaven-headed Australian soldiers wearing wrap-around sunglasses struck nonchalant poses for the TV cameras, while the Australian commander-in-chief, Major-General Peter Cosgrove, was barely articulate, the chin-strap of his slouch hat (a crucial sartorial element in the ANZAC myth[4]) apparently preventing him from opening his mouth properly. In such images, Australian militarism followed a American strategic example, modified by the unmistakable influence of contemporary commodified macho genre, but also of laconic bush manhood (somewhat in the tradition of the famous photo of a slouch-hatted soldier carving the sardonic inscription 'heaven' in the stucco wall of the railway station in Tobruk).

Not only military policy but also economic exchange with the US has also come to supplant the earlier primacy of trade with Britain, and US-Australian trade relations have also had their ups and down in the half-century since the war. What is notable about the post-war relations between Australia and the US is that this 'constitutive relationship is not embedded in a cultural tradition in the ways in which the relationship with Britain was, and to a certain extent, continues to be. The rich cultural inheritance which has for two centuries afforded a wide range of cultural icons and discourses of the British-Australian relationship, from the image of the colonial new chum (the naive and inexperienced British immigrant in the bush newly arrived from "the old country") or stereotypes of effete English aristocrats, to the rhetoric of cricket and affectionate "Pommie-bashing", is lacking for the dependence on America . . .'[5] This apparent cultural vacuum is all the more curious given the profound and widespread effects of American culture on Australian society, evident in such everyday phenomena as the design of road signs (only one Australian state, Tasmania, has consciously based its traffic signs on the British model). Symptomatic in this context, for instance, is the perplexity patently experienced by the prominent Australian art critic and historian Patrick McCaughey in finding a contemporary common denominator in the domain of culture in his introduction to a combined US-Australian exhibition of early colonial landscape painting in the two ex-British settler colonies.[6] Contemporary Australia still lacks a cultural framework within which the all-pervasive relationship with the US can be reflected and debated. It is possible that these difficulties in developing a public discourse of the history of Australian-American relations may have been entrenched by Australian eagerness not to remember the shameful Vietnam episode of the 1960s and early 1970s. There have been frequent thematizations of Americans in Australia in

3 Ronald, McKie, *We Have No Dreaming* (Syndey: Collins, 1989), 236.

4 Helen Gilbert, *Sightlines: Race, Gender and Nation in Contemporary Australian Theatre* (Ann Arbor: University of Michigan Press, 1998), 191.

5 John Rickard, *Australia: A Cultural History* (London: Longman, 1995), 218; Richard White, *Inventing Australia: Images and Identity 1688–1980* (Sydney: George Allen & Unwin, 1981), 79–81.

6 Patrick McCaughey, 'Likeness and Unlikeness: The American-Australian Experience', in Elizabeth Johns, Andrew Sayers, Elizabeth Mankin Kornhauser and Amy Ellis (eds), *New Worlds from Old: 19th Century Australian and American Landscapes* (Canberra: National Gallery of Australia/Hartford, Conn.: Wadsworth Atheneum, 1998), 15–21.

films from the fifth continent.[7] *Crocodile Dundee* none the less represents a new departure, in that it actively approaches the deep interlocking of the two cultures. An earlier popular national hero abroad had been the Australian comic figure Bazza McKenzie, who, at large in the UK in Bruce Bereford's 1972 film The Adventures of Barry McKenzie, articulated the complexities of a still-close British-Australian relationship. *Crocodile Dundee* is notable as the most powerful recent attempt to give expression to the Australian-American relationship in its two-way functioning, in part because that relationship is articulated in terms of gender, the most familiar, everyday and deep-seated system of binary logic structuring representations of social existence.

In 1974 the German performance artist Joseph Beuys staged a three-day action in New York entitled 'I like America and America likes me,' in which the European artist and a wild American coyote cautiously approached one another in a gradual process of reciprocal familiarization.[8] *Crocodile Dundee* undertakes a similar project, albeit in a rather different manner, with Sue's cry across the crowded subway station at the end of film, 'I love you,' being multiplied and relayed from person to person, so that it becomes the staging of a collective love affair, modelled along hegemonic heterosexual lines, spoken into existence by the film's own incantatory power. It is this aspect of the film which demands closer examination and thereby a reconsideration of national identity in conjunction with some recent innovations in film theory.

Recent developments in film theory have shifted the focus of gender interrogation from the female body on the screen, to the less discussed aspect of masculinity. In reviewing some recent writing on film, Steven Cohan and Ina Rae Hark point out that: 'In concentrating upon the female body as the primary stake of cinematic representation, . . . even the most acute and insightful of [the discussions following upon Laura Mulvey's essay on visual pleasure] have ignored the problem of masculinity which motivates that system.'[9] They go on to elucidate their position in the following terms:

> While we certainly do not minimize the importance of exposing the disadvantaged positioning of the female spectator and the women within the diegesis in Hollywood cinema, the scant attention paid to the spectacle of men ends up reinforcing the apparent effacement of the masculine as a social construction in American culture. The male's seeming exemption from visual representation may work very hard to preserve the cultural fiction that masculinity is not a social construction, but American movies have always served as one of the primary sites through which the culture, in the process of promulgating that fiction, has also exposed its workings as a mythology. The male image on the cinema screen is therefore as significant a representational stake as the female.[10]

7 O'Regan, *Australian National Cinema*, 52.

8 Caroline Tisdall, *Joseph Beuys: Coyote*, trans. Dominique Le Bourg (Paris: Hazan, 1988); Uwe M. Schneede and Joseph Beuys, *Die Aktionen: Kommentiertes Werkverzeichnis mit fotographischen Dokumentationen* (Stuttgart: Gerd Hatje, 1994), 330–353.

9 Steven Cohan and Ina Rae Hark, 'Introduction', in Steven Cohan and Ina Rae Hark (eds), *Screening the Male: Exploring Masculinities in Hollywood Cinema* (London: Routledge, 1993), 1.

10 Cohan/Hark, *Introduction*, 2–3.

The following analysis assumes that the representation of gender, and in particular of masculinity, in the film possesses a crucial role in the formation of public consciousness and collective experiences of social life. This assumption in turn obliges one to ask the question of which forms of community the representation of gender in film may contribute to moulding. In general this question is not asked, the relevant social context being assumed as a given. At the point at which the question of gender is linked to that of national identity, however, a further gap in research comes to light. In an apparently throwaway line in his classic work on the formation of national identity, Benedict Anderson writes that: 'in the modern world everyone can, should, will 'have' a nationality, as he or she 'has' a gender.'[11] But the problem has rarely been addressed in its reverse form: does a nation have a gender? Several writers on the sociology of the nation comment that until recently, the literature on nationalism had been blind to issues of gender. As McClintock notes that: 'Nationalism becomes . . . radically constitutive of people's identities through social contests that are frequently violent and always gendered. Yet, if the invented nature of nationalism has found wide theoretical currency, explorations of the gendering of the national imagery have been conspicuously paltry.'[12] This imbalance has been righted in recent years, with some attention to the place of women in nationalism, but none the less this literature has neglected to examine men as an equally constructed category.[13] Mayer argues 'that the national ego is intertwined with male and female ego, that it is inseparable from gender and sexuality,' and 'that nationalism becomes the language through which sexual control and repression (specifically, but not exclusively, of women and homosexuals) is justified, masculine prowess is expressed and exercised'; similarly, Nira Yuval-Davies enumerates ways in which nationalist traditions 'are used as ways of legitimizing the control and oppression of women.'[14] These theses are illuminating and helpful, but in the context of *Crocodile Dundee* it is worthwhile asking, conversely, about the ways nationalism is *constructed* on the basis of gender characteristics. This direction of reflection is implicitly suggested for instance by Mayer's claim that: 'Because nationalism, gender and sexuality are all socially and culturally constructed, they frequently play an important role in constructing one another – by invoking and helping to construct the "us" versus "them" distinction and the exclusion of the Other.'[15] Such a reversal of the terms of the causal link may then allow one to understand better how the construction of nation with the help of gender imagery probably in turn assists in the justification of sexual oppression in the name of nationalism. Mayer's conclusion, then, is particularly relevant for the case of film as an instance in which national identity is both constructed and gendered: 'The nation is comprised of sexed subjects whose "performativity" constructs not only their own gender identity but the

11 Benedict Anderson, *Imagined Communities: Reflections on the Origin and Spread of Nationalism*, 2nd ed. (London: Verso, 1991), 5.

12 Anne McClintock, *Imperial Leather: Race, Gender and Sexuality in the Colonial Contest* (New York: Routledge, 1995), 353.

13 Nira Yuval-Davis, *Gender & Nation* (London: Sage, 1997), 1; Tamar Mayar, 'Gender Ironies of Nationalism: Setting the Stage', in Tamar Mayer (ed.). *Gender Ironies of Nationalism: Sexing the Nation*. (London: Routledge, 2000), 5.

14 Mayer, *Gender Ironies*, 1; Yuval-Davis, *Gender & Nation*, 46.

15 Mayer, *Gender Ironies*, 1.

identity of the entire nation as well.'[16] In what follows the question of performativity, in particular the forms of performativity evident in film, will be considered in the light of the agency of binary oppositions in constructing notions of male selfhood and of national selfhood.

Chiasmus and entwining in masculinity and national identity

Australia as a modern nation was created in 1901 by the Act of Federation which united the hitherto disparate British colonies on the Australian continent, only shortly before the First World War, which signalled the end of the political importance of the large dynasties, and thereby the historical high-water mark of the nation-state.[17] None the less, Australian national identity has been marked from its inception by a high degree of instability, being caught up in a constant process of 're-invention.'[18] *Crocodile Dundee* would thus appear to participate in an ongoing project of national self-definition, and can be understood as an instance of what Tom O'Regan has called 'national cinema.' National cinema functions as a social bond, uniting and excluding diverse people, constituting an object of knowledge 'which narratively and discursively connects Australia, society, the cinema, genre and various cultural differences,' 'representing Australia to itself.'[19] Significantly, Mick Dundee combines a number of well-known masculine personifications of Australia: the bushman, the larrikin outlaw, the digger abroad. But at the same time, there is something slightly antiquated about this notion of national cinema, particularly when looking at a film such as *Crocodile Dundee*. For it is virtually impossible to think about the nation today without placing it in an international, indeed global context, which increasingly casts the concept of the nation-state into the shadow.[20] What is remarkable about the film is its project, based on the financial necessity of releasing the film simultaneously in the US and in Australia, and thus addressing two publics, the Australian and the American, at the same time. Thus the question of national identity is inherently situated in a relational context, rather than being assumed to be some sort of autonomous entity. This is reflected directly in the narrative structure of the film, which is divided into two equal halves set in the Australian outback and New York respectively, and balanced symmetrically by a chiastic construction: the American journalist Sue visits Mick Dundee in his outback homeland, and he accompanies her back to her home in the Big Apple. Tom O'Regan speaks of the pronounced tendency of some Australian films to effect 'border-crossings' which then subject them to 'productive mis-readings.'[21] In *Crocodile Dundee*, such border-crossings are pre-programmed in a film which was designed from the outset to speak to quite disparate audiences, and whose very plot

16 Mayer, *Gender Ironies*, 5.
17 Anderson, *Imagined Communities*, 85–86.
18 Richard White, *Inventing Australia: Images and Identity 1688–1980* (Sydney: George Allen & Unwin, 1981).
19 O'Regan, *Australian National Cinema*, 10, 35.
20 Ulrich Beck, *Was ist Globalisierung?* (Frankfurt/Main: Suhrkamp, 1997).
21 O'Regan, *Australian National Cinema*, 59.

maps the history of a border transit. International border-crossing is the precondition of the film, the constitutive framework which its plot self-reflexively mimics.

The inbuilt border-crossing process is not, however, the result of a symmetrical relationship. At all levels the relationship between Australia and the US is an unequal one, as demonstrated by Australia's fawning to the US in matters of military assistance, and the United States' refusal to reciprocate that assistance in the 1999 East Timor crisis. In the immediate context of the Australian film industry, Meaghan Morris has drawn attention to the funding cuts in government film subsidies which meant that Australian films had to gain pre-selling guarantees, preferably in the United States, in order to buttress investment at home.[22] The film does little more than point, via a bold *mise-en-abyme*, to its own conditions of production, namely, the radical financial dependence of the Australian film industry upon America. The small Australian media industry is not independent on the world market; the very chiastic, two-part structure of the film thus constitutes a loud expression of dependence of national selfhood on Otherness. In the interests of narcissism-driven box-office takings, both audiences had to be able to recognize themselves not only in the representations of their respective countries, but also in the 'other' national site in the film. The ubiquitous pervasiveness of American elements in the Australian part of the film – from the Wild-West saloon fight to the very un-Australian tassels festooning Mick's leather waistcoat and cowboy boots, or from Mick's proclaiming himself as Fred Astair to the country music overlaid upon tourist-industry panoramas of the natural beauty of Kakadu National Park. Later on, elements of the Australian environment will be translated into the New York context, with Mick replacing his cowboy tassels with a snakeskin jacket, and echoing his 'Out of the way dopey!' (originally addressed to the ponderous water buffalo blocking the outback track) for the benefit of a New York motorist driving on the 'wrong' (right) side of the street. Similarly, the multicultural face of New York society, whether plebeian or upper-crust, mirrors a prominent aspect of contemporary Australian society which is otherwise elided by the exclusively outback setting of the Antipodean half of the film. These are all forms of chiasmus which declare a radical interdependence of Australian and American culture. O'Regan comments that: 'this seeming dependence on "other cinemas" and their norms, genres and so on – is actually one of the most fascinating aspects of Australian cinema, enabling it to speak so powerfully to local and international audiences alike in *Strictly Ballroom*, *Mad Max II (The Road Warrior)*, *My Brilliant Career* and *Crocodile Dundee*.'[23]

Chiasmus, however, is not just a figure of radical dependence upon an opposed Other; it is also a way of masking that dependence, of presenting it as symmetrical and mirroring. The most prominent figure of mystificatory chiasmus in the film is that of a gender reversal. The traditional association of masculinity with power and femininity with powerlessness could not be allowed to remain intact in the film, for the simple reason that for the film to function for two audiences, the balance of power must be equal. In contrast to the real historical situation of the thousands of Australian World War Two war-wives, where the journey was largely one way, and

22 Morris, *The Pirate's Fiancée*, 247–48.
23 O'Regan, *Australian National Cinema*, 71.

where Australia figured in the exchange as the female partner, the film inverts the usual gender hierarchy, figuring Australia as the masculine Mick Dundee, and America as the female journalist Sue. In this manner, the film suggests a equilibrium between essential masculine and feminine attributes: America's power is toned down by virtue of its being incorporated in a woman (which accords with the iconic feminine figure of the statue of liberty, but also allows the blunt facts of American world dominance to be recast in the equally patent fact of women's restricted access to social and political power). Simply ignoring political realities is in no way an effective ideological strategy, and so the superior power of the US must be surreptitiously acknowledged, but in such a way as to mask the imbalance. This chiastic strategy affords the possibility of articulating whilst simultaneously disavowing America's status as a potent object of desire on the part of Australians (Sue is alternately desired by the kangaroo hunter in the Walkabout Creek Pub, by the crocodile, by Mick, by Wally). Thus, in the Australian section of the film, Mick is portrayed as sexist but deeply impressed by his American guest, while Sue is presented as the liberated, independent modern girl but who is incapable of defending herself in the bush. Conversely, in the American section of the film, Mick is shown to be celebrated but finally defenceless before American wealth, Richard's priority as Sue's fiancé, and the violence of the pimps respectively. In a nutshell, Sue is powerful by virtue of her derived (American) power, but as a woman can be seduced by Mick (thus devolving to him a 'minor' form of agency).

This attempted compromise between the realities of geopolitical power imbalances, and the necessity to pander to viewers' nationalist-narcissistic sensibilities, based upon chiasmus, tends however to produce major contradictions, particularly in the images of body which are proposed to the public. Benedict Anderson suggests: 'The nation is imagined as *limited* because even the largest of them, encompassing perhaps a billion living human beings, has finite, if elastic, boundaries, beyond which lie other nations. No nation imagines itself coterminous with mankind.'[24] Psychic identity is constructed upon the establishment of bodily limits,[25] and this establishment of identity through the delineation of borders is particularly apposite as a figure for the formation of national identity. The perforation or fraying of the community's limits or the points where it is constituted or dissolves – for instance in the threshold moments of birth, initiation, marriage, or death – is a cause for much concern, particularly when the nation is figured as a gendered body, often feminine.[26] The imagined vulnerability of Australia to invasion from the North has been a persistent trope in the nation's foreign-policy discourse. The presence of American GIs in Australia during the Second World War has frequently been described, both in popular and historical accounts, as an 'invasion,' thus implying a

24 Anderson, *Imagined Communities*, 5.

25 Sami-Ali, *L'Espace imaginaire* (Paris: Gallimard/Tel., 1982); Didier Anzieu, *Le Moi-peau* (Paris: Dunod, 1985).

26 Mary Douglas, *Purity and Danger: An Analysis of the Concepts of Pollution and Taboo* (London: Routledge and Kegan Paul, 1980); Victor Turner, *From Ritual to Theatre: The Human Seriousness of Play* (New York: PAJ Publications, 1982); Jerry Brotton, 'Mapping the early modern nation: cartography along the English margins', *Paragraph* 19:2 (July 1996), 139–55.

threat to Australian femininity, with distinct overtones of rape.[27] Yet the perforation of the national body is presumably even more disturbing when a national selfhood figured as *masculine*, and therefore as penetrating rather than as penetrable, is threatened from outside. Here it is worth mentioning the importance of the journey abroad as a rite of passage for Australian masculinity, the classic example being the ANZACs' campaigns overseas in the first half of the century, and the year overseas for the youth of the second half; as George Johnston famously wrote, the Australian male 'has been obliged to look elsewhere for the great adventures, the necessary challenges to flesh and spirit. This is why his wars must be fought for other causes than his own – and often for strange ones – and always in faraway places.'[28] That *Crocodile Dundee* re-enacts such a conquest narrative in the second half of the film, is perhaps indicative of a sense of needing to re-establish equilibrium following a traumatic symbolic experience of loss of (national) boundaries. For masculinity is predicated upon the construction of boundaries against Others, in particular against the mother and femininity in general, and equally, upon the refusal of the desire which inevitably accompanies a converse and equally constitutive identification with masculinity.[29] The undermining of such boundaries threatens the very constitution of masculinity, as has been shown in film studies by Silverman's work on the permeability of the margins of the masculine body which bring it close to femininity, and Krutnik's analyses of the instability of the ostensibly autonomous masculine self in the American detective film.[30] If it is on the basis of self-differentiation that masculine gender is formed, and upon the maintenance of a limit between the two genders that the stability of masculinity is upheld, then gender chiasmus represents a perilous and fraught process. A precedent for this aspect of *Crocodile Dundee* can be found in the films of Anthony Mann, where the recurring motif of a chiastic love/hate rapport of the charming 'villain' and the near-psychotic 'hero' dramatizes the danger of the masculine hero becoming his enemy – to whom, moreover, he is often related by blood.[31] Gender chiasmus represents a 'catastrophe' for identity in the sense of René Thom's catastrophe theory, the point at which a coherent mathematical structure meets another structure and undergoes a radical structural transformation.[32] Whence Mick's oath as the plane takes off from Australian soil for New York, and his nervous negotiation of the escalator at JFK Airport, with its critical point of transition, its visual, mechanical tectonic-plate-like divide between two cultures and the respective realms of two genders. The end of the escalator at JFK also figures a brutal fine-toothed maw which will mince up anyone

[27] Gilbert, *Sightlines*, 187–88, 245 n3.

[28] George Johnston, *My Brother Jack* (1964; Blackburn, Victoria: Collins Fontan, 1981), 271.

[29] Nancy Chodorow, *The Reproduction of Mothering: Psychoanalysis and the Sociology of Gender* (London: University of California Press, 1978); Dorothy Dinnerstein, *The Rocking of the Cradle and the Ruling of the World* (London: The Women's Press, 1987); Judith Butler, 'Melancholy Gender/Refused Identification', in Berger, Wallis and Watson (eds), *Constructing Masculinity* (New York: Routledge, 1995), 21–36.

[30] Kaja Silverman, *Male Subjectivity at the Margins* (New York: Routledge, 1992); Frank Krutnik, *In a Lonely Street: Film Noir, Genre, Masculinity* (London: Routledge, 1991).

[31] Paul Willemen, 'Anthony Mann: Looking at the Male', *Framework* 15–17 (1981), 16.

[32] See also René Thom, *Paraboles et catastrophes: Entretiens sur les mathématiques, la science et la philosophie* (Paris: Flammarion, 1983).

getting caught in its embrace, a pair of metal jaws which signals once again the vulnerability of the masculine body (as it now enters 'feminine' US territory). The chiastic structure which brings together Australia/America and masculinity/femininity threatens to rip open the closure of the masculine persona. In bringing masculinity and femininity into close contact, and even more, exchanging their various attributes in a chiastic inversion, the film threatens to undo its very constitutive terms, and to destroy the masculinity with which the Australian nation is endowed (it is worth asking whether such a chiastic inversion and concomitant blending would have the same results for feminine identity: the answer may be negative[33]). Significantly, the encounter with the toothed escalator is accompanied by an even more ambiguous, but utterly banal phenomenon: as Mick dithers in front of the tectonic intersection, a young woman moves past him, virtually ignoring him (a dramatization of the feared dissolution of a genderless, and thus non-differentiated self) but for a fleeting, disinterested glance (the feared catastrophe as absolute anticlimax).

Other symptoms of this vulnerability to invasion, intrusion or perforation are to be found in the film. Sue's friendly attempts at empathy for Mick are refused, taken as attempts to occupy Mick's home territory. In reflecting about his mauling by a crocodile, she says: 'I reckon I know how you must have felt. Or how I would have felt if I was you.' Mick scoffs: 'You out here alone? A city girl like you? You wouldn't last five minutes out here love. This is a man's country.' At which point, deeply offended and determined to set out her own through the bush towards the day's destination, she takes up the rifle he presents her for the case of an emergency. When Mick patronizingly tells her 'That's the dangerous end,' Sue fires a shot at his feet which barely misses penetrating his boot. Here feminine (near)-perforation of the masculine body is presented as a concomitant of feminine penetration of masculine territory, the masculinized outback heart of Australian national identity. A similar risk of penetration of the male body is also presented in terms of a gendered relationship when Mick self-deprecatingly describes his leg wounds from the crocodile's attack as 'just a love bite'; this predatory feminine intrusion into the body of the masculine incorporation of Australian identity will be almost immediately reversed into masculine pursuit of Sue, with the obese kangaroo hunter in the pub 'just want[ing] to get a bite' (of Sue, though his snide remarks are addressed to her dancing partner, Mick), and the crocodile also directing its attentions to the American journalist a short while later. The perforation of the masculine body is such a threat because it erases the very borders upon which the gendering of that body is predicated. These possibilities, however, can barely be articulated by the film's gender topographies. Within the political project of *Crocodile Dundee*, the two sides of the gendered equation must inevitably be bonded to each other with a distribution of strength and weakness which implicitly questions the gender divide. Explicitly, however, this blurring of gender power must be controlled and recuperated, and

33 See in particular Luce Irigaray, *Ethique de la différence sexuelle* (Paris: Minuit, 1984), *Je, Tu, Nous: Pour une culture de la différence* (Paris: Grasset, 1990) and *J'aime à toi: Esquisse d'une félicité dans l'histoire* (Paris: Grasset, 1992).

cannot be allowed to question the very schema used to portray power and its equalization.

Silence, reserve and litotes

One way this fraying of the boundaries of masculine identity can be controlled is by strategies of reserve, understatement or silence. When Sue's point-blank rifle shot barely misses Mick's foot, his only response is a sort of startled high-pitched grunt. The speechlessness produced by her sudden emergence out of the protective cocoon of stereotypical feminine behaviour is in part evidence of Mick's abrupt disarray – but also, the sign of a very effective system of defence. 'I hope you're not going to be the strong silent type,' Sue says as she sets out to interview Mick Dundee – to which he replies that he is his own favourite topic of conversation. But the whole emphasis of *Crocodile Dundee* is upon Australian masculinity as a form of reserve involving minimal speech, minimal action, minimal violence, reserved energy – what Meaghan Morris refers to as the film's '"masculine" refusal of overkill, hyperbole, and hysteria as principles of action.'[34] This is all part of the Australian male stereotype of laconic speech, easy loose-limbed gait, evinced in combination, for instance, in the shot where Mick turns back to the truck after having hypnotized the water buffalo. Thus Mick's reactions to the overblown violence of the kangaroo hunters is to employ the object of their terror (the kangaroo itself) to scare away the intruders; in the same way, the American male, with its overblown rhetoric and false elegance, connoting forms of effeminacy (Richard with his Italian and Italianate posturing and elegant words, the pimp with his exaggerated Latino sarcasm) are silenced with one carefully measured blow. Thus the film presents Australia in understated terms, making no claims to be a powerful nation. In so doing, the film attenuates the power of Australian masculinity (or masculine Australia) in accord with the realities of geopolitical power, while accommodating that attenuation to a national stereotype of low-keyed masculinity, whose strength is evinced, paradoxically, in the indexical absence of force. This masculinity operates according to the rhetorical figure of restraint, that of litotes, which reins in excessive emotion by ironic negation. Rather than admiring the palatial hotel suite Sue has reserved for him in New York, Mick's dry response is: 'It's a bit rough, but I'll manage.' Popular wisdom, which has it that the Australian vernacular is characterized by opening one's mouth as little as possible, exemplifies a pragmatic, somatic instance of litotes. The prominence of litotes in the film – Mick Dundee is a past master of this laconic form – is symptomatic of a (gendered) relation to Otherness embedded in language itself. According to Steve Neale, masculine silence is linked to an attempt to overcome the symbolic castration associated with the entry into language, which profoundly threatens the narcissism of early childhood: 'language is a process (or a set of processes) involving absence and lack, and these are what threaten any image of the self as totally enclosed, self-sufficient, omnipotent.'[35] Within Lacanian theory,

34 Morris, *The Pirate's Fiancée,* 252.

35 Steve Neal, 'Masculinity as Spectacle: Reflections on men and mainstream cinema', in Steven Cohan and Ina Rae Hark (eds), *Screening the Male: Exploring Masculinities in Hollywood Cinema* (London: Routledge, 1993), 12–13.

language signals the subject's dependence upon the upon the Symbolic, upon the Name of the Father; more prosaically, language stands in for the object, and the usage of a word highlights the fact of the absence of the object being spoken of, which therefore constitutes a lack. Masculinity, which typically figures itself as fullness in contrast to feminine lack, has a particular interest in concealing its connections with its Other in order to paper over its own lacunae. If language displays the manner in which the self is dependent upon and implicated in, indeed, constituted by Otherness, then the laconic structure of the whole film dramatizes restraint as a form of recuperation and masking of loss of power. A significant expression of Mick's desire for Sue is his roundabout comparison of himself to the crocodile, which, in her words 'was going to eat me alive.' Mick's growled comment ('The same thought had crossed by mind once or twice') expresses affection through deadly aggression. Thereupon he puts his hat over his face and goes to sleep, thus terminating face-to-face contact, sealing off language and silencing the symptoms of sexual or emotional hunger. Reserve is thus a means of dealing with implicit powerlessness, configured here under the sign of gender. Reserve is a way of reworking the imbalance of power and the intimate imbrication with the Other who limits the power of the self, as a form of what Lyotard has called 'retorsion': the capacity to seize effects wielded by a stronger power, and to reroute those effects in a manner radically opposed to the original imbalance of forces.[36] The reserve and litotic elements of the film thus implicitly reveal in masculinity a structure which is in no way autonomous, but predicated upon its Other; the film necessarily works to admit this fact, and simultaneously to elide it.

It is in this perspective that the film's apparent contesting of gender stereotypes needs to be regarded. *Crocodile Dundee* is replete with apparent subversion of images of traditional masculine power. In the inaugural pub scene, Mick kisses Donk on the lips, thus replacing the traditional punch in the stomach which always fails to spill the glass of beer balanced on the muscle-man's head. Mick openly deflates his own elevated tone or his puncturing of images of hyper-masculinity: when shaving in the bush, he smartly replaces his razor with the enormous bush-knife as soon as Sue appears in the corner of the frame, but cannot help laughing at his own patently staged backwoodsman pose. In reply to Sue's admiration of her defender on the New York streets with the epithet 'Tarzan,' Mick utters not a bellow but something resembling a bleat. He partakes of Aboriginal knowledge, with his appearance as barefoot tracker, his supernatural capacity to hypnotize animals, instances of appropriation of bush knowledge which Nev, the Aboriginal lad from the city, no longer possesses. The self-deprecating deflation of stereotypical masculinity which repeatedly occurs in *Crocodile Dundee* can be seen, on the one hand, as part of the film's comedy, which constantly takes aim at masculine pretensions to power. On the other, more disturbingly, they can be conceived as aspects of the litotic thrust of the film, by which hegemonic masculinity is recast in a ironic, negative form in order to pre-empt signs of its own deep vulnerability.

36 Jean-François Lyotard, *Rudiments païens: genre disseratif* (Paris: UGE 10/18, 1977), 66, 127.

Recuperation

The gender characteristics of *Crocodile Dundee* are not utilized in the film merely to figure the place of the Australian nation in relation to the US; as suggested above, they also work to describe the position of the diminutive Australian film industry in relation to its Hollywood counterpart. Significantly, at the end of the film, Mick Dundee walks over the heads of a cheering American crowd in the subway station, a proleptic *mise-en-abyme* of the film's resounding success. Tom O'Regan suggests it is precisely the Australian film industry's engagement on Hollywood's own terrain – a gendered engagement, because the Australian film industry is small and not particularly powerful on the American cinema stage – which reveals to what extent Australian film is closely linked to the other national cinemas in competition with whom it quite consciously defines itself. O'Regan speaks of strategies which work 'to transform what is the culturally weak Australian position into a comic vehicle that turns the tables on the culturally strong: moving from outright mimicry, to ironic imitation, adjustment, negotiation, transformation, resistance and subversion. All these movements entail relations of implication, not violent resistance.'[37] A similar complicity is revealed, ironically, in Mick's confession, when asked about his nickname 'Crocodile,' that it was suggested by Wally: 'He reckons it makes me more colourful for the tourist business.' Thus the very name which has since become an international synonym for stereotypical outback Australianness is quite openly admitted to be a strategy for inviting the world to intrude upon the Red Centre of Australia. Thus the film directly addresses not only the imbrication of self and Other, of masculinity and femininity, but also, more cannily, that of vulnerability and recuperation for an immensely successful marketing ploy.

The penetration of the American woman into the realm of Australian masculinity is figured by Sue's camera, whose brand name, Canon, signals its close connection with the rifle which nearly perforates Mick's foot. The journalist's camera in turn is a metonymy of the gaze in its double capacity in this film. The gaze can undermine masculine confidence, as in the episode when Mick, fearing the intrusion of the chambermaid Rosina into the New York hotel bathroom, seizes his bush hat in a movement of panic to cover up his vulnerable private parts. Likewise, his own hypnotic gaze, capable of overwhelming water buffalos and dogs, fails to subdue the pimp and his sidekick thugs. And in sexually liberated New York, Mick's mistrustful gaze functions as an index of his own anxiety about the erasure of gender difference as he finds himself obliged to carry out manual verification of the gender of transexuals. Yet on the other hand, it is precisely in New York, where Mick's masculinity is most tested by the danger of the loss of differentiation, the same telephoto lens which tracks him in the outback subsequently establishes him as a form of photogenic and commodifiable difference. Thus Mick's conquest of New York is captured by Sue's camera as Mick stands atop the Empire State Building, pointing across the panorama with a deictic gesture which appropriates the mastery endowed by the photographic gaze – that of Sue's camera, in turn replicated by that of the cinematic camera. Here the film makes a self-reflexive gesture about its own

[37] O'Regan, *Australian National Cinema*, 234.

offering of a narcissistic view of an Australian national identity – an identity simultaneously emasculated *and* masculine in its engagement with the powerful forces of Hollywood film industry. For it is this gaze, both at home and abroad, which has guaranteed the establishment of an artificial yet immensely successful version of Australian identity subsequently marketed by other commercial enterprises such as Foster's.

The anxious gaze trying to ascertain sexual difference in danger of erasure ('just making sure') indicates one potential consequence of the problematic process of chiasmus and interlocking which the film undertakes in order to equalize the patently unequal relationship between Australia the US. The mapping of masculinity and femininity onto Australia and the US and their subsequent spatial exchange comes close to endangering its own project, because chiasmus and interlocking threaten to blur the very boundaries upon which gendered national identity are predicated. The escalator at JFK where Mick dithers before the corrugated meshing of the moving steps – a machine in which Same and Other meet, and blend together in a vicious toothed embrace – figures the process by which two genders meet. If the escalator figures, in comic form, the possibly dire consequences for the individual identity being carried by the process, the same escalator also explains how the film successfully averts the possible melting of gendered identity. For in actual fact, at the point on the escalator where self and Other meet, difference *is* maintained, despite the 'catastrophic' moment at which the two structures intersect and blend. Here the film gives a visual image of the way sexual difference is both eroded and maintained, by being co-opted for a project of commodification of cultural and gender difference. In that image of the moving steps, radical differences meet and indeed interlock in a process of unceasing dissolution of one of the structures, without the structure itself disappearing.

To recapitulate, the principle shift in the film occurs between two versions of masculinity. The Australian-US relationship is articulated in gender terms, partly to make it accessible and tangible to the public, and partly to rework a patently unequal power relation by playing off a gender hierarchy against a political hierarchy. This chiastic reversal of hierarchies has the secondary effect of bringing out the intimate connections between the two genders. That connection in turn carries with it the danger of the eradication of gender difference, something that is thematized in the second part of the film in Mick's encounters with transexuals. This problem is in turn resolved by converting masculinity as a structure involved in a difference-suppressing chiastic relationship, into masculinity as a commodified difference whose regional origin can be assimilated to a commercial process. Lawrence Grossberg has proposed that

> [i]n its originary – colonial – mode of operation, the discursive machine apparently operated – somewhat like an ideology – by hiding the primacy of difference and producing what appeared to be essential (at least for the colonizer, positive) identities.

> This is no longer true: the machine not only tolerates but seems to demand the visible production of difference everywhere.[38]

Rather than being suppressed, difference becomes the principle product of global media:

> My argument is that media produces the local – (as territories or places – whether as the village, the nation, or the region) – in fact, a heterogeneity of locales. . . . Globalization is producing a reality in which differences proliferate in a highly reterritorialized world (hence, there is a reinvestment in the local and identities as places). . . . This constructed equivalence of place and identity constitutes in my opinion the primary power of the media as a global force.[39]

If Grossberg's suspicions are founded, then the cultural difference of Mick Dundee is a dramatized, staged commodification of a distinct identity linked to a specific place whose broad outlines are sketched out in the first part of the film, and whose marketing abroad is proleptically indicated in a grand *mise-en-abyme* in the second half of the film. *Crocodile Dundee* is a perfect example of what Grossberg sees as a modern community identity which is

> less a matter of relations than of images of lifestyles (themselves defined by the aura of commodities) embodying imaginations of "becoming American" [read: Australian], i.e. of entering into the auratic space of the commodity located in specific imagined places.[40]

More importantly, the cultural difference which is so successfully commodified in *Crocodile Dundee* (both within its own fictional world, and in the success enjoyed by the film itself) is based upon a gender difference, one whose threatened erasure is subsequently recuperated as a further form of difference. For the masculinity produced by *Crocodile Dundee* is both traditionally sexist and conservative and, at the same time, quixotically naive and close to the feminine. In a very pertinent warning to cultural studies, Grossberg cautions: 'If this is the case, it makes the current faith in difference (and even hybridity) as the form and site of resistance and agency quite problematic.'[41] The same warning could be recast for the exponents of an anti-ideological gender studies.

Finally, as noted above, the gaze which so threatens Mick Dundee is the key to his success on the New York scene, and as a film icon internationally. Regarding the visibility of masculinity, Jonathon Rutherford has written that masculine identity 'is an identity that is in continual struggle to assert its centrality in cultural life, yet it attempts to ensure its absence, and to evade becoming the object of discourse.'[42]

[38] Lawrence Grossberg, 'Globalization and the "Economisation" of Cultural Studies', in Bundesministerium für Wissenschaft und Verkehr/Internationales Forschungszentrum Kulturwissenschaften (ed.), *The Contemporary Study of Cultures* (Vienna: Turia + Kant, 1999), 39.

[39] Grossberg, 'Globalization', 41.

[40] Grossberg, 'Globalization', 43.

[41] Grossberg, 'Globalization', 39.

[42] Jonathan Rutherford, 'Who's That Man?', in Rowena Chapman and Mike Rutherford (eds), *Male Order: Unwrapping Masculinity* (London: Lawrence & Wishart, 1988), 23.

Following Foucault, it is the invisibility of power which ensures its perfect functioning.[43] Yet Frank Mort's work on the recent prominence of highly stylized masculinity in fashion advertising and lifestyle magazines has shown that an intense spotlight cast upon the masculine body as a visual icon in no way necessarily implies a genuine questioning of male social power, but can go hand in hand with the continued exclusion of women from public space and positions of power.[44]

The 'difference' of a masculinity rendered visible does not necessarily lead to the demystification of its ideological underpinning, to the detachment of its 'metaphoric' adherence to a naturalized real for the 'metonymic' shifting of hitherto manipulated signifiers. Far more, enhanced mobility injected into the illusory 'metaphorical' fullness of the signifier can lead to an eternal metonymic succession of signifiers desired as commodities; each impulse towards the impossible 'metaphorical' act of possession of the commodity only triggers a further metonymical desire for acquisition. In the words of Fredric Jameson, these impulses 'are initially awakened within the very texts [or commodities] that seek to still them.'[45] Precisely this transformation can be seen at work in the episode of the swish New York party. 'Just checking,' explains a relieved Mick, having grabbed at the drag queen Ben's nether regions and thus re-established the clear dividing lines of gender difference; thereupon Sue is left to justify Mick's behaviour: 'Don't worry, he's Australian.' This scene marks exactly the point of suture where the anxious gaze verifying the presence of clearly delineated sexual difference is recycled as commodified national difference. Here, masculinity abroad as a structure undermined by its proximity to its constitutive Other, which threatens it with the loss of boundary-based difference, is rescued as commodified difference. Exemplary of this troubled border is Mick's statement of derived phallic superiority, ridiculing a New York switchblade with a flourish of his oversize Outback machete – 'That's not a knife, *that's* a knife,' perhaps the film's most famous one-liner – which pithily summarizes the film's gender project, that of shoring up endangered difference in service of profitable (inter)cultural capital. In this second phase, the 'lack' displayed by the naive lad from the bush – his sexual innocence, his ignorance of drugs, his inability to adapt to the anonymity of a large metropolis – become part of his 'aura,' that of unpolluted and nostalgic purity.

The commodification of masculinity, and not its demystification through the denaturalizing work of the intensely visual culture of the 80s and 90s, is expressed by Mort's succinct description of the motivations of the artists and designers working in the men's magazine scene: 'What were the contours of this consumption-led discourse, and how did the new form of magazine publishing hope to intervene in men's lives? Publishers and journalists confronted these matters not as ethical or political dilemmas, but as business questions demanding practical solutions. Shifting the boundaries of masculinity, defining new identities and styles of life were

43 Michael Foucault, *Histoire de la sexualité, 1: La Volonté de savoir* (Paris: Gallimard, 1976), 113.

44 Frank Mort, *Cultures of Consumption: Masculinities and Social Space in late Twentieth-Century Britain* (London: Routledge, 1996), Part One.

45 Fredric Jameson, *The Political Unconscious: Narrative as a Socially Symbolic Act* (London: Methuen, 1981), 287.

immediately bound up with the search for markets . . .'[46] Clearly, Paul Hogan's Mick Dundee character is a far cry from the slick fashion boys of contemporary men's lifestyle magazines. What this unlikely juxtaposition should illuminate, however, is the links between masculinity, an increasing degree of visual attention to differentiated masculine identity, and consumerism, as evinced in the chiastic relationships between Foster's Lager and *Crocodile Dundee*, explored at the beginning of this chapter.

Anne McClintock provocatively writes: 'All nationalisms are gendered, all are invented and all are dangerous.'[47] Given the worldwide resonance of *Crocodile Dundee*, and conversely, its success within Australia, its significance as a moulder of social representations and values, in particular in the field of gender and national identity, cannot be underestimated. What the film *elides* should be of some concern.

There is no real confrontation with American and Australia's participation in American overseas policy (including, for instance, the presence of American military bases on Australian territory, and Australia's ongoing participation in American-led or –sponsored wars). There is no mention of and therefore no reflection on Australia as a multicultural, urban society located in South-East Asia. The *active* symbolic work of the film is equally concerning. *Crocodile Dundee* cannot be seen as a politically progressive film. Typical of its apparently innocuous, but in the last analysis deep conservatism is, for instance, Mick's opinion of Aboriginal land rights. When interrogated by Sue on Aboriginal demands for restitution of their land, he replies that the Aborigines do not own the land but that they belong to it, thus co-opting one partial aspect of Aboriginal lore in order to dismiss their political activism. This ostensibly well-informed riposte, which claims to reflect the Aborigines' own cultural standpoint over against a 'politicized' stance (invented by white activists?), merely echoes the findings of Justice Blackburn in 1971 which rejected Aboriginal claims in the Milirrpum case on the ground that the Aboriginal people had a sense of obligation to the land rather than a relationship of possession, thus disqualifying them from proprietary interest in tribal lands.[48] The profoundly disturbing character of the film's contribution to the further history of relations between black and white Australia becomes evident when one reflects that the Australian governments have often restricted the process of transfer of land to indigenous custodians, and reconciliation with indigenous Australians. *Crocodile Dundee*'s active contribution to gender politics is equally reactionary. The identification by men of their selfhood with the nation as described by Hroch[49] means that gendered figures of nationhood can in turn be appropriated by individual men within their everyday lives, with the association of nationhood and masculinity serving as legitimization for a particular masculine habitus of domination, a phenomenon

46 Mort, *Cultures of Consumption*, 44.

47 Anne McClintock, *Imperial Leather: Race, Gender and Sexuality in the Colonial Contest* (New York: Routledge, 1995), 352.

48 Galarrwuy Yunupingu, 'From the Bark Petition to Native Title', in Galarrwuy Yunupingu (ed.), *Our Land is Our Life: Land Rights: Past, Present, Future* (Brisbane: University of Queensland Press, 1997), 4.

49 M. Hroch, 'From national movement to fully formed nation: the nation-building proces in Europe', in G. Balakrishnan (ed.), *Mapping the Nation* (London: Verso, 1996), 90–91.

epitomized in Mick Dundee's 'This's a man's country love.' The few aspects of an alternative, non-hegemonic masculinity which are offered to the audience in *Crocodile Dundee* are rapidly recuperated for a commodified version of victorious masculinity. In terms of gender politics, *Crocodile Dundee* presents traditional hegemonic masculinity (uncommunicative, sexist, racist, violent); its areas of weakness are revealed by contact with a strong and assertive form of femininity, but those weaknesses are rapidly turned to its own advantage, helping to get the public on its side.

Crocodile Dundee can be thus seen as belonging to a genre of contemporary films which '[put] masculinity into crisis' without '[offering] a radical critique either of masculinity or of violence'; Mick Dundee can be regarded as exemplifying a generic hero 'who redeems himself through loss.'[50] The notion of redemption through failure has particularly strong cultural resonance in Australia, whose popular mythology of masculist national identity reposes upon the ANZAC legend and the military debacle at Gallipoli in 1915, a myth of stoic soldier heroism seriously eroded by Australian participation as an ally of the US in the Vietnam war – and, significantly, a myth which numerous films and plays have attempted to rehabilitate in recent years.[51] These strategies of recuperation of hegemonic versions of masculinity have a broad base in social practices. Like other erstwhile liberal Western societies enthusiastically embracing neo-liberal economic policies and dismantling socially progressive state services for its citizens, Australia has also experienced a vehement reaction against transformations in gender practices in private and public life. Ronald McKie for instance has recently bemoaned the encroachment of feminism upon Australian males' privileges:

> His bewilderment grows as his position and status is undermined. His certainties have degenerated into uncertainties as his place as a man is being more and more assaulted. This . . . is such a profound historical and emotional change that it is impossible to guess how far the [feminist] movement will go and what damage it will do, since it is only just beginning. If the movement slows down in the years ahead, largely through the natural commonsense of women, evolutionary change rather than revolutionary may be more easily absorbed and the influence on the individual and the family may be more easily accepted. But a female revolution which destroys male position and self-confidence, and attempts to make the male virtually obsolete, could produce a community that is a social disaster – and not only for the male. What women do not seem to have yet understood is that they are in grave danger of losing those characteristics which make them such a strong, perceptive, compassionate and superb sex – their essential dignity and their hidden power.
>
> I have only seen one matriarchy, and its male components were miserable and demoralised specimens.[52]

McKie's simplistic populist stance is symptomatic of a strong trend in Australian society in times of social change coupled with the constant threat of economic recession. It is at this point that images of national identity, particularly when propa-

50 Pam Cook, 'Masculinity in Crisis? Tragedy and Identification in *Raging Bull*', *Screen* 23, 3–4 (1982), 39–40.

51 Gilbert, *Sightlines*, 190–91, 246 n6–7.

52 McKie, *We Have No Dreaming*, 245–246.

gated by a cultural medium as seductive and suggestive as film, need to be scrutinized in their legitimating force within everyday practices of employment, educational opportunities, social services resources and so on. *Crocodile Dundee* projected an image of masculine Australia and of Australian masculinity on the international screen which gestured towards acceptance of such change in gender patterns while in reality offering renewed legitimization to traditional hegemonic masculinity, and sealing that legitimization with the seal of success on the international market for identity commodities and corresponding global fame.

12 The Traumas of Translation and the Translation of Trauma: Translation and Cultural Plurality in Fremd and Yasbincek

How would it be to heed David Malouf's injunction to cease 'seeing [Australia] as . . . a second-hand Europe,' and to replace it with a vision of Australia as 'a Europe translated – not just transported, but translated' – and to take it literally?[1] Malouf's rhetoric of translation is generally understood in a metaphorical sense, and in that way the novelty of what he is saying can easily be cushioned. Australia is a nation constructed of translation – and mistranslation. Curiously enough, Malouf's own autobiography, as noted in chapter 7 above, records the failure of translation: the Lebanese émigré grandfather, isolated in his native Arabic, speaks neither with son nor protagonist grandson in *12 Edmondstone Street*.[2] But the Penguin edition of that memoir also describes his polyglot domicile in a Maremma village, in a gesture which may appear significantly compensatory. When *Remembering Babylon*, a novel quintessentially about cross-cultural (mis)communication, was being translated into French, Malouf invited the translator, Robert Pépin to stay with him in the Maremma. Pépin worked in the same room where most of the novel had been written.[3] This anecdote may show how densely layered and overlaid translation, expatriation, settlement and identity-formation can be in the Australian context, occupying the same space, squatting under the same roof.[4]

Yet silence reigns over translation in Australian literary studies (try searching the standard companions or literary histories). The elision of manifold processes of translation from Australian literature cannot but appear as a major lacuna when one considers just how much immigration and thus polylingualism has marked the culture of the nation. In this chapter I wish to pursue the issue of translation and its elision, or, conversely, its textual marking, in two recent Australian novels published ten years apart: Angelika Fremd's *Heartland* (1989) and Morgan Yasbincek's *liv* (2000). My contention is that translation, whether linguistic, historiographical, geographical or cultural, has been a generically traumatic experience in twentieth-century history, and one that has been rendered more traumatic in the Australian context by a deep-seated resistance to the phenomenon it indexes, namely, polylingualism. The rhetorical burden of this chapter is sharpened by a sense that with the demise of state-sponsored multiculturalism, issues of polylingualism and translation have lost the little attention they might, for a brief period, have received in the humanities. The relocation to Canada of one of Australia's most prominent scholars in this area, Sneja Gunew, could be taken as symptomatic of this shift of priorities in the

1 Malouf in interview with Jim Davidson in James Tulip (ed.) *David Malouf: Johnno, Short Stories, Poems, Essays and Interviews* (St Lucia: University of Queensland Presss, 1990), 289.

2 David Malouf, *12 Edmonstone Street* (Harmondsworth: Penguin, 1986), 5–7.

3 See the conversation between Malouf and Pépin in 'In conversation: Translating David Malouf', http://www.literarytranslation.com/workshops/inconversation/davidmalouf/. Accessed 19 March 2007.

4 See Antoine Berman, *La Traduction et la Lettre: ou, l'auberge du lointain* (Paris: Seuil, 1999).

academy. This increasing neglect is nothing if not concerning when one considers that in the current climate of global politics such issues are more pressing than ever.

Michael Clyne has observed that there is 'a paradox between the linguistic diversity of our population and our gross under-utilisation of this diversity.' He goes on to suggest that the 'greatest impediment to recognising, valuing and utilising our language potential is a persistent monolingual mindset. Such a mindset sees everything in terms of monolingualism being the norm . . . in spite of our own linguistic diversity. It views multilingualism as outside the possible experience of "real Australians."'[5] The stigma placed upon linguistic diversity has a long tradition in Australia: a Queensland senator ranted in 1914 that Chinese immigrants could heard 'jeering in their own lingo at white men and women' (how did he know?); German Jewish refugees in the late 1930s were advised, 'Above all, do not speak German in the streets and in trams. Do not make yourself conspicuous anywhere by walking with a group of persons all of whom are speaking loudly in a foreign language.'[6] The stigma of polylingualism retains its currency today: the Prime Minister John Howard, in his 2007 Australia Day speech, intoned that 'it's very important that we embrace as our common method of communication with each other a single language, and that is the English language, because citizenship and interaction with each other is impossible unless we can effectively communicate with one another.'[7] Underlying both the aversion of a public presence of polylingualism, and the implicit claim that such polylingualism hinders communication, is the monolingual majority's fear that it may find itself excluded from polylingual communication in its own land.

For all its elision or demonization in public discourse, translation *is* present in Australia – massively so, in a society with over 250 ethnic languages, and census returns in 2001 indicating that at least one in six persons (16 per cent of the population) used a language other than English at home. In the cities the rates were even higher: 29 per cent of Sydneysiders and 27 per cent of Melburnians.[8] (By way of comparison the previous 1996 census had produced returns of 14.6 per cent home LOTE-speakers.) The trend is a rising one, as more and more Australians effect quotidian transactions between ethnic languages and the national *lingua franca*.[9] Increasingly, Lotman's claim that 'the elementary act of thinking is translation' takes on a concrete everyday relevance.[10] For persons who are polylingual, translation is often something which has become totally reflexive, happening in unmarked ways as they engage in code-switching or cognate bridging practices. It becomes explicit when polylingual children are asked to translate for older relatives in situa-

5 Michael Clyne, *Australia's Language Potential* (Crows Nest, NSW: UNSW Press, 2005), x–xi.

6 David Day, *Claiming a Continent: A New History of Australia* (1996; Sydney: HarperCollins, 2005), 196; Hilary L. Rubenstein, *The Jews in Australia: A Thematic History* (Melbourne: Heinemann, 1991), I, 214.

7 John Howard's 2007 Australia Day speech. http://www.pm.gov.au/news/speeches/speech 2344. html. Accessed 13 February 2007.

8 Clyne, *Australia's Language Potential*, 3.

9 See for example Mary Besemeres & Anna Wierzbicka (eds), *Translating Lives: Living with Two Languages and Cultures* (St Lucia : University of Queensland Press, 2007).

10 Yuri M. Lotman, *Universe of the Mind: A Semiotic Theory of Culture*, trans. Ann Shukman (London: I. B. Tauris, 1990), 143.

tions such as medical visits. Australia does acknowledge the necessity of translation, by providing a telephone interpreter service, or making available interpreters for courts and hospitals. It provides translations on ballot sheets and other government publications. Yet a fundamental suspicion of 'foreign' languages – this exclusionary appellation appears to be gaining ground again – remains present and active in public discourse. Literature, I posit, may be one of the sites where the traumas associated with translation may be worked through.

One would expect translation to be a very visible preoccupation in postcolonial studies – an area of enquiry that re-envisages the forcible meetings of cultures under colonialism and launches a concomitant 'politics of translation designed to transform the conditions of the present.'[11] But with the exception of a few scholars such as Gayatri Chakravorty Spivak, Tejaswini Niranjana or Paul Carter, translation as a constitutive aspect of the 'contact zone' has been largely neglected as a subject of enquiry[12] – though it has re-emerged in the wake of 9/11 in the guise of the 'translation zone.'[13] The cross-lingual encounters of the colonial epoch were unevenly pitched, almost always in favour of the colonizer, with a one-sided politics of language making up part of the armoury of the militarily sanctioned civilizing mission: '*Learn to speak English*' was one of the demands placed upon the indigenous tribes by John Hindmarsh, the founding governor of South Australia.[14] Subsequently, perhaps because postcolonial studies has been predominantly pursued in the erstwhile colonial metropolis or settler colonies, the erasure of the problematics of translation has been preserved largely intact. For this reason, I suggest, translation remains the site of a colonial trauma, one which has not yet been adequately addressed or acknowledged within postcolonial studies, or its avatar Australian literary studies.

Why then this aversion to translation and its vicissitudes? One may surmise that the suspicion of translation reposes upon the fact that the translative process lays bare the ineluctable fact of polylingualism in a given interactional context. Where translation takes place, linguistic difference is manifestly present, and, virtually insurmountable … except by the means of translation. Translation, as Derrida has shown, is, paradoxically, evidence both of the possibility of interlingual communi-

11 Robert J. C. Young, *Postcolonialism: An Historical Introduction* (Oxford: Blackwell, 2001), 66.

12 See Gayatri Chakravorty Spivak, 'The Politics of Translation', in Lawrence Venuti (ed.), *The Translation Studies Reader* (London: Routledge, 2000), 397–416; Tejaswini Niranjana, *Siting Translation: History, Post-Structuralism and the Colonial Context* (Berkeley: University of California Press, 1992); Paul Carter, 'Translation: On Salvaging Words, Carrying Meanings', in Paul Carter and Ruark Lewis (eds), *Depth of Translation/The Book of Raft* (Burnley VIC: NMA Publications, 1999), 22–109. A theatre project I conducted with Paul Carter in Berlin in June 2002 focussed on the question of translation in the colonial context. See Russell West-Pavlov, *Transcultural Graffiti: Diasporic Writing and the Teaching of Literary Studies* (Amsterdam/New York: Rodopi, 2005), 182–207; Paul Carter, 'The empty space is a wall: The role of theatrical translation in the public re-inscription of the other', *Performance Research* 10: 2 (2006), 79–91. See also Susan Bassnett and Harish Trivedi (eds), *Postcolonial Translation Theory* (London: Routledge, 2005).

13 Emily Apter, *The Translation Zone: A New Comparative Literature* (Princeton, NJ: Princeton University Press, 2005).

14 Day, *Claiming a Continent*, 103.

cation – and of its impossibility.[15] This is so for several reasons. First, logically, though translation is predicated upon the claim for translatability, the very act of translation, as a performative operation which displays the difference of languages, undermines communication by the stark fact of its own necessity. Second, more empirically, there is always a supplement of untranslatable meaning, a sector of the source language which simply resists translation, and will thus be abandoned, though possibly compensated by new shades of meaning acquired in the target language. Translation, whether vitiated by its own logical (im)possibility, or dogged by the pragmatic vicissitudes of linguistic transfer, will relentlessly advertise the brute fact of linguistic difference. Translation cannot but be a thorn in the eye of any society that wishes to be or believes itself monolingual. Indeed, the difference between languages evinced by the act of translation may even transpire to be a contamination. Interlingual translation may possess the potential to point up the differences within the ostensibly singular mono-language itself. Translation may already be endemic to the source language (as speakers of disparate 'englishes' often discover as they struggle to communicate with each other). A language which is from the outset not identical with itself will display translation processes within its own boundaries. It is perhaps this potentially destablizing force of interlingual translation, with its power to lay bare the intralingual translation always already at work in any language, which unconsciously draws the ire of monolinguals.

What relevance does all this have for literature? Literature is a secondary modelling system, according to Lotman – an aesthetic system constructed on the basis of a linguistic system.[16] If translation is immanent to the primary system itself, and literature is a secondary, therefore derivative, translated system, then translation by implication should be omnipresent within its fabric. This is all the more so given that literature is more or less permanently concerned with interrogating its own meaning – with self-translation. This is implicitly the claim made by Bakhtin's theory of dialogism, which posits an inherent interweaving of mutually foreign sociolects within a single language and a single text.[17] To what extent that self-reflexive hermeneutic drive is also directed at its own intra- and not merely interlingual semantics is an index of its awareness of the ambient polylingualism which may or may not register in the text itself or in its constitutive context.

In this chapter, translation is addressed at several levels. First, I cast a gaze over the way in which polylingual inserts in literary texts are translated (or, less often, not translated).[18] Secondly, I scrutinize the manner in which immigration, the 'translation' of persons from one culture to another ('We are translated men' says Rushdie on several occasions[19]) is represented with regard to the linguistic experiences of the

15 Jacques Derrida, 'Des tours de Babel', trans. J. F. Graham, in J. F. Graham (ed.), *Difference in Translation* (Ithaca, NY/London: Cornell University Press, 1985), 165–208.

16 See Jurij Lotman, *The Structure of the Artistic Text*, trans. Gail Lenhoff and Ronald Vroon (Ann Arbor: University of Michigan – Department of Slavic Languages and Literatures, 1977).

17 See Mikhail Bakhtin, *The Dialogic Imagination: Four Essays by M. M. Bakhtin*, ed. Michael Holquist (Austin, TX: The University of Texas Press, 1981).

18 See Marion Gymnich, *Metasprachliche Reflexionen und sprachliche Gestaltungsmittel im englischsprachigen postkolonialen und interkulturellen Roman* (Trier: WVT, 2007), 63–96.

19 Salman Rushdie, *Imaginary Homelands: Essays and Criticism 1981–91* (London: Granta, 1991), 16; *Shame* (1983; London: Picador, 1984), 29.

subject. Thirdly, I consider the manner in which subjective experience as it is encoded in a literary narrative may itself repose upon or evince a translative process (the recasting of experience into conscious and unconscious material, and the construction of memory, Andrew Benjamin has suggested, are pre-eminent examples of translation at work[20]). The chiastic pair 'the trauma of translation' and 'the translation of trauma' summarize for me the second and third senses of translation. The polylingual inserts in the first sense can be taken as being doubly symptomatic of translation as a fraught process at the story level ('the trauma of translation') and the discourse level ('the translation of trauma') of the literary text. My contention is that these crossed terms are causally linked: a society which resists translation as a symptom of polylingualism will do little to facilitate the working-through of the traumas which in many cases trigger emigration but are carried intact across the caesura of immigration. The culture which does not 'translate' its pasts may well be condemned to repeat them.

Manifestly, in the literary texts read here, immigration is a traumatic process of transculturation carried out with little assistance from either the source culture (divided Germany in Fremd's *Heartland* or socialist Yugoslavia in Yasbincek's *liv*) or the target culture (post-war Australia). At the same time, the young protagonists bring with them the burden of a past which they cannot access or articulate and which must be decoded, translated, against the resistance of the parental generation – and also of the host country: 1950s migrants were told that Australia was prepared to assimilate them 'AS HUMAN BEINGS' but was 'NOT prepared to assimilate their old-world hatreds and vendettas,' which in many cases meant turning a blind eye to immigrants' bloody histories.[21] The assimilation expected of the first generation of post-war immigrants evinced a notion of translation which erased all traces of the source language and demanded a seamless integration into the target culture and language. This assimilation left little space for transition, acknowledged no in-between spaces of polylingualism, and did little to cushion the traumas of immigration. It went hand in hand with a culture that sought to smooth over the conflicts of the past, repressing rather than working through the European conflicts which the immigrants inevitably brought with them as memories – or as ongoing traumas. Whence my eponymous chiasmus of the trauma of translation and the translation of trauma addressed by Fremd's *Heartland* and Yasbincek's *liv*. These double, mutually entwined struggles are materialized in the opacity of the words on the page. The literal encoding of translation in the text indexes the material site where the crossing between the traumas of immigration-as-translation and the fraught translation-of-trauma occurs – in language itself, where the 'foreign' and the native converge.

20 See Andrew Benjamin, *Translation and the Nature of Philosophy: A New Theory of Words* (London: Routledge, 1989), 109–49.

21 John Rickard, *Australia: A Cultural History* (Melbourne: Longman Cheshire, 1988), 231.

The failure of translation

In Angelika Fremd's *Heartland*, the failure of translation, or its perversion, appears to predominate.[22] Very few German words subsist in this text about a family of post-war immigrants from Germany. One of the few, *Mäuschen* (diminutive 'mouse' = darling), Karl's term of affection for his perennially reluctant wife, gathers an aura of lechery about it. It resonates with the cajoling of a husband whose wife, already pregnant to another soldier, has married him in wartime desperation, and now immigrates under duress. *Mäuschen* resonates with the attentions which, in the face of his wife's sexual reluctance, Karl turns upon his daughter Inge. The very fabric of the text is thus marked with the incestuous stigma of the 'foreign word.'

The novel is dominated by the mother's non-acculturation into the Australian context, her inability to ever find some sort of connection with Australia, concomitant with her inability to love the husband she had married out of necessity and then accompanied to Australia. The mother's subjective non-translation culminates in her suicide upon learning of the husband's attempts to sexually abuse the protagonist daughter (*Heartland* 153–54).

The text is also overshadowed by the non-translation, mnemonic this time, of the father's concealed past. This past resurges in his anti-Semitism, which comes to light at moments of stress (*Heartland* 115). The trace of the past is to be found, corporeally, in the scar left on his left arm, which betrays the removal of an SS tattoo (*Heartland* 124). The father's gift for survival (evinced in his chameleon-like self-translation into the roles of controversial municipal painter and then art teacher at the local high school), reposes precisely upon his capacity to conceal the evidence of translation. This self-effacing translation proceeds, however, at the cost of others, trumpeting its contempt for the weak – such as the hobo murdered in the abandoned house opposite the family home (*Heartland* 84). This self-translation at the cost of others is shared by the mother. Her ruthlessness is evinced during the perilous flight from the Soviet sector into West Germany prior to immigration to Australia. In danger of discovery by the border police, the mother is quite prepared to suffocate her second daughter, Monika, so as to prevent the child's crying betraying their whereabouts (*Heartland* 50).

Self-translation at the potential cost of one's own children is metonymically connected to linguistic translation and the way in which it is imposed upon a young generation of new Australians:

> [Mr Cooke, the headmaster] now cursed the war that had sent him this array of disinherited human flotsam. Broken dolls to be mended. Unwilling tongues to be got around a 'th'. He remembered Inge's essay for a moment and the thought flashed through his mind that this angry, withdrawn child in front of him had understood that as a baby, she had been considered expendable for the sake of survival. Could a baby know this? These were uneasy thoughts and he dismissed them, but he was glad that he had never had to make such a decision. (*Heartland* 57–58)

[22] Angelika Fremd, *Heartland* (St Lucia: University of Queensland Press, 1989). All references in the text.

The text remains elusive – what connects linguistic assimilation, a toddler's intuition of its own expendability, and a teacher's sense of unease? Certainly this teacher is busy inculcating other avatars of sacrificial survival techniques. As an educator, Mr Cooke is convinced he must also sacrifice the language of the newcomers in the interests of their survival in Australia – he is the one who enforces the suppression of linguistic otherness:

> Mr Cooke loomed large before them. . . .
> 'Inge, Nate, what were my instructions?' he thundered.
> 'Not to speak German, because she has to learn English,' Renate replied, with an accusing glance towards Inge. . . .
> 'It's for your own good, Inge,' Mr Cooke went on in a kindlier tone.
> (*Heartland* 17–18)

The aggression towards the linguistic other, directed against the children who fail to eradicate it (Inge has let slip an inadvertent 'ja'), modulates rapidly into the self-censorship of the 'kindlier tone' and the self-legitimization of the 'for your own good.' The 'own good' acts as an alibi for aggression by setting up the other in its own circuit of imposed responsibility;[23] it is the other which must be protected from itself, from the dire consequences of being other. In 1950s assimilationist, rural Australia, that foreignness is unacceptable and must cede to the regime of bland sameness.

The irony, of course, is that the linguistic obstacle blocking the path of assimilation ('Unwilling tongues to be got around a "th" ' – *Heartland* 57) is an obstacle for the natives even before it is declared one for the newly arrived: '"Here is a new pupil for you, Miss White, by the name of Inge Heinrich." Mr Cooke had trouble getting his tongue around the name, pronouncing it in a way almost unrecognisable to Inge' (*Heartland* 15). Mr Cooke is the one who finds the articulate path of his sentence obstructed by the foreign name. This obstruction, however, is then laid at the door of the immigrants, who cannot get *their* tongues 'around' such refractory phonemes as /θ/ or /ð/.

The fault-bearing victim, the immigrant as recalcitrant other, accepts the burden of assimilation: Inge ostentatiously throws away her German books upon leaving home so as to make the break with her German-speaking family:

> Her mind was clearer than it ever had been. She would take with her the things that fitted into her new life, nothing else. She picked out two dresses, hand-me-downs from Mrs Gerhard's eldest daughter, and wrapped them in a blanket. I'll destroy them as soon as I can, she thought. She took each one of the books off her shelf – German books, history books, a few novels. Without much hesitation she deposited the German books in the paper bin. (*Heartland* 158)

The break with the parents is complete. The daughter leaves the incestuous father and his half-concealed, half-perpetuated Nazi past, and the mother with her coupled

23 See Jennifer Rutherford, *The Gauche Intruder: Freud, Lacan and the White Australian Fantasy* (Carlton South: Melbourne University Press, 2000).

self-hatred and hatred of a once-loved daughter. But of more consequence, precisely because it marks the abrupt terminus of the novel, is the betrayal of the sister. Inge's departure entails abandoning her sister: 'As the bike began to move, Inge turned to see Monika standing at the front gate, moving her small arm like a drowning person' (*Heartland* 159). Self-preservation is bought at the cost of breaking with the past and with the language of the past, but also with the immediate present, the shared legacy with the younger sister. Like her mother, Inge must treat her sister as 'expendable for the sake of survival' (*Heartland* 57).

That this departure constitutes a major break with the mother tongue is indexed by an odd note in the final passage. She decides to flee with David, a boyfriend she only half loves, but who promises her a possibility of escape:

> Inge started to leave her room. She caught her reflection in the full-length mirror. Her image made her uncomfortable. 'You don't love him,' it hissed. 'He'll make you live his way, fill you with his foreignness. Take care.' She moved closer to her image until she touched it, then composed herself. (*Heartland* 158)

Ironically, Inge is repeating here her own mother's calculating liaison with a man she did not love, and who would father the daughter she would later regard as expendable, Monika. In this moment of prevarication, the native, offering the route to survival via assimilation, an assisted passage into the 'heartland' of Australia, is registered as 'foreign.' Here, a thread still connects the protagonist and her sister. The moment of self-scission, and self-address anticipating the pending self-alienation of a cynical, pragmatically motivated partnership, cedes to self-composition. In the very moment of departure, the text thus registers that flight into the sameness of 1960s Australia is a saving break with a mortiferous diachronic translation, but also with the synchronic solidarity of sisterly translation.

Heartland is thus a narrative of broken-off translations. The text cannot restore them, but it does locate the exact moment of rupture. Ironically, however, the author does retain the translation process in her name, 'Fremd' (literally, 'foreign'), thus compensating at the level of the paratext a last residue of an alterity otherwise banished from the body of the book.

Translation regained?

Whereas in *Heartland*, the failure of translation in a post-war immigration context appears to extend right through to a rupture of the fragile solidarity between sisters, in Yasbincek's *liv* it is a sense of solidarity between women, a tenuous mode of communication across and between the languages, which rescues ruined subjectivities.[24] *liv* contains the same harrowing composite of traumas of linguistic and cultural translation (a painful immigration to Australia) and the untranslatability of traumas (war crimes committed in Europe by a paternal figure, and an ongoing history of sexual and physical abuse against women and children over successive generations).

[24] Morgan Yasbincek, *liv* (Fremantle: Fremantle Arts Centre Press, 2000). All references in the text.

As in *Heartland*, with its sparing use of German inserts, *liv* is cautious in its shop-fronting of Croatian. Terms of affection mark the presence of this intimate foreignness, but in contradistinction to Fremd's text, Yasbincek translates. '– Moje srtce [*sic*], moje srtce' is rendered as 'My darling heart, my darling heart,' and '– Moja tata, moja tata' as 'My dadda, my dadda,' with a declination which obviously seeks to minimize the difference between languages and effect their convergence (*liv* 145–46). There are other sites in the text where translation also happens, but in paradoxical and perverse ways.

The first-generation immigrant Lydia's fluent but garbled English is a masked translation which even the eponymous narrator Olivia, her granddaughter, appears not to recognize as such: 'Lydia repeats her simple-past verbs alongside the past-participle. Like rivals, they will not be separated: *I voz gone* to Fremantle, *She voz* laughed to me' (*liv* 41). The author's ingenious – and ingenuous – explanation of a synchronic grammatical hybrid elides the fact of an all-too-literal transposition of Croatian structures. Lydia is merely constructing sentences in an approximation of the Croatian composite past, which uses the verb *biti* ('to be') with the past participle. She is translating faithfully, but by so doing, evinces a radical recalcitrance to the demands of the target system. Lydia's unwillingness to assimilate via self-effacing translation remains the comical hallmark of her communication throughout the text (e.g. *liv* 139–40).

Of equal significance as an instance of resistance to the target system is the unique occasion where a Croatian insert remains untranslated. In one of the novel's episodes, Olivia and her sister Adrienne find a stray dog and bring it home to keep it as a pet. Their grandmother, Lydia, wakes in the morning and sees the creature bending over her bed. She does not recognize it as a dog but takes it for a bear, and screams in terror to her daughter Sancha: 'OI, OI, STA TO, STA TO, SANCHA!' (*liv* 165) [Oi, Oi, what is it, what is it, Sancha!]. This cry of terror remains untranslated, and in a sense is untranslatable, for it indexes the Real in the Lacanian sense – that which cannot be represented, a resurgence of something so awful it temporarily erases Lydia's broken English. It is significant that the English text even erases the superscript marks signalling the /ʃ/ ('sh') consonant ('Šta to, šta to'), thus censoring the body of the language no less than its semantics. This is no coincidence, for it is the bodily experience of trauma – sexual abuse and physical violence – which is most untranslatable in *liv*.

At this point the trauma of translation, the constantly threatening 'stress of not being able to understand' which dogs the immigrant (*liv* 82), intersects with the translation of trauma. The creature which can only be registered, in a moment of blank terror, as a bear, is coextensive with the other horrors the text can likewise often do nothing more than index: the grandfather's shadowy past as a member of the fascist Ustashi and his participation in genocide (*liv* 148, 172, 233, 249), the ongoing physical and sexual abuse of the mother, the daughter and the granddaughter by the grandfather and various other men: 'Sancha . . . hopes what happened last time doesn't happen again. It doesn't feel real to her any more' (*liv* 114).[25]

Indeed, the text goes so far as to suggest that the impossibility of translation of trauma is not merely retrograde, arising out of the trauma imprint's incompatibility with other modes of representation[26] – but rather, that this violence is enacted deliberately, proleptically, in order to vitiate representation:

> Why did my grandfather perform strange ceremonies upon me? Why did he torture me and offer me to strangers to play with? Why did he set out to thoroughly and mercilessly cripple every possible continuity with myself? . . . I was only a baby. He saw the pure blue flame behind my eyes, perceiving him, perceiving everything he had ever done and been and wanted to put it out. . . . He knew that even if one day I were to remember, clear narrative memories would not be possible for me, no one would ever believe me. (*liv* 173–74)

Much of the text is preoccupied with the attempt to translate the past in such a way as to fill the existential and representational gap at the heart of these shattered female subjectivities – while warding off the potential danger that what may be revealed may be so horrific that it obliterates the precarious sense of selfhood laboriously pieced together by the mutely suffering woman: 'I can only write what I can bear to know' (*liv* 291).

In *liv*, translation occurs under the sign of association. It operates indexically rather than metaphorically. Where translation, against all odds, does succeed, it is by virtue of discontinuity, not in spite of it. Translation in this context of massive, untranslatable trauma, occurs in a mode which is indicated by the passage cited above describing Lydia's shaky grammar: '*I voz gone* to Fremantle, *She voz* laughed to me. As matriarch she speaks with authority. Because of her we are here. Because of her we speak a different language' (*liv* 41).

For the over-literal authority of bad (and badly masked) translation is the same authority which guarantees a tenuous connection between past and present generations. Olivia, Lydia's granddaughter, and thus the third generation in the narrative, reports:

> Comments are made on the awkwardness of my syntax; school reports, assignments. It is true: my idiolect has my mother's veins in it, my grandmother's corpuscles. On the bus when I listen to the elastic phonemes of second generation Australians, I can hear strains resonant with the tones of my own speech. (*liv* 115)

Far from lamenting the immigrant condition, this passage registers a tenacious and ineluctably plural cultural identity. Lydia's unwitting refusal of linguistic assimilation guarantees a matrilinear line of succession which somehow, against all odds, can be sustained down the generations. If Lydia's sentences are 'odd and discontinued' (*liv* 41), this will be the mode of writing adopted by the text: 'I chose

25 The gruesome instances of abuse, more or less explicitly described, abound in *liv*: 72, 112, 114–15, 124, 146, 162, 172, 212, 241, 244, 292, 293, 295.

26 See Dominick LaCapra, *Writing History, Writing Trauma* (Baltimore: Johns Hopkins University Press, 2000), 107.

to test the fragment' (*liv* 303); 'Piece by piece I collect a shaping of myself ' (*liv* 45). This painstaking work of reconstruction, posited upon a continuity of matrilinear (un)translation, does not, however, result in quietism. Rather, it leads back to war-torn Croatia in the 1990s. Olivia has a vision of one of the victims of the 1990s war: 'her mouth is open and she is crying out in another language; a language I recognize. It's Sancha's language. Lydia's language' (*liv* 36). Olivia goes even further: 'I am the mother tongue and the second language and the idiolect' (*liv* 300). The traumas of the past may never be dis-encrypted, but those of the present can be identified (with). It is at this moment, then, that via language and the difficult work of 'translation,' that a sense of solidarity emerges which is very different to *Heartland*'s sisterly betrayal. The self is imagined as a collection of disparate languages, and subjectivity as a process of translation which cannot but generate connections, however fragmentary, beyond the self.

A singular 'monolingual' sense of selfhood may sit comfortably with the absence of suffering, but it would appear to merely generate exclusion elsewhere: 'Language is only a fragment. Does the disaster which underscores our culture perform itself because it tries to encode?' (*liv* 255). This interrogation might in turn lead us to ask about the possibilities of a culture which did not encode but rather in-code, gathering together plurality in a loose confederation rather than imposing a singular rule. Australia is an example of a society which has achieved an approximation of such a confederation. It repeatedly has its moments of aporia and contradiction, but its pluralism is tenacious and deserves to be defended against critics and pessimists alike.[27]

The translator within

Why, then, does translation as an index of cultural plurality receive so little attention in Australian literature and in Australian literary studies? The discipline has been hampered by a constitutive monolingual perspective, perhaps because it is professed, for the most part, by scholars with little or no access to polylingualism. The discipline has been largely indifferent to the fact that, as Robert Dixon has recently pointed out, writers such as Henry Handel Richardson, Patrick White, or David Malouf were or are polylingual and deeply embedded in a polycultural context going beyond the Australian shores.[28] I try to suggest in this chapter that a salutary reminder of the constitutive role of polylingualism, indexed by the process of translation, may come from many Australian literary texts themselves.

Does Australian Literary Studies have an Anglo bias? The erstwhile connection between Australian versions of high culture and Britain is obvious. The emergence of Australian literary studies as part of a reaction to an Anglocentric 'cultural cringe' in the main did not, however, translate into a concomitant openness to pluriculturalism outside of the English language. There are poets, of course, who translate (Vivian Smith, Chris Wallace-Crabbe, Chris Andrews; Les Murray was

27 See Bob Hodge & John O'Carroll, *Borderwork in Multicultural Australia* (Crows Nest NSW: Allen & Unwin, 2006).

28 Robert Dixon, 'Australian Literature – International Contexts', in *Southerly* 2007 issue on Elizabeth Webby.

once a translator by profession) and some writers have utilized experimental modes to index the rupture of English-language monolingualism (see, for instance, Ania Walwicz's 'translate'[29]). Some Australian literary researchers do work across multilingual borders (e.g. Sonia Mycak), though their position in the academy tends to be marginal; other such iconic scholars as Sneja Gunew have left the country, thus indexing some fundamental unease in their discipline.[30] Others work overseas, like the many non-Australian practitioners and advocates of Australian Studies abroad (a representative figure might be Xavier Pons at Toulouse-le-Mirail), or expatriates such as the late Anna Rutherford (some subsequently return home), but again their status is an ambivalent one, 'doing it and (not) being here' (to invert the title of a famous essay by Anne Freadman).

In the main, then, Australian literary studies would appear to remain hegemonically Anglo in its constitution and attitudes, an anomaly in our polylingual and polycultural society. Gunew's calls to destabilize received notions of Australian literature by introducing subject positions located outside the customary Anglo-Celtic cultural domain, or to implement a 'stuttering pedagogy' which in Deleuzian terms would 'render the native language foreign or discover the foreignness within it' seem to have gone largely unheeded.[31] Doubtless this late-colonial hangover has its socio-economic explanations, but one might have thought that several decades of freely accessible tertiary education would have dismantled elitist barricades to a greater extent and produced more scholars who are hyphenated-Australian in background, transcultural in theoretical orientation, and internationally known as scholars of Australian (literary) studies (for instance Nikos Papastergiadis).

Texts such as Fremd's *Heartland* and Yasbincek's *liv* implicitly issue a call to literary studies to take cognisance of the ambient linguistic pluralism and the omnipresent strategies of translation out of which they emerge, but which have been hitherto largely ignored. Ngũgĩ wa Thiong'o has observed that in 'English education and in English culture generally, the art of translation does not enjoy the same status as the other arts.'[32] Other theorists have remarked upon this phenomenon. Laurence Venuti writes: 'The marginality of translation reaches even to educational institutions, where it is manifested in a scandalous contradiction: on the one hand, an utter dependence on translated texts in curricula and research; on the other hand, a general tendency, in both teaching and publications, to elide the status of translated texts as translated.'[33] In contrast to this desolate monolingual hegemony, Ngũgĩ imagines a world in which translation would be acknowledged as the dominant mode of cultural and intellectual exchange:

29 Ania Walwicz, *Boat* (North Ryde NSW: Angus & Robertson, 1989), 83–85.

30 See also Gillian Whitlock, 'Leaving "ME" ', *Australian Humanities Review* (June 2002), http://www.lib.latrobe.edu.au/AHR/archive/Issue-June-2002/whitlock2.html. Accessed 17 March 2007.

31 Sneja Gunew, *Framing Marginality: Multicultural Literary Studies* (Carlton South: Melbourne University Press, 1994), 118, and *Haunted Nations: The Colonial Dimensions of Multiculturalisms* (London: Routledge, 2004), 126.

32 Ngũgĩ wa Thiong'o, *Moving the Centre: The Struggle for Cultural Freedoms* (Oxford: Currey, 1993), 40.

33 Lawrence Venuti, *The Scandals of Translation: Towards an Ethics of Difference* (London: Routledge, 1998), 89.

> the different languages should be encouraged to talk to one another through the medium of interpretation and translation. Each country should encourage the teaching of language from the five continents of the earth. There is no reason why each child should not master at least three languages as a matter of course. The art of translation and interpretation should be an integral subject in schools.[34]

Such a paradigm is one we could well profit from in our ineluctably polylingual Australian context. It would remind us in salutary manner of translation as a core element of the Australian way of life, one which is all around us but all too often imperceptible for our (predominantly, hegemonically) monolingual ears.

[34] Ngũgĩ wa Thiong'o, *Moving the Centre*, 39–40.

13 Translation History as a Provocation for Australian Literary Studies

In Rushdie's *The Satanic Verses*, a minor character remarks in passing, 'The trouble with the Engenglish is that their hiss hiss history happened overseas, so they dodo don't know what it means.'[1] This chapter sketches an approach to a similar deficit: namely, the gap in most nations' literary histories, a gap constituted by those large tracts of national literary history which happen overseas. The chapter reflects upon work done elsewhere, namely, the compilation of the first complete catalogue of German translations of Australian literature.[2] The count of extant translations completed between 1789 and early 2010 registered almost 3000 German-language titles, with the number of translations rising exponentially in the last decade covered by the survey. The implications of this cataloguing project have the potential to revolutionize literary studies by levering the study of literary history out of its customary national framework. The chapter stages 'translation history,' to appropriate Jauß's famous title, 'as a provocation for literary studies.'[3]

Translation studies have long had a relatively peripheral status within the academy, relating to something that was seen primarily as a 'craft.'[4] In recent years, however, translation studies, with the help of allies such as systems theory, postcolonial studies, deconstruction and psychoanalytic theory, have become a more prominent subdiscipline in the humanities. Moreover, with recent theorists such as Lotman declaring that 'the elementary act of thinking is translation,'[5] translation has also advanced to the status of a key epistemological instrument for understanding other cultural operations. The emphasis in this chapter is not so much upon the epistemological status of translation, but rather starts from the massive empirical reality of translation history, positing this as a hitherto neglected facet of a nation's literary history which calls into question the very notion of national literature itself.

The translation of Australian literature overseas is a huge area of literary production as evinced not only by the number of translations but more significantly by the sharp rise in translation activity particulary since 2000. This area of 'offshore' Australian literary production generally remains invisible to Australians themselves. Yet literary translation represents one of the major ways in which complex and differentiated conceptions of Australia as a cultural nation become accessible to

1 Salman Rushdie, *The Satanic Verses* (London: Vintage, 1998), 343.

2 Russell West-Pavlov & Jens Elze-Volland, *Australian Literature in German Translation: A Catalogue of Titles, Translators and Trends* (Berlin: Institut für Englische Philologie, Freie Universität Berlin, 2010). The data included in this catalogue are currently being uploaded onto the online database of the 'AustLit' project run by the University of Queensland and the National Library of Australia.

3 Hans Robert Jauß, *Literaturgeschichte als Provokation* (Frankfurt/Main: Suhrkamp, 1970), 144–207.

4 Lawrence Venuti, 'Introduction', in Lawrence Venuti (ed.), *Rethinking Translation: Discourse, Subjectivity, Ideology* (London: Routledge, 1992), 2–4.

5 Juri Lotman, *Universe of the Mind: A Semiotic Theory of Culture*, trans. Ann Shukman (Bloomington: Indiana University Press, 1990), 143.

educated, internationally networked, globally mobile and financially influential populations around the world. The translation of Australian literature abroad has some financial support from Australian cultural institutions such as the Australia Council,[6] but in general this involvement remains *ad hoc* and piecemeal, thus relinquishing to a large extent any significant handle on this aspect of Australia's self-imaging abroad.

This chapter sketches the theoretical underpinnings for a broader project, one which would go well beyond the limited purview of the German-language translations already catalogued. The project in its wider scope would aim to rectify the astounding lack of information about the translation of Australian literature in Europe and elsewhere. The broader project would assume a new transnational paradigm of Australian literary space so as to comprehensively map patterns and trends in the translation of Australian Literature in different parts of the world, though such a brief would clearly exceed the comptenecies of a single scholar and would assume a team of researchers. Such an empirical task would seek to provide, in the long run, a knowledge base upon which authors, translators, literary agents, publishers and cultural institutions could draw in order to participate in the global project of translating Australian literature in better informed and more coherently oriented ways.

Deficits of the national literary paradigm

Australia's 'psychogeography' presents a seductively neat isomorphism of continental coastline and national identity,[7] making it particularly tempting to think of its culture in terms which are similarly insular. Gillian Whitlock has recently commented that Australian 'literary scholars remain deeply attached to representations of Australia as a nation apart. . . . A preference for thinking about Australian literature as a literature on its own remains intact.'[8] Yet as Graham Huggan has noted, there is a 'widespread feeling that, even if the paradigm of identity itself is not completely exhausted, the corresponding view of Australian literature as a container for *national* identity is increasingly under threat.'[9] Indeed, as Huggan has pointed out, 'to invoke the national specificity of Australia and/or Australian literature is thus often a conspicuously *trans*national activity.'[10] It is a small step from such recognitions to abandoning the assumption that there is a one-to-one fit between mainland or continent as the place of residence and the language and cultural affiliation for any given writer (such assumptions tend to assume that English and

6 Australia Council for the Arts. 'Arts Funding Guide' 2009.http://www.australiacouncil.gov.au grants/arts_funding_guide. Accessed 29 April 2010.

7 See Ien Ang. 'Racial/Spatial Anxiety: "Asia" in the psychogeography of Australian whiteness', in Ghassan Hage and Roanne Couch (eds), *The Future of Australian Multiculturalism: Reflections of the Twentieth Anniversary of Jean Martin's 'The Migrant Presence'* (Sydney: The Research Institute for Humanities and Social Sciences, 1999),189–204.

8 Gillian Whitlock, 'Australian Literature: Points for Departure', *Australian Literary Studies* 19.2 (1999), 153.

9 Graham Huggan, A*ustralian Literature: Postcolonialism, Racism, Transnationalism* (Oxford: Oxford University Press, 2007), 10.

10 Huggan, *Australian Literature*, 2.

Anglophone connections as a linguistic default mode). From there, it is only another step to reconceptualizing translations of Australian literature as an integral part of that mainland literary heritage. Just as Australia is slowly taking on board the idea that its large expatriate population (5% at any one time) may be a significant off-shore contingent of the national body politic,[11] so too it may be time to begin including translations of Australian literature as a non-negligible offshore sector of the literary corpus of the national cultural heritage.

However, because Australia's hegemonic culture is still predominantly, if no longer exclusively, Anglophone and monolingual, much of what happens to Australian culture when it goes offshore remains out of sight of decision-makers at home. Things may look very different if one descends below the threshold of elite culture, with much immigrant writing, often self-published, cast in community languages and dealing with transnational thematic clusters.[12] Such alternative perspectives notwithstanding, translation as a phenomenon is, in general, particularly vulnerable to neglect by hegemonic but myopic cultural perspectives.

The invisibility of such translational facets of the national literary field is evinced in the Australian context by reiterated demands for a broadening of the literary canon to encompass multiple cultural domains. The frequency of such calls may play a merely indexical role, pointing to a lack which may be deceptively palliated and paradoxically perpetuated by a now-ritualized demand: critics have been wondering since the 1990s why 'the cry for more comparative studies . . . *keeps* reappearing as a lack'[13] As if to instantiate this observation, we find Robert Dixon, Chair of Australian Literature at Sydney University, and thus a representative of the literary establishment and literary institutions, a decade later asking, 'What might a transnational practice of Australian literary criticism look like? What kinds of research questions would it ask? What kinds of data, criticism and reading would we need to develop a transnational perspective?'[14] Dixon's investigation of the emergent internationalization of Australian literary studies merely translates into a series of fundamental and presumably as-yet-unanswered questions, though his more recent work, while reiterating these questions almost word for word, has begun to fill some of the gaps, albeit tentatively:

> Literary influences, intellectual formations, careers in writing, and the processes of editing, publication, translation, reception and reputation-making take place both within and beyond the nation, and in more than one language. What might a trans-

11 Nicholas Brown, 'The Changing Resonance of "the International" in Australian Politics and Culture', in Russell West-Pavlov (ed), *Who's Australia? – Whose Australia?: Contemporary Politics, Society and Culture in Australia* (Trier: WVT, 2005. 43–64); Australian Parliament, Senate, Legal and Constitutional References Committee, 'They still call Australia home: Inquiry into Australian Expatriates' (March 2005), *Parliament of Australia: Department of the Senate: Homepage*. http://www.aph.gov.au/senate/Committee/legcon_ctte/completed_inquiries /2004-07/ex pats03/report/report.pdf. Accessed 29 April 2010.

12 Gunew, Sneja, L. Houbein, A. Karakostas-Seda and J. Mahyuddin (eds), *A Bibliography of Australian Multicultural Writers* (Geelong VIC: Deakin University Press, 1992).

13 David Carter, 'Australia/Post: Australian Studies, Literature and Post-Colonialism', in Wenche Ommundsen and Helen Rowley (eds), *From a Distance: Australian Writers and Cultural Displacement* (Geelong VIC: Deakin University Press, 1996), 107.

14 Robert Dixon, 'Australian Literature – International Contexts', *Southerly* 67.1–2 (2007), 22.

> national practice of Australian literary criticism that aimed to overcome the translator's invisibility look like? What kinds of research questions would it ask?
>
> What kinds of data and readings would we need to develop a transnational perspective, to see Australian literature in the translation zone?[15]

One practical way of rectifying these deficits would be to compile detailed empirical evidence for a truly transnational face of Australian literary production in the form of overseas translations. To take on board this idea, however, a further conceptual re-orientation is necessary: namely, a transformed notion of the globalized literary field.

Theories of post-national literary fields

The first notion which may facilitate the re-conceptualization of Australian literature beyond a national paradigm is that of the world literary field. The term 'Weltliteratur' was coined by Goethe,[16] was predicted by Marx's meditations upon an emergent capitalist world economy[17] and has re-emerged into prominence in recent years as a salient domain of literary conceptualization in the wake of theorization on globalization.[18] Theories of world literature build upon Luhmann's or Lotman's systems theories[19] or world-system theory[20] to analyze global economic

15 Robert Dixon, 'Australian Literature in the Translation Zone: Robert Dessaix and David Malouf', in Katherine Bode and Robert Dixon (eds), *Resourceful Reading: The New Empiricism, eResearch and Australian Literary Culture* (Sydney: Sydney University Press, 2009), 88. Answers are beginning to emerge: see Ken Gelder, 'Proximate Reading: Australian Literature in Transnational Reading Frameworks', *JASAL* special issue 2010, 'Common Readers and Cultural Critics'. http://www.nla.gov.au/openpublish/index.php/jasal/article/viewFile/1535/2082, accessed 11 April 2011; Oliver Haag, 'Australia and Its German-Speaking Readers. A Study of How German Publishers Have Imagined Their Readers of Australian Literature', also in *JASAL* special issue 2010, 'Common Readers and Cultural Critics'. http://www.nla.gov.au/open publish/ index.php/jasal/article/viewFile/1478/2089, accessed 11 April 2011.

16 Johann Peter Eckermann, *Conversations with Goethe*, trans. John Oxenford (Oxford: Da Capo, 1998), 165–66, or Johann Peter Eckermann, *Gespräche mit Goethe in den letzten Jahren seines Lebens* (Leipzig: Insel, 1968), 204–5; H. J. Schrimpf, *Goethes Begriff der Weltliteratur* (Stuttgart: Metzler, 1968).

17 Karl Marx, and Friedrich Engels, *Manifest der kommunistischen Partei* (Berlin: Dietz, 1953), 10–11, or Karl Marx, and Friedrich Engels, *The Communist Manifesto*, trans. Samuel Moore (Penguin: Harmondsworth, 1967), 83–84.

18 Pascale Casanova, *The World Republic of Letters*, trans. M. B. DeBevoise (Cambridge, MA: Harvard University Press, 2004), or Pascale Casanova, *La république mondiale des lettres* (Paris: Seuil/Points, 2008); David Damrosch, *What is World Literature?* (Princeton, NJ: Princeton University Press, 2003); Franco Moretti, 'More Conjectures', *New Left Review* 20 (March–April 2003): 73–81; Franco Moretti, 'Conjectures on World Literature', in Christopher Prendergast (ed.), *Debating World Literature* (London: Verso, 2004), 148–62; Franco Moretti, 'Evolution, World-Systems, *Weltliteratur*', in G. Lindberg-Wada (ed.), *Studying Transcultural Literary History* (Berlin: De Gruyter, 2006. 113–21); Christopher Prendergast (ed.), *Debating World Literature* (London: Verso, 2004); Haun Saussy (ed.), *Comparative Literature in an Age of Globalization* (Baltimore, MD: Johns Hopkins University Press, 2006).

19 Niklas Luhmann, *Soziale Systeme: Grundriß einer allgemeinen Theorie* (Frankfurt/Main: Suhrkamp, 1984); Lotman, *Universe of the Mind*, 1990.

patterns according to relationships of centre and periphery, thus allowing an articulation of the complex differentials of cultural capital and the dynamics of the cultural field on the world market. Recent pioneering analyses of translation history implementing a systemic approach[21] have demonstrated the potential of this conceptual instrument.

World-system or global field theories of literature entail a number of significant methodological shifts which have important implications for literary studies. The first of these is the shift from a hermeneutics of translation analysis towards an 'empirical' systemic description.[22] By 'empirical' analysis Schmidt means renouncing the replicative interpretation also dismissed by Foucault,[23] in favour of a descriptive analysis of the dynamic network of relationships in which 'producing, mediating, receiving and processing literary objects' takes place.[24] Such an approach would, for instance, reveals very different domains of German-language translation of Australian literature – with the GDR reception/translation privileging a quite distinct corpus of works (notably writers with explicit left-wing political tendencies, Frank Hardy, Dymphna Cusack, or producers of socio-historical panoramas, such as Marcus Clarke) from the corpus assembled by translation policies in the Federal Republic.

Such a paradigmatic shift implies a re-orientation of the analytic methodology from individual textual analysis to systemic analysis, from 'literary texts' to 'literary objects' – so as to de-fetishize the text and produce 'a notion of "literature" which is as inclusive as necessary in order to get into the field under investigation all relevant phenomena.'[25] This systemic approach works to 'deemphasize the traditional text-centeredness of literary studies by redefining the object domain.'[26] To take the central terms of Lotman's work, it involves a turn from the structure of the artistic text (1977) towards the semiosphere (1990). According to the provocative formulation of Franco Moretti, it implies a zooming-out from the time-honoured method of 'close reading' to what he calls 'distant reading': 'distance . . . *is a condition of knowledge* . . . [and] allows you to focus on units that are much smaller or larger than the text: devices, themes, tropes – or genres and systems.'[27] In a more judicious choice of

20 Emmanuel Wallerstein, *The Modern World-System. Volume I: Capitalist Agriculture and the Origins of the Modern World-Economy in the Sixteenth Century* (New York: Academic Press, 1974); Emmanuel Wallerstein, *The Modern World-System. Volume II: Mercantilism and the Consolidation of the European World-Economy, 1600–1750* (New York: Academic Press, 1980); Emmanuel Wallerstein, *The Modern World-System. Volume III: The Second Great Expansion of the Capitalist World-Economy, 1730–1840s* (San Diego: Academic Press, 1989).

21 See, for example, André Lefevere, *Translation, Rewriting and the Manipulation of Literary Fame* (London: Routledge, 1995).

22 Siegfried J. Schmidt, *Grundriß der Empirischen Literaturwissenschaft* (Frankfurt/Main: Suhrkamp, 1991).

23 Michel Foucault, *Naissance de la clinique* (1963; Paris: PUF/Quadrige, 1980), xii–xiii; Michel Foucault, *The Birth of the Clinic: An Archaeology of Medical Perception*, trans. Alan Sheridan (London: Tavistock, 1973), xvi–xvii.

24 Siegfried J. Schmidt, '*Empirische Literaturwissenschaft* as Perspective', *Poetics* 8 (1979), 562.

25 Schmidt, *Empirische Literaturwissenschaft*, 562, n8.

26 Helmut Hauptmeier and Reinhold Viehoff, 'Empirical Research on the Basis of Bio-Epistemology: A New Paradigm for the Study of Literature?', *Poetics Today* 4.1 (1983), 154.

27 Moretti, 'Conjectures on World Literature', 151.

vocabulary, he has suggested that we need to abandon the *longue durée* concept of literary history understood as an *histoire événementielle* positing a small number of individual works and authors whose role is to triumph over the norm, thereby marking significant moments of rupture of genre; rather, systemic literary theory would turn its gaze back to literary genres which conform to convention and have hitherto been neglected by literary history.[28] In this understanding of literary analysis, individual texts are merely the scoria of the system, just as for Foucault, the subjects that compose them are merely extrusions of discourse.[29] In the domain of translation, 'close reading' produces the method of comparative translation analysis most recently and brilliantly theorized by Berman.[30] I have undertaken such analyses elsewhere;[31] the systemic study of translations represents a significant shift away from that prior mode of analysis, in an effort to gain a larger perspective calibrated to a countervailing scale of economy.

The second shift is away from evaluation towards description. World-system analysis does not pursue the inherently 'universalizing' project underlying Pascale Casanova's 'world republic of letters,'[32] an approach critiqued especially from the perspective of postcolonial studies.[33] Rather, it assumes a pragmatic logic which is that of the global market of literary production, distribution and consumption. Consequently, the world-systemic approach ignores traditional literary hierarchies. In the realm of translation, hitherto denigrated or disregarded genres abruptly take on a new significance, based upon their statistical weight rather than the value accorded to them by literary critical elites.[34] In our study, genres such as children's literature (e.g. Ivan Southall), detective literature (e.g. Peter Corris, Arthur Upfield), or romance literature (e.g. Colleen McCullough) abruptly become highly prominent genres making up substantial segments of the body of Australian literature in translation. This is in stark contrast, for instance, to a tradition of condemnation of popular ideology reaching back to Adorno. Within this non-evaluative perspective, questions of ideology must also, at least initially, be bracketed off. Niranjana has dictated that '[t]he post-colonial translator must be wary of essentialist anti-colonial narratives; in fact, s/he must attempt to deconstruct them, to show their complicity in the master narrative of imperialism.'[35] Certainly our own prior translation analyses have targeted the tendency in German translations (for instance of White or Dessaix) to

28 Franco Moretti, *Signs Taken for Wonders: On the Sociology of Literary Forms* (London: Verso, 2005), 12–13, 15.

29 Gilles Deleuze, *Foucault* (Paris: Minuit, 1988), 101–30; Gilles Deleuze, *Foucault*, trans. Seán Hand (Minneapolis: University of Minnesota Press, 1988), 94–123.

30 Antoine Berman, *Pour une critique des traductions: John Donne* (Paris: Gallimard/NRF, 1995).

31 See for instance Russell West-Pavlov, *Transcultural Graffiti: Diasporic Writing and the Teaching of Literary Studies* (Amsterdam/New York: Rodopi, 2005), 61–80, 97–109.

32 Casanova, *La république mondiale des lettres,* xiv–xvi.

33 Debjaly Ganguly, 'Global Literary Reflections: Reading Pascale Casanova's *The World Republic of Letters* in the Post-Cold War Era', *English Academy Review* 25.1 (May 2008.), 4–19.

34 Barbara Hernstein Smith, *Contingencies of Value* (Cambridge, MA: Harvard University Press, 1988).

35 Tejaswini Niranja, *Sitting Translation: History, Post-Structuralism and the Colonial Context* (Berkeley, University of California Press, 1992), 167.

privilege 'what is seen abroad as "Australian" in markedly – marketably – stereotypical terms'[36] and edit out elements that may contradict common conceptions of a mythologized Australia.[37] However, the task of systemic analysis is, in the first instance, to map these trends and assess them empirically.

Translation may none the less be a phenomenon which necessitates some modifications to the systemic model. Translation as a cultural phenomenon demands that disciplines of national literary studies exceed their own borders and explore the entanglements of a given national literary heritage with the cultural archives of other nations, cultures and languages. This imperative in turn modifies the standard picture of systemic interaction. Rather than imagining discrete systems as being connected by interfaces along a border region,[38] the very notion of 'the translation zone'[39] is resistant to such linear-interface paradigms. If original and translation are positioned along each side of a border, then as the two versions of a single text, they evidence far more a phenomenon Luhmann has termed 'systemic interpenetration,'[40] or Even-Zohar systemic 'interference.'[41] Far more radically, however, translation as a phenomenon implies that one imagines these regions of 'interpenetration' stretching in some cases to the heart of the neighbouring cultural territory: 'Increasingly . . . we find that Western society as a whole has turned into an immense contact zone, where intercultural relations contribute to the internal life of all national cultures.'[42] Such phenomena necessarily evince multiple vectors of influence: 'While the bulk of translation traffic today goes from English into other languages, the borders of cultural productions in English expand, becoming increasingly diasporic, occupying larger and larger chunks of territory.'[43] For our purposes, it becomes possible to speak of an Australian-German literary interface which may take Australian literature as a field deep into the realm of German middle- to highbrow culture.

A second modification to systemic world literature theory which may be caused by the phenomenon of translation is the aspect of power relations, which is integral to that model. At the heart of systemic analysis are the apparently oxymoronic notions of binarism and asymmetry.[44] According to Even-Zohar, 'There is no symmetry in literary interference. A target literature is, more often than not, interfered with by a source literature which completely ignores it.'[45] In Moretti's formulation, the world-system is one but uneven,[46] characterized as it is by 'grossly

36 Huggan, *Australian Literature*, xii.
37 West-Pavlov, *Transcultural Graffiti*, 61–80, 97–109.
38 Lotman, *Universe of the Mind*, 142.
39 Emily S. Apter, *The Translation Zone: A New Comparative Literature* (Princeton, NJ: Princeton University Press, 2005).
40 Luhmann, *Soziale Systeme*, 290–91.
41 Even-Zohar Itamar, 'Laws of Literary Interference', *Poetics Today* 11.1 (Spring 1990), 53–72; Even Zohar Itamar, 'System, Dynamics and Interference in Culture: A Synoptic View', *Poetics Today* 11.1 (Spring 1990), 85–94.
42 Sherry Simon, *Gender in Translation: Cultural Identity and the Politics of Transmission* (London: Routledge, 1996), 161.
43 Simon, *Gender in Translation*, 153–54.
44 Lotman, *Universe of the Mind*, 124.
45 Even-Zohar, 'Laws of Literary Interference', 62.
46 Moretti, *Conjectures on World Literature*, 150.

unequal cultural exchanges between the hegemonic English-language nations, particularly the United Sates, and their others in Europe, Africa, Asia, and the Americas.'[47] Yet these observations regarding asymmetry are contradicted by frequent observations to the effect that peripheral literatures are highly significant for the world system, as cultural innovation inevitably comes from the border regions.[48] The most visible phenomena of this kind have certainly been the post-1960s 'boom' literatures from Latin America (García Márquez, Vargas Llosa, Cortázar etc.), often falsely equated with magic realism, and their widespread translation into and reception in all European languages; this reception has significantly influenced literary production in the US and Europe since the 1970s. Innovation from the margins has also taken place in the US, where the often bilingual literatures of Mexican-Americans, Puerto Ricans and Cubans have conquered a significant share of the middlebrow book market and increasingly entered university syllabi. Translation as a global phenomenon obliges systemic analysis to complicate and refine its mapping of systemic asymmetry.

Australian literature, for instance, is a relatively peripheral subsystem within the literary world system. However, in accordance with its status as the literary manifestation of a Pacific-Rim outpost of Anglo-European society, it none the less commands a certain cultural prestige (just as its well-marketed national image commands market prestige, particularly in the domain of tourism). This recognition was perhaps pioneered by the makers of the classic film *Crocodile Dundee* (1986), which in turn contributed decisively to the international distribution of a particular cultural stereotype of Australianness.[49] The gradual European rise of interest in Australian literature has gone hand in hand with shifts in international perceptions of Australia itself: from colonial backwater, via destination of economic migration, to receptacle for tourism and lifestyle fantasies. At the same time, this shift of perceptions has been accompanied by a broadening of the palette of cultural products[50] available from Australia on the international market, from film (most recently, for instance, Baz Luhrman's hyperbolic *Australia* [2008]) and TV (e.g. soaps, from *Neighbours* to *McLeod's Daughters*) via music (e.g. Midnight Oil), to indigenous art commanding a considerable global market. Australian literature, which has had a long period of reception to outside influences (from the colonial period through to the residual 'cultural cringe' of the 1950s[51]), has increasingly entered a sending phase.[52] This sending phase roughly corresponds, internally, with the rise of the discipline of Australian literature in universities and with substantial public funding for Australian literary creation since the Whitlam era; and externally,

47 Venuti, 'Introduction', 5.

48 Casanova, *La république mondiale des lettres*, 253–58; Casanova, *The World Republic of Letters*, 175–79; Lotman, *Universe of the Mind*, 134; Itamar Even-Zohar, 'The Position of Translated Literature within the Literary Polysystem', in Lawrence Venuti (ed.), *The Translation Studies Reader* (London: Routledge, 2000), 193.

49 Meaghan Morris, *The Pirate's Fiancée: Feminism, Reading, Postmodernism* (London: Verso, 1988), 241–69.

50 See Lotman, *Universe of the Mind*, 124.

51 A. A. Philips, *A. A. Phillips on the Cultural Cringe* (Carlton VIC: Melbourne University Press, 2006).

52 Lotman, *Universe of the Mind*, 144–47.

with the changing international status of Australia from a destination for economic migration to a destination for lifestyle migration or tourism. Clearly these multiple systemic factors are heavily overdetermined and are often contradictory or conflictual (the refugee scandal in the 1990s, for instance, temporarily disrupted German fantasies of Australia as the moral Antipodes of old Europe[53]). None the less, these factors converge in a general trend which evinces a steadily rising number of translations of Australian literature into German spread across an increasing number of niche markets.

Consequences for literary canons

The benefit of this expanded version of the national literary canon, encompassing both the native-language originals and their foreign-language translations, is that it allows us to extend the notion of responsibility to offshore domains of the Australian literary system. If translations of Australian literary works belong, in part at least, to a cross-border national literary system, then it becomes incumbent upon Australian literary institutions to further and foster that cognate literary culture rather than leaving it to its own devices. To that end, however, it becomes imperative to understand what foreign (in this case European) markets are taking from the field of Australian literary production, which translators are active, which publishers are dominant, and what readers expect or are taught to expect. Robert Dixon enquires:

> How important is the agency of the author and translator in relation to other personnel, including authors' and publishers' agents, publishers, editors, and publishers' scouts, in commissioning translations? Increasingly, it seems that overseas rights and translation contracts are initiated by publishers and their scouts at events such as the Frankfurt and London trade fares. Are these commercial arrangements similar throughout the world or do they vary from one culture to another?[54]

This knowledge is in many cases not available to authors or publishers in far-off Australia. Dixon concurs: 'As if confirming Venuti's claim for the translator's "invisibility", there is to date no systematic, empirically informed account of this translation zone in Australian literary scholarship.'[55] Our catalogue of German translations of Australian literature aims to provide such information by offering detailed data on the German translation domain to potential end users. Such expertise can be put at the disposal of authors and agents seeking appropriate channels to introduce their work onto other markets. With this expertise at hand, they can decide best how to lodge their work in ways that the market will be able to assimilate, but which may also challenge and modify consumer expectations.

53 See for example Richard Herzinger, 'Die Lippen zugenäht',*Die Zeit* 6. 31 January 2002. http://www.zeit.de/2002/06/Die_Lippen_zugenaeht. Accessed 27 October 2009.
54 Dixon, 'Australian Literature in the Translation Zone', 97.
55 Dixon, 'Australian Literature in the Translation Zone', 97.

Australian literature in German translation: A preliminary survey

Our catalogue of German translations of Australian literature generated a trawl of almost 3000 translation entries. The database was configured in four different listings according to date of translation, author, publisher and translator. A very rough survey of the results allowed us to reach some tentative and provisional conclusions about the history and current state of German translations of Australian literature, as well as making some prognoses and recommendations.

The total yield of translations (beginning with a virtually immediate translation of Tench's *Narrative of an Expedition to Botany Bay* in 1789 and culminating with newly published titles at the beginning of 2010) was close on 3000. It is worth pointing out that unlike historical empirical literary research carried out by scholars such as Moretti[56] or St. Clair,[57] this field of research is constantly fluctuating, with new translations appearing regularly. The catalogue did not count titles as such, but rather, disparate translations, so that new editions, reprints with a new publisher (often signalling a transfer from hardback to paperback, or a reprint under licence, e.g. in a book club) or changes of medium (e.g. from print to audio book) are registered separately, as they are clear indices of market impact and successful sales results. On the basis of the data gathered, a few provisional tendencies and trends can be identified.

First of all, it is clear that the volume of translations, with the exception of a thirty-year period of stagnation from 1960 to 1990, has been rising from the outset, with a steadily accelerating rate of increase. Translation from 1900–1950 was minimal, with around 50 titles (around 2% of the total translation volume to date). Translation of Australian literature in Germany really got under way after roughly 1950. The decade 1950–1960 saw approximately 5% of the total yield (around 150 titles). The decades 1960–1970, 1970–1980 and 1980–1990 saw production rising abruptly and then remaining stable. Each of these three decades saw between 300 and 350 titles a year, that is, 10–12% of the total yield for each decade. After 1990, the translation volume climbed steeply, with over 500 titles in the 1990s (almost 20% of the total volume). The most striking development has been the explosion of translation work since 2000 (over 1000 titles), meaning that over 40% of the total volume has been produced in this last decade alone.

Second, it is clear that there is a disparity between canonicity and translation volume. Canonical 'literary' or highbrow literature actually makes up a fairly small sector of the overall translation volume. The vast majority of translations are of popular genres such as romance, fantasy, science-fiction novels, crime, thrillers and children's literature, which in most literary markets make up the vast majority of the texts produced. Among the most popular 'popular' authors, one can count Nevil Shute, translated from 1945 onwards with over 40 translations, Di Morrissey with 43 translations, Colleen McCullough with 73 translations, and Patricia Shaw with 115 translations. Shaw provides a perfect example of the increasing tendency to add an

56 Morretti, *Signs Taken for Wonders*, 2005.

57 William St. Clair, *The Reading Nation in the Romantic Period* (Cambridge: Cambridge University Press, 2004).

explicit 'Australian' marketing tag to the title (*Die große Australiensaga*, *Ein Australienthriller*, *Eine australische Familiengeschichte*), often relabelling reprints of translations produced before the 1980s and 1990s. Such subtitles certainly try to cash in on Australia's popularity in Europe and especially Germany (particularly eastern Germany) as an actual tourist destination but also as an imaginary ideal associated with freedom, expanse, nature and the wish for a radically different life-style in a faraway and supposedly radically different place. This trend is evident, however, as early as 1954, when the translation of Eleanor Dark's *The Timeless Land* carried the tag 'Australienroman.'

Non-highbrow literature translations frequently occupy clear niche markets such as crime fiction (for instance Arthur Upfield with 65 translations), romance (for instance Maysie Greig with 60 titles remaining in print from 1954 to 1990). A significant sector here is that of children's literature, beginning with classics from the 1960s or 1970s (Alan Marshall with 5 translations, and Ivan Southall or Colin Thiele with 22 translations each). More recently translated children's authors are Morris Gleitzmann, Melina Marchetta or John Marsden (the latter with 21 translations).

Top-shelf popular (i.e. middle- to highbrow) authors with a large translation presence include Kathy Lette with 17 translations, Ruth Park with 21 translations, Lily Brett with 34, and Morris West with an astounding 122 translations. Lily Brett is an interesting case as she is the only Australian author to be published by Suhrkamp, perhaps the most prestigious middle-to-highbrow publisher in the German-speaking domain, thus indicating the persistently peripheral status of Australian literature within the global field of literary canonicity.[58]

Highbrow authors are led, hardly surprisingly, by the 1973 and 2003 Nobel Prize winners Patrick White and J. M. Coetzee (Coetzee typifies the not-infrequent trans-national or polylingual affiliation of many of the translated authors: he left South Africa for Australia in 2002 and took on Australian citizenship in 2006). Thus he only retroactively became Australia's second Nobel laureate for literature, though he was already resident in Australia at the time of the award). Coetzee tops the list with 38 translations, followed by Patrick White with 35 translations. Interestingly, White's popularity in Germany did not simply come with the Nobel, as he was already substantially translated (7 translations by 1973) from the 1950s onwards (*inter alia* by another future Nobel laureate, Heinrich Böll). Other prominent highbrow authors, in ascending order of numbers of translations, are Christopher Koch and Christina Stead with 4 translations each, Rodney Hall with 7 translations, Elizabeth Jolley with 9 translations, Thomas Keneally with 10 translations, David Malouf with 11 translations, Tim Winton with 12 translations, and Peter Carey with 20 translations. The younger generation of literary authors are certainly present on the market, but surprisingly, are often fairly sparsely translated: writers such as Brian Castro, Gail Jones, Nicholas Jose or Christos Tsiolkas are hardly translated (1 title each in general); Robert Dessaix fares better with 2, Murray Bail and Janette Turner Hospital with 3 each, Richard Flanagan with 4, and Kate Grenville with 5

58 Simon, During, *Exit Capitalism: Literary Culture, Theory, and Post-Secular Modernity* (New York: Routledge, 2010), 94.

translations (though before *The Secret River* Grenville was hardly present on the German market). This is one area where the overseas translation of Australian literary works could benefit from enhanced sponsorship and enhanced expertise regarding where best to place Australian literary works (i.e. with which agents, translators, or publishers). Poetry translations, as one might expect, in general remain rare, with Les Murray and Lily Brett as lonely representatives of the genre, alongside Hans-Joachim Zimmermann's 1999 bilingual collection entitled *Schwarzaustralische Gedichte*, which gathered a selection from disparate poetry collections by Jack Davis, Lionel Fogarty, Kevin Gilbert, Oodgeroo Noonuccal (Kath Walker), Mudrooroo Narogin (Colin Johnson) and Roberta Sykes.

The colonial classics have been well represented from the outset. Henry Handel Richardson's *Maurice Guest* (1908) was translated within four years – unsurprisingly, given its German setting and theme. Ralf Boldrewood's *Robbery under Arms* (1888) was translated in 1927 and reprinted in 1928; Marcus Clarke's *For the Term of his Natural Life* appeared in a GDR translation in 1957 (alongside other hand-picked socialist writers such as Dymphna Cusack, Frank Hardy, whose *Power without Glory* [1950] was translated and published within two years, or Katherine Susannah Prichard, who was translated from 1954 onward – Christina Stead apparently fell through the net).

It comes as something of a surprise, given the enormous popularity of indigenous culture in Germany, to discover that remarkably few indigenous authors have been translated. Sally Morgan and Mudrooroo top the list, with 6 translations each, followed by David Unaipon, Oodgeroo Noonuccal, Roberta Sykes (1 translation each). As mentioned above, a number of indigenous poets are represented in Hans-Joachim Zimmermann's 1999 collection of poems in translation. It would seem that the public interest in indigenous culture far outstrips the real production of translations in this area. This is one domain where the empirical data made available by the pilot project could be used to enhance the public representation of a historically underprivileged sector of the Australian polity and in so doing combat ongoing modes of cultural discrimination.

Third, it is possible to make a few tentative remarks not merely about the spread of translation genres and representative authors, but also about the respective longevity of the translation editions. Here the numerical relationship between quantity and 'quality' (by virtue of which highbrow literature, with a few exceptions, makes up the smallest proportion of the translations), is inverted, though some popular authors possess a long shelf life. The more enduring classics of the popular variety (Morris West, McCullough) join the middle- and highbrow authors like Patrick White, J. M. Coetzee, Tim Winton, or Thomas Kenneally to constitute the more resilient branch of Australian literature translated into German. Texts from this branch remain reprinted long after their original publications – if sometimes sporadically (as is the case with Patrick White). Most of the less successful popular texts remain confined to one or two printings and then vanish into what a future *longe dureé* analysis of translation of Australian literature into German and probably of Australian literature *per se* may reveal as 'the great unread.'[59] As the temporal

[59] Moretti, 'More Conjectures', 149.

distance to the original publication of a text increases, the dichotomy between more successful texts and 'the great unread' increasingly seems to manifest itself as the distinction between high- and lowbrow literature – despite the evidence of some immensely successful popular authors mentioned above. It would seem that the ongoing academic reception of a text and a broad consensus about the aesthetic quality, cultural relevance and innovativeness of a text play a major role in ensuring its survival.

Manifestly, these provisional results are only the harvest of a first superficial assessment of the data. More deeply probing and multivariate statistical analyses would reveal connections between genres and publishers, between translators and specific thematic bundles, etc. A combination of quantitative and qualitative research would factor in potentially significant extraneous data such as reviewing trends, prizes, international events, sponsorship by so-called 'translator advocates,' synergies between simultaneous or cognate translations and their impacts in different countries/languages, and so on.[60] A more rigorous analysis of the data of this type, however, goes well beyond the brief of this chapter, whose purpose is merely to give an initial glimpse of the translation field and furnish further research with a basis for subsequent analysis.

The offshore canon

In general, Australia makes little effort to 'market' its culture overseas. The relatively unimportant status of culture within foreign policy is reflected in the absence of any Australian equivalent to the Confucius Institute, the Goethe-Institut, the Alliance Française or the British Council. It is striking, for instance, that the Australia Council for the Arts, which does not have the brief of creating an overseas interface between Australian culture at home and other national cultures, is only very sparsely represented in Australian missions abroad. This problem has been recognized, as is evinced in a recent Australian Parliament report, which expresses concern about the neglect of what it calls global 'public diplomacy.'[61] In fact, it is other cultures which do the 'exporting' of Australian literary culture according to their own criteria. Effectively, current laissez-faire policy releases Australian culture into the public domain overseas and relinquishes potential modes of intervention or influence upon it once it takes on a foreign guise. It is this striking imbalance in the involvement in the 'export' of Australian cultural commodities that a systemic analysis of translations of Australian literature abroad would seeks to rectify.

Admittedly, the Australia Council or the Arts has recognized the need to foster overseas translations of Australian fiction. The Publishing and Promotion support scheme administered by the Literature Board of the Australia Council makes grants

60 See Dixon, *Australian Literature in the Translation* Zone, 2009b.

61 Australian Parliament, Senate, Standing Committee on Foreign Affairs, Defence and Trade, 'Australia's Public Diplomacy: Building Our Image' (2007), *Parliament of Australia: Department of the Senate: Homepage*. http://www.aph.gov.au/senate/Committee/fadt_ctte/completed_inquiries /2004-07/public_diplomacy/report/index.htm. Accessed 19 May 2010.

of up to A$10,000 to translate Australian literary works into other languages.[62] This is a very small-scale initiative, with only modest sums earmarked for the promotion of Australian literature via translation. This contrasts markedly, for instance, with the German rights sales of a single Australian fiction publisher, Allen and Unwin, which reportedly had sold rights to 16 Australian fiction titles by mid 2009 alone. Wondering about 'the spatial, temporal and economic arrangements of translation as a literary and commercial practice, and the extent to which individual instances of translation are connected across an author's body of work, or between one language and another,' Robert Dixon concludes that '[a] major factor remains the sheer commercial power of a publishing house to commission translations independently of the initiatives of authors and translators, whose role appears at times to have been relatively reactive.'[63] Such contrasts are indicative of the relatively low priority outward-bound translation holds within the sphere of cultural politics in Australia in comparison with the more hard-headed policies of the cultural marketing business. These contrasts are all the more crass when set in the context of the generally very astute 'branding' of Australian culture in the global public sphere. They are also indicative of a knowledge gap which appears to work to the advantage of the global publishing consortia at the expense of the primary producers of global literary culture: namely, authors and translators. A number of current projects by scholars in Australian (for instance the translation studies group at Monash University) and abroad seek to establish a database which will right that imbalance of knowledge distribution and access. It is increasingly imperative to create new possibilities for literary institutions or individual authors or translators to intervene in translation trends. More easily accessible information about current translation trends, information a number of researchers are working to make available, would contribute to an enhanced potential to influence those trends.

These cultural-policy and market considerations may appear far removed from the concerns of literary studies. However, if literary studies, conceived as a global rather than a merely national undertaking (and the overseas avatars of national literary disciplines, such as 'Englische Philologie' or 'Anglistik' in the German-speaking world, are by definition symptoms of such transnational projects) are to retain their relevance in our day and age, they must be prepared to extend their purview to encompass not only literary history and literary theory, but also more empirical concerns such as literary markets.[64] Translation as an object of 'distant reading' and systemic analysis seeks to radicalize the received paradigm of national literary studies, aims to make a contribution to the enhanced purchase of literary studies in the field of contemporary cultural production.

(co-written with Jens Elze)

62 Australia Council for the Arts, 'Arts Funding Guide' (2009). http://www.australiacouncil.gov.au/ grants/arts_funding_guide. Accessed 29 April 2010.

63 Dixon, *Australian Literature in the Translation Zone*, 104.

64 See by way of comparison William Paulson, *Literary Culture in a World Transformed: A Future for the Humanities* (Ithaca: Cornell University Press, 2001).

Bibliography

Aczel, Richard. 'Rhetorical Figures as Narrative Strategies in English Renaissance Prose Fiction' in Bernhard Reitz and Sigrid Reuwerts (eds), *Anglistentag 1999 Mainz: Proceedings* (Trier: WVT, 1999), 451–61.

Agamben, Giorgio. *Homo Sacer: Sovereign Power and Bare Life*, trans. Daniel Heller-Roazen (Stanford, Cal.: Stanford University Press, 1998).

———. *State of Exception*, trans. Kevin Attell (Chicago: University of Chicago Press, 2005).

Albertazzi, Silvia. 'Beautiful Travellers: Some Notes on Postmodern Fiction', *Commonwealth Essays and Studies* 11:2 (Spring 1989), 53–62.

Alomes, Stephen. *When London Calls: The Expatriation of Australian Creative Artists to Britain* (Cambridge: Cambridge University Press, 1999).

Anderson, Benedict. *Imagined Communities: Reflections on the Origin and Spread of Nationalism*, 2nd ed. (London: Verso, 1991).

———. *Imagined Communities: Reflections on the Origin and Spread of Nationalism*, 2nd ed (London: Verso, 2001).

Ang, Ien. 'Asians in Australia: A Contradiction in Terms?' in John Docker and Gerhard Fischer (eds), *Race, Colour and Identity in Australia and New Zealand* (Sydney: University of New South Wales Press, 2000), 115–30.

———. 'Introduction: Alter/Asian Cultural Interventions for 21st Century Australia', in Ien Ang, Sharon Chalmers, Lisa Law and Mandy Thomas (eds), *Alter/Asians: Asian-Australiian Identities in Art, Media and Popular Culture.* (Annadale, NSW: Pluto Press, 2000), xiii–xxx.

———. 'Racial/Spatial Anxiety: "Asia" in the psychogeography of Australian whiteness' in Ghassan Hage and Roanne Couch (eds), *The Future of Australian Multiculturalism: Reflections of the Twenetieth Anniversary of Jean Martin's 'The Migrant Presence'* (Sydney: The Research Institute for Humanities and Social Sciences, 1999), 189–204.

Anzieu, Didier. *Le Moi-pea* (Paris: Dunod, 1985).

———. *Une Peau pour la pensée: Entretiens avec Gilbert Tarrab* (Paris: Clancier-Guérard, 1986).

Apter, Emily. *The Translation Zone: A New Comparative Literature* (Princeton, NJ: Princeton University Press, 2005).

ATSIC. Aboriginal and Torres Straits Islanders Commission Homepage. http://www.atsic.gov.au. Accessed 15 April 2011.

Attwood, Bain. 'Historical Controversies and the History wars', in Russell West-Pavlov and Jennifer Wawrzinek (eds), *Frontier Skirmishes: Literary and Cultural Debates in Australia since 1992* (Heidelberg: Winter, 2010), 33–44.

———. *In the Age of Mabo: History, Aborigines and Australia* (St. Leonards NSW: Allen & Unwin, 1996).

Australia Council for the Arts. 'Arts Funding Guide' 2009. http://www.australia council.gov.au/grants/arts_funding_guide. Accessed 29 April 2010.

Bachelard, Gaston. *La Poétique de l'espace* (1957; Paris: PUF/Quadrige, 1994).

Bail, Murray. *Eucalyptus* (London: Harvill, 1999).
Bakhtin, Mikhail. *The Dialogic Imagination: Four Essays by M. M. Bakhtin, ed. Michael Holquist* (Austin, TX: The University of Texas Press, 1981).
Barrett, Charles. *White Blackfellows: The Strange Adventures of Europeans Who Lived among the Savages* (Melbourne: Hallcraft, 1948)
Barta, Tony. 'Sorry, and not sorry, in Australia: How the Apology to the Stolen Generations Buried a History of Genocide', *Journal of Genocide Research* 10:2 (June 2008), 201–214.
Bassnett, Susan and Harish Trivedi (eds). *Postcolonial Translation Theory* (London: Routledge, 2005).
Beck, Ulrich. *Risikogesellschaft. Auf dem Weg in eine andere Moderne* (Frankfurt/Main: Suhrkamp, 1986).
———. *Was ist Globalisierung?* (Frankfurt/Main: Suhrkamp, 1997).
Benjamin, Andrew. *Translation and the Nature of Philosophy: A New Theory of Words* (London: Routledge, 1989), 109–49.
Benjamin, Walter. *Illuminations*, trans. Harry Zohn (London: Pimlico, 1999).
Benstock, Bernhard (ed.). *Essays on Detective Fiction* (London: Macmillan, 1983).
Benterrak, Krim, Stephen Muecke and Paddy Roe. *Reading the Country: Introduction to Nomadology* (Fremantle: Fremantle Arts Centre Press, 1984).
Benveniste, Emile. *Problèmes de linguistique générale* (Paris: Gallimard, 1966).
Berman, Antoine. *La Traduction et la Lettre: ou, l'auberge du lointain* (Paris: Seuil, 1999).
———. *Pour une critique des traductions: John Donne* (Paris: Gallimard/NRF, 1995).
Bernhard, Thomas. 'Ein junger Schriftsteller' in Wolfgang Schneider (ed.), *Männerbilder: Ein Lesebuch* (Frankfurt/Main: Suhrkamp, 1998).
Besemeres, Mary & Anna Wierzbicka (eds). *Translating Lives: Living with Two Languages and Cultures* (St Lucia: University of Queensland Press, 2007).
Blainey, Geoffrey. 'Drawing up a balance sheet of our history', *Quadrant* 37: 7–8 (July–August 1993), 10–15.
Blanchot, Maurice. *Le Livre à venir* (Paris: Gallimard/ Folio essais, 1986).
———. 'Literature and the Right to Death', in P. Adams Sitney (ed.), *The Gaze of Odysseus and Other Literary Essays* (Barry Town, NY: Station Hill, 1981), 21–62.
Bonheim, Helmut. 'Conative Solicitude and the Anaphoric Pronoun in the Canadian Short Story', in Werner Wollte (ed.), *Sprachtheorie und angewandte Linguistik: Festschrift für Alfred Wollmann zum 60. Geburtstag* (Tübingen: Narr, 1982), 77–86.
———. 'Narration in the second person', *Recherches anglaises et américaines* 16 (1983), 69–80.
Bourdieu, Pierre. *Homo academicus* (Paris: Minuit, 1984).
Bowen, Deborah. 'Borderline Magic: Janette Turner Hospital and Transfiguration by Photography', *Studies in Canadian Literature/Etudes en littérature canadienne* 16:2 (1991), 182–96.
Boyce, James. 'Fantasy Island', in Robert Manne (ed.), *Whitewash: On Keith Windschuttle's Fabrication of Aboriginal History* (Melbourne: Black Inc, 2003), 17–78.

———. 'Journeying home: A new look at the British invasion of Van Diemen's Land: 1803–1823', *Island Magazine* 66 (Autumn 1996), 38–63.

———. *Van Diemen's Land* (Melbourne: Black Inc, 2008).

Brewster, Anne. 'Aboriginal Women's Autobiography: Alice Nannup's *When the Pelican Laughed*', in Dieter Riemenschneider and Geoffrey V. Davis (eds), *Aratjara: Aboriginal Culture and Literature in Australia* (Amsterdam/Atlanta, GA: Rodopi, 1997), 121–27.

———. *Reading Aboriginal Women's Autobiography* (Sydney: Sydney University Press, 1996).

Bringing them Home. Report of the National Inquiry into the Separation of Aboriginal and Torres Strait Islander Children from Their Families (Australian Commonwealth Government). April1997. http://www.austlii.edu.au/au/special /rsj project/ rsjlibrary/hreoc /stolen/prelim.html. Accessed 16 April 2011.

Bromley, Roger. *Narratives for a New Belonging: Diasporic Cultural Fictions* (Edinburgh: Edinburg University Press, 2000).

Brotton, Jerry. 'Mapping the early modern nation: cartography along the English margins.' *Paragraph* 19,2 (July 1996), 139–155.

Brown, Nicholas. 'The Changing Resonance of "the International" in Australian Politics and Culture', in Russell West-Pavlov (ed.), *Who's Australia? – Whose Australia?: Contemporary Politics, Society and Culture in Australia* (Trier: WVT, 2005), 43–64.

Brydon, Diana. 'The Stone's Memory: An Interview with Janette Turner Hospital', *Commonwealth Novel in English* (Spring 1991), 14–23.

Bürger, Peter. *Theorie der Avantgarde* (Frankfurt/Main: Suhrkamp, 1974).

———. *Theory of the Avant-Garde*, trans. Michael Shaw (Minneapolis: University of Minnessota Press, 1989).

Burgin, Victor. *In/Different Spaces: Place and Memory in Visual Culture* (Berkeley: University of California Press, 1996).

Butcher, Melissa and Mandy Thomas (eds). *Ingenious: Emerging Youth Cultures in Urban Australia* (Sydney: Pluto Press, 2000).

Butler, Judith. *Giving an Account of Oneself* (New York: Fordham University Press, 2005).

———. 'Melancholy Gender/Refused Identification", in Berger, Wallis and Watson (eds), *Constructing Masculinity* (New York: Routledge, 1995), 21–36.

———. *Precarious Life: The Powers of Mourning and Violence* (London: Verso, 2004).

Callahan, David. 'Acting in the Public Sphere and the Politics of Memory in Janette Turner Hospital', *Tulsa Studies in Women's Literature*, 15:1 (1996), 73–81.

Carr, Julie. *The Captive White Woman of Gipps Land: In Pursuit of the Legend* (Melbourne: Melbourne University Press, 2001).

———. 'The White Blackfellow', *Island Magazine* 56 (Spring 1993), 71–72.

Carter, David. 'Australia/Post: Australian Studies, Literature and Post-Colonialism', in Wenche Ommundsen and Helen Rowley (eds), *From a Distance: Australian Writers and Cultural Displacement* (Geelong VIC: Deakin University Press, 1996), 103–116.

Carter, Paul. 'The empty space is a wall: The role of theatrical translation in the public re-inscription of the other', *Performance Research* 10: 2 (2006) 79–91.

———. 'Translation: On Salvaging Words, Carrying Meanings', in Paul Carter and Ruark Lewis (eds), *Depth of Translation/The Book of Raft* (Burnley VIC: NMA Publications, 1999), 22–109.
———. and David Malouf. 'Spatial History', *Textual Practice* 3:2 (1989), 173–183.
———. *Living in a New Country: History, Travelling and Language* (London: Faber, 1992).
———. *The Lie of the Land* (London: Faber, 1996).
———. *The Road to Botany Bay* (London: Faber & Faber, 1988).
———. *The Road to Botany Bay: An Essay in Spatial History* (London: Faber, 1987).
Casanova, Pascale. *La république mondiale des lettres* (Paris: Seuil/Points, 2008).
———. 'Literature as a World', *New Left Review* 31 (January–February 2005), 71–90.
———. *The World Republic of Letters*, trans. M. B. DeBevoise (Cambridge, MA: Harvard University Press, 2004).
Castro, Brian. *Birds of Passage* (St. Leonards, NSW: Allen & Unwin, 1983).
———. *Looking for Estrellita* (St Lucia, QLD: University of Queensland Press, 1999).
Chakravorty Spivak, Gayatri. 'The Politics of Translation', in Lawrence Venuti (ed.), *The Translation Studies Reader* (London: Routledge, 2000), 397–416.
Chambers, Ross. *Room for Maneuver: Reading (the) Oppositional (in) Narrative* (Chicago: University of Chicago Press, 1991).
Chodorow, Nancy. *The Reproduction of Mothering: Psychoanalysis and the Sociology of Gender* (London: University of California Press, 1987).
Clarke, Danielle and Elizabeth Clarke (eds). *'This Double Voice': Gendered Writing in Early Modern England* (London: Macmillan, 2000).
Clifton, Tony. 'Talking Trash', Newsweek [Australian edition] (5 October 1998).
Cloran, Phil. Review of Andrew McGahan, *The White Earth*, *API Review of Books* 25 (July 2004). http://www.api-network.com/cgi-bin/reviews/jrbview.cgi?n=1741141478. Accessed 12 December 2005.
Clutterbuck, Charlotte. 'A Shared Depository of Wisdom: Connection and Redemption in *The Tiger in the Tiger Pit* and *Possession*', *Southerly* 52:3 (June 1993) 121–29.
Clyne, Michael. *Australia's Language Potential* (Crows Nest, NSW: UNSW Press, 2005).
Cohan, Steven and Ina Rae Hark. 'Introduction' in Steven Cohan and Ina Rae Hark (eds), *Screening the Male: Exploring Masculinities in Hollywood Cinema* (London: Routledge, 1993), 1–8.
Collins, Felicity and Therese Davis. *Australian Cinema after Mabo* (Cambridge: Cambridge University Press, 2004)
Connor, John. *The Australian Frontier Wars 1788–1838* (Sydney: University of New South Wales Press, 2002).
Cook, Pam. 'Masculinity in Crisis? Tragedy and Identification in *Raging Bull*', *Screen* 23, 3–4 (1982), 39–46.
Cowley, Julian. '"Violent Times": Janette Turner Hospital's Art of Memory and the History of the Present', in Sarah Sceats and Gail Cunningham (eds), *Image and Power: Women and Fiction in the Twentieth Century* (London: Longman, 1996), 173–83.

Culler, Jonathan. *The Pursuit of Signs: Semiotics, Literature, Deconstruction* (London: Routledge and Kegan Paul, 1981).

Curnow, Wystan. *Imants Tillers and the 'Book of Power'* (North Ryde, NSW: Craftsman House, 1998).

Currie, Mark. *About Time: Narrative, Fiction and the Philosophy of Time* (Edinburgh: Edinburgh University Press, 2007).

Damrosch, David. *What is World Literature?* (Princeton, NJ: Princeton University Press, 2003).

Dark, Eleanor. *The Timeless Land* (1941; Sydney: Angus & Robertson, 2002).

Davis, Jack. *Black Life: Poems* (St Lucia: University of Queensland Press, 1992).

———. *Plays from Black Australia* (Sydney: Currency Press, 1989).

———. *The First Born and Other Poems* (Sydney: Angus and Robertson, 1970)

Davison, Liam. *The White Woman* (St Lucia, QLD: University of Queensland Press, 1994).

Day, David. *Claiming a Continent: A New History of Australia* (1996; Sydney: HarperCollins, 2005).

De Certeau, Michel. *L'Ecriture de l'histoire* (Paris: Gallimard, 1975).

Deleuze, Gilles and Félix Guattari. *Capitalisme et schizophrénie: Mille Plateaux* (Paris: Minuit, 1980).

Deleuze, Gilles. *Foucault* (Paris: Minuit, 1988).

———. *Foucault*, trans. Seán Hand (Minneapolis: University of Minnesota Press, 1988).

Derrida, Jacques. 'Des tours de Babel', trans. J. F. Graham, in J. F. Graham (ed.), *Difference in Translation* (Ithaca, NY/London: Cornell University Press, 1985), 165–208.

Dinnerstein, Dorothy. *The Rocking of the Cradle and the Ruling of the World* (London: The Women's Press, 1987).

Dixon, Robert. 'Australian Fiction and the World Republic of Letters, 1890–1950', in Peter Pierce (ed.), *The Cambridge History of Australian Literature* (Port Melbourne: Cambridge University Press, 2009), 223–254.

———. 'Australian Literature – International Contexts', *Southerly* 67.1–2 (2007), 15–27.

———. 'Australian Literature in the Translation Zone: Robert Dessaix and David Malouf', in Katherine Bode and Robert Dixon (eds), *Resourceful Reading: The New Empiricism, eResearch and Australian Literary Culture* (Sydney: Sydney University Press, 2009), 87–104.

Dollimore, Jonathan. *Sexual Dissidence: Augustine to Wilde, Freud to Foucault* (Oxford: Oxford University Press, 1991).

Donaldson, Tamsin. 'Australian Tales of Mystery and Miscegenation', *Meanjin* 50 (1991), 341–52.

Douglas, Mary. *Purity and Danger: An Analysis of the Concepts of Pollution and Taboo* (London: Routledge and Kegan Paul, 1980).

Drew, Philip. *The Coast Dwellers: A Radical Reappraisal of Australian Identity* (Ringwood: Penguin, 1994).

Dunker, Michael. *Beeinflussung und Steuerung des Lesers in der englischsprachigen Detektiv- und Kriminalliteratur* (Frankfurt/Main: Lang, 1991).

During, Simon. *Exit Capitalism: Literary Culture, Theory, and Post-Secular Modernity* (New York: Routledge, 2010).
———. 'Out of England: Literary Subjectivity in the Australian Colonies, 1788–1867', in Judith Ryan & Chris Wallace-Crabbe (eds), *Imagining Australia: Literature and Culture in the New World* (Cambridge, Mass.: Harvard University Press, 2004), 3–21.
———. *Patrick White* (Melbourne: Oxford University Press, 1996).
Eckermann, Johann Peter. *Conversations with Goethe*, trans. John Oxenford (Oxford: Da Capo, 1998).
———. *Gespräche mit Goethe in den letzten Jahren seines Lebens* (Leipzig: Insel, 1968).
Eggington, Robert. 'Jangga Meenya Bomunggur (The Smell of the White Man is Killing Us)', in Anne Brewster, Angeline O'Neill, Rosemary van den Berg (eds), *Those who Remain Will Always Remember: An Anthology of Aboriginal Writing* (Fremantle: Fremantle Arts Centre Press, 2000).
Elfyn, Menna. *Detholiad o Gerddi – Selected Poems 1978–1994* (Llandysul: Gomer, 1995).
Eliot, T. S. *The Complete Poems and Plays of T. S. Eliot* (London: Faber, 1982).
Even-Zohar, Itamar. 'Laws of Literary Interference', *Poetics Today* 11.1 (Spring 1990), 53–72.
———. 'Polysystem Theory', *Poetics Today* 1.1–2 (Autumn 1979), 287–310.
———. 'System, Dynamics and Interference in Culture: A Synoptic View', *Poetics Today* 11.1 (Spring 1990), 85–94.
———. 'The Position of Translated Literature within the Literary Polysystem', in Lawrence Venuti (ed.), *The Translation Studies Reader* (London: Routledge, 2000), 192–197.
Fish, Stanley. *Is There a Text in this Class? The Authority of Interpretive Communities* (Cambridge, Mass.: Harvard University Press, 1980).
Flanagan, Richard. *Death of a River Guide* (Ringwood, VIC: Penguin, 1996).
Fludernik, Monika. 'Introduction: Second-Person Narrative and Related Issues', *Style* 28: 3 (1994), 281–311.
———. *The Fictions of Language and the Languages of Fiction: The Linguistic Representation of Speech and Consciousness* (London: Routledge, 1993), 72–82.
Flusser, Vilém. *Von der Freiheit des Migranten: Einsprüche gegen den Nationalismus* (Bensheim: Bollmann Verlag, 1994).
Fogarty, Lionel. *New and Selected Poems: Munaldjali, Mutuerjaraera* (Melbourne: Hyland House. 1992).
———. *Yoogum Yoogum* (Ringwood, VIC: Penguin, 1982).
Foucault, Michel. *Histoire de la sexualité, 1: La Volonté de savoir* (Paris: Gallimard, 1976).
———. *Naissance de la clinique* (1963; Paris: PUF/Quadrige, 1980).

———. 'Nietzsche, Genealogy, History', in Donald F. Bouchard (ed.), *Language, Counter-Memory, Practice: Selected Essays and Interviews*, trans. Donald F. Bouchard and Sherry Simon (Ithaca: Cornell University Press, 1977), 139–64.

———. 'Nietzsche, la généalogie, l'histoire', in Daniel Defert and François Ewald (eds), *Dits et écrits 1954–1988* (Paris: Gallimard, 1994), Vol. 2: 1970–1975, 136–56.

———. *The Birth of the Clinic: An Archaeology of Medical Perception*. Trans. Alan Sheridan (London: Tavistock, 1973).

Fremd, Angelika. *Heartland* (St Lucia: University of Queensland Press, 1989).

Frow, John. 'A Politics of Stolen Time', in Jon May and Nigel Thrift (eds), *TimeSpace: Geographies of Temporality* (London: Routledge, 2001), 73–88.

Gadamer, Hans Georg. *Truth and Method*, trans. W. Glen-Doepel, 2nd ed. (London: Continuum, 1989).

———. *Wahrheit und Methode: Grundzüge einer philosophischen Hermeneutik*, 2nd ed. (Tübingen: Mohr Siehbeck, 1965).

Ganguly, Debjaly. 'Global Literary Reflections: Reading Pascale Casanova's *The World Republic of Letters* in the Post-Cold War Era', *English Academy Review* 25.1 (May 2008.), 4–19.

Gardner, Peter D. *Gippsland Massacres: The Destruction of the Kurnai Tribes 1800–1860*, 2nd ed. (Ensay, VIC: Ngarak Press, 1993).

Gelder, Ken. 'Proximate Reading: Australian Literature in Transnational Reading Frameworks', *JASAL* special issue 2010, 'Common Readers and Cultural Critics': http://www.nla.gov.au/openpublish/index.php/jasal/article/viewFile/1535/2082. Accessed 11 April 2011.

Gelder, Ken and Jane M. Jacobs. *Uncanny Australia: Sacredness and Identity in Postcolonial Australia* (Melbourne: Melbourne University Press, 1998).

Gibson, Ross. *Seven Versions of an Australian Badland* (St Lucia, QLD: University of Queensland Press, 2002).

Gilbert, Helen. *Sightlines: Race, Gender and Nation in Contemporary Australian Theatre* (Ann Arbor: University of Michigan Press, 1998).

Gilbert, Kevin. *Black from the Edge* (Melbourne: Hyland House, 1994).

———. 'Black Policies', in Jack Davis and Bob Hodge (eds), *Aboriginal Writing Today*, Papers from the First National Conference on Aboriginal Writers, Perth, Western Australia, 1983 (Canberra: Australian Institute of Aboriginal Studies, 1985).

———. *The Blackside: People ARE Legends and other poems* (Melbourne: Hyland House, 1990).

Gilbert, Pam. *Coming Out from Under: Contemporary Australian Women Writers* (London/Sydney: Pandora/Unwin Hyman, 1988).

Gillet, Sue. 'Charades: Searching for Father Time: memory and the Uncertainty Principle', *New Literatures Review* 21 (Summer 1991), 68–81.

Gilroy, Paul. *There Ain't No Black in the Union Jack: The Cultural Politics of Race and Nation* (London: Routledge, 1993).

Glissant, Edouard. *Mahogany* (Paris: Seuil, 1987).

Goodall, Heather. 'Too Early Yet or Not Soon Enough?: Reflections on Sharing Histories as Process', in Kate Darian Smith (ed.), *Challenging Histories: Reflections on Australian History* (Special Issue of Australian Historical Studies 118 [2002]), 7–24.

Gooneratne, Yasmine. *A Change of Skies* (Sydney: Pan Macmillan Picador, 1991).

Grandin, Greg. 'Katrina Time', *London Review of Books* 33.1 (6 January 2011), 27–8.

Gray, Stephen. 'In Black or White, or Beyond the Pale?: The "Authenticity" Debate and Protection for Aboriginal Culture, Pointing the Literary Bone', *Australian Feminist Law Journal* 15 (December 2001), 105–20.

———. *The Artist is a Thief* (Sydney: Angus & Robertson, 2001).

Greer, Germaine. *Whitefella Jump Up: The Shortest Way to Nationhood, Quarterly Essay* 11 (2003).

Grenville, Kate. *The Secret River* (Melbourne: Text, 2005).

Grigorescu Pana, Irina. *The Tomis Complex: Exile and Eros in Australian Literature* (Berne, Frankfurt/Main: Peter Lang, 1996).

Grimshaw, Pat. 'Federation as a Turning Point in Australian History', *Australian Historical Studies*, Special Issue 'Challenging Histories', 118 (2002), 25–41.

Grossberg, Lawrence. 'Globalization and the "Economisation" of Cultural Studies', in Bundesministerium für Wissenschaft und Verkehr/Internationales Forschungszentrum Kulturwissenschaften (ed.), *The Contemporary Study of Cultures* (Vienna: Turia + Kant, 1999), 23–46.

Guha, Ranajit. 'On Some Aspects of the Historiography of Colonial India', in Ranajit Guha (ed.), *Selected Subaltern Studies* (New York: Oxford University Press, 1988), 37–44.

Gunew, Sneja. 'Constructing Australian Subjects: Critics, Writers, Multicultural Writers' in Peter Quartermaine (ed.), *Diversity Itself: Essays in Australian Arts and Culture* (Exeter: University of Exeter, 1986), 51–62.

———. *Framing Marginality: Multicultural Literary Studies* (Melbourne: Melbourne University Press, 1994).

———. *Haunted Nations: The Colonial Dimensions of Multiculturalisms* (London: Routledge, 2004).

———. L. Houbein, A. Karakostas-Seda and J. Mahyuddin (eds). *A Bibliography of Australian Multicultural Writers* (Geelong VIC: Deakin University Press, 1992).

———. 'Women's Experimental Writing' in Anna Couani and Sneja Gunew (eds), *Telling Ways: Australian Women's Experimental Writing* (Adelaide: Australian Feminist Studies, 1988), 5–8.

Gymnich, Marion. *Metasprachliche Reflexionen und sprachliche Gestaltungsmittel im englischsprachigen postkolonialen und interkulturellen Roman* (Trier: WVT, 2007).

Haag, Oliver. 'Australia and Its German-Speaking Readers. A Study of How German Publishers Have Imagined Their Readers of Australian Literature', also in *JASAL* special issue 2010, 'Common Readers and Cultural Critics': http://www.nla.gov.au/openpublish/index.php/jasal/article/viewFile/1478/2089. Accessed 11 April 2011.

Haebich, Anna. *Broken Circles: Fragmenting Indigenous Families 1800–2000* (Fremantle: Freemantle Arts Centre Press, 2000).

Hage, Ghassan. *Against Paranoid Nationalism: Searching for Hope in a Shrinking Society* (Annadale, NSW: Pluto/London: Merlin, 2003).

Hall, Rodney. *The Second Bridegroom* (London: Faber & Faber, 1992).

Hall, Stuart. 'Cultural Identity and Diaspora', in Jonathan Rutherford (ed.), *Identity: Community, Culture, Difference* (London: Lawrence and Wishart, 1990), 222–237.

Hamelin, Christine. '"Novelist as Urgent Quester": An Interview with Janette Turner Hospital', *Australian and New Zealand Studies in Canada* 9 (June 1993), 106–11.

Handel Richardson, Henry. *The Fortunes of Richard Mahony* (London: Heinemann, 1930).

Harvey, David. *The Condition of Postmodernity: An Enquiry into the Origins of Cultural Change* (Oxford: Basil Blackwell, 1989).

Hauptmeier, Helmut and Reinhold Viehoff. 'Empirical Research on the Basis of Bio-Epistemology: A New Paradigm for the Study of Literature?', *Poetics Today* 4.1 (1983), 153–171.

Healy, Chris. *From the Ruins of Colonialism: History as Social Memory* (Cambridge: Cambridge University Press, 1997), 159–89.

Healy, J. J. *Literature and the Aboriginal in Australia*. 2nd ed. (St Lucia: University of Queensland Press, 1989).

Heidegger, Martin. *Holzwege*, 5th ed. (Frankfurt/Main: Klostermann, 1972).

Herzinger, Richard. 'Die Lippen zugenäht'. *Die Zeit*, 31 January 2002. http://www.zeit.de/2002/06/Die_ Lippen_zugenaeht. Accessed 27 October 2009.

Hodge, Bob and John O'Carroll, *Borderwork in Multicultural Australia* (Crows Nest NSW: Allen & Unwin, 2006).

———. and Vijay Mishra. *Dark Side of the Dream: Australian Literature and the Postcolonial Mind* (Sydney: Allen and Unwin, 1991).

Hooks, Bell. *Teaching to Transgress: Education as the Practice of Freedom* (New York: Routledge, 1994).

Hooton, Joy. 'First Person Narratives', *Overland* 103 (July 1986), 60–62.

Hope, A. D. 'Australia', in John Tranter & Philip Mead (eds), *The Penguin Book of Modern Australian Poetry* (Camberwell VIC: Penguin, 1991), 16.

Horne, Donald. *The Lucky Country: Australia in the Sixties* (Ringwood, VIC: Penguin, 1964).

Howard, John. 2007 Australia Day speech, http://www.pm.gov.au/news/speeches/ speech2344.html. Accessed 13 February 2007.

Hroch, M. 'From national movement to fully formed nation: the nation-building proces in Europe', in G. Balakrishnan (ed.), *Mapping the Nation* (London: Verso, 1996), 78–97.

Huggan, Graham. *Australian Literature: Postcolonialism, Racism, Transnationalism* (Oxford: Oxford University Press, 2007).

———. 'Orientalism Reconfirmed? Stereotypes of East-West Encounters in Janette Turner Hospital's *The Ivory Swing* and Yvon Rivard's *Les Silences du corbeau*', *Canadian Literature* 16:2 (1991), 182–96.

Hughes d'Aeth, Tony. 'Which Rabbit-Proof Fence? Empathy, Assimilation, Hollywood', Australian Humanities Review. http://www.australianhumanities review.org/archive/Issue-September-2002/hughesdaeth.html#essay. Accessed 7 October 2009.

Hughes, John. *The Idea of Home: Autobiographical Essays* (Artarmon NSW: Giramondo, 2004).

Hughes, Robert. *The Fatal Shore: A History of the Transportation of Convicts to Australia 1787–1868* (London: Pan/Collins, 1988).

Hutcheon, Linda. *A Poetics of Postmodernism: History, Theory, Fiction* (London: Routledge, 1988).

Irigaray, Luce. *Ethique de la différence sexuelle* (Paris: Minuit, 1984).

———. *J'aime à toi: Esquisse d'une félicité dans l'histoire* (Paris: Grasset, 1992).

———. *Je, Tu, Nous: Pour une culture de la différence* (Paris: Grasset, 1990).

Irwin, John T. *The Mystery to a Solution: Poe, Borges, and the Analytical Detective Story* (Baltimore: Johns Hopkins University Press, 1994).

Iser, Wolfgang. *Der Akt des Lesens: Theorie ästhetischer Wirkung* (München: Fink/UTB, 1976).

———. *Der implizite Leser: Kommunikationsformen des Romans von Bunyan bis Beckett*, 3rd ed. (München: Fink, 1994).

———. *Die Appellstruktur der Texte: Unbestimmtheit als Wirkungsbedingung literarischer Prosa* (Konstanz: Konstanzer Universitätsreden, 1974).

Jaireth, Subhash. 'The "I" in Sally Morgan's *My Place*: writing of a monologised self', *Westerly* 40: 3 (Spring 1995), 69–78.

Jameson, Fredric. *Postmodernism, or, The Cultural Logic of Late Capitalism* (London/New York: Verso, 1992).

———. *The Political Unconscious: Narrative as a Socially Symbolic Act* (London: Methuen, 1981).

Jauß, Hans Robert. *Ästhetische Erfahrung und literarische Hermeneutik* (Frankfurt/Main: Suhrkamp, 1982).

———. *Literaturgeschichte als Provokation* (Frankfurt/Main: Suhrkamp, 1970).

Johnson, Colin. *Doctor Wooreddy's Prescription for Enduring the End of the World* (Melbourne: Hyland House, 1983).

Johnston, Anna. 'Australian Autobiography and the Politics of Narrating Post-Colonial Space', *Westerly* 41:2 (Winter 1996), 73–80.

Johnston, George. *My Brother Jack* (1964; Blackburn, Victoria: Collins Fontana, 1981).

Keller, Thomas. 'Einleitung: Ein Leben in und zwischen verschiedenen Kulturen führen', in Bernd Thum and Thomas Keller (eds), *Interkulturelle Lebensläufe* (Tübingen: Stauffenberg, 1998), 1–10.

Kelly Tipping, Richard. 'An Interview with David Malouf', *Southerly* 3 (September 1989), 492–502.

Khoo, Tsee. 'Re-Siting Australian Identity', in Wenche Ommundsen (ed.), *Bastard Moon: Essays on Chinese-Australian Writing* [special issue of *Otherland Literary Journal* 7 (July 2001), 95–109.

Kidd, Rosalind. *Black Lives, Government Lies* (Sydney: UNSW Press, 2000).

Knight, Stephen. *Form and Ideology in Crime Fiction* (London: Macmillan, 1980).

Kramer, Leonie and Adrian Mitchell (eds). *The Oxford Anthology of Australian Literature* (Melbourne: Oxford University Press 1985).

Kristeva, Julia. *Etrangers à nous-mêmes* (Paris: Fayard, 1988).

Krutnik, Frank. *In a Lonely Street: Film Noir, Genre, Masculinity* (London: Routledge, 1991).

Kunz, Egon Frank. 'The Settlers: Hungarians', in James Jupp (ed.), *The Australian People* (Melbourne: Angus & Robertson, 1988), 536–41.

Lacan, Jacques. *Ecrits II* (Paris: Seuil/Points, 1971).

LaCapra, Dominick. *Writing History, Writing Trauma* (Baltimore: Johns Hopkins University Press, 2001).

Laing, Rosemary. 'Welcome to Australia', Large format colour photograph, 110.8cm x 239.3 cm, part of the series 'To walk on a sea of salt', 2004 (currently in Bendigo Art Gallery, National Gallery of Victoria, Melbourne, Australia).

Langer, Beryl. 'The Real Thing: Cliff Hardy and Cocacola-Nisation', *SPAN* 31 (1991), 29–44.

Langford Ginibi, Ruby. 'Koori Dubays', in Dale Spender (ed.), *Heroines* (Ringwood, VIC: Penguin, 1991).

Lawrence, Anthony. *Skinned by Light: Poems 1989–2002* (St Lucia QLD: University of Queensland Press, 2002).

Leer, Martin. 'Sheer Edge: Geography and the Imagination in David Malouf', *Australian Literary Studies* 12:1 (May 1985), 3–21.

Lefevere, André. *Translation, Rewriting and the Manipulation of Literary Fame* (London: Routledge, 1995).

Lévinas, Emmanuel. *Autrement qu'être ou au-delà de l'essence* (Paris: Livre de poche/Biblio essais, 1990).

———. *Ethique et infini* (Paris: Livre de poche/Biblio essais, 1988).

Lévi-Strauss, Claude. *Tristes tropiques* (1955; Paris: UGE 10/18, 1966).

Libretti, Tim. 'Lucha Corpi and the Politics of Detective Fiction', in Adrienne Johnson Gosselin (ed.), *Multicultural Detective Fiction: Murder from the "Other" Side* (New York: Garland, 1999), 61–82.

Longley, Kateryna Olijnyk. 'Autobiographical Storytelling by Australian Aboriginal Women', in Sidonie Smith and Julia Watson (eds), *De/Colonising the Subject: The Politics of Gender in Women's Autobiography* (Minneapolis: University of Minnesota Press, 1992), 370–84.

Lotman, Jurij M. *Die Struktur des künstlerischen Textes*, trans. Rainer Grübel, Walter Kroll and Hans Eberhard Seidel (Frankfurt/Main: Suhrkamp, 1973).

———. *The Structure of the Artistic Text*, trans. Gail Lenhoff and Ronald Vroon (Ann Arbor: University of Michigan – Department of Slavic Languages and Literatures, 1977).

———. *Universe of the Mind: A Semiotic Theory of Culture*, trans. Ann Shukman (Bloomington: Indiana University Press, 1990).

Luhmann, Niklas. *Soziale Systeme: Grundriß einer allgemeinen Theorie* (Frankfurt/Main: Suhrkamp, 1984).

Luke, Allan and Carmen Luke. 'The Difference Language Makes: The Discourses on Language of Inter-Ethnic Asian-Australian Families', in Ien Ang, Sharon Chalmers, Lisa Law and Mandy Thomas (eds), *Alter/Asians: Asian-Australian Identities in Art, Media and Popular Culture* (Annadale, NSW: Pluto Press, 2002), 42–67.

Lyotard, Jean-François. *Rudiments païens: genre disseratif* (Paris: UGE, 1977).

Malouf, David. *12 Edmondstone Street* (Harmondsworth: Penguin, 1986).

———. *An Imaginary Life* (London: Chatto & Windus, 1978).

———. 'A Spirit of Play - The Making of the Australian Consciousness' (Australian Broadcasting Corporation 1998 Boyer Lectures), Lecture 1, broadcast on 15 November 1998.

———. *Child's Play*, with *Eustace* and *The Prowler* (Ringwood VIC: Penguin, 1983).

———. *Fly Away Peter* (London: Chatto & Windus, 1982).

———. Interview with Jim Davidson in James Tulip (ed.), *David Malouf: Johnno, Short Stories, Poems, Essays and Interviews* (St Lucia: University of Queensland Presss, 1990), 285–298.

———. Interview with Nikos Papastergiadis, *Dialogues in the Diasporas: Essays and Conversations on Cultural Identity* (London: Rivers Oram Press, 1998).

———. *Johnno* (Ringwood VIC: Penguin, 1976).

———. *Remembering Babylon* (New York: Vintage, 1994).

———. *The Conversations at Curlew Creek* (London: Chatto and Windus, 1997).

———. *The Great World* (London: Chatto & Windus, 1990).

Martin, David. *Fox on My Door: A Journey through my Life* (Melbourne: Collins Dove, 1987).

———. *My Strange Friend: An Autobiography* (Chippendale, NSW: Picador, 1991).

Marx, Karl and Friedrich Engels. *Manifest der kommunistischen Partei* (Berlin: Dietz, 1953).

———. *The Communist Manifesto*, trans. Samuel Moore (Penguin: Harmondsworth, 1967).

Mayer, Tamar. 'Gender Ironies of Nationalism: Setting the Stage', in Tamar Mayer (ed.), *Gender Ironies of Nationalism: Sexing the Nation* (London: Routledge, 2000), 1–22.

Mbembe, Achille. *On the Postcolony* (Berkeley: University of California Press, 2001).

McCaughey, Patrick. 'Likeness and Unlikeness: The American-Australian Experience', in Elizabeth Johns, Andrew Sayers, Elizabethn Mankin Kornhauser and Amy Ellis (eds.), *New Worlds from Old: 19th Century Australian and American Landscapes* (Canberra: National Gallery of Australia/Hartford, Conn.: Wadsworth Atheneum, 1998), 15–21.

McClintock, Anne. *Imperial Leather: Race, Gender and Sexuality in the Colonial Contest* (New York: Routledge, 1995).

McGahan, Andrew. *The White Earth* (Crows Nest, NSW: Allen & Unwin, 2004).

McKie, Ronald. *We Have No Dreaming* (Syndey: Collins, 1998).

McLean, Ian. *White Aborigines: Identity Politics in Australian Art* (Cambridge: Cambridge University Press, 1998).

Mercer, Kobena. 'Welcome to the Jungle: Identity and Diversity in Postmodern Politics', in Jonathon Rutherford (ed.), *Identity, Community, Culture, Difference* (London: Lawrence and Wishart, 1990), 43–71.

Moretti, Franco. 'Conjectures on World Literature', in Christopher Prendergast (ed.), *Debating World Literature* (London: Verso, 2004), 148–162.

———. 'Evolution, World-Systems, *Weltliteratur*', in G. Lindberg-Wada (ed.), *Studying Transcultural Literary History* (Berlin: De Gruyter, 2006), 113–121.

———. 'More Conjectures', *New Left Review* 20 (March–April 2003), 73–81.

———. *Signs Taken for Wonders: On the Sociology of Literary Forms* (London: Verso, 2005).
Morgan, Sally. *My Place* (Fremantle: Fremantle Arts Centre Press, 1987).
Morris, Meaghan. 'Metamorphoses at Sydney Tower', *New Formations* 11 (Summer 1990), 5–18.
———. *The Pirate's Fiancée: Feminism, Reading, Postmodernism* (London: Verso, 1988).
Mort, Frank. *Cultures of Consumption: Masculinities and Social Space in late Twentieth-Century Britain* (London: Routledge, 1996).
Muecke, Stephen, *Ancient and Modern: Time, Culture and Indigenous Philosophy* (UNSW Press, 2004).
———. With Paddy Roe and Krim Benterrak. *Reading the Country: Introduction to Nomadology* (Fremantle: Fremantle Arts Centre Press, 1984).
———. *Textual Spaces: Aboriginality and Cultural Studies* (Kensington, NSW: University of New South Wales Press, 1992).
Murray, Les. *Collected Poems* (London: Minerva, 1992).
———. *Größer im Liegen* (Berlin/Hörby: Edition Rugerup, 2011),
Napier, A. David. *Foreign Bodies: Performance, Art, and Symbolic Anthropology* (Berkeley: University of California Press), 1992.
Narogin, Mudrooroo. *The Garden of Gethsemane: Poems from the Lost Decade* (Melbourne: Hyland House, 1991).
———. *Writing from the Fringe: A Study of Modern Aboriginal Literature* (Melbourne: Hyland House, 1990).
Neal, Steve. 'Masculinity as Spectacle: Reflections on men and mainstream cinema', in Steven Cohan and Ina Rae Hark (eds), *Screening the Male: Exploring Masculinities in Hollywood Cinema* (London: Routledge, 1993), 9–20.
Neilsen, Philip. *Imagined Lives: A Study of David Malouf* (St Lucia: University of Queensland Press, 1990).
Nicoll, Fiona. *From Diggers to Drag Queens: Reconfigurations of Australian Identity* (Annadale, NSW: Pluto Press, 2001).
Nietzsche, Freidrich. *Die nachgelassenen Fragmente: Eine Auswahl*, ed. Günter Wohlfart (Stuttgart: Reclam, 1996).
Niranjana, Tejaswini. *Siting Translation: History, Post-Structuralism and the Colonial Context* (Berkeley: University of California Press, 1992).
Noonuccal, Oodgeroo. *My People: A Kath Walker Collection* (Milton QLD: Jacaranda, 1970).
O'Regan, Tom. *Australian National Cinema* (London: Routledge, 1996).
Otto, Peter. 'Forgetting Colonialism', *Meanjin* 52:3 (1993), 545–58.
Papastergiadis, Nikos. 'The invasion complex: the abject other and spaces of violence', *Geografiska Annaler (Series B)*, 88.4 (2006), 429–442.
Parliament of Australia: Department of the Senate. Legal and Constitutional References Committee. 'They still call Australia home: Inquiry into Australian Expatriates'. March 2005. http://www.aph.gov.au/senate/Committee/legcon_ctte/completed_inquiries/2004-07/expats03/report/report.pdf. Accessed 29 April 2010.
Paulson, William. *Literary Culture in a World Transformed: A Future for the Humanities* (Ithaca, NY: Cornell University Press, 2001).

Perera, Suvendrini. 'Unspeakable Bodies: Representing the Aboriginal in Australian Critical Discourse', *Meridian* 13: 1 (1994), 15–16.

Philips, A.A. *A.A. Phillips on the Cultural Cringe* (Carlton VIC: Melbourne University Press, 2006).

Phillip, Arthur. 'Governor Phillip to Lord Sydney. Sydney Cove, New South Wales, May 15th, 1788', Historical Records of New South Wales, Vol 1, Part 2 – Phillip 1783–1792 (Sydney: Charles Porter, Government Printer, 1892).

Pilkington/Nugi Garimara, Doris. *Follow the Rabbit-Proof Fence* (St Lucia QLD: University of Queensland Press, 1996).

Pons, Xavier. 'History and Her Story: The Deconstruction and Reconstruction of the Past in Janette Turner Hospital's *Charades*', *Caliban* 29 (1992), 145–55.

Pred, Allan. 'Re-Presenting the Extended Present Moment of Danger: A Meditation on Hypermodernity, Identity and the Montage Form', in Georges Benko and Ulf Strohmeyer (eds), *Space and Social Theory: Interpreting Modernity and Postmodernity* (Oxford: Blackwell, 1997), 117–40.

Prendergast, Christopher (ed.). *Debating World Literature* (London: Verso, 2004).

Prengel, Annedore. *Pädagogik der Vielfalt* (Opladen: Leske & Budrich, 1993).

Probyn, Elspeth. 'Eating Skin', in Sara Ahmed and Jackie Stacey (eds), *Thinking Through the Skin* (London: Routledge, 2001), 89–90.

Rabbit-Proof Fence. Dir. Phillip Noyce. Miramax 2001.

Reynolds, Henry. *Aboriginal Sovereignty: Three Nations, One Australia?* (Crows Nest NSW: Allen & Unwin, 1996).

———. *Fate of a Free People* (Ringwood VIC: Penguin, 1995).

Rickard, John. *Australia: A Cultural History* (Melbourne: Longman Cheshire, 1988).

———. *Australia: A Cultural History* (London: Longman, 1995).

Robertson, Craig. *Buckley's Hope: A Novel* (Melbourne: Scribe, 1997).

Rowley, C. D. *The Destruction of Aboriginal Society* (Ringwood, Victoria: Penguin, 1972).

Rowse, Tim. *After Mabo: Interpreting Indigenous Traditions* (Melbourne: Melbourne University Press, 1993).

———. *Contesting Assimilation* (Perth: API Network/Curtin University of Technology, 2005).

Rubenstein, Hilary L. *The Jews in Australia: A Thematic History* (Melbourne: Heinemann, 1991).

Rudd, Kevin. Apology to Australia's Indigenous Peoples, Speech in House of Representatives, Parliament House, Canberra, 13 February 2008. http://www.pm.gov.au/media/speech/2008/speech_0073.cfm. Accessed 26 May 2009.

Ruppert, James. 'Mediation and Multiple Narrative in Contemporary Native American Fiction', *Texas Studies in Literature and Language* 28 (1986): 209–25

———. 'Mediation and Multiple Narrative in Love Medicine', *North Dakota Quarterly* 59 (1991): 229–41.

Rushdie, Salman. *Imaginary Homelands: Essays and Criticism 1981–91* (London: Granta, 1991).

———. *Shame* (1983; London: Picador, 1984).

———. *The Satanic Verses* (London: Vintage, 1998).

Rutherford, Jennifer. 'Homeland in Absentia: Ireland as a Trope in Contemporary Australian Narratives of Belonging', paper given at a conference on 'The Dilemma of Identity and Exile: Myths and Realities in the English-Speaking World', Université d'Avignon, March 1998 (Proceedings forthcoming with the Presses Universitaires d'Avignon).

———. *The Gauche Intruder: Freud, Lacan and the White Australian Fantasy* (Carlton South: Melbourne University Press, 2000).

Ryan, Lyndall. 'Waterloo Creek, Northern New South Wales, 1838', in Bain Attwood and S. G. Foster (eds), *Frontier Conflict: The Australian Experience* (Canberra: National Museum of Australia, 2003), 33–43.

Said, Edward. W. *Culture and Imperialism* (London: Vintage, 1994).

———. 'Orientalism Reconsidered', in Francis Baker et al. (eds), *Literature, Politics and Theory*: Papers from the Essex Conference 1976–84 (London: Methuen, 1986), 210–29.

———. *The World, the Text and the Critic* (London: Faber, 1984).

Sami-Ali. *L'Espace imaginaire* (Paris: Gallimard/Tel, 1982).

Sanders Peirce, Charles. *Collected Papers*, ed. Charles Hartshorne and Paul Weiss (Cambridge, Mass.: Harvard University Press, 1974).

Saussy, Haun (ed.). *Comparative Literature in an Age of Globalization* (Baltimore, MD: Johns Hopkins University Press, 2006).

Schaffer, Kay. *In the Wake of First Contact: The Eliza Fraser Stories* (Cambridge: Cambridge University Press, 1995).

Schenkel, Elmar. *Sense of Place: Regionalität und Raumbewußtsein in der neueren britischen Lyrik* (Tübingen: Niemeyer, 1993).

Schlunke, Katrina. *Bluff Rock: Autobiography of a Massacre* (Fremantle WA: Curtin University Books/Fremantle Arts Centre Press, 2005).

Schmidt, Siegfried J. '*Empirische Literaturwissenschaft* as Perspective', *Poetics* 8 (1979), 557–68.

———. *Grundriß der Empirischen Literaturwissenschaft.* (Frankfurt/Main: Suhrkamp, 1991).

Schneede, Uwe M. *Joseph Beuys: Die Aktionen: Kommentiertes Werkverzeichnis mit fotographischen Dokumentationen* (Stuttgart: Verlag Gerd Hatje, 1994), 330–353.

Schrimpf, H.J. *Goethes Begriff der Weltliteratur* (Stuttgart: Metzler, 1968).

Schwarz, Anja and Justine Lloyd. 'The Pacific Solution meets Fortress Europe: Emerging Parallels in Transnational Refugee Regimes', in Anja Schwarz and Russell West-Pavlov (eds), *Polyculturalism and Discourse* (Amsterdam: Rodopi, 2007), 247–70.

———. 'Beached: A Postcolonial Reading of the Australian Shore', unpublished PhD thesis, Free University of Berlin, 2008.

Scott, Kim. 'Apologies, Agency and Resilience', in Russell West-Pavlov and Jennifer Wawrzinek (eds), *Frontier Skirmishes: Literary and Cultural Debates in Australia after 1992* (Heidelberg: Winter, 2010), 57–68.

———. *Benang: From the Heart* (Fremantle: Fremantle Arts Centre Press, 1999).

———. *That Deadman Dance* (Sydney: Picador, 2010).

Shklovsky, Viktor. *Theory of Prose (1925/1929)*, trans. Benjamin Sher (Elmswood Park, IL: Dalkey Archive Press, 1990).

Silverman, Kaja. *Male Subjectivity at the Margins* (New York: Routledge, 1992).
Simon, Sherry. *Gender in Translation: Cultural Identity and the Politics of Transmission* (London: Routledge, 1996).
Smith, Barbara Hernstein. *Contingencies of Value* (Cambridge, MA: Harvard University Press, 1988).
Soja, Edward W. *Postmodern Geographies: The Reassertion of Space in Critical Social Theory* (London: Verso, 1989).
St. Clair, William. *The Reading Nation in the Romantic Period* (Cambridge: Cambridge University Press, 2004).
Stanner, W. E. H. *After the Dreaming: The 1968 Boyer Lectures* (Sydney: Australian Broadcasting Commission, 1969).
Stewart, Michelle Pagni. '"A Rose by Any Other Name": A Native American Detective Novel by Louis Owens', in Adrienne Johnson Gosselin (ed.), *Multicultural Detective Fiction: Murder from the "Other" Side* (New York: Garland, 1999), 167–83.
Stratton, Jon. *Race Daze: Australia in Identity Crisis* (Annadale, NSW: Pluto Press).
Swain, Tony. *A Place for Strangers: Towards a History of Australian Aboriginal Being* (Cambridge: Cambridge University Press, 1993).
Tani, Stefano. *The Doomed Detective: The Contribution of the Detective Novel to Postmodern American and Italian Fiction* (Carbondale and Edwardsville: Southern Illinois University Press, 1984).
Temby, Kate. 'Gender, power and postmodernism in *The Last Magician*', *Westerly* 40:3 (Spring 1995), 47–55.
Tench, Watkin. *A Narrative of the Expedition to Botany Bay*, in Tim Flannery (ed.), *1788. Comprising A Narrative of the Expedition to Botany Bay, and A Complete Account of the Settlement at Port Jackson*. (Melbourne: Text, 1996).
Teo, Hsu-Ming. 'Future Fusions and a Taste for the Past: Literature, History and the Imagination of Australianness', in Kate Darian-Smith (ed.), *Challenging Histories: Reflections on Australian History*, Special issue of *Australian Historical Studies* 118 (2000), 128–9.
———. *Love and Vertigo* (Crows Nest, NSW: Allen & Unwin, 2000).
Thiong'o, Ngũgĩ wa. *Moving the Centre: The Struggle for Cultural Freedoms* (Oxford: Currey, 1993).
Thom, René. *Paraboles et catastrophes: Entretiens sur les mathématiques, la science et la philosophie* (Paris: Flammarion, 1983).
Thomsen, Mads. *Mapping World Literature: International Canonization and Transnational Literatures* (London: Continuum, 2008).
Tillers, Imants. 'Locality fails', *Art & Text* 6 (1982), 51–61.
Tisdall, Caroline. *Joseph Beuys: Coyote*, trans. Dominique Le Bourg (Paris: Hazan, 1988).
Todorov, Tzvetan. *La Notion de littérature et autres essais* (Paris: Seuil/Points, 1987).
———. *Poétique de la prose suivi de Nouvelles recherches sur le récit* (Paris: Seuil/Points, 1980).
Turner Hospital, Janette. *Borderline* (London: Virago, 1990).
———. *Charades* (London: Virago, 1983).
———. 'Letter to a New York Editor', *Meanjin*, 47:3 (Spring 1988), 562.

———. *Oyster* (London: Virago, 1996).
———. *The Last Magician* (London: Virago, 1992).
Turner, Victor. *From Ritual to Theatre: The Human Seriousness of Play* (New York: PAJ Publications, 1982).
Ullmann, Stephen. *Language and Style* (Oxford: Blackwell, 1964).
Upfield, Arthur. *Bony and the Black Virgin* (Sydney: Pan Books/Heinemann, 1984).
Van Krieken, Robert. 'Assimilation and Liberal Government', in Tim Rowse (ed.), *Contesting Assimilation* (Perth: API Network/Curtin University of Technology, 2005), 39–47.
Van Toorn, Penny. *Writing Never Arrives Naked: Early Aboriginal Cultures of Writing in Australia* (Canberra: Aboriginal Studies Press, 2006).
Venuti, Lawrence. 'Introduction', in Lawrence Venuti (ed.), *Rethinking Translation: Discourse, Subjectivity, Ideology* (London: Routledge, 1992), 1–17.
———. *The Scandals of Translation: Towards an Ethics of Difference* (London: Routledge, 1998).
Virilio, Paul. *Esthétique de la disparition* (1980; Paris: Livre de poche/Biblio essais, 1994).
———. *L'Espace critique* (Paris: Christian Bourgeois, 1984).
———. *Vitesse et politique: Essai de dromologie* (Paris: Galilée, 1977).
Wallerstein, Emmanuel. *The Modern World-System. Volume I: Capitalist Agriculture and the Origins of the Modern World-Economy in the Sixteenth Century* (New York: Academic Press, 1974).
Walwicz, Ania. *Boat* (North Ryde NSW: Angus & Robertson, 1989).
Waterhouse, Richard. 'Cultural Transmissions' in Hsu-Ming Teo and Richard White (eds), *Cultural History in Australia* (Sydney: University of New South Wales Press, 2003), 113–26.
Wenz, Karin. *Raum, Raumsprache und Sprachräume: Zur Textsemiotik der Raumbeschreibung* (Tübingen: Gunter Narr, 1997).
West-Pavlov, Russell and Jens Elze-Volland. *Australian Literature in German Translation: A Catalogue of Titles, Translators and Trends* (Berlin: Institut für Englische Philologie, Freie Universität Berlin, 2010).
———. *North-South/East-West: Global Entanglements in Post-Imperial Writing in French and German* (Trier: WVT, 2010).
———. *Spaces of Fiction/Fictions of Space: Postcolonial Place and Literary DeiXis* (Basingstoke: Palgrave Macmillan, 2010).
———. *Transcultural Graffiti: Diasporic Writing and the Teaching of Literary Studies* (Amsterdam/New York: Rodopi, 2005).
White, Patrick. *The Tree of Man* (1956; Ringwood: Penguin, 1961/1965).
———. *A Fringe of Leaves* (Harmondsworth: Penguin, 1983).
White, Richard. *Inventing Australia: Images and Identity 1688–1980* (Sydney: George Allen & Unwin, 1981).
Whitlock, Gillian. 'Australian Literature: Points for Departure', *Australian Literary Studies* 19.2 (1999), 152–162.
———. 'Leaving "ME" ', *Australian Humanities Review* (June 2002), http://www.lib.latrobe.edu.au/AHR/archive/Issue-June-2002/whitlock2.html. Accessed 17 March 2007.

Willbanks, Ray. 'A Conversation with David Malouf', *Antipodes* 4:1 (Spring 1990), 13–18.

Willemen, Paul. 'Anthony Mann: Looking at the Male', *Framework* 15/17 (1981), 16.

Williams, Barbara and Shelagh Rogers. 'Two Interviews with David Malouf', *Australian and New Zealand Studies in Canada 5* (Spring 1991), 81–94.

Windschuttle, Keith. *The Fabrication of Aboriginal History. Volume 1: Van Diemen's Land 1803–1847* (Sydney: Macleay Press, 2002).

Winterson, Jeanette. *Art Objects: Essays on Ecstsay and Effrontery* (London: Vintage, 1996).

Wolf, Christa. *Im Dialog: Aktuelle Texte* (Frankfurt/Main: Luchterhand Literaturverlag, 1990).

Wolf, Eric. *Europe and the People Without History* (Berkeley: University of California Press, 1982).

Yasbincek, Morgan. *liv* (Fremantle: Fremantle Arts Centre Press, 2000).

Young, Robert J. C. *Postcolonialism: An Historical Introduction* (Oxford: Blackwell, 2001).

Yu, Ouyang. 'An Interview with Brian Castro' in Wenche Ommundsen (ed.), *Bastard Moon: Essays on Chinese-Australian Writing*, Special Issue of *Otherland Literary Journal* 7 (July 2001), 73–82.

Yunupingu, Galarrwuy. 'From the Bark Petition to Native Title', in G. Yunupingu (ed.), *Our Land is Our Life: Land Rights: Past, Present, Future* (Brisbane: University of Queensland Press, 1997), 1–17.

Zima, Peter V. *Modern/Postmoderne: Gesellschaft, Philosophie, Literatur* (Tübingen/Basel: Francke/UTB, 1997).

———. *Theorie des Subjekts: Subjektivität und Identität zwischen Moderne und Postmoderne* (Tübingen: Francke/UTB, 2000).

Zimmermann, Hans Joachim (ed.). *Schwarzaustralische Gedichte: Oodgeroo Noonuccal, Jack Davis, Kevin Gilbert, Bobbi Sykes, Mudrooroo Narogin, Lionel Fogarty*, trans. Hans-Joachim Zimmermann (Heidelberg: Mattes, 1999).